murach's
HTML5
and CSS3

Zak Ruvalcaba

Anne Boehm

TRAINING & REFERENCE

murach's HTML5 and CSS3

Zak Ruvalcaba

Anne Boehm

MIKE MURACH & ASSOCIATES, INC.

4340 N. Knoll Ave. • Fresno, CA 93722

www.murach.com • murachbooks@murach.com

Editorial team

Authors:	Zak Ruvalcaba
	Anne Boehm
Editors:	Mike Murach
	Ben Murach
Cover design:	Zylka Design
Production:	Maria Pedroza David

Books for web developers

Murach's HTML5 and CSS3

Murach's JavaScript and DOM Scripting

Murach's PHP and MySQL

Murach's Java Servlets and JSP (Second Edition)

Murach's ASP.NET 4 Web Programming with C# 2010

Murach's ASP.NET 4 Web Programming with VB 2010

Books on Java, C#, and Visual Basic

Murach's Java Programming

Murach's C# 2010

Murach's Visual Basic 2010

Books for database programmers

Murach's SQL Server 2008 for Developers

Murach's Oracle SQL and PL/SQL

Murach's MySQL for Developers

Murach's ADO.NET 4 Database Programming with C# 2010

Murach's ADO.NET 4 Database Programming with VB 2010

For more on Murach books, please visit us at www.murach.com

Printed in the United States of America

10 9 8 7 6 5 4 3 2 1
ISBN: 978-1-890774-66-0

Contents

Expanded contents

Chapter 8   How to work with images

Chapter 9   How to work with tables

Chapter 10   How to work with forms

Section 3 JavaScript and jQuery skills

Chapter 13 How to use JavaScript to enhance your web pages

Chapter 14 How to use jQuery to enhance your web pages

Chapter 15 How to use jQuery Mobile to build mobile web sites

Chapter 18   **How to deploy a web site on a web server**

Introduction

HTML5 is changing the way that web pages are developed. Just one of the reasons why is that the new HTML5 semantic tags make it easier to develop web pages and format them with CSS. These tags also improve user accessibility and are allowing search engines to return ever more relevant results. For those reasons alone, you should start using HTML5 right away.

You can do that because the best HTML5 features are already supported by all modern browsers. In addition, you can make HTML5 work on older browsers by implementing some simple workarounds. You'll also find that it's relatively easy to modify the HTML and CSS for your current pages so they use HTML5 and CSS3. In fact, every web developer should start using the best features of HTML5 starting today.

The trick of course is learning how to use HTML5 and CSS3 as quickly, as easily, and as sensibly as possible. That's where this book comes in. Unlike other HTML5 books, this one integrates all of the HTML5 and CSS3 skills that you need today with the proven instructional approach that made the first edition of this book so effective. As a result, you'll learn how to use the new features at the same time that you see where they fit in with the old features.

That's why this is the right book for web developers who want to expand and update their skills. That includes web designers, JavaScript and jQuery programmers, and server-side programmers who use PHP, ASP.NET, Java servlets and JSP, or other scripting languages. But that's also why this is the right book for novices who are learning HTML and CSS for the first time.

What this book does

- To get you started right, the six chapters in section 1 show you how to use HTML and CSS to develop web pages at a professional level. These chapters are designed to teach you what you need to know faster and better than ever, and they include all of the relevant HTML5 and CSS3 features that you can start using right away.

  In chapter 3, for example, you'll learn how to use the new HTML5 semantic elements to structure a web page, and that's the game changer. Then, chapters 4 through 6 show you how to use CSS and CSS3 to format the

HTML of your pages, including how to use the new CSS3 properties for text and border shadows, background gradients, and text columns.

- When you finish the first 6 chapters, you will have the perspective and skills you need for developing professional web pages. Then, you can add to those skills by reading any of the chapters in the next 3 sections...and you don't have to read those sections or chapters in sequence. In other words, you can skip to any of the last three sections after you finish section 1.

- The chapters in section 2 let you learn new skills whenever you need them...like having a mentor right at your side, showing you how to do whatever you need to know next. If, for example, you want to learn more about using images, you can skip to chapter 8. If you want to learn how to use the new data validation features for forms, you can skip to chapter 10. And if you want to learn how to use the new HTML5 audio and video tags, you can skip to chapter 11.

- Because most modern web sites use some JavaScript, chapters 13 and 14 of section 3 show you how to use JavaScript and jQuery (today's most popular library of ready-to-use JavaScript routines) to add special features to a web site. Then, in chapter 15, you can learn how to use jQuery Mobile for developing web sites for mobile devices, which by itself should pay for this book. And in chapter 16, you can learn how to use advanced HTML5 features like embedded fonts, geolocation, web storage, and canvas.

- Finally, section 4 presents two related subjects that you can skip to whenever you're ready for them. In chapter 17, you can learn the basic principles for designing a web site. In chapter 18, you can learn how to deploy a web site and get it into the search engines.

Why you'll learn faster and better with this book

Like all our books, this one has features that you won't find in competing books. That's why we believe you'll learn faster and better with our book than with any other. Here are a few of those features.

- From the first page to the last, this book shows you how to use HTML and CSS the modern, professional way, with HTML for the structure and content of each page and CSS for the formatting and page layout. That way, your web pages and your web sites will be easier to create and maintain.

- Because HTML5 and CSS3 are integrated throughout the book, you won't learn these features out of context, which is the way they're treated in most competing books. Instead, you'll learn exactly where these features fit into the overall context of web site development.

- Because section 1 presents a complete subset of HTML and CSS in just 6 chapters, you are ready for productive work much sooner than you are when you use competing books. In most competing books, for example, you won't learn how to use CSS for page layout until late in the book, even though that's a critical part of web page development.

- If you page through this book, you'll see that all of the information is presented in "paired pages," with the essential syntax, guidelines, and examples on the right page and the perspective and extra explanation on the left page. This helps you learn faster by reading less...and this is the ideal reference format when you need to refresh your memory about how to do something.

- To show you how HTML and CSS work together, this book presents all the code for complete web pages that range from the simple to the complex. To see how that works, take a quick look at the four sets of web pages and code that start in figures 4-17, 5-6, 5-13, and 6-5 in chapters 4, 5, and 6. As we see it, studying complete examples is the best way to master HTML and CSS because they show the relationships between the segments of code. And yet, most competing books limit themselves to snippets of code that don't show these relationships.

- Of course, this book also presents dozens of short examples. So it's easy to find an example that shows you how to do whatever you need to do as you develop web pages. And our "paired pages" presentation method makes it much easier to find the example that you're looking for than it is with traditional presentations where the code is embedded in the text.

What software you need

To develop web pages with HTML and CSS, you can use any text editor that you like. However, a text editor that includes syntax coloring and auto-completion will help you develop applications more quickly and with fewer errors. That's why we recommend Aptana Studio 3 for both Windows and Mac OS users. Although Aptana is free, it provides many powerful features.

Then, to test a web page, you need multiple web browsers. Because Internet Explorer is the browser that deviates the most from the standards, you should always test your pages in IE. But we also recommend that you test your pages in a standard browser that has excellent support for HTML5 and CSS3, like Mozilla Firefox, Opera, Apple's Safari, or Google's Chrome. The one(s) you choose will depend on which browsers your site visitors are using. But here again, all of these browsers are free.

To help you install these products, Appendix A provides the web site addresses and procedures that you'll need.

How our downloadable files can help you learn

If you go to our web site at www.murach.com, you can download all the files that you need for getting the most from this book. These files include:

- the HTML and CSS files for all of the applications and examples in this book

- the HTML and CSS files that you will use as the starting points for the exercises

These files let you test, review, and experiment with the code. They also let you copy and paste any of the source code into your own files. Here again, appendix A shows you how to download and install these files.

Support materials for trainers and instructors

If you're a corporate trainer or a college instructor who would like to use this book for a course, we offer an Instructor's CD that includes: (1) a complete set of PowerPoint slides that you can use to review and reinforce the content of the book; (2) instructional objectives that describe the skills a student should have upon completion of each chapter; (3) test banks that measure mastery of those skills; and (4) additional student materials.

To learn more about this Instructor's CD and to find out how to get it, please go to our web site at www.murach.com and click on the Trainers link or the Instructors link. Or, if you prefer, you can call Kelly at 1-800-221-5528 or send an email to kelly@murach.com.

Related books

If you want to learn client-side or server-side web programming when you finish this book, we offer several books that will help you. Our JavaScript and DOM scripting book will help you get the most from JavaScript. Our ASP.NET books will show you how to develop web applications with C# or Visual Basic. Our servlets and JSP book will show you how to develop web applications with Java. And our PHP and MySQL book will show you how to develop web applications with PHP as the scripting language and MySQL as the database.

To find out more about our new books and latest editions, please go to our web site at www.murach.com. There, you'll find the details for all of our books, including complete tables of contents.

Please let us know how this book works for you

From the start of this project, we had three goals. First, we wanted to simplify and improve the first edition to help you learn even faster. Second, we wanted to integrate the new HTML5 and CSS3 features into the proven approach of the first edition because we know that's the right way to teach those features. Third, we wanted to raise the level of expertise of the first edition to make the new edition work even better for professional developers.

Now, we hope we've succeeded. We thank you for buying this book. We wish you all the best with your web development. And if you have any comments, we would appreciate hearing from you.

Anne Boehm, Author
anne@murach.com

Zak Ruvalcaba
zak@modulemedia.com

Section 1

A crash course
in HTML and CSS

The six chapters in this section are designed to get you off to a fast start. First, chapter 1 presents the concepts and terms that you need for using HTML and CSS. Then, chapter 2 shows you how to enter, edit, test, and validate the HTML and CSS for the web pages of a web site. These chapters provide all of the background that you need for learning the coding details of HTML and CSS.

Then, chapter 3 shows you how to code the HTML that defines the content and structure for a web page. Chapter 4 shows you how to code the CSS that does basic formatting to the HTML content. Chapter 5 shows you how to use the CSS box model for spacing, borders, and backgrounds. And chapter 6 shows you how to use CSS for page layout.

When you complete these chapters, you'll be able to develop web pages at a professional level. Then, you can expand your skills by reading the other chapters in this book.

Please note, however, that you don't have to read the chapters in the other sections in sequence. Instead, you can skip to the chapter that presents the skills that you want to learn next. In other words, the six chapters in this section present the prerequisites for all of the other chapters, and all of the other chapters are written as independent learning modules. As a result, you can read any of those chapters whenever you need its skills.

1

Introduction to web development

This chapter introduces you to the concepts and terms that you need to work with HTML and CSS. When you're finished with this chapter, you'll have the background you need for learning how to build web sites.

How web applications work

The *World Wide Web*, or web, consists of many components that work together to bring a web page to your desktop over the *Internet*. Before you start web pages of your own, you should have a basic understanding of how these components work together.

The components of a web application

The first diagram in figure 1-1 shows that web applications consist of *clients* and a *web server.* The clients are the computers, tablets, and mobile devices that use the web applications. They access the web pages through programs known as *web browsers*. The web server holds the files that make up a web application.

A *network* is a system that allows clients and servers to communicate. The Internet in turn is a large network that consists of many smaller networks. In a diagram like this, the "cloud" represents the network or Internet that connects the clients and servers.

In general, you don't need to know how the cloud works. But you should have a general idea of what's going on. That's why the second diagram in this figure gives you a conceptual view of the architecture of the Internet.

To start, networks can be categorized by size. A *local area network* (*LAN*) is a small network of computers that are near each other and can communicate with each other over short distances. Computers on a LAN are typically in the same building or in adjacent buildings. This type of network is often called an *intranet*, and it can be used to run web applications for use by employees only.

In contrast, a *wide area network* (*WAN*) consists of multiple LANs that have been connected together over long distances using *routers*. To pass information from one client to another, a router determines which network is closest to the destination and sends the information over that network. A WAN can be owned privately by one company or it can be shared by multiple companies.

An *Internet service provider* (*ISP*) is a company that owns a WAN that is connected to the Internet. An ISP leases access to its network to other companies that need to be connected to the Internet.

The Internet is a global network consisting of multiple WANs that have been connected together. ISPs connect their WANs at large routers called *Internet exchange points* (*IXP*). This allows anyone connected to the Internet to exchange information with anyone else.

This diagram shows an example of data crossing the Internet. Here, data is being sent from the client in the top left to the server in the bottom right. First, the data leaves the client's LAN and enters the WAN owned by the client's ISP. Next, the data is routed through IXPs to the WAN owned by the server's ISP. Then, it enters the server's LAN and finally reaches the server. All of this can happen in less than 1/10th of a second.

The components of a web application

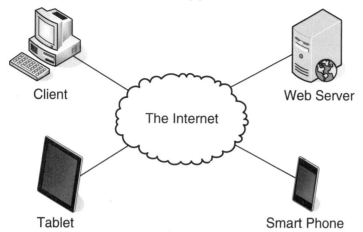

The architecture of the Internet

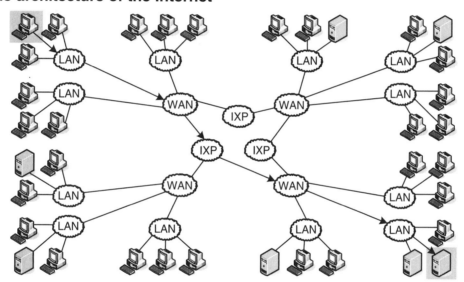

Description

- A web application consists of clients, a web server, and a network. The *clients* use programs known as *web browsers* to request web pages from the web server. The *web server* returns the pages that are requested to the browser.

- A *local area network* (LAN) directly connects computers that are near each other. This kind of network is often called an *intranet*.

- A *wide area network* (WAN) consists of two or more LANs that are connected by *routers*. The routers route information from one network to another.

- The *Internet* consists of many WANs that have been connected at *Internet exchange points* (IXP). There are several dozen IXPs located throughout the world.

- An *Internet service provider* (ISP) owns a WAN and leases access to its network. It connects its WAN to the rest of the Intenet at one or more IXPs.

Figure 1-1   The components of a web application

How static web pages are processed

A *static web page* like the one at the top of figure 1-2 is a web page that only changes when the web developer changes it. This web page is sent directly from the web server to the web browser when the browser requests it.

The diagram in this figure shows how a web server processes a request for a static web page. This process begins when a client requests a web page in a web browser. To do that, the user can either type the address of the page into the browser's address bar or click a link in the current page that specifies the next page to load.

In either case, the web browser builds a request for the web page and sends it to the web server. This request, known as an *HTTP request*, is formatted using the *hypertext transport protocol* (HTTP), which lets the web server know which file is being requested.

When the web server receives the HTTP request, it retrieves the requested file from the disk drive. This file contains the *HTML (HyperText Markup Language)* for the requested page. Then, the web server sends the file back to the browser as part of an *HTTP response*.

When the browser receives the HTTP response, it *renders* (translates) the HTML into a web page that is displayed in the browser. Then, the user can view the content. If the user requests another page, either by clicking a link or typing another web address into the browser's address bar, the process begins again.

In this book, you'll learn how to use HTML to create static web pages. You can spot these pages in a web browser by looking at the extension in the address bar. If the extension is .htm or .html, the page is a static web page.

A static web page at http://www.valleytownhall.com/toobin.html

How a web server processes a static web page

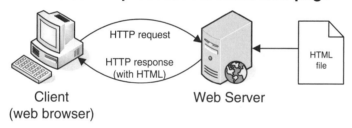

Client
(web browser)

Web Server

Description

- *Hypertext Markup Language* (*HTML*) is the language used to design the web pages of an application.

- A *static web page* is an HTML document that's stored on the web server and doesn't change. The filenames for static web pages have .htm or .html extensions.

- When the user requests a static web page, the browser sends an *HTTP request* to the web server that includes the name of the file that's being requested.

- When the web server receives the request, it retrieves the HTML for the web page and sends it back to the browser as part of an *HTTP response*.

- When the browser receives the HTTP response, it *renders* the HTML into a web page that is displayed in the browser.

Figure 1-2   How static web pages are processed

How dynamic web pages are processed

A *dynamic web page* like the one in figure 1-3 is a page that's created by a program or script on the web server each time it is requested. This program or script is executed by an *application server* based on the data that's sent along with the HTTP request. In this example, the HTTP request identified the book that's shown. Then, the program or script retrieved the image and data for that book from a *database server*.

The diagram in this figure shows how a web server processes a dynamic web page. The process begins when the user requests a page in a web browser. To do that, the user can either type the URL of the page in the browser's address bar, click a link that specifies the dynamic page to load, or click a button that submits a form that contains the data that the dynamic page should process.

In each case, the web browser builds an HTTP request and sends it to the web server. This request includes whatever data the application needs for processing the request. If, for example, the user has entered data into a form, that data will be included in the HTTP request.

When the web server receives the HTTP request, the server examines the file extension of the requested web page to identify the application server that should process the request. The web server then forwards the request to the application server that processes that type of web page.

Next, the application server retrieves the appropriate program or script from the hard drive. It also loads any form data that the user submitted. Then, it executes the script. As the script executes, it generates the HTML for the web page. If necessary, the script will request data from a database server and use that data as part of the web page it is generating.

When the script is finished, the application server sends the dynamically generated HTML back to the web server. Then, the web server sends the HTML back to the browser in an HTTP response.

When the web browser receives the HTTP response, it renders the HTML and displays the web page. Note, however, that the web browser has no way to tell whether the HTML in the HTTP response was for a static page or a dynamic page. It just renders the HTML.

When the page is displayed, the user can view the content. Then, when the user requests another page, the process begins again. The process that begins with the user requesting a web page and ends with the server sending a response back to the client is called a *round trip*.

Dynamic web pages let you create interactive *web applications* that do all of the types of processing that you find on the Internet including eCommerce applications. Although you won't learn how to develop dynamic web pages in this book, you will learn how to create the HTML forms that send user data to the web server. Once you master HTML, you can learn how to use server-side languages like JSP, ASP, or PHP to create the dynamic pages that a web site needs.

A dynamic web page at amazon.com

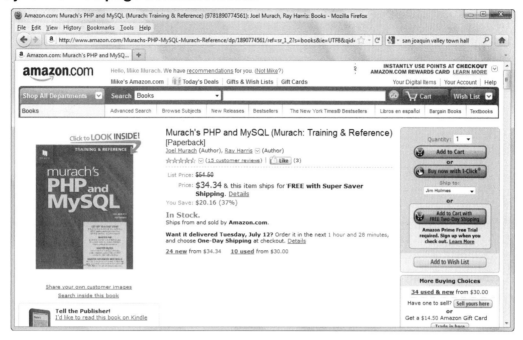

How a web server processes a dynamic web page

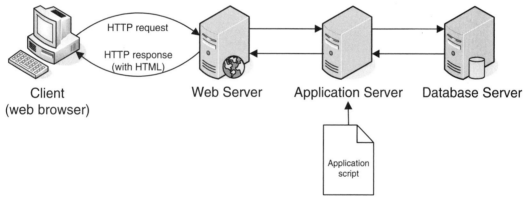

Description

- A *dynamic web page* is a web page that's generated by a server-side program or script.

- When a web server receives a request for a dynamic web page, it looks up the extension of the requested file to find out which *application server* should process the request.

- When the application server receives a request, it runs the specified script. Often, this script uses the data that it gets from the web browser to get the appropriate data from a *database server*. This script can also store the data that it receives in the database.

- When the application server finishes processing the data, it generates the HTML for a web page and returns it to the web server. Then, the web server returns the HTML to the web browser as part of an HTTP response.

Figure 1-3   How dynamic web pages are processed

A survey of web browsers
and server-side scripting languages

Figure 1-4 summarizes the five web browsers that are used the most today. Microsoft's Internet Explorer (IE) is the browser that comes with Windows. It has long been the most widely-used browser, but other browsers have been catching up in recent years.

Firefox is available for Windows, Mac OS, Linux, and other operating systems. Firefox was built using source code from the original Netscape Navigator web browser, and many web developers use it as their primary browser because they like its many features including its debugging features.

Google's Chrome is a recent addition to the most popular web browsers, and its popularity is growing fast. Chrome is based on the WebKit rendering engine, which is the same one that Safari uses.

Safari and Opera are used by a smaller percentage of users. Safari is the default web browser on Mac OS, but it is also available for Windows. Opera is available for Windows, Mac OS, Linux, and other operating systems.

Next, this figure summarizes the most common *scripting languages* for web servers. These are the languages that let you develop dynamic web pages. For instance, ASP.NET is a Microsoft product. JSP is a free, open-source language that is commonly used with Java servlets. And PHP is another free, open-source language. To develop dynamic web pages, you need to choose the scripting language that you will use for *server-side processing*.

When you choose the scripting language, you also determine what web server you're going to need. For instance, JSP and PHP run on an *Apache web server*, which was developed by the Apache Software Foundation. It is an open-source software project that's available for free, and it runs on most operating systems, especially Linux systems. In contrast, ASP.NET runs on Microsoft's *Internet Information Services* (*IIS*), which isn't open source and runs on a Windows system.

Web browsers

Browser	Published by	Available on
Internet Explorer	Microsoft	Windows
Firefox	Mozilla Corporation	All major operating systems
Chrome	Google	All major operating systems
Safari	Apple	Macintosh and Windows
Opera	Opera Software	All major operating systems

Server-side scripting languages

Language	Description
ASP.NET	Runs on a Microsoft IIS web server. Its pages have the .aspx extension.
JSP	A free, open-source language that is commonly used with Java servlets. It runs on an Apache web server, and its pages have the .jsp extension.
PHP	A free, open-source language that is typically used with an Apache web server. Its pages have the .php extension.
ColdFusion	A commercial scripting language from Adobe that integrates well with Adobe Flash and Flex. Its pages have the .cfml file extension.
Ruby	A free, open-source language that is typically combined with the Rails framework to simplify development. Its pages have the .rb extension.
Perl	A free, open-source language that was originally designed for use at the UNIX command line to manipulate text. Its pages have the .pl extension.
Python	A free, open-source language that can be used to develop many types of applications besides web applications. Its pages have the .py extension.

Description

- When you develop a web site for general use, you need to test it on all five of the web browsers listed above including all versions that are still in common use.
- To develop dynamic web pages, you use a *server-side scripting language* like ASP.NET, JSP, or PHP.
- The scripting languages are designed to run on specific web servers. The two most popular web servers are Microsoft IIS (Internet Information Services) and Apache.

Figure 1-4   A survey of web browsers and server-side scripting languages

How client-side JavaScript fits into web development

In contrast to the server-side processing that's done for dynamic web pages, *JavaScript* is a scripting language that provides for *client-side processing*. In the web site in figure 1-5, for example, JavaScript is used to change the images that are shown without using server-side processing.

To make this work, all of the required images are loaded into the browser when the page is requested. Then, if the user clicks on one of the color swatches below a shirt, the shirt image is changed to the one with the right color. This is called an *image swap*. Similarly, if the user moves the mouse over a shirt, the image is replaced by a close-up image of the shirt. This is called an *image rollover*.

The diagram in this figure shows how JavaScript processing works. When a browser requests a web page, both the HTML and the related JavaScript are returned to the browser by the web server. Then, the JavaScript code is executed in the web browser by the browser's *JavaScript engine*. This takes some of the processing burden off the server and makes the application run faster. Often, JavaScript is used in conjunction with dynamic web pages, but it can also be used with static web pages.

Besides image swaps and rollovers, there are many other uses for JavaScript. For instance, another common use is to validate the data that the user enters into an HTML form before it is sent to the server for processing. This saves unnecessary trips to the server. Other common uses of JavaScript are to run slide shows, rotate headlines or products in one area of a web page, and provide animation. In fact, whenever you see a portion of a web page cycle through a series of text blocks or images, that's probably being done by JavaScript.

In this book, you won't learn how to code JavaScript. However, you will learn how to use existing JavaScript routines in section 3 of this book. For instance, chapter 13 shows you how to use JavaScript to enhance your web pages with features like image swaps, slide shows, and data validation. Chapter 14 shows you how to use a JavaScript library called jQuery to add features like carousels, accordions, and sortable lists. And chapter 15 shows you how to use a JavaScript library called jQuery Mobile to develop web sites for mobile devices.

A web page with image swaps and rollovers

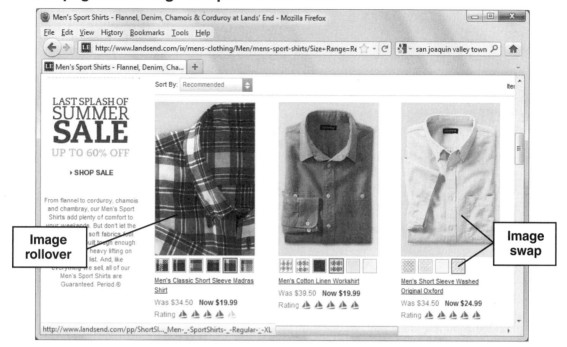

How JavaScript fits into this architecture

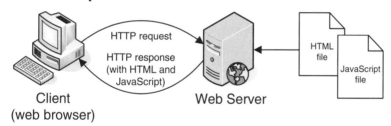

Three of the common uses of JavaScript

- Data validation
- Image swaps and rollovers
- Slide shows

Description

- *JavaScript* is a *client-side scripting language* that is run by the *JavaScript engine* of a web browser and controls the operation of the browser.
- When the browser requests an HTML page that contains JavaScript or a link to a JavaScript file, both the HTML and the JavaScript are loaded into the browser.
- Because JavaScript runs on the client, not the server, it provides functions that don't require a trip back to the server. This can help an application run more efficiently.

Figure 1-5   How client-side JavaScript fits into web development

An introduction to HTML and CSS

To develop a web page, you use HTML to define the content and structure of the page. Then, you use CSS to format that content. The topics that follow introduce you to HTML and CSS.

The HTML for a web page

HyperText Markup Language (*HTML*) is used to define the content and structure of a web page. In figure 1-6, for example, you can see the HTML for a web page followed by a browser that shows how that page is displayed in the Firefox browser. Although you're going to learn how to code every aspect of an HTML page in this book, here's a brief introduction to what's going on.

The code for the entire page is called an *HTML document*. This document starts with a *DOCTYPE declaration* that is followed by *tags* that identify the *HTML elements* within the document. The *opening tag* for each element consists of the element name surrounded by angle brackets, as in <html>. And the *closing tag* consists of a left angle bracket, a forward slash, the element name, and the right angle bracket, as in </html>.

The basic structure of an HTML document consists of head and body elements that are coded within the html element. The head section contains elements that provide information about the document. The body section contains the elements that will be displayed in the web browser. For instance, the title element in the head section provides the title that's shown in the title bar of the web browser, while the h1 element in the body section provides the heading that's displayed in the browser window.

Many elements can be coded with *attributes* that identify the element and define the way the content in the element is displayed. These attributes are coded within the opening tag, and each attribute consists of an attribute name, an equals sign, and the attribute value. For instance, the <img> tag in this example has two attributes named src and alt. In this case, the src attribute provides the name of the image file that should be displayed and the alt attribute provides the text that should be displayed if the image can't be found.

The code for an HTML file named javascript_book.html

```
<!DOCTYPE html>
<html lang="en">
    <head>
        <meta charset="utf-8">
        <title>JavaScript book</title>
    </head>
    <body>
        <h1>JavaScript and DOM Scripting</h1>
        <img src="javascriptbook.jpg" alt="JavaScript Book">
        <p>Today, web users expect web sites to provide advanced
            features, dynamic user interfaces, and fast response times. To
            deliver that, web developers need to know the JavaScript
            language. Beyond that, though, they need to know how to use
            JavaScript to script the Document Object Model (or DOM).</p>
        <p>Now, at last, your trainees can learn both JavaScript and DOM
            scripting in this one great book. To find out how this book does
            it, <a href="">read more...</a></p><br><br><br>
    </body>
</html>
```

The HTML displayed in a web browser

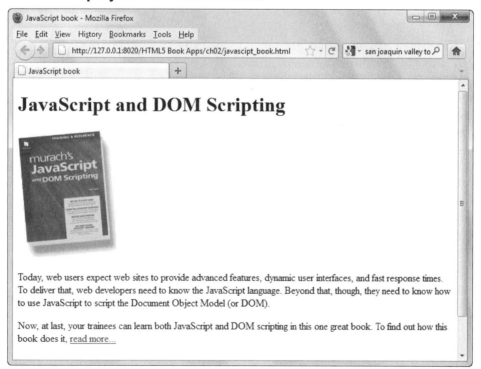

Description

- *HTML (HyperText Markup Language)* is used to define the structure and content of a web page.

Figure 1-6   The HTML for a web page

The CSS for a web page

Not long ago, HTML documents were coded so the HTML not only defined the content and structure of the web page but also the formatting of that content. However, this mix of structural and formatting elements made it hard to edit, maintain, and reformat the web pages.

Today, however, *Cascading Style Sheets* (*CSS*) let you separate the formatting from the content and structure of a web page. As a result, the formatting that was once done with HTML should now be done with CSS.

In most cases, the best way to apply a *style sheet* to an HTML document is to code the styles in a separate file called an *external style sheet*. Then, to apply the style sheet, you code a link element in the head section of the HTML document as shown at the top of figure 1-7. Here, the href attribute of the tag says that the style sheet in the file named book.css should be applied to the HTML document.

After this link element, you can see the CSS that's in the book.css file. This is followed by a browser that shows how the web page is displayed after the style sheet has been applied to it. If you compare this to the browser in the previous figure, you can see that the page is now centered with a border around it, the heading is larger, the font for the text has been changed, there's less spacing between paragraphs, and the text is displayed to the right of the book image. This gives you a quick idea of how much you can do with CSS.

Although you're going to learn how to code CSS in chapters 4, 5, and 6, here's a brief introduction to how the CSS works. First, this CSS file consists of four *rule sets*. Each of these rule sets consists of a *selector* and a *declaration block*. The selector identifies an HTML element, and the declaration block specifies the formatting for the element. Within the declaration block are one or more *declarations* (or *rules*) that specify the formatting for the element.

For instance, the first rule set applies to the body element. Its first rule says that the font family for the content should be Arial, Helvetica, or the default sans-serif type, in that order of preference. Then, the second rule says that the font-size should be 82.5% of the browser's default font size. These rules change the font and font size for the elements that are coded within the body.

The third rule for the body sets its width to 500 pixels. Then, the fourth rule sets the top and bottom margins to zero and the left and right margins to auto, which centers the page in the browser window. Finally, the fifth rule sets the padding within the body to 1 em (a unit that you'll learn about in chapter 4), and the sixth rule adds a solid, navy border to the body.

Similarly, the second rule set formats the h1 element in the HTML with a larger font size and the navy color. The third rule set formats the image by floating it to the left so the <p> elements are displayed to its right. And the fourth rule set changes the spacing between p elements.

You will of course learn all of the details for coding rule sets in this book, but this should give you the idea of what's going on. In short, the HTML defines the content and structure of the document, and the CSS defines the formatting of the content. This separates the content from the formatting, which makes it easier to create and maintain web pages.

The element in the head section of the HTML file that links it to the CSS file

```
<link rel="stylesheet" href="book.css" >
```

The code for the CSS file named book.css

```
body {
    font-family: Arial, Helvetica, sans-serif;
    font-size: 82.5%;
    width: 500px;
    margin: 0 auto;
    padding: 1em;
    border: 1px solid navy;
}
h1 {
    margin: 0;
    padding: .25em;
    font-size: 250%;
    color: navy;
}
img  {
    float: left;
    margin: 0 1em;
}
p {
    margin: 0;
    padding-bottom: .5em;
}
```

The web page displayed in a web browser

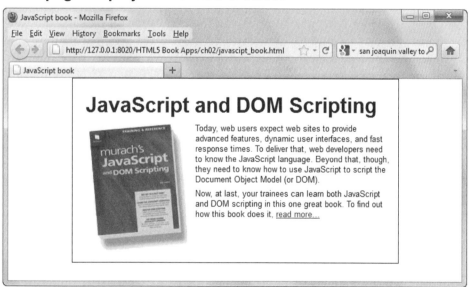

Description

- *Cascading Style Sheets* (*CSS*) are used to control how web pages are displayed by specifying the fonts, colors, borders, spacing, and layout of the pages.

Figure 1-7   The CSS for a web page

A short history of the HTML and CSS standards

As figure 1-8 shows, HTML is a standardized language that has been around since the early 1990's. The last version of HTML (4.01) was released in December 1999. Then, XHTML 1.0 was introduced in January 2000.

XHTML (eXtensible HTML) is a modified version of HTML that supports the same elements as HTML 4.01, but uses the syntax of XML. This is a stricter syntax that allows XHTML to be read and manipulated by automated tools. This also allows XHTML editors to identify errors in the document structure more easily.

Today, HTML 5 is a specification that provides many new features and replaces the old HTML and XHTML standards with a single standard. Although this standard won't be officially adopted for several more years, all current browsers support many of its features. Because these features improve the way that web pages are developed, you should start using them right now.

As this figure also shows, CSS is a standardized language that goes back to 1996. However, it wasn't widely used as the right way to format HTML pages until the 2000's. Today, CSS 3.0 is the latest draft standard, and many of its features are supported by all modern browsers. Here again, these features improve the way web pages are developed so it makes sense to start using them right now.

In this book, you're going to learn how to use HTML 5 and CSS 3 to develop web pages. That means that you're going to learn the HTML and CSS that hasn't changed because that's still essential for developing web pages. But you're also going to learn the new features of HTML 5 and CSS 3 that are currently supported by all modern browsers, plus the new features that are most likely to be supported in the next couple of years. That way, you'll be developing web pages that take advantage of the best features of HTML 5 and CSS 3.

What about older browsers that don't support the new features? This book will also show you how to get your web pages to work in those browsers. Often, though, you won't have to do anything because the new features will just be ignored by the old browsers with no harm done. If, for example, you use CSS 3 to provide for rounded corners or shadows on HTML boxes, these features will improve the graphics in modern browsers but be ignored in older browsers.

This figure also presents two web sites that you ought to become familiar with. The first is for the *World Wide Web Consortium*, which is commonly referred to as *W3C*. This is the group that develops the standards, and this site should be one of your primary sources for HTML and CSS information.

The second web site is for the *Web Hypertext Application Technology Working Group (WHATWG)*. This is a community of people interested in evolving HTML and related technologies, and this site should be another primary source for HTML and CSS information.

Incidentally, from this point forward, we'll refer to HTML 5 and CSS 3 as *HTML5* and *CSS3*. In particular, we'll use these terms to identify the new features of HTML5 and CSS3 so you won't miss them.

Highlights in the development of the HTML standards

Version	Description
HTML 1.0	A draft specification released in January 1993 that was never adopted as a standard.
HTML 2.0	Adopted in November 1995.
HTML 4.0	Adopted in December 1997. It formalized new features that were used by web browsers and deprecated older features.
HTML 4.01	Adopted in December 1999 and updated through May 2001.
XHTML 1.0	Adopted in January 2000 and revised in August 2002. It reformulates HTML 4 using the syntax of XML, which makes it easier to parse the web page. This allows automated tools to find errors in a web page.
XHTML 1.1	Adopted in May 2001. The control of the presentation of content is now done through CSS.
HTML 5	Released as a working draft in January 2008. Originally, it defined an HTML version called HTML 5 and an XHTML version called XHTML 5. Today, the draft has been enhanced into a new HTML specification that replaces both HTML 4 and XHTML 1.

Highlights in the development of the CSS standards

Version	Description
1.0	Adopted in December 1996.
2.0	Adopted in May 1998.
2.1	First released as a candidate standard in February 2004, it returned to working draft status in June 2005. It became a candidate standard again in July 2007.
3.0	A modularized version of CSS with the earliest drafts in June 1999.

Two web sites that you should become familiar with

*   The *World Wide Web Consortium* (*W3C*) is an international community in which member organizations, a full-time staff, and the public work together to develop Web standards. It's web site address is: www.w3.org.

*   The *Web Hypertext Application Technology Working Group* (*WHATWG*) is a community of people interested in evolving HTML and related technologies. It's web site address is: www.whatwg.org.

Description

*   Today, HTML 5 is an HTML specification that replaces both HTML 4 and XHTML 1. As a result, there will no longer be a distinction between HTML and XHTML.

*   At this writing in 2011, the HTML5 and CSS3 standards still haven't been accepted and it may be several years before they are.

*   Nevertheless, all modern browsers support many of the best features of HTML5 and CSS3. Those are the features that this book emphasizes, and those are the features that you should start implementing right now.

Figure 1-8   A short history of the HTML and CSS standards

Tools for web development

To create and edit the HTML and CSS files for a web site, you need either a text editor or an IDE for web development. To deploy a web site on the Internet, you also need an FTP program to upload the files from your computer or network server to the web server. You'll learn about these tools next.

Text editors for HTML and CSS

Although you can use any text editor to enter and edit HTML and CSS files, a better editor can speed development time and reduce coding errors. For that reason, we recommend Aptana Studio 3. It is a free editor that runs on both Windows and Mac OS systems, and it has many excellent features. For instance, Aptana provides syntax highlighting and auto-completion lists that let you select an item after you enter the first characters.

Aptana's auto-completion feature is illustrated in figure 1-9. Here, the developer has entered the first letter of an <img> tag, and the auto-completion list shows the words that start with that letter. At that point, the developer can move the cursor to the right word in the list and press the Tab key to enter that word into the code. Then, Aptana finishes the opening tag and adds the ending tag so the developer can type the content between the two tags.

In the next chapter, you'll learn how to use Aptana Studio 3 to develop your web pages. That will help you appreciate the many features that it provides. Please note, however, that you can use any text editor that you like for developing your web pages. Or, you can use an IDE like one of those in the next figure.

Aptana Studio 3 with open HTML and CSS files

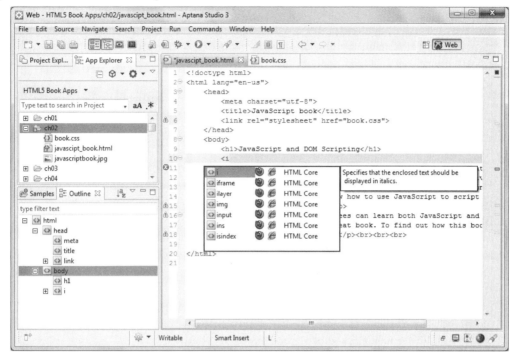

Three free text editors that you can use with this book

Editor	Runs on
Aptana Studio 3	Windows, Macintosh, Linux
Notepad++	Windows
TextWrangler	Macintosh

Description

- A text editor lets you enter and edit the HTML and CSS files for a web application.

- Some common features of a text editor for HTML and CSS are syntax highlighting and auto-completion.

- Today, there are many text editors for developing web applications with HTML and CSS. Most of them are either free or inexpensive.

- For this book, we recommend the use of Aptana Studio 3 because it's free; it runs on Windows, Macintosh, and Linux; and it has many excellent features.

- In chapter 2, you'll learn how to use Aptana Studio 3, but you don't have to use it to do the exercises for this book.

Figure 1-9   Text editors for HTML and CSS

IDEs for web development

After you get some experience with a text editor like Aptana Studio 3, you may be interested in an *Integrated Development Environment* (*IDE*) for web development. For instance, Adobe Dreamweaver has long been the most popular commercial IDE for web development.

As you can see in figure 1-10, Dreamweaver lets you edit HTML or CSS code in one panel of its window while it shows you how the web page will look in another panel. Dreamweaver also lets you generate code instead of entering it by dragging the symbols for common elements onto the HTML document. It provides the starting code for an HTML document whenever you start a new file. It helps you manage the folders and files for the web site. It provides an FTP program that uploads the pages from your development server to your Internet server. And it has many other features.

In general, an IDE like Dreamweaver can help you make dramatic improvements in your productivity. That's why professional web developers often use IDEs for web development. Note, however, that IDEs vary considerably in features and price. For instance, some IDEs offer features that let you integrate your HTML and CSS development with JavaScript and server-side scripting languages like PHP, Perl, and Python. So before you buy an IDE, you need to find the IDE that best suits your requirements and budget.

At the highest level, an IDE for web development can include all of the programs that are required for developing a web site. IDEs like this are often referred to as *suites*. For example, the Design Premium edition of the Adobe Creative Suite includes Photoshop for editing photos and images, Illustrator for creating and editing illustrations, Flash for adding animation and interactivity to web pages, and several other programs that are related to web development. Similarly, Microsoft Expression Studio provides a variety of related products for developing web pages.

Adobe Dreamweaver

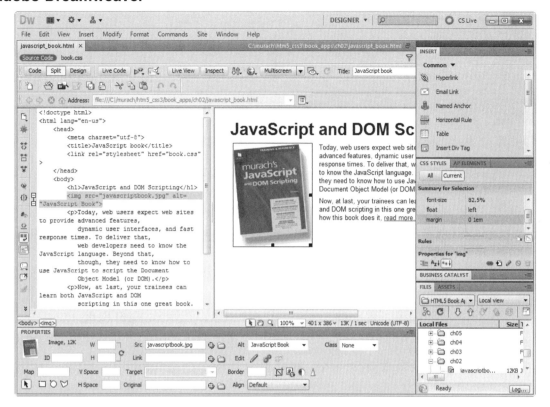

Popular IDEs for web development

IDE	Runs on
Adobe Dreamweaver	Windows and Macintosh
Microsoft Expression Web	Windows

Popular suites for web development

IDE	Runs on
Adobe Creative Suite	Windows and Macintosh
Microsoft Expression Studio	Windows

Description

- An *Integrated Development Environment* (*IDE*) goes beyond text editing to provide other features for the development of web sites.
- *Suites* are IDEs that provide all of the software components that you need for the development of a web site.

Figure 1-10   IDEs for web development

FTP programs for uploading files to the web server

If you want to *deploy* (or *publish*) your web site on the Internet, you need to transfer the folders and files for your web site from your computer or network to a web server with Internet access. To do that, you use an *FTP program* like one of those listed in figure 1-11. This type of program uses *File Transfer Protocol* to transfer files to or from the web server.

Some text editors like Aptana Studio 3 include FTP programs, and IDEs like Dreamweaver typically include them. If your text editor doesn't provide an FTP program, you may be able to find a *plug-in* for an FTP program. Then, you can access that FTP program from your text editor.

If you don't already have an Internet web server, one option is to find an *Internet Service Provider* (*ISP*) that provides *web hosting*. If you search the web, you'll be able to find many ISPs that provide web hosting, often for a small monthly fee.

If you're going to use dynamic web pages on your web site, you need to find an ISP that supports the server-side language and the database that you're going to use. If, for example, you're going to use PHP with a MySQL database, which is a common combination, you need to find an ISP that supports that.

When you select a web host, you get an *IP address* like 64.71.179.86 that uniquely identifies your web site (IP stands for Internet Protocol). Then, you can get a *domain name* like www.murach.com. To do that, you can use any number of companies on the Internet, and sometimes you can get the domain name from your ISP. Until you get your domain name, you can use the IP address to access your site.

After you get a web host, you use your FTP program to upload the files for your web site to the web server of the web host. Then, you can test your web site on the Internet. When you're through testing, you can announce your web site to the world and let it go live.

FileZilla as it is used to upload files to the web server

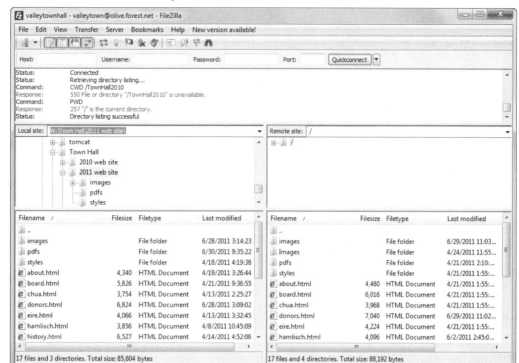

Some popular FTP programs

Program	Description
FileZilla	A free program for Windows, Macintosh, and Linux.
FTP Voyager	An inexpensive program for Windows.
CuteFTP	An inexpensive program for Windows and Macintosh.
Fetch	An inexpensive program for Macintosh.

Description

- To *deploy* (or *publish*) a web site on the Internet, you need to transfer the folders and files for the web site from your computer or network to a web server on the Internet. To do that, you use an *FTP program* that uses *File Transfer Protocol*.

- An FTP program not only lets you transfer files from a client to a web server but also from a web server to a client.

- Most IDEs and some text editors have built-in FTP programs. For instance, both Dreamweaver and Aptana Studio 3 provide FTP.

- If you're using some text editors, you may have to use a separate FTP program or add a plug-in FTP program to your editor.

- For more information on deploying an application to a web server, please see chapter 18.

Figure 1-11   FTP programs for uploading files to the web server

How to view deployed web pages

Next, you'll learn how to view a web page in a web browser and how to view the source code for a web page that's displayed in the browser. These are valuable skills as you test your own web pages or study the pages on other sites.

How to view a web page

Figure 1-12 shows you how to view a web page on the Internet. One way is to enter a *uniform resource locator* (*URL*) into the address bar of your browser. The other is to click on a link on a web page that requests another page.

As the diagram at the start of this figure shows, the URL for an Internet page consists of four components. In most cases, the *protocol* is HTTP. If you omit the protocol, the browser uses HTTP as the default.

The second component is the *domain name* that identifies the web server that the HTTP request will be sent to. The web browser uses this name to look up the address of the web server for the domain. Although you can't omit the domain name, you can often omit the "www." from the domain name.

The third component is the *path* where the file resides on the server. The path lists the folders that contain the file. Forward slashes are used to separate the names in the path and to represent the server's top-level folder at the start of the path. In this example, the path is "/ourwork/".

The last component is the name of the file. In this example, the file is named index.html. If you omit the filename, the web server will search for a default document in the path. Depending on the web server, this file will be named index.html, default.htm, or some variation of the two.

If you want to view an HTML page that's on your own computer or an intranet, you can use the Open command (IE) or Open File command (Firefox) in the File menu of the browser. However, it's easier to use your text editor or IDE to do that, and you'll learn more about that in the next chapter.

At the bottom of this figure, you can see our naming recommendations for your folders and files. In general, we recommend that folder and filenames should only contain lowercase letters, numbers, underscores or hyphens, and the period. In the examples in this book, you'll see the author's preference, which is to use underscores instead of hyphens to separate the words in a name. But some developers use hyphens instead of underscores.

The other recommendation is to create names that clearly indicate the contents of your folders and web pages. This can improve search engine optimization (SEO), which you'll learn more about in a moment.

Incidentally, Linux/Apache web servers are case-sensitive. Then, if a URL specifies a folder named "Images", but the folder on the server is actually named "images", the web server will report that it cannot find the file. By using lowercase letters only, you avoid this problem.

The components of an HTTP URL

```
http://www.modulemedia.com/ourwork/index.html
```
| protocol | domain name | path | filename |

The web page at http://www.modulemedia.com/ourwork/index.html

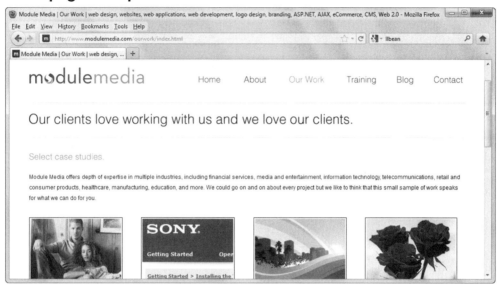

What happens if you omit parts of a URL

- If you omit the protocol, the default of http:// will be used.
- If you omit the filename, the default document name for the web server will be used. This is typically index.html, default.htm, or some variation.

Two ways to access a web page on the Internet

- Enter the URL of a web page into the browser's address bar.
- Click on a link in the current web page to load the next web page.

Two ways to access a web page on your own server or computer

- Use the File→Open command with Internet Explorer or the File→File Open command with Firefox.
- Use the features of your text editor or IDE.

Naming recommendations for your own folders and files

- Create names for folders and files that consist of lowercase letters, numbers, underscores or hyphens, and the period.
- Use filenames that clearly indicate what a page contains. This is good for search engine optimization (see figure 1-16).

Figure 1-12   How to view a web page

How to view the source code for a web page

When a web page is displayed by a browser, you can use the techniques in figure 1-13 to view the HTML code for the page in a separate window. If, for example, you're using the Firefox browser, you can usually use the View→Page Source command to see the HTML code. In this example, the HTML code for the page in the previous figure is shown.

Viewing the source code can be useful when you're testing an application. But you can also use this technique to view the HTML for the pages of other sites on the Internet. This can be a good way to learn how other sites work. Although some sites use various techniques to hide their code, a lot of the code for Internet sites is available.

If the CSS for an HTML page is stored in an external file, you can sometimes use the Firefox browser to open that file by clicking on the path in the HTML code. In the code in this figure, for example, you can click on styles/core.css to access the first of the three css files that this site uses. This lets you analyze how the CSS code works.

If you're using Internet Explorer, you can view the CSS code in an external file by entering the URL for the CSS file in the browser's address bar. For instance, for the first CSS file that's identified by the link element in the HTML code in this figure, you can enter this address into the browser:

```
http://www.modulemedia.com/styles/core.css
```

Then, when you press the Enter key, the file is opened in another browser window. In chapter 3, you'll learn more about the relative addresses that are used in HTML code so you'll be able to determine what their URLs are.

When you view the HTML code for a web page, keep in mind that it may include embedded CSS code or JavaScript code. Beyond that, you'll find that all but the simplest sites are quite complicated. Once you finish this book, though, you should be able to figure out how the HTML and CSS for most sites work. And you'll learn a lot by studying how the best sites are coded.

The HTML source code for the page in figure 1-12

```
Source of: http://www.modulemedia.com/ourwork/index.html - Mozilla Firefox

File  Edit  View  Help

<!DOCTYPE html PUBLIC "-//W3C//DTD XHTML 1.0 Transitional//EN" "http://www.w3.org/TR/xhtml1/DTD/xhtm
<html xmlns="http://www.w3.org/1999/xhtml" dir="ltr" lang="en-US" xml:lang="en">
<head>
    <title>Module Media | Our Work | web design, websites, web applications, web development, logo d
    <meta http-equiv="Content-Type" content="text/html; charset=UTF-8" />
    <link href="../favicon.ico" rel="shortcut icon" />

    <link rel="stylesheet" href="../styles/core.css" media="screen" type="text/css" />
    <link rel="stylesheet" href="../styles/layout.css" media="screen" type="text/css" />
    <link rel="stylesheet" href="../styles/ourwork.css" media="screen" type="text/css" />

    <!--[if IE 6]><link rel="stylesheet" type="text/css" href="../styles/ie6.css" media="screen" /><
    <!--[if IE 7]><link rel="stylesheet" type="text/css" href="../styles/ie7.css" media="screen" /><

    <script type="text/javascript" src="../scripts/jquery-1.3.2.min.js"></script>
    <script type="text/javascript" src="../scripts/jquery-ui-1.7.2.js"></script>
        <script type="text/javascript" src="../scripts/application.js"></script>
</head>

<body class="ourwork">

Line 31, Col 15
```

How to view the HTML source code for a web page

- Use the View→Source or View→Page Source command.
- Right-click on the page and select the Source, View Source, or View Page Source command.

How to view the CSS code in an external CSS file

- In Firefox, click on the link in the link element that refers to it.
- In Internet Explorer, enter the URL for the CSS file in the address bar of your web browser.

Description

- When you view the source code for a web page in a web browser, the HTML code is opened in a separate window.
- If the CSS is stored in the HTML file, you'll be able to see both the HTML and CSS code in the one file.
- If the CSS for the page is stored in an external file, you can often view that file by using the techniques above.

Figure 1-13   How to view the source code for a web page

Three critical web development issues

Whenever you develop a web application, you should be aware of the three issues that are presented in the next three figures. Then, as you progress through this book, you will be given guidelines for coding the tags and attributes that help provide for cross-browser compatibility, user accessibility, and search engine optimization.

Cross-browser compatibility

If you want your web site to be used by as many visitors as possible, you need to make sure that your web pages are compatible with as many browsers as possible. That's known as *cross-browser compatibility*. That means you should test your applications on as many browsers as possible, including the five browsers summarized in figure 1-14 and the older versions of those browsers.

The table in this figure shows the current release numbers of these browsers and their rating for HTML5 support. To get an updated version of this information, though, you can go to the web site at www.html5test.com. This web site will also rate the browser that you're using when you access it.

In general, Internet Explorer gives web developers the most problems because it's the least standard. In contrast, the other four browsers generally support the same features so if a web page runs on one of them, it will also run on the others. The other four browsers also provide for automatic updates, but IE typically hasn't done that. As a result, the other four browsers are most likely to support the latest features of HTML5 and CSS3.

To provide for browsers that don't support the HTML5 and CSS3 features that are presented in this book, this book shows you the workarounds that you need to use. However, it's difficult to test your web pages in older browsers because (1) you can't get them anymore and (2) you can't put all versions of the old browsers on one system even if you could get them.

If you're a student, you probably won't need to test your web pages on old browsers. But for production applications, that type of testing is essential. To help you do it, you can search the Internet for web sites or software products that provide ways to test your pages on old browsers.

To do the exercises in this book, you can get by with just the current versions of IE and Firefox. That's why the appendix shows you how to install those browsers. But if you're using a Mac OS system, you won't be able to install IE so you can skip any steps that require it or substitute Safari for IE references. For a production system, of course, you need to install all five browsers and make sure your web pages work on all of them.

The current browsers and their HTML5 ratings (perfect score is 450)

Browser	Release	HTML5 Test Rating
Google Chrome	12	343
Opera	11	286
Mozilla Firefox	8	313
Apple Safari	5	293
Internet Explorer	9	141

The web site for these ratings

`http://www.html5test.com`

Guidelines for cross-browser compatibility

- Test your web pages on all of the major browsers, including the older versions of these browsers.
- Use the HTML5 and CSS3 features that are supported by all of the modern browsers, which are the features that are presented in this book. But use the workarounds so those features will work in the older browsers too.

How to test your web pages in older browsers

- One of the problems in cross-browser testing is that you can't install all of the old browsers on one system. In particular, Windows doesn't let you install more than one version of IE at the same time.
- The solution is to use programs or web sites that offer this type of testing. To find out what's available, try searching for "browser testing software" or "cross browser testing".

Description

- As a web developer, you want your web pages to work on as many different web browsers as possible. This is referred to as *cross-browser compatibility*.
- When you develop a web site for general use, you need to test it on all five of the web browsers listed above including all releases that are still in common use.
- Although Internet Explorer is still the most-used browser, it gives web developers the most problems because it is the least standard and because it hasn't provided for automatic updates.
- In this book, you'll be alerted to cross-browser compatibility problems, and you'll learn to use the workarounds that you need for older browsers.
- Eventually, all browsers will support HTML5 and CSS3 so the workarounds won't be necessary.
- When you access www.html5test.com, it will automatically rate the browser you're using.

Figure 1-14   The issue of cross-browser compatibility

User accessibility

The second major issue is *user accessibility*, or just *accessibility*. This refers to the qualities that make a web site accessible to as many users as possible, especially disabled users.

For instance, visually-impaired users may not be able to read text that's in images so you need to provide other alternatives for them. Similarly, users with motor disabilities may not be able to use the mouse, so you need to make sure that all of the content and features of your web site can be accessed through the keyboard.

To a large extent, this means that you should develop your applications so the content of your web site is still usable if images, CSS, and JavaScript are disabled. A side benefit of doing that is that your site will also be more accessible to search engines, which rely primarily on the text portions of your pages.

In this book, you will be given guidelines for providing accessibility as you learn the related HTML. However, there's a lot more to accessibility than that. As a result, we recommend that you learn more on your own by going to the sites that are identified in this figure.

The Articles tab of the WebAIM site

Accessibility laws that you should be aware of

- The Americans with Disabilities Act (ADA).
- Sections 504 and 508 of the federal Rehabilitation Act.
- Section 255 of the Telecommunications Act of 1996.

Types of disabilities

- Visual
- Hearing
- Motor
- Cognitive

Information sources

- The WebAIM web site provides a good starting point for learning about accessibility at http://www.webaim.org.
- The World Wide Web Consortium (W3C) provides a full set of accessibility guidelines at http://www.w3.org/TR/WCAG.
- W3C also provides a specification called WAI-ARIA (Web Accessibility Initiative—Accessible Rich Internet Applications) that shows how to make rich internet applications more accessible to the disabled at http://www.w3.org/TR/wai-aria.

Description

- *Accessibility* refers to the qualities that make a web site accessible to users, especially disabled users.
- As you go through this book, you'll be given guidelines for coding the elements and attributes that provide accessibility. However, there's a lot more to accessibility than that.

Figure 1-15   The issue of user accessibility

Search engine optimization

Search engine optimization, or *SEO*, refers to the goal of optimizing your web site so your pages rank higher in search engines like Google, Bing, and Yahoo. In figure 1-16, for example, what causes the links that are shown to be returned by Google?

Since SEO is critical to the success of a web site, this book presents SEO guidelines as you learn the related HTML. For instance, the title element in the head section of an HTML document is one of the most important elements for SEO. In this book, then, you'll learn how to code this element and all elements like it that affect SEO.

In the future, the new HTML5 structural elements are expected to affect the way that search engines rank pages. In particular, these elements should help the search engines find pages that are more relevant to the search term. That's one of the reasons for starting to implement these elements right away, and this book will show you the right way to do that.

Note, however, that SEO goes way beyond the way HTML pages are coded. So here again, you need to do some independent research. To start, you can search the Internet for information on SEO, but you might also want to buy a book or two on the subject.

The Google search results for "HTML5 documentation"

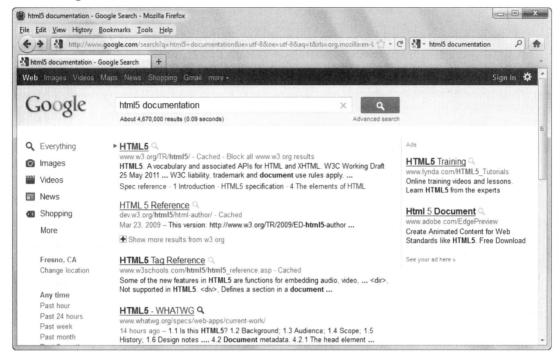

The most popular search engines

- Google
- Yahoo
- Bing

Description

- *Search engine optimization* (*SEO*) refers to the goal of optimizing your web site so its pages will rank high in the search engines that are used to access them.
- Although the search algorithms that are used by the search engines are changed frequently, there are some common coding techniques that will help your pages do better in the search engines.
- HTML5 has some new elements that are designed to help search engines deliver results that are more relevant.
- As you go through this book, you'll be given guidelines for coding the elements and attributes that will help your web sites place better in the search engine results. However, there's a lot more to SEO than that.

Figure 1-16   The issue of search engine optimization

Perspective

Now that you know the concepts and terms that you need for developing web sites with HTML and CSS, you're ready to learn how to develop a web page. So in the next chapter, you'll learn how to enter, edit, test, and validate a web page. After that, you'll be ready to learn all the details of HTML and CSS that you need for developing the pages of a web site.

Terms

World Wide Web
Internet
client
web browser
web server
network
local area network (LAN)
intranet
wide area network (WAN)
router
Internet service provider (ISP)
Internet exchange point (IXP)
static web page
HTTP request
HTTP (HyperText Transport Protocol)
HTML (HyperText Markup Language)
HTTP response
render a web page
dynamic web page
application server
database server
round trip
web application
scripting language
server-side processing
Apache web server
IIS (Internet Information Services)
JavaScript
client-side processing
image swap
image rollover
JavaScript engine
HTML document
DOCTYPE declaration
HTML element

tag
opening tag
closing tag
attribute
CSS (Cascading Style Sheets)
style sheet
external style sheet
rule set
selector
declarative block
declaration
rule
XHTML (eXtensible HTML)
W3C (World Wide Web Consortium)
WHATWG (Web Hypertext Application Technology Working Group)
IDE (Integrated Development Environment)
suite
deploy
publish
FTP program
FTP (File Transfer Protocol)
FTP plug-in
ISP (Internet Service Provider)
web hosting
IP address
domain name
URL (Uniform Resource Locator)
protocol
domain name
path
cross-browser compatibility
user accessibility
SEO (Search Engine Optimization)

Summary

- A web application consists of clients, a web server, and a network. *Clients* use *web browsers* to request web pages from the web server. The *web server* returns the requested pages.

- A *local area network* (*LAN*) connects computers that are near to each other. This is often called an *intranet*. In contrast, a *wide area network* (*WAN*) uses *routers* to connect two or more LANs. The *Internet* consists of many WANs.

- To request a web page, the web browser sends an *HTTP request* to the web server. Then, the web server retrieves the HTML for the requested page and sends it back to the browser in an *HTTP response*. Last, the browser *renders* the HTML into a web page.

- A *static web page* is a page that is the same each time it's retrieved. The file for this type of page has .html or .htm as its extension, and its HTML doesn't change.

- The HTML for a *dynamic web page* is generated by a server-side program or script, so its HTML can change from one request to another.

- *JavaScript* is a *scripting language* that is run by the *JavaScript engine* of a web browser. It provides for *client-side processing*.

- *HTML* (*HyperText Markup Language*) is the language that defines the structure and contents of a web page. *CSS* (*Cascading Style Sheets*) are used to control how the web pages are formatted.

- To develop web pages, you can use a text editor like Aptana Studio 3 or an *Integrated Development Environment* (*IDE*) like Adobe Dreamweaver.

- To *deploy* (or *publish*) a web site on the Internet, you need to transfer the folders and files for your site from your computer to a web server with Internet access. To do that, you use an *FTP program* that uses *File Transfer Protocol* .

- To view a web page, you can enter the *URL* (*Uniform Resource Locator*) into a browser's address bar. A URL consists of the *protocol*, *domain name*, *path*, and filename.

- To view a web page that's on your own computer or server, you can use the browser's File→Open or File→File Open command.

- To view the HTML for a web page, right-click on the page and select View Source or View Page Source. Or, you can use your browser's View→Source or View→Page Source command. Then, to view the CSS for a page, you can click on its link in the source code or enter its URL in the address bar.

- Three critical issues for web development are *cross-browser compatibility*, *user accessibility*, and *search engine optimization* (*SEO*). In this book, you'll learn the HTML and CSS techniques that are related to these issues.

Before you do the exercises for this book...

Before you do the exercises for this book, you should download and install the Firefox browser. You should also download and install the applications for this book. The procedures for installing the software and applications for this book are described in appendix A.

Exercise 1-1   Visit some Internet web sites

In this exercise, you'll visit some Internet web sites and view the source code for those sites.

Visit the author's web site with Firefox

1. Start Firefox.

2. Enter www.modulemedia.com into the address bar and press the Enter key or click on the arrow at the right side of the address bar. That should display the home page for this web site. Here, JavaScript is used to rotate the images at the top of the page.

3. If you're using a Windows system, enter "modulemedia" into the address bar, hold down the Ctrl key, and press the Enter key. If this works, it will add www. and .com to your entry. This is a quick way to enter the URL for a .com address.

4. Use one of the techniques in figure 1-13 to view the HTML file for the home page. In the source code, the three link elements identify the CSS files that do the formatting for the page. This is followed by three script elements that identify JavaScript files.

5. If you scroll through this code, it probably looks overwhelming, even though this site is relatively simple. By the time you complete this book, though, you should understand the HTML and CSS that it uses.

6. Click on the underlined value of the href attribute in the first link element. That should open the first CSS file for this page. This shows how easy it is to access the HTML and CSS code for many (but not all) sites.

Visit other web sites

7. Go to www.landsend.com, find a page like the one in figure 1-5, and experiment with the image swaps and rollovers. Those are done by JavaScript after all of the images are loaded with the page.

8. Use Firefox to visit other web sites and view the source code for those sites. When you're through experimenting, go to the next exercise.

Exercise 1-2   View the application for this chapter

In this exercise, you'll visit the book page that was used as an example in figures 1-6 and 1-7.

Open the book page in Firefox

1. Start Firefox if it isn't already open.

2. Use the File→Open File command to open this HTML file:

   `c:\murach\html5_css3\book_apps\ch01\javascript_book.html`

3. Right-click on the page and choose View Page Source to display the HTML file for this page.

4. Click on book.css in the link element in the HTML code to display the CSS file for this page.

Open the book page in IE (if you're using a Windows system)

5. Start Internet Explorer if it isn't already open.

6. Use the File→Open command to open the same HTML file as in step 2.

7. Use the View→Source command to open the HTML file for this page.

8. Click on book.css in the link element in the HTML code to try to display the CSS file for this page. Note that this doesn't work with IE.

Exercise 1-3   View other applications and examples

1. Open this file in the Firefox browser:

   `c:\murach\html5_css3\book_apps\ch06\town_hall\index.html`

   Then, click on the link for Scott Sampson to see that page. This is the application that's presented at the end of chapter 6, and this gives you some idea of what you'll be able to do when you complete section 1. Note, however, that only the Scott Sampson link has been implemented for this application.

2. Open this file in the Firefox browser:

   `c:\murach\html5_css3\book_examples\ch05\12_gradients.html`

   This is the example for figure 5-12 in chapter 5. Here, the 12 in the filename refers to the figure number. As you do the exercises for this book, you may want to copy code from the examples to your exercise solution.

3. Open this file in the Firefox browser.

   `c:\murach\html5_css3\book_examples\ch14\04_carousel\index.html`

   This is the example for figure 14-4 in chapter 14. Note that the figure number is in the folder name this time. This is true for all of the examples that require more than one file.

Exercise 1-4   Learn more about HTML5, accessibility, and SEO

1. Go to www.w3.org. This is the web site for the group that develops the HTML5 and CSS3 standards. It provides all sorts of useful information including HTML5 documentation.

2. Go to www.whatwg.org. This is the web site for a community that is interested in evolving HTML and its related technologies. It also provides all sorts of useful information including HTML5 documentation.

3. Go to www.html5test.com, and view the HTML5 rating for your browser. Then, review the other browser data that this site provides.

4. Use Google to search for "cross browser testing" or "browser testing software". That will return some sites that provide products or services for testing your web pages on older browsers.

5. Go to www.webaim.org. Then, review the information about accessibility that this site provides.

6. Use Google to search for "search engine optimization". Then, click on the first google.com link for this subject to get more information about it. You may also want to download and print the PDF on SEO that Google offers.

2

How to code, test, and validate a web page

In this chapter, you'll learn how to create and edit HTML and CSS files. Then, you'll learn how to test those files to make sure they work correctly. Last, you'll learn how to validate the code in HTML and CSS files to make sure that it doesn't have any errors. When you're through with this chapter, you'll be ready to learn all the details of HTML and CSS coding.

The HTML syntax

When you code an HTML document, you need to adhere to the rules for creating the HTML elements. These rules are referred to as the *syntax* of the language. In the four topics that follow, you'll learn the HTML syntax.

The basic structure of an HTML document

Figure 2-1 presents the basic structure of an *HTML document*. As you can see, every HTML document consists of two parts: the DOCTYPE declaration and the document tree.

When you use HTML5, you code the *DOCTYPE declaration* exactly as it's shown in this figure. It will be the first line of code in every HTML document that you create, and it tells the browser that the document is using HTML5. If you've developed web pages with earlier versions of HTML or XHTML, you will be pleased to see how much this declaration has been simplified.

The *document tree* starts right after the DOCTYPE declaration. This tree consists of the *HTML elements* that define the content and structure of the web page. The first of these elements is the html element itself, which contains all of the other elements. This element can be referred to as the *root element* of the tree.

Within the html element, you should always code a head element and a body element. The head element contains elements that provide information about the page itself, while the body element contains the elements that provide the structure and content for the page. You'll learn how to code these elements in the next chapter.

You'll use the elements shown in this figure in every HTML document that you create. As a result, it's a good practice to start every HTML document from a template that contains this code or from another HTML document that's similar to the one you're going to create. Later in this chapter, you'll learn how you can use Aptana to do that.

When you use HTML5, you can code elements using lowercase, uppercase, or mixed case. For consistency, though, we recommend that you use lowercase unless uppercase is required. The one exception we make is in the DOCTYPE declaration because DOCTYPE has historically been capitalized (although lowercase works too). You will see this use of capitalization in all of the examples and applications in this book.

The basic structure of an HTML5 document

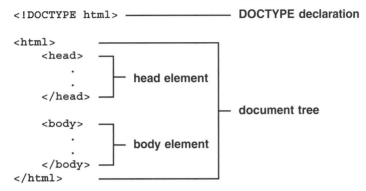

```
<!DOCTYPE html> ────────────── DOCTYPE declaration

<html>
    <head>
        .
        .
    </head>

    <body>
        .
        .
    </body>
</html>
```

A simple HTML5 document

```
<!DOCTYPE html>
<html lang="en">
    <head>
        <meta charset="utf-8">
        <title>San Joaquin Valley Town Hall</title>
    </head>
    <body>
        <h1>San Joaquin Valley Town Hall</h1>
        <p>Welcome to San Joaquin Valley Town Hall.</p>
        <p>We have some amazing speakers in store for you this season!</p>
        <p><a href="speakers.html">Speaker information</a></p>
    </body>
</html>
```

General coding recommendations for HTML5

- Although you can code the HTML using lowercase, uppercase, or mixed case, we recommend that you do all coding in lowercase because it's easier to read.

Description

- An *HTML document* contains *HTML elements* that define the content and structure of a web page.

- Each HTML5 document consists of two parts: the DOCTYPE declaration and the document tree.

- The *DOCTYPE declaration* shown above indicates that the document is going to use HTML5. You'll code this declaration at the start of every HTML document.

- The *document tree* starts with the html element, which marks the beginning and end of the HTML code. This element can be referred to as the *root element* of the document.

- The html element always contains one head element that provides information about the document and one body element that provides the structure and content of the document.

Figure 2-1   The basic structure of an HTML document

How to code elements and tags

Figure 2-2 shows you how to code elements and tags. As you have already seen, most HTML elements start with an *opening tag* and end with a *closing tag* that is like the opening tag but has a slash within it. Thus, <h1> is the opening tag for a level-1 heading, and </h1> is the closing tag. Between those tags, you code the *content* of the element.

Some elements, however, have no content or closing tag. These tags are referred to as *empty tags*. For instance, the <br> tag is an empty tag that starts a new line, and the <img> tag is an empty tag that identifies an image that should be displayed.

The third set of examples in this figure shows the right way and the wrong way to code tags when one element is *nested* within another. In short, the tags for one element shouldn't overlap with the tags for another element. That is, you can't close the outer element before you close the inner element.

From this point on in this book, we will refer to elements by the code used in the opening tag. For instance, we will refer to head elements, h1 elements, and img elements. To prevent misreading, though, we will enclose single-letter element names in brackets. As a result, we will refer to <a> elements and <p> elements. We will also use brackets wherever else we think they will help prevent misreading.

Two elements with opening and closing tags

```
<h1>San Joaquin Valley Town Hall</h1>
<p>Here is a list of links:</p>
```

Two empty tags

```
<br>
<img src="logo.gif" alt="Murach Logo">
```

Correct and incorrect nesting of tags

Correct nesting

```
<p>Order your copy <i>today!</i></p>
```

Incorrect nesting

```
<p>Order your copy <i>today!</p></i>
```

Description

- Most HTML elements have an opening tag, content, and a closing tag. Each tag is coded within a set of brackets (<>).

- An element's *opening tag* includes the tag name. The *closing tag* includes the tag name preceded by a slash. And the *content* includes everything that appears between the opening and closing tags.

- Some HTML elements have no content. For example, the <br> element, which forces a line break, consists of just one tag. This type of tag is called an *empty tag*.

- HTML elements are commonly *nested*. To nest elements correctly, though, you must close an inner set of tags before closing the outer set of tags.

Figure 2-2   How to code elements and tags

How to code attributes

Figure 2-3 shows how to code the *attributes* for an HTML element. These attributes are coded within the opening tag of an element or within an empty tag. For each attribute, you code the attribute name, an equals sign, and the attribute value.

When you use HTML5, the attribute value doesn't have to be coded within quotation marks unless the value contains a space, but we recommend that you use quotation marks to enclose all values. Also, although you can use either double or single quotes, we recommend that you always use double quotes. That way, your code will have a consistent appearance that will help you avoid coding errors.

In the examples in this figure, you can see how one or more attributes can be coded. For instance, the second example is an opening tag with three attributes. In contrast, the third example is an empty img element that contains a src attribute that gives the name of the image file that should be displayed plus an alt attribute that gives the text that should be displayed if the image file can't be found.

The next example illustrates the use of a *Boolean attribute*. A Boolean attribute can have just two values, which represent either on or off. To turn a Boolean attribute on, you code just the name of the attribute. In this example, the checked attribute turns that attribute on, which causes the related check box to be checked when it is rendered by the browser. If you want the attribute to be off when the page is rendered, you don't code the attribute.

The next set of examples illustrates the use of two attributes that are commonly used to identify HTML elements. The id attribute is used to uniquely identify just one element, so each id attribute must have a unique value. In contrast, the class attribute can be used to mark one or more elements, so the same value can used for more than one class attribute. You'll see these attributes in a complete example in figure 2-6.

How to code an opening tag with attributes

An opening tag with one attribute
```
<a href="contact.html">
```

An opening tag with three attributes
```
<a href="contact.html" title="Click to Contact Us" class="nav_link">
```

How to code an empty tag with attributes
```
<img src="logo.gif" alt="Murach Logo">
```

How to code a Boolean attribute
```
<input type="checkbox" name="mailList" checked>
```

Two common attributes for identifying HTML elements

An opening tag with an id attribute
```
<div id="page">
```

An opening tag with a class attribute
```
<a href="contact.html" title="Click to Contact Us" class="nav_link">
```

Coding rules

- An attribute consists of the attribute name, an equals sign (=), and the value for the attribute.
- Attribute values don't have to be enclosed in quotes if they don't contain spaces.
- Attribute values must be enclosed in single or double quotes if they contain one or more spaces, but you can't mix the type of quotation mark used for a single value.
- Boolean attributes can be coded as just the attribute name. They don't have to include the equals sign and a value that's the same as the attribute name.
- To code multiple attributes, separate each attribute with a space.

Our coding recommendation

- For consistency, enclose all attribute values in double quotes.

Description

- *Attributes* can be coded within opening or empty tags to supply optional values.
- A *Boolean attribute* represents either an on or off value.
- The id attribute is used to identify a single HTML element so its value can be used for just one HTML element.
- A class attribute with the same value can be used for more than one HTML element.

Figure 2-3   How to code attributes

How to code comments and whitespace

Figure 2-4 shows you how to code *comments*. Here, the starting and ending characters for the two comments are highlighted. Then, everything within those characters is ignored when the page is rendered.

One common use of comments is to describe or explain portions of code. That is illustrated by the first comment.

Another common use of comments is to *comment out* a portion of the code. This is illustrated by the second comment. This is useful when you're testing a web page and you want to temporarily disable a portion of code that you're having trouble with. Then, after you test the rest of the code, you can remove the comments and test that portion of the code.

This figure also illustrates the use of *whitespace*, which consists of characters like tab characters, return characters, and extra spaces. For instance, the return character after the opening body tag and all of the spaces between that tag and the next tag are whitespace.

Since whitespace is ignored when an HTML document is rendered, you can use the whitespace characters to format your HTML so it is easier to read. In this figure, for example, you can see how whitespace has been used to indent and align the HTML elements.

That of course is a good coding practice, and you'll see that in all of the examples in this book. Note, however, that the code will work the same if all of the whitespace is removed. In fact, you could code all of the HTML for a document in a single line.

Although whitespace doesn't affect the way an HTML document is rendered, it does take up space in the HTML file. As a result, you shouldn't overdo your use of it. Just use enough to make your code easy to read.

An HTML document with comments and whitespace

```
<!DOCTYPE html>
<!--
    This document displays the home page
    for the web site.
-->

<html>
    <head>
        <title>San Joaquin Valley Town Hall</title>
    </head>

    <body>
        <h1>San Joaquin Valley Town Hall</h1>
        <h2>Bringing cutting-edge speakers to the valley</h2>
        <!-- This comments out all of the HTML code in the unordered list
        <ul>
            <li>October 19, 2011: Jeffrey Toobin</li>
            <li>November 16, 2011: Andrew Ross Sorkin</li>
            <li>January 18, 2012: Amy Chua</li>
            <li>February 15, 2012: Scott Sampson</li>
            <li>March 21, 2012: Carlos Eire</li>
            <li>April 18, 2012: Ronan Tynan</li>
        </ul>
        The code after the end of this comment is active -->
            <p>Contact us by phone at (559) 444-2180 for ticket information.</p>
    </body>
</html>
```

Our coding recommendations

- Use whitespace to indent lines of code and make them easier to read.
- Don't overdo your use of whitespace, because it does add to the size of the file.

Description

- An HTML *comment* is text that appears between the <!-- and --> characters. Since web browsers ignore comments, you can use them to describe or explain portions of your HTML code that might otherwise be confusing.

- You can also use comments to *comment out* elements that you don't want the browser to display. This can be useful when you're testing a web page.

- An HTML comment can be coded on a single line or it can span two or more lines.

- *Whitespace* consists of characters like tab characters, line return characters, and extra spaces.

- Since whitespace is ignored by browsers, you can use it to indent lines of code and separate elements from one another by putting them on separate lines. This is a good coding practice because it makes your code easier to read.

Figure 2-4   How to code comments and whitespace

The CSS syntax

Like HTML, CSS has a syntax that must be adhered to when you create a CSS file. This syntax is presented next.

How to code CSS rule sets and comments

A CSS file consists of *rule sets*. As the diagram in figure 2-5 shows, a rule set consists of a *selector* followed by a set of braces. Within the braces are one or more *declarations*, and each declaration consists of a *property* and a *value*. Note that the property is followed by a colon and the value is followed by a semicolon.

In this diagram, the selector is h1 so it applies to all h1 elements. Then, the rule set consists of a single property named color that is set to the color navy. The result is that the content of all h1 elements will be displayed in navy blue.

In the CSS code that follows, you can see four other rule sets. Three of these contain only one declaration (or *rule*), but the third example is a rule set that consists of two rules: one for the font-style property, and one for the border-bottom property.

Within a CSS file, you can also code comments that describe or explain what the CSS code is doing. For each comment, you start with /* and end with */, and anything between those characters is ignored. In the example in this figure, you can see how CSS comments can be coded on separate lines or after the lines that make up a rule set.

You can also use comments to comment out portions of code that you want disabled. This can be useful when you're testing your CSS code just as it is when you're testing your HTML code.

The parts of a CSS rule set

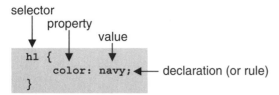

A simple CSS document with comments

```
/*********************************************************
* Description: Primary style sheet for valleytownhall.com
* Author:       Anne Boehm
*********************************************************/
/* Adjust the styles for the body */
body {
    background-color: #FACD8A;        /* This is a shade of orange. */
}

/* Adjust the styles for the headings */
h1 {
    color: #363636;
}
h2 {
    font-style: italic;
    border-bottom: 3px solid #EF9C00;  /* Adds a line below h2 headings */
}

/* Adjust the styles for the unordered list */
ul {
    list-style-type: square;           /* Changes the bullets to squares */
}
```

Description

- A CSS *rule set* consists of a selector and a declaration block.
- A CSS *selector* consists of the identifiers that are coded at the beginning of the rule set.
- A CSS *declaration block* consists of an opening brace, zero or more declarations, and a closing brace.
- A CSS *declaration* (or *rule*) consists of a *property*, a colon, a *value*, and a semicolon.
- To make your code easier to read, you can use spaces, indentation, and blank lines within a rule set.
- CSS *comments* begin with the characters /* and end with the characters */. A CSS comment can be coded on a single line, or it can span multiple lines.

Figure 2-5   How to code CSS rule sets and comments

How to code basic selectors

The selector of a rule set identifies the HTML element or elements that the rules should be applied to. To give you a better idea of how this works, figure 2-6 shows how to use the three basic selectors for CSS rule sets. Then, in chapter 4, you'll learn how to code all types of selectors.

The first type of selector identifies HTML elements like body, h1, or <p> elements. For instance, the selector in the first example applies to the body element. But if h1 were coded instead of body, the rule set would apply to all h1 elements. This type of selector is called a *type selector*.

The second type of selector starts with the pound sign (#) and applies to the single HTML element that's identified by the id attribute. For instance, #main applies to the HTML element that has an id attribute with a value of main. As you can see, that's the div element in the HTML code. Similarly, #copyright applies to the last <p> element in the HTML code.

The third type of selector starts with a period (.) and applies to all of the HTML elements that are identified by the class attribute with the named value. For instance, .base_color applies to all elements with class attributes that have a value of base_color. In the HTML code, this includes the h1 element and the last <p> element.

Starting with chapter 4, you'll learn all of the coding details for rule sets. But to give you an idea of what's going on in this example, here's a quick review of the code.

In the rule set for the body element, the font-family is set either to Arial (if the browser has access to that font) or the sans-serif type that is the default for the browser. This font is then used for all text that's displayed within the body element, unless it's overridden later on by some other rule set. So in this example, all of the text will be Arial or sans-serif, and you can see that font in the browser display.

In the rule set for the div element (#main), the width of the division is set to 300 pixels, and the padding between the contents and the border is set to 1 em, which is the height of the default font. Then, in the rule set for the second <p> element (#copyright), the font size is set to 75% of the default font size, and the text is right-aligned. Here again, you can see how these rule sets are applied in the browser display.

Last, in the rule set for the class named base_color, the color is set to blue. This means that both of the HTML elements that have that class name (the h1 element and the second <p> element) are displayed in blue.

This example shows how easy it is to identify the elements that you want to apply CSS formatting to. This also shows how the use of CSS separates the formatting from the content and structure that is defined by the HTML.

HTML elements that can be selected by element type, id, or class

```
<body>
    <div id="main">
        <h1 class="base_color">Student materials</h1>
        <p>Here are the links for the downloads:</p>
        <ul id="links">
            <li><a href="exercises.html">Exercises</a></li>
            <li><a href="solutions.html">Solutions</a></li>
        </ul>
        <p id="copyright" class="base_color">Copyright 2012</p>
    </div>
</body>
```

CSS rule sets that select by element type, id, and class

Type

```
body {
    font-family: Arial, sans-serif;
}
```

ID

```
#main {
    width: 300px;
    padding: 1em;
}
#copyright {
    font-size: 75%;
    text-align: right;
}
```

Class

```
.base_color {
    color: blue;
}
```

The elements in a browser

Description

- To code a selector for an HTML element, you simply name the element. This is referred to as a *type selector*.
- If an element is coded with an id attribute, you can code a selector for that id by coding a pound sign (#) followed by the id value, as in #main.
- If an element is coded with a class attribute, you can code a selector for that class by coding a period followed by the class name, as in .base_color.

Figure 2-6   How to code basic selectors

How to use Aptana to work with HTML and CSS files

In chapter 1, you were introduced to text editors like Aptana Studio 3. This is the text editor that we recommend because it's free; it runs on Windows, Mac OS, and Linux; and it has some excellent features. In the topics that follow, you'll learn how to use Aptana for common development functions.

If you're going to use a different editor as you work with the applications for this book, you may still want to browse these topics because they will give you a good idea of what an editor should be able to do. They may also encourage you to give Aptana a try.

How to create a project

In Aptana, a *project* consists of the folders and files for a complete web application. Once you create a project, it's easier to work with its folders and files, to create new files for the project, and so forth.

To create a project, you use the procedure in figure 2-7. The result of this procedure is that you end up with a named project that starts with the top-level folder for the application. Then, you can easily access the folders and files for the application by using the App Explorer window that's shown in the next figure.

To make it easier to work with the applications for this book, we recommend that you create an Aptana project that includes all of them. To do that, you can create a project named HTML5 Book Apps that starts with the path shown in this figure. The final dialog box for doing this is displayed in this figure.

The last dialog box for creating an Aptana project

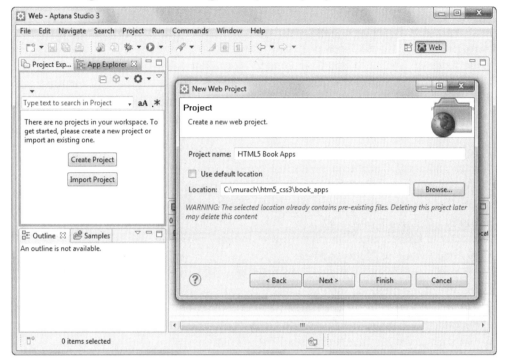

The folder that contains the folders for all of the book applications

```
C:\html5_css3\book_apps
```

How to create a project

- Use the File→New→Web Project command to display the New Web Project dialog box that's shown above. Or, in the App Explorer window, click on the Create Project button, select Web Project in the dialog box that's displayed, and click the Next button to display the New Web Project dialog box.

- In the New Web Project dialog box, enter a name for the project. Next, uncheck the Use Default Location box, click on the Browse button, and select the top-level folder for the project. If a warning message appears, read it so you realize that deleting the project in Aptana may also delete the project on the disk drive. Then, click the Finish button.

Description

- Aptana works the best when you set up projects for the web applications that you're developing and maintaining.

- In general, each Aptana *project* should contain the folders and files for one web application. For the purposes of this book, however, you can set up one project for all of the book applications and another project for all of the exercises.

Figure 2-7   How to create a project in Aptana

How to open an HTML file

Figure 2-8 shows how to open an HTML file after you've created a project. Here, the HTML5 Book Apps project is shown in the App Explorer window on the left side of Aptana. If you have created more than one project, you can switch from one to another by using the drop-down project list that's at the top of the App Explorer window.

Once you have the correct project open, you can drill down to the file that you want to open by clicking on the plus signs for the folders. In this example, the ch02 folder has been expanded so you can see the three files for the application for chapter 2. Then, to open a file, you just double-click on it.

When you open an HTML file in Aptana, it is opened in a new tab. This means that you can have several files open at the same time and move from one to another by clicking on a tab. This makes it easy to switch back and forth between the HTML and CSS files for a web page. This also makes it easy to copy code from one file to another.

If you want to open a file that isn't part of a project, you can do that by using one of the methods shown in this figure. First, you can use the Project Explorer window to locate the file on your computer and then double-click on it. Second, you can use the File→File Open command to open a file the way you would with any other file. (Incidentally, this notation means to drop-down the File menu and select the File Open command, and this notation will be used throughout this book.)

When a file is open and selected, its outline is displayed in the Outline window in the lower left corner of Aptana. Then, you can drill down to see all of the elements in the HTML document. When you select one of them in the outline, it is also selected in the HTML.

Aptana with a project in the App Explorer and an HTML file in the first tab

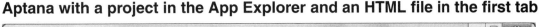

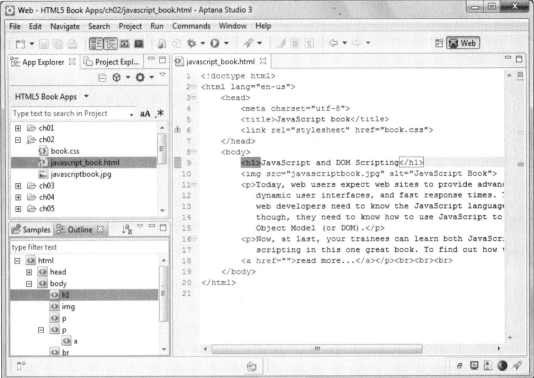

How to open an HTML file within a project

- Use the drop-down list in Aptana's App Explorer to select the project. Then, locate the file and double-click on it.

Two ways to open an HTML file that isn't in a project

- Use Aptana's Project Explorer to locate the file. Then, double-click on it.
- Use the File→Open File command.

Description

- When you open an HTML file, the file is opened in a new tab and its outline is displayed in the Outline window.

Figure 2-8   How to open an HTML file in Aptana

How to start a new HTML file

Because all HTML documents contain the same DOCTYPE declaration and the same starting tags for the document tree, it makes sense to start each new HTML file from a *template* that includes the starting code or from an HTML document that's similar to the one you're going to create. If you're using projects, Aptana makes that easy to do.

The first procedure in figure 2-9 shows how to start a new HTML file from your own template. To do that, you can use the File→New→File command, and complete the dialog box as shown in this figure. In this case, a new file named php_book.html is going to be created from the template.html file that's stored in the ch02 folder for the book applications.

The second procedure in this figure shows how to start a new HTML file from an existing HTML file. If, for example, you're going to create a second book page that's similar to an existing book page, it makes sense to start the new file from the old file. To do that, you just open the old file and save it with a new name. Then, you can delete the parts of the old file that the new page doesn't need and add the new parts.

Another option is to start a new HTML file from Aptana's HTML5 template. However, this template contains code and comments that you're going to want to delete. As a result, you're better off using a template that is designed for the application that you're working on. In fact, for most web sites, you should have one template for each type of page that you're developing.

As you become more familiar with HTML, you can create your own templates. If, for example, you're going to develop several pages that have the same general content, you can create an HTML template for those pages. That will make it easier for you to develop those pages.

Incidentally, an IDE like Dreamweaver provides templates that you can use for a variety of page layouts. For instance, there's a template for a page that has a header, a footer, and a two-column body as well as a template for a page that has a header, a footer, and a three-column body. Templates like those give you both the HTML and CSS files that you need, which not only increases your productivity but helps you learn the right way to code those layouts.

If you're using a text editor that doesn't provide for the use of templates, you can get the same result by opening a file that contains a template and then saving it right away with a new name before you modify the file. That way, the original template file remains unchanged. The main problem with this is that you're likely to forget to save the template with a new name and modify its code before you realize it.

Aptana's dialog box for creating a new HTML file from a template

How to start a new HTML file from any template

- Select the File→New→File command. In the New File dialog box that's displayed, select the folder that the new file should be stored in and enter a filename for the new file including its .html extension.

- Still in the New File dialog box, click on the Advanced button, check the Link to File in the File System box, click on the Browse button, and select the template that you want to start the new file from. Then, click the Finish button.

How to start a new HTML file from another HTML file

- Open the file that you want to base the new file on. Then, use the File→Save As command to save the file with a new name.

Description

- Because all HTML files require the same starting elements, it's a good practice to start a new file from a *template* that contains those elements. When you use projects, Aptana makes that easy to do.

- If you're going to create a new file that's similar to an existing file, you can open the existing file and save it with a new name.

- Although you can use the File→New From Template→HTML→HTML 5 Template command to start a new file from the Aptana HTML5 template, it's usually better to start your files from a template that's specifically designed for your HTML documents.

Figure 2-9   How to start a new HTML file in Aptana

How to edit an HTML file

Figure 2-10 shows how to edit an HTML file. When you open a file with an html extension, Aptana knows what type of file you're working with so it can use color to highlight the syntax components. That makes it easier to spot errors in your code.

As you enter a new line of code, the auto-completion feature presents lists of words that start with the letters that you've entered. This type of list is illustrated by this figure. Here, the list shows the choices after the letter *i* has been entered. Then, you can select a word and press the Tab key to insert it into your code. This causes Aptana to close the opening tag and add the closing tag so all you have to do is enter the content for the tag.

This figure also lists some common coding errors. Often, the color coding will help you spot the first three types of errors. If, for example, you misspell an attribute name or if you forget to code a closing quotation mark, the color coding will indicate that the code isn't correct.

Beyond that, Aptana provides error markers and warning markers that help you find and correct errors. In this figure, for example, you can see an error marker and four warning markers. Then, to get the description of the error or warning, you can hover the mouse over the marker.

On the other hand, Aptana has no way of knowing what the correct code should be for file references in link, img, or <a> elements. As a result, you must discover those errors when you test the web page. If, for example, the file reference for a style sheet in a link element is incorrect, the CSS won't be applied. If the file reference in an img element is incorrect, the image won't be displayed and the value of the alt attribute will be displayed. And if the file reference for an <a> element is incorrect, the browser won't access the correct page.

Please note that this figure also shows how to change the colors that are used to highlight the syntax. Because the default colors are hard to read, this is something that you probably will want to do.

Aptana with an auto-completion list for an HTML file

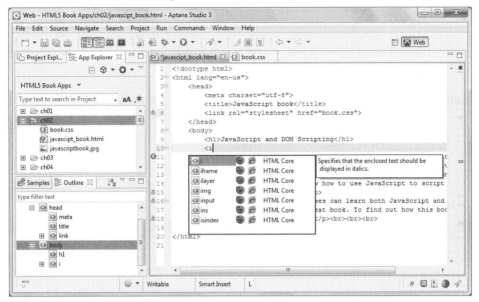

Common coding errors

- An opening tag without a closing tag.
- Misspelled tag or attribute names.
- Quotation marks that aren't paired.
- Incorrect file references in link, img, or <a> elements.

How to set the colors that are used to highlight the syntax

- Use the Window→Preferences command to open the Preferences dialog box. Then, click on Aptana Studio, click on Themes, and choose a theme from the drop-down list. (In this book, we use the Dreamweaver theme.)

Description

- Aptana displays the different parts of a file in different colors so they're easy to recognize. This helps you spot some of the common errors. For this to work, the file must have the html extension.
- The auto-completion feature displays a list of elements that start with what you've typed. To insert one of those terms, double-click on it or use the arrow keys to highlight it and press the Tab key. Aptana automatically adds the closing tag or /> for an empty tag (although our coding recommendation is to change the /> to just > for an empty tag).
- An error marker is a red circle that contains a white X at the start of a line. A warning marker is a yellow triangle that contains an exclamation mark. These markers are displayed as you enter and edit code.
- To get a description of the error or warning, hover the mouse over the marker.

Figure 2-10   How to edit an HTML file in Aptana

How to open or start a CSS file

In general, you use the same methods for opening and starting CSS files that you use for opening and starting HTML files. For instance, the easiest way to open a file that's part of a project is to find it in the App Explorer window and double-click on it.

Similarly, to start a CSS file from a template that contains the starting code, you use the procedure in figure 2-11. Here again, you can start a new CSS file from your own template or from the Aptana template. In this case, though, the Aptana template consists of just an empty rule set for the body type. As a result, you're better off using a template that's specific to the application that you're developing.

When you're creating a web site, for example, you will often use the same rule sets for many of the pages. That will give your pages a consistent look. For instance, all your pages are likely to use the same rule sets for common elements like the body, h1, h2, <p>, and <a> elements. Then, you can save these rule sets in a template and use that template to start new CSS files.

The other alternative is to start a new CSS file from an existing CSS file. To do that, you just open the file in Aptana and save it with a new name. This makes sense when the new file will use many of the same styles as the old file. Then, you just delete the styles that you don't need and add the files that you do need.

Aptana's dialog box for creating a new CSS file from a template

How to start a new CSS file for a project from any template

- Select the File→New→File command. In the New File dialog box that's displayed, select the folder that the new file should be stored in, and enter a filename for the new file, including its .css extension.

- Still in the New File dialog box, click on the Advanced button, check the Link to File in the File System box, click on the Browse button, and select the template that you want to start the new file from. Then, click the Finish button.

How to start a new CSS file from another CSS file

- Open the file that you want to base the new file on. Then, use the File→Save As command to save the file with a new name.

Description

- Because all CSS files require some of the same elements, it's good to start a new file from a template that contains those elements. Aptana makes that easy to do.

- If you're going to create a new file that's similar to an existing file, you can open the existing file and save it with a new name.

- Although you can use the File→New From Template→CSS→CSS Template command to start a new file from the Aptana CSS template, it's better to use your own templates.

Figure 2-11   How to start a new CSS file from a template in Aptana

How to edit a CSS file

In general, when you use Aptana to edit a CSS file, you use the same techniques that you use for editing an HTML file. This is summarized in figure 2-12.

When you open a file with the css extension, Aptana knows what type of file you're working with so it can use color to highlight the syntax components. When you type the first letter of a property, the auto-completion feature displays a list of properties so you can select the one you want. After you select one, Aptana automatically adds the colon after it, so you can enter the property specification.

Beyond that, Aptana provides error and warning markers that help you spot errors. In this figure, for example, you can see an error marker at the start of the line for the padding property. It's there because padding is spelled wrong, and the color coding also indicates that.

These features help you avoid the first three common errors that are listed in this figure. On the other hand, Aptana has no way of knowing if you code an id or class name incorrectly. Instead, you'll find that out during testing when you notice that the rule sets that you've specified for the elements haven't been applied.

Aptana with an auto-completion list for a CSS file

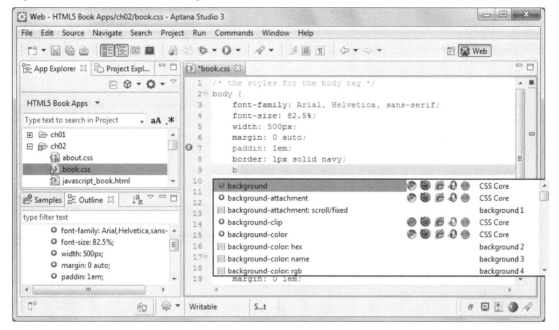

Common coding errors

- Braces that aren't paired correctly.
- Missing semicolons.
- Misspelled property names.
- Id or class names that don't match the names used in the HTML.

Description

- To edit a CSS file, you can use the same techniques you use to edit an HTML file. Here again, the color coding and the error markers will help you spot syntax errors. For this to work, the file must have the css extension.

- The auto-completion feature displays a list of properties that start with what you've typed. To insert one of those properties, double-click on it or use the arrow keys to highlight it and press the Tab key. Aptana automatically adds the colon after the property name.

- When you type the left brace after a selector, Aptana automatically adds the right brace. Then, you can enter the rules between the braces.

Note

- Aptana's color coding indicates that a measurement like .5em is incorrect because it looks for a digit before the decimal point as in 0.5em. However, the digit before the decimal point isn't required by browsers or the CSS standards, so an entry like .5em will be rendered correctly.

Figure 2-12   How to edit a CSS file in Aptana

How to preview and run an HTML file

Figure 2-13 shows how to preview and run an HTML file from Aptana. To preview the document, you select the tab that contains the open file and click on the Show Preview button in the toolbar. That shows the preview in another tab of the editor window. This is a quick way to see how the changes that you've made to an HTML or CSS file are displayed, but the preview may have rendering errors that you won't find in browsers.

To run an HTML file in the default browser, you again select the tab of the open file. Then, you click on the Run button. This opens the default browser and runs the file in that browser. This is the preferred way to see what a web page looks like because the preview can't be trusted.

To run an HTML file in another browser, you use the drop-down list to the right of the Run button. In this figure, this list has been dropped down, and it shows that the default browser is Firefox. Then, to run the file in Internet Explorer, you click on that option.

Incidentally, if you click on the Show Preview or Run button when an HTML file isn't selected, nothing happens. Also, you need to save any changes to an HTML file and its related CSS file before you can preview and run it. To do that, you can click on the Save or Save All button in the toolbar. But if you forget to do that, Aptana will warn you.

The Show Preview and Run buttons

Show
Preview
button

Run
button

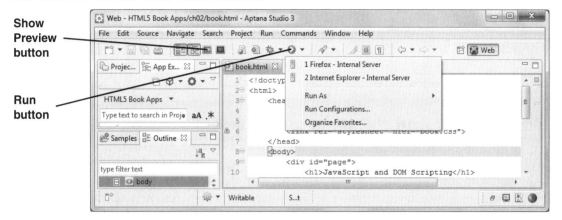

The preview of the javascript_book.html file

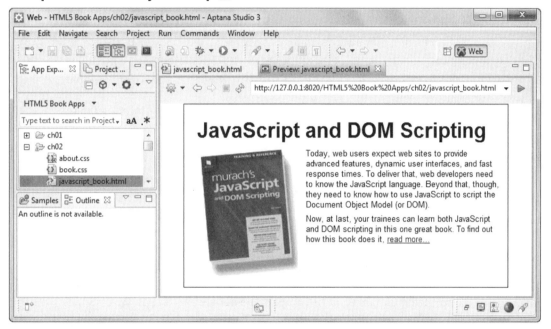

Description

- To preview an HTML file in an Aptana tab, open the HTML file, select its tab, and click on the Show Preview button.
- To run an HTML file in the default browser, open the file, select its tab, and click on the Run button.
- To run an HTML file in another browser, click the down-arrow to the right of the Run button and select the browser.
- Before you preview or run a file, you should save any changes that you've made to it or its related CSS file. To do that, you can click on the Save or Save All button in the toolbar. But if you forget to save the files, Aptana will warn you.

Figure 2-13   How to preview and run an HTML file from Aptana

How to test, debug, and validate HTML and CSS files

Now that you know how to create and edit HTML and CSS files, you're ready to learn how to test, debug, and validate those files.

How to test and debug a web page

When you *test* a web page, you run the file on all the browsers that are likely to access the file and try to identify all of the problems. When you *debug* a web page, you find the causes of the problems, fix them, and test again.

To run a web page, you can use one of the techniques in figure 2-14. If you're using Aptana, though, you can just click on the Run button. Once the page is displayed in the browser, you study it to make sure that it looks the way you want it to. You should also make sure that all of the links work.

If you find errors, you need to change the HTML, the CSS, or both, and test the page again. When you test a page for the second time, though, you don't need to run it again. Instead, you can click on the Reload or Refresh button in the browser's toolbar.

Often, the changes you make as you test a web page are just minor adjustments or improvements. But sometimes, the web page doesn't look at all the way you expected it to. Often, these errors are caused by trivial coding problems like missing tags, quotation marks, and braces, but finding these problems can be hard to do when your files consist of dozens of lines of code.

When you test a web page on more than one browser, you will often find that a web page will work on one browser, only to find that it doesn't work on another. That's usually because one of the browsers makes some assumptions that the other browser doesn't. If, for example, you have a slight coding error in an HTML file, one browser might make an assumption that fixes the problem, while the other doesn't.

To fix problems like these, it often helps to validate the HTML or CSS file. That should clearly identify the coding errors. You'll learn how to do that in the next two figures.

The HTML file displayed in the Firefox browser

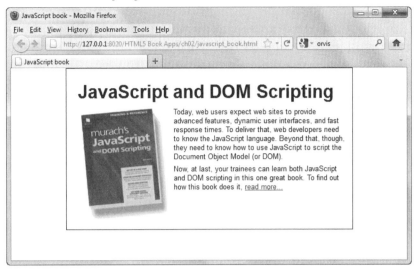

Three ways to run a web page that's on an intranet or your own computer

- Start your browser, and use the File→Open or Open File command to open the file. Or, type the complete path and filename into the address bar, and press Enter.

- On a Windows system, use Windows Explorer to find the HTML file, and double-click on it.

- If you're using Aptana, select the HTML file and click the Run button to open the file in the default browser. If you're using another text editor or IDE, look for a similar button or command.

How to rerun a web page from a browser after you change its source code

- Click the Reload or Refresh button in the browser.

How to test a web page

- Run the page in all of the browsers that are likely to access your site.

- Check the contents and appearance of the page to make sure it's correct in all browsers.

- Click on all of the links to make sure they work properly.

How to debug a web page

- Find the causes of the errors in the HTML or CSS code, make the corrections, and test again.

Description

- When you *test* a web page, you try to find all of the errors.

- When you *debug* a web page, you find the causes of the errors in the HTML or CSS code, correct them, and test the page again.

Figure 2-14   How to test and debug the HTML and CSS for a web page

How to validate an HTML file

To *validate* an HTML document, you use a program or web site for that purpose. One of the most popular web sites for validating HTML is the one for the W3C Markup Validation Service that's shown in figure 2-15.

When you use this web site, you can provide the HTML document that you want to validate in three ways. You can provide the URL for the page. You can upload the document. And you can copy and paste the document into their Validate by Direct Input tab.

In this figure, the Validate by File Upload tab is shown. Then, you click on the Browse button to find the file that you want to validate. Once that's done, you click on the Check button to validate the document.

Another way to validate an HTML document is to use the Aptana command for doing that, which is explained in this figure. Then, the results of the validation are displayed in one tab of the editor window, as shown in the next figure. This makes it much easier to validate a document, which is another reason for using Aptana Studio 3. Note, however, that you may get slightly different results with Aptana because it uses the HTML Tidy validator and W3 uses its own validator.

The home page for the W3C validator

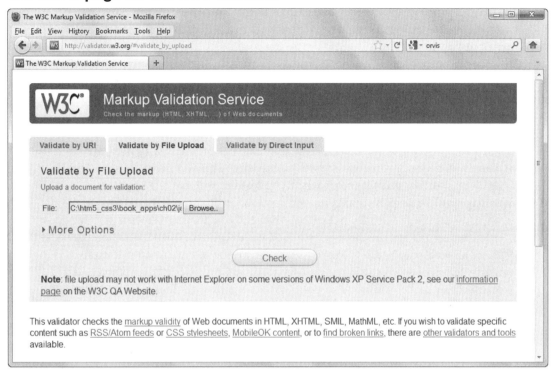

How to use the W3C Markup Validation Service

- Go to the URL that follows, identify the file to be validated, and click the Check button:

  `http://validator.w3.org/`

How to validate an HTML file from Aptana

- Select the file. Then, issue the Commands→HTML→Validate Syntax (W3C) command.

Description

- To *validate* the HTML for a page, you can use a program or web site for that purpose. One of the most popular web sites is the W3C Markup Validation Service.

- When you use the W3C Markup Validation Service, if the file you want to validate has already been uploaded to a web server, you can validate it by entering its URL on the Validate by URI tab. If the file you want to validate hasn't been uploaded to a web server, you can validate it by locating it on the Validate by File Upload tab.

- With the W3C Markup Validation Service, you can also validate HTML by copying and pasting it into the Validate by Direct Input tab.

- If you're using Aptana, you can validate an HTML file by using the command above. However, you may get slightly different results because Aptana uses the HTML Tidy validator and W3 uses its own validator.

Figure 2-15   How to validate an HTML file (part 1 of 2)

If the HTML code is valid when a document is validated, the validator displays a message to that effect. However, it may still display one or more warning messages. At this writing, two warnings are displayed for the web pages in this book.

On the other hand, if the code contains errors, the message will indicate the number of errors that were detected. Then, you can scroll down to a list of the errors like the one in the second part of this figure. Here, the validation results are shown in an Aptana tab.

In this example, the three error messages for line 11 in the HTML were caused by a missing > at the end of the img element on line 10. In this case, Aptana would display an error marker so this error shouldn't slip by you. And if it did, you should catch that error when you test the web page. But sometimes, a web page will be displayed okay in one browser, even though it contains an error or two, although it may not display correctly in another browser.

Should all HTML documents be validated, even though it's estimated that 99% of all web pages aren't? We say, yes! As we see it, validation is a useful practice that will solve some testing problems, and programs like Aptana and Dreamweaver make validation so easy that it's well worth doing. Besides that, validation may help your SEO results because clean code gets better results.

The Aptana validator output for an HTML file with a missing >
at the end of the img element

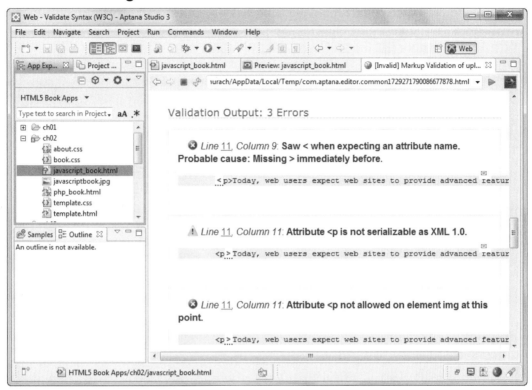

Description

- If the HTML document is valid, the validator will indicate that the document passed the validation. However, one or more warnings may still be displayed.
- If the HTML document isn't valid, the validator will indicate the number of errors that were detected. Then, you can scroll down to a description of the errors.

Figure 2-15   How to validate an HTML file (part 2 of 2)

How to validate a CSS file

You can validate a CSS file the same way you validate an HTML file, either with a validation program that may be part of a text editor or an IDE, or with a web site service like the W3C CSS Validation Service. If you use the W3C Validation Service, the opening page looks like the one for markup validation. Then, you can use any one of the three tabs to validate a CSS file.

If the file contains errors, the validation service will display a screen like the one in figure 2-16. Here, the error was caused by a missing semi-colon at the end of a rule. Although you would normally catch this type of error with Aptana's error markers and color coding, CSS validation is useful when the file is large, the CSS isn't working right, and you can't spot any errors. CSS validation may also mean that your CSS will work on an infrequently-used browser that isn't one of the browsers that you're using for testing.

The CSS Validation Service with errors displayed

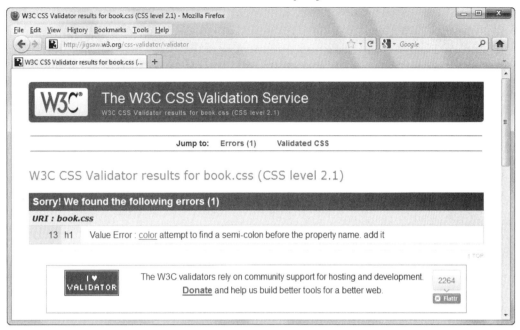

How to use the W3C CSS Validation Service

* Go to the URL that follows, identify the file to be validated, and click the Check button:

```
http://jigsaw.w3.org/css-validator/
```

How to validate a CSS file from Aptana

* Select the file. Then, issue the Commands→CSS→Validate Selected CSS (W3C) command.

Description

* To validate the CSS for a page, you can use a program or web site for that purpose. One of the most popular web sites is the W3C CSS Validation Service. This web site works the same as the W3C Markup Validation Service.

* If the CSS for a page is valid, the CSS Validation Service displays a message that indicates that no errors were found.

* If you're using Aptana, you can validate a CSS file by using the command above. However, you may get slightly different results because Aptana uses the CSS Tidy validator and W3 uses its own validator.

Figure 2-16   How to validate a CSS file

Perspective

Now that you've completed this chapter, you should be able to create and edit HTML and CSS files using Aptana or the editor of your choice. Then, you should be able to test those files by displaying their web pages in your web browser and in any other web browsers that your users might use. You should also be able to validate the HTML and CSS files for a web page.

At this point, you're ready to learn the coding details for HTML and CSS. So, in the next chapter, you'll learn the details for coding the HTML elements that define the structure and content for a web page. And in chapters 4, 5, and 6, you'll learn the details for coding the CSS rule sets that format the HTML content.

Terms

syntax	whitespace
HTML document	rule set
DOCTYPE declaration	selector
document tree	declaration block
HTML element	declaration
root element	rule
opening tag	property
closing tag	value
content of an element	type selector
empty tag	template
nested elements	Aptana project
attribute	testing
Boolean attribute	debugging
comment	HTML validation
comment out	CSS validation

Summary

- An *HTML document* consists of a *DOCTYPE declaration* that indicates what version of HTML is being used and a *document tree* that contains the *HTML elements* that define the content and structure of a web page.

- The *root element* in a document tree is the html element, which always contains a head element and a body element. The head element provides information about the page, and the body element provides the structure and content for the page.

- Most HTML elements consist of an *opening tag* and a *closing tag* with *content* between these tags. When you *nest* elements with HTML, the inner set of tags must be closed before the outer set.

- *Attributes* can be coded in an opening tag to supply optional values. An attribute consists of the name of the attribute, an equal sign, and the attribute value. To code multiple attributes, you separate them with spaces.

- An *HTML comment* can be used to describe or explain a portion of code. Because comments are ignored, you can also use comments to *comment out* a portion of HTML code so it isn't rendered by the browser. This can be helpful when you're testing your HTML code.

- *Whitespace* consists of characters like tab characters, line return characters, and extra spaces that are ignored by browsers. As a result, you can use whitespace to indent and align your code.

- A *CSS rule set* consists of a selector and a declaration block. The *selector* identifies the HTML elements that are going to be formatted. Three of the common CSS selectors select by element (called a *type selector*), ID, and class.

- The *declaration block* in a CSS rule set contains one or more *declarations* that do the formatting. Each declaration (or *rule*) consists of a *property*, a colon, a *value*, and a semicolon.

- *CSS comments* work like HTML comments. However, CSS comments start with /* and end with */, and HTML comments start with <!-- and end with -->.

- Aptana is a text editor that can be used to edit HTML or CSS code. To help you read the code, Aptana displays the syntax components with different colors. It also provides auto-completion lists, and error checking that detects common entry errors.

- When you start a new HTML or CSS file, it's best to start from a *template* or an old file that's similar to the new file that you're going to create.

- To *test* an HTML file, you run it on all of the browsers that your clients may use. Then, if you discover problems, you need to *debug* the code and test it again.

- To *validate* an HTML or CSS file, you can use a program or web site for that purpose. Often, a validation program will detect errors in a file, even though the web page displays the way you want it to on all browsers.

Before you do the exercises for this book...

If you haven't already done it, you should install the Firefox browser and the applications, examples, and exercises for this book. If you're going to use Aptana Studio 3 as your text editor, you should also download and install that product. The procedures for doing all three are in appendix A.

Exercise 2-1   Get started right with Aptana

This exercise is for readers who are going to use Aptana Studio 3 with this book. It guides you through the process of creating projects that provide easy access to the book applications, examples, and exercise starts that you've downloaded.

Create the projects

1. Use the procedure in figure 2-7 to create a project for the book applications that are stored in this folder:

    `c:\murach\html5_css3\book_apps`

    This project should be named HTML5 Book Apps, and the entries for the last dialog box should be just like those in this figure.

2. Use the same procedure to create a project named HTML5 Examples for the book examples that are stored in this folder:

    `c:\murach\html5_css3\book_examples`

3. Use the same procedure to create a project named HTML5 Exercises for the exercises that are stored in this folder:

    `c:\html5_css3\exercises`

Use the projects that you've created

4. Use the drop-down list in the App Explorer to select the HTML5 Book Apps project. This provides access to all of the applications that are in this book.

5. Click on the plus sign before ch02 to display the files in this folder. Then, double-click on the file named javascript_book.html to open that file.

6. Delete the l in the opening tag for the h1 element and note how Aptana highlights this error. Then, undo this change. (To use the keyboard to undo a change, press Ctrl+Z.)

7. Start a new element after the h1 element and note how Aptana provides auto-completion. Then, undo this change and save the file if necessary.

8. Click on the Show Preview button shown in figure 2-13 to preview the file in Aptana. Then, click on the tab for the HTML file and click on the Run button shown in figure 2-13 to run the file in your default browser.

9. Use the drop-down list in the App Explorer to select the HTML5 Exercises project. This provides access to all of the starting files for the exercises.

10. Right-click on one of the tabs in the editor window, and select Close All to close all of the tabs. Then, experiment on your own if you like.

Exercise 2-2   Edit and test the book page

In this exercise, you'll edit and test the book page that is shown in figure 2-14. You should do this exercise whether you're using Aptana or another text editor.

Open the HTML and CSS files for the book page

1. Start your text editor.

2. Open this HTML file in your text editor:

    `c:\html5_css3\exercises\ch02\javascript_book.html`

    For Aptana users, this will be in the project named HTML5 Exercises.

3. Open the CSS file named book.css that's in the same folder. This should open in a new tab.

Test the book page in Firefox and Internet Explorer

4. Run the HTML file in Firefox.

5. Run the HTML file in Internet Explorer. Notice that the page looks the same in both browsers.

Modify the HTML and CSS code and test again

6. Go to the javascript_book.html file in your text editor, and delete just one of the <br> tags near the end of the body element. Then, save the file.

7. Refresh the page in the Firefox browser by clicking on the Reload button. Then, refresh the page in the IE browser by clicking on the Refresh button. Is there a difference in the pages? If so, this illustrates why you need to test a web page in more than one browser. But this does depend on the browser versions.

8. Go back to your text editor, undo the change that you made in step 6. Then, save the file and test the page in the IE browser to make sure that the page has been corrected.

9. Go back to your text editor and click on the tab for the book.css file. Then, change the float property for the img element from left to right, and save the file. Now, test this change in one or both browsers.

10. Go back to the book.css file, and change the color for the h1 element to "red" and change the font-size to 200%. Then, save the file and test the change in one or both browsers.

11. Go back to the javascript_book.html file, and add a <p> element at the bottom of the page that has this content:

    `For customer service, call us at 1-555-555-5555.`

    Then, save the file and test this change.

12. Go to the javascript_book.html file and add an id attribute with the value "service" to the <p> element that you just entered. Then, go to the book.css file and enter a rule set for the <p> element with that id. This rule set should use the color property to change the text to red. If you need help doing this, refer to figures 2-5 and 2-6. Now, save both the html and css files, and test these changes.

Validate the HTML and CSS files

13. In the HTML file, delete the ending > for the img tag, and save the file. Then, go to the site in figure 2-15, and use the Validate by File Upload tab to validate the file. If you scroll down the page when the validation is done, you'll see 3 error messages, even though the file contains just one error.

14. In the CSS file, delete the semi-colon for the color rule in the h1 rule set, and save the file. Then, go to the site in figure 2-16, and use the Validate by File Upload tab to validate the file. This time, you'll see 1 error message.

15. If you're using Aptana, note the error marker in the HTML file. Then, validate the HTML file by using the command in figure 2-15. This shows how much easier it is to validate files within the text editor or IDE that you're using.

16. If you're using Aptana, note the error marker in the CSS file. Then, validate the CSS file by using the command in figure 2-16. Note here that the validation found no errors, which differs from the results for step 14.

17. Now, undo the errors in the files, save the file, and validate the HTML page again. This time, it should pass with two warnings. Then, test the web page one last time.

Exercise 2-3   Start a new web page

In this exercise, you'll start HTML and CSS files from templates in this folder:

```
c:\html5_css3\exercises\ch02
```

For Aptana users, this will be in the project named HTML5 Exercises.

Start your files from templates

1. Create a new HTML file named testpage.html from the template named template.html. If you're using Aptana, you can use the first procedure in figure 2-9. Otherwise, you can use the second procedure in this figure.

2. Create a new CSS file named testpage.css from the template named template.css. If you're using Aptana, you can use the first procedure in figure 2-11. Otherwise, you can use the second procedure in this figure.

Add some content to the HTML file and test it

3. In the title element, change the content to "Test page".

4. In the link element, enter the value "testpage.css" for the href attribute.

5. Add an h1 element to the body of the HTML file that says: "This is a test page." Then, save the file, and test the page by running it in Firefox or IE.

6. This illustrates how fast you can get started with a new web page when you start the html and css files from templates. Now, if you want to add more elements to the HTML or more rules or rule sets to the CSS, give it a try.

7. When you're through experimenting, close the files in your editor.

3

How to use HTML to structure a web page

In chapter 2, you saw the basic structure of an HTML document, you learned the basic techniques for coding the elements that make up a document, and you learned that these elements specify the structure and content of a page when it's displayed in a browser. Now, in this chapter, you'll learn how to code the HTML elements that you'll use in most of the documents you create. Then, in the next three chapters, you'll learn how to use CSS to format those HTML elements.

How to code the head section

The head section of an HTML document contains elements that provide information about the web page rather than the content of the page. In chapter 1, for example, you learned that the title element sets the text that's displayed in the browser's title bar. Now, you'll learn more about this element as well as some other elements that you can code in the head section.

How to code the title element

The head section of every page should include a unique title element that describes the content of the page. This title is used by search engines for search engine optimization, and it appears in the results of a search to help the users decide whether they want to go to that page. That's why you should follow the SEO guidelines in figure 3-1 when you code this element.

As you can see in this figure, the content of this element is also displayed in the browser's title bar and in the tab for the page. In this example, the title tag gives the name of the organization followed by the keywords *speakers* and *luncheons*.

How to link to a favicon

The link element is an optional element that you can use to specify a file that should be linked to the web page. In figure 3-1, the link element is used to link a custom icon, called a *favicon*, to the web page. This causes the icon to be displayed at the left side of the URL in the browser's address bar and to the left of the title in the tab for the page. Note that you typically name this icon favicon.ico as shown in this figure.

When you code the link element, you typically include two attributes. The rel attribute indicates the relationship of the linked resource to the document. For a favicon, you use the value "shortcut icon".

The href attribute provides the URL of the resource. In this example, the favicon is in the same folder as the HTML file, so the URL is just the filename. If the file is in a different location, though, you can use an absolute or relative URL to identify that location. You'll learn how to code absolute and relative URLs later in this chapter.

If you're using an older version of Internet Explorer, you should realize that it won't display a favicon if the page is displayed from your local file system. To test a favicon in this browser, then, you need to upload the page to a server and display it from that server.

A browser that shows the title and favicon

A head section that specifies a title and links to a favicon

```
<head>
    <title>San Joaquin Valley Town Hall | speakers and luncheons</title>
    <link rel="shortcut icon" href="favicon.ico">
</head>
```

SEO guidelines for the title tag

- Always code a title tag in the head section.
- The title should accurately describe the page's content, and it should include the one or two keywords that you want the page ranked for.
- The title should be interesting enough to entice the reader to click on it when it's shown in the search results for a search engine.
- The title should be unique for each page in your web site.
- Limit the length of your titles to around 65 characters because most search engines don't display more than that in their results.

Description

- The title element specifies the text that's displayed in the browser's title bar.
- The title is also displayed in the tab for the web page, and it is used as the name of a favorite or bookmark for the page.
- A custom icon, called a *favicon*, is typically named favicon and must have the extension .ico to work correctly with Internet Explorer. A favicon typically appears to the left of the URL in the browser's address bar. It may also appear to the left of the title in a tab, and it may be used in a favorite or bookmark.
- To specify a favicon for a page, you use a link tag exactly like the one shown above.
- To create an ico file, you can use an icon editor, a program that converts an image to an ico file, or a web-based converter. You may also be able to find an icon on the Internet by searching for "web icons". For more information, see chapter 8.

Internet Explorer note

- A favicon isn't displayed in older versions of Internet Explorer if the page is served from your local file system. It is only displayed if the page is served from the web server.

Figure 3-1   How to code the title element and link to a favicon

How to include metadata

The meta element is another optional element that you can code within the head element. You use it to specify *metadata*, which provides information about the content of the document.

The head element in figure 3-2 includes three meta elements. The first one specifies the character encoding used for the page, and UTF-8 is the encoding that's commonly used for the World Wide Web. Since this element is required for HTML5 validation, you should include it in the head section of every HTML document, and it should be one of the first elements in the head section.

The next two meta elements in this figure provide metadata that can be used by search engines to index the page. Here, the first element uses the name attribute with the value "description" to indicate that the content attribute that follows contains a description of the web page. This can be a longer description than the one in the title element, and it should also be unique for each page in your web site.

The second meta element uses the name attribute with the value "keywords" to indicate that the content attribute contains a list of keywords related to the page. At one time, the keywords were an important factor for search engine optimization, but they have been de-emphasized in recent years, partly because some web masters used keywords to misrepresent what a page contained.

At present, there is some debate about how search engines use the description and keywords metadata. In fact, the algorithms that search engines use are frequently changed, so it's hard to know what the best use of metadata is. There is also the danger that you might change the content of a page and forget to change the metadata. In that case, a search engine might index the page incorrectly. Nevertheless, it's still a good practice to provide the description and keywords metadata for at least the important pages of a web site. Just make sure that your descriptions and keywords accurately represent the contents of your pages.

A head section that includes metadata

```
<head>
    <title>San Joaquin Valley Town Hall | speakers and luncheons</title>
    <meta charset=utf-8">
    <meta name="description" content="A yearly lecture series with speakers
        that present new information on a wide range of subjects">
    <meta name="keywords" content="san joaquin, town hall, speakers,
        lectures, luncheons">
</head>
```

Three attributes of the <meta> tag

Attribute	Description
charset	A required tag in HTML5 that specifies the type of character encoding to be used for the page. UTF-8 is the encoding that's commonly used for the World Wide Web.
name	Specifies the type of metadata being added to the document. The values "description" and "keywords" can be used to specify content that's used by some search engines.
content	Specifies the value to be used for the item specified by the name attribute.

SEO guidelines

- Code the description metadata for each page of your web site. It should summarize the contents of the page, it should be unique for each page, and it can be longer than the title tag. When it is displayed in the search-engine results, it should encourage users to click on your link.

- Code the keywords metadata for each page of your web site. It should consist of no more than 10 keywords or phrases, and it should be unique for each page.

Description

- The meta element provides information about the HTML document that's called *metadata*.

- The charset metadata is required for HTML5 validation.

- All or part of the description metadata may be displayed in the search results of some search engines.

- Although the keywords metadata has been de-emphasized by some search engines, it's still a good practice to include this data.

Figure 3-2   How to include metadata

How to code text elements

Within the body of a document, you can code two types of elements: block elements and inline elements. In the topics that follow, you'll learn how to code a variety of block and inline elements that define the text for a document.

How to code headings and paragraphs

Headings and paragraphs are the most common content of a web page. These are defined by the HTML elements shown in figure 3-3. These elements are called *block elements*, and each one begins on a new line when it is displayed.

If you review the example in this figure, you shouldn't have any trouble understanding how these elements work. Here, the HTML uses the h1, h2, and <p> elements to generate the text that's shown. When these elements are displayed by a browser, each element has a default font and size that's determined by the base font of the browser. This base font is typically Times New Roman in 16 pixels.

When you use the h1 through h6 elements, you should use them to provide a logical structure for your document, not to format the text. That means that the first heading on a page should always be an h1 element. That also means you should only go down one level at a time, not jump down two or more levels to indicate less importance. In other words, the first heading level after an h2 should be an h3, not an h4.

For example, the h1 element in this figure is used to mark the most important heading on the page, and the h2 elements are used to mark the next level of importance. Then, if the first h2 element required two subheadings below it, they would both be coded at the h3 level. This structure helps search engines index your site properly, and it makes your pages more accessible to devices like screen readers. Then, you can use CSS to size and format the text in these elements, as shown in the next chapter.

Common block elements for headings and paragraphs

Element	Description
h1	Creates a level-1 heading with content in bold at 200% of the base font size.
h2	Creates a level-2 heading with content in bold at 150% of the base font size.
h3	Creates a level-3 heading with content in bold at 117% of the base font size.
h4	Creates a level-4 heading with content in bold at 100% of the base font size.
h5	Creates a level-5 heading with content in bold at 83% of the base font size.
h6	Creates a level-6 heading with content in bold at 67% of the base font size.
p	Creates a paragraph of text at 100% of the base font size.

HTML that uses the block elements

```
<h1>San Joaquin Valley Town Hall Programs</h1>
<h2>Pre-lecture coffee at the Saroyan</h2>
<p>Join us for a complimentary coffee hour, 9:15 to 10:15 a.m. on the day
    of each lecture. The speakers usually attend this very special event.</p>

<h2>Post-lecture luncheon at the Saroyan</h2>
<p>Extend the excitement of Town Hall by purchasing tickets to the
    luncheons</p>
```

The block elements in a web browser

San Joaquin Valley Town Hall Programs

Pre-lecture coffee at the Saroyan

Join us for a complimentary coffee hour, 9:15 to 10:15 a.m. on the day of each lecture. The speakers usually attend this very special event.

Post-lecture luncheon at the Saroyan

Extend the excitement of Town Hall by purchasing tickets to the luncheons.

SEO guidelines

- Use the heading tags to show the structure and importance of the content on a page. Always start with an h1 tag and decrease one level at a time to show subsequent levels of importance.
- Don't use heading levels as a way to size text. Instead, use CSS to size the headings.

Description

- *Block elements* are the main building blocks of a web site and can contain other elements. Each block element begins on a new line.
- The base font size and the spacing above and below headings and paragraphs are determined by the browser, but you can change these values by using CSS.

Figure 3-3   How to code headings and paragraphs

How to code special blocks of text

In addition to the elements for headings and paragraphs, HTML provides some elements that you can use to code special blocks of text. For instance, three of the most common elements are described in figure 3-4.

You typically use the pre element to display preformatted blocks of code. When you use this element, any whitespace or line breaks that appear in the content is maintained. In addition, the content is displayed in a monospaced font. In this figure, the pre element is used to display two lines of JavaScript code.

You typically use the blockquote element to display an actual quote like the one shown in this figure. Depending on the browser, this element may cause the content to be indented from the left side of the block element that contains it or from both the left and right sides. But note that this doesn't add quotation marks to the text.

You can use the address element to display contact information for the developer or owner of a web site. In this figure, the address element is used to display a phone number and an email address. As you can see, the browser displays this information in italics.

Although these elements provide some default HTML formatting, you shouldn't think of these elements that way. Instead, you should use these elements to identify specific types of content. Then, you can use CSS to format these elements so they look the way you want them to.

Block elements for special types of text

Element	Description
pre	Used for portions of code that are formatted with line breaks and spaces. Creates a block of preformatted text that preserves whitespace and is displayed in a monospaced font.
blockquote	Used for quotations. Can be used with the cite and <q> elements of figure 3-5.
address	Used for contact information for the developer or owner of a web site.

HTML that uses the block elements

```
<p>How to use JavaScript to display the year:</p>
<pre>
        var today = new Date();
        document.writeln( today.getFullYear() );
</pre>

<p>Ernest Hemingway wrote:</p>
<blockquote>Cowardice, as distinguished from panic, is almost always
    simply a lack of ability to suspend the functioning of the imagination.
</blockquote>

<p>How to contact Mike Murach &amp; Associates:</p>
<address>1-800-221-5528<br>
    <a href="emailto:murachbooks@murach.com">murachbooks@murach.com</a>
</address>
```

The block elements in a web browser

How to use JavaScript to display the year:

```
        var today = new Date();
        document.writeln( today.getFullYear() );
```

Ernest Hemingway wrote:

> Cowardice, as distinguished from panic, is almost always simply a lack of ability to suspend the functioning of the imagination.

How to contact Mike Murach & Associates:

1-800-221-5528
murachbooks@murach.com

Description

- These block elements identify the type of content that they contain. That's consistent with the way the HTML5 semantic elements are used (see figures 3-9 and 3-10).

Figure 3-4   How to code special blocks of text

How to code inline elements for formatting and identifying text

In contrast to a block element, an *inline element* doesn't start on a new line. Instead, an inline element is coded within a block element. In this topic, you'll learn how to code some of the most common inline elements for identifying and formatting.

The first table in figure 3-5 presents five elements for formatting text. for instance, the <i> element is used to italicize text, and the <b> element is used to boldface text. With the exception of the <br> element, each element must have both an opening and a closing tag. Then, the appropriate formatting is applied to the content between these tags.

In contrast, the <br> element starts a new line of text. You can use this to start a new line within an element, but you shouldn't use it to provide space between block elements. Instead, you should use CSS to control the space between block elements.

The second table in this figure presents elements that are used for identifying inline content. For instance, you can use the abbr element to identify an abbreviation, the <q> element to identify a quotation, and the cite element to identify the source of a block element like a quotation.

Unlike the blockquote element, which is a block element, the browser adds quotation marks to a <q> element. Also, these quotation marks are curly instead of straight. In the examples, you can see that a <q> element is used for a quotation within a paragraph, but this inline element could also be used within a blockquote element to add the quotation marks.

In general, you should use the elements in the second table to identify the type of text whenever some meaning is implied. Then, you can use CSS to format those elements. In contrast, you should only use the elements in the first table to format text when no meaning is implied.

This is different from the way the <i> and <b> elements were used before CSS become available. Previously, these elements were commonly used to apply formatting. Now, it's more common to use em and strong and to use CSS to apply the appropriate formatting.

Inline elements for formatting text

Element	Description
i	Displays the content in italics.
b	Displays the content in bold.
sub	Displays the content as a subscript.
sup	Displays the content as a superscript.
br	An empty element that starts a new line of text.

Inline elements for identifying content

Element	Description
abbr	Used for abbreviations.
cite	Used to indicate a bibliographic citation like a book title.
code	Used for computer code, which is displayed in a monospaced font.
dfn	Used for special terms that can be defined elsewhere (definitions).
em	Indicates that the content should be emphasized, which is displayed in italics.
kbd	Used for keyboard entries, which is displayed in a monospaced font.
q	Used for quotations, which are displayed within quotation marks.
samp	Used to mark a sequence of characters (sample) that has no other meaning.
strong	Indicates that the content should be strongly emphasized, which is displayed in bold.
var	Used for computer variables, which are displayed in a monospaced font.

HTML that uses some of the inline elements

```
<p>If you don't get 78% or more on your final, <em>you won't pass.</em></p>
<p>Save a bundle at our <strong>big yearend sale</strong>.</p>
<p>When the dialog box is displayed, enter <kbd>brock21</kbd>.</p>
<p>The chemical symbol for water is H<sub>2</sub>O.</p>
<p><q>To sleep, perchance to dream-ay, there's the rub.</q></p>
```

The inline elements in a web browser

If you don't get 78% or more on your final, *you won't pass.*

Save a bundle at our **big yearend sale**.

When the dialog box is displayed, enter `brock21`.

The chemical symbol for water is H_2O.

"To sleep, perchance to dream-ay, there's the rub."

Description

- An *inline element* is coded within a block element and doesn't begin on a new line.
- The formatting elements should be used when no special meaning is implied.
- The content elements should be used to convey meaning. Then, you can use CSS to format them.

Figure 3-5 .   How to code inline elements for formatting and identifying text

How to code character entities

Many of the web pages you develop will require special characters such as a copyright symbol and opening and closing "curly" quotes. To display these special characters, you use *character entities*. Figure 3-6 presents the most common of these entities.

As you can see, all character entities start with an ampersand (&) and end with a semicolon (;). Then, the rest of the entity identifies the character it represents. To insert the copyright symbol (©), for example, you use the © character entity.

Because the & character marks the start of each character entity, you shouldn't use this character within an HTML document to represent an ampersand. Instead, you should use the & entity. Similarly, because the left bracket (<) and right bracket (>) are used to identify HTML tags, you shouldn't use those characters within an HTML document to represent less-than and greater-than signs. Instead, you should use the < and > entities.

Besides the entities for characters, you may sometimes need to insert a non-breaking space to force a browser to display a space. To do that, you use the   character entity. In the third paragraph in this figure, for example, this character entity is used to indent the first line of the paragraph four spaces. However, because you can accomplish the same thing with CSS, you probably won't use the   character entity this way.

Common HTML character entities

Entity	Character
&	&
<	<
>	>
©	©
®	®
™	™
¢	¢
°	°
±	±
‘	' (opening single quote).
’	' (closing single quote or apostrophe).
“	" (opening double quote).
”	" (closing double quote).
	A non-breaking space.

Examples of character entities

```
<p>It&rsquo;s time to start your Christmas shopping!</p>

<p>President John F. Kennedy said, &ldquo;And so, my fellow Americans,
ask not what your country can do for you; ask what you can do for
your country.&rdquo;</p>

<p>    Turning fear into hope, medical futurist
Dr. Alan J. Russell will discuss the science of regenerating damaged
or diseased human body parts, while offering real hope for the future
of human health.</p>

<p>&copy; 2012 Mike Murach &amp; Associates, Inc.</p>
```

The character entities in a web browser

It's time to start your Christmas shopping!

President John F. Kennedy said, "And so, my fellow Americans, ask not what your country can do for you; ask what you can do for your country."

Turning fear into hope, medical futurist Dr. Alan J. Russell will discuss the science of regenerating damaged or diseased human body parts, while offering real hope for the future of human health.

© 2012 Mike Murach & Associates, Inc.

Description

- *Character entities* can be used to display special characters in an HTML document.
- HTML provides a variety of character entities in addition to the ones above.

Figure 3-6   How to code character entities

How to code the core attributes

Besides the attributes you've learned about so far, HTML provides some core attributes that you can use with most elements. In figure 3-7, you can see the core attributes that you're most likely to use.

You use the id attribute to uniquely identify an HTML element. Then, you can use CSS to work with the element.

The class attribute is similar, except it doesn't have to be unique. That lets you assign more than one element to the same class. Then, you can use CSS to apply the same formatting to all the elements in the class. When you use the class attribute, you can also assign more than one class to a single element.

In the example in this figure, you can see that the input element has an id attribute with the value "email". As you'll see in the next chapter, CSS can be used to apply unique formatting to elements with id attributes.

In this example, you can also see that a class attribute is used to assign a class named "first" to the first <p> element. Then, another class attribute is used to assign two classes to the second <p> element. These classes are "first" and "field". Later, you can use CSS to apply formatting to the elements in each class.

You can use the title attribute to provide additional information for an element. In the example in this figure, this attribute is used to provide a tooltip for an input field that lets the user enter an email address (you'll learn more about input fields in chapter 10). Then, when the cursor is moved over this field in the browser, the tooltip is displayed. For some elements, though, a tooltip isn't displayed so the title attribute has no purpose.

The lang attribute lets you specify the language used by a document. For instance, we recommend that you code this attribute on the html element to specify the language for the entire document. For English-speaking countries, you typically code this attribute like this:

```
<html lang="en">
```

This can help a screen reader pronounce words correctly. However, you can also code this attribute for individual elements. If a sentence on a web page is written in French, for example, you can code this attribute for the element that contains the sentence.

Core HTML attributes

Attribute	Description
id	Specifies a unique identifier for an element that can be referred to by CSS.
class	Specifies one or more class names that can be referred to by CSS, and the same name can be used for more than one element. To code more than one class name, separate the class names with spaces.
title	Specifies additional information about an element. For some elements, the title appears in a tooltip when the user hovers the mouse over the element.
lang	Identifies the language that the content of the element is written in.

HTML that uses these attributes

```
<html lang="en">
<body>
    <h1>San Joaquin Valley Town Hall</h1>
    <p class="first">Welcome to San Joaquin Valley Town Hall.</p>
    <form action="subscribe.php" method="post">
        <p>Please enter your e-mail address to subscribe to our
            newsletter.</p>
        <p class="first field">E-Mail:
        <input type="text" name="email" id="email"
                title="Enter e-mail here."></p>
        <p><input type="submit" value="Subscribe"></p>
    </form>
</body>
</html>
```

The HTML in a web browser with a tooltip displayed

Accessibility guideline

- Always code the lang attribute on the html element to identify the language for the page.

Description

- The core attributes can be coded for most HTML elements.
- ID and class names are case sensitive, should start with a letter, and can include letters, numbers, underscores, hyphens, colons, and periods.
- The lang attribute is typically used to assist screen readers to read content correctly and to provide for searches that are restricted by language.

Figure 3-7   How to code the core attributes

How to structure the content of a page

The new structural elements are one of the key features of HTML5. Before you learn how to use those elements, though, you should learn how the div and span elements of HTML4 are used.

How to code div and span elements

Figure 3-8 shows how to code the div and span elements that have traditionally been used to structure a page and to format portions of inline content. You need to know how these elements are used because you're sure to see them in the HTML for pages that haven't yet been converted to HTML5. For new pages, though, you should use the HTML5 elements that are presented in the next figure.

The div element is a block element that you can use to divide an HTML document into divisions. In the example in this figure, you can see that the content of the document is divided into three divisions. The first division contains the header for the page, the second division contains the main contents of the page, and the third division is for the footer. If you look at this web page as it's displayed in the browser, you can see that these div elements don't affect the appearance of the page.

For each div element, the id attribute is used to indicate the contents of the division. Later, as you'll see in the next chapter, this id can be used as the selector that's used to apply CSS formatting to each division. In the next two figures, though, you'll see how the new HTML5 structural tags can simplify this.

The other element that's presented in this figure is the span element. This inline element has traditionally been used to identify content so CSS can be used to format it. For instance, the <p> element in the main division in this figure contains an inline span element. Here again, the span element doesn't affect the appearance of the page, but its id attribute can be used as the selector for CSS formatting.

For modern web sites, though, div and span elements should only be used when more specific tags don't apply. Instead of div elements, you should use the HTML5 semantic elements of the next two figures. Instead of span elements, you should use the block elements of figure 3-4 and the inline elements of figure 3-5 to identify the content types. By using these elements instead of div and span elements, you not only improve accessibility but also SEO.

A block element for structuring a web page

Element	Description
div	Lets you divide a page into divisions that can be formatted and positioned with CSS.

An inline element for formatting text

Element	Description
span	Lets you identify text that can be formatted with CSS.

A page that's structured with div and span elements

```html
<body>
    <div id="header">
        <h1>San Joaquin Valley Town Hall</h1>
    </div>
    <div id="main">
        <p><span id="welcome">Welcome to San Joaquin Valley Town
            Hall.</span>
            We have some fascinating speakers for you this season!</p>
    </div>
    <div id="footer">
        <p>&copy; Copyright 2012 San Joaquin Valley Town Hall.</p>
    </div>
</body>
```

The page displayed in a web browser

San Joaquin Valley Town Hall

Welcome to San Joaquin Valley Town Hall. We have some fascinating speakers for you this season!

© Copyright 2012 San Joaquin Valley Town Hall.

Accessibility and SEO guidelines

- Use div tags only when the HTML5 semantic elements don't apply.
- Use span tags only when the tags for identifying content don't apply.

Description

- Before HTML5, div elements were used to define divisions within the body of a document. Now, the HTML5 semantic elements will be replacing div elements.
- Before HTML5, span elements were used to identify portions of text that you could apply formatting to. Today, a better practice is to use the elements in figures 3-4 and 3-5 to identify content and to use CSS to format that content.

Figure 3-8   How to code the div and span elements

How to structure a page with the HTML5 semantic elements

Figure 3-9 presents the new HTML5 *semantic elements* that improve the way you can structure a page. For instance, the example in this figure shows how the header, section, and footer elements can be used to replace the three div tags of the previous figure. This makes it easier to see the structure of the page by looking at the HTML tags. This also makes it easier to code the selectors that you need for formatting these elements.

Using the new structural elements is often referred to as *HTML5 semantics*. The implication is that you do a better job of creating meaning when you use the new elements. In contrast, the div elements were generic elements with no meaning implied. In the long run, using HTML5 semantics may mean that search engines will be able to do a better job of coming up with relevant pages. For that reason, you should start using the semantic elements right away.

Although this figure only illustrates the use of three of the six elements in the table, you'll see the nav element used in the web page at the end of this chapter. Then, in chapter 6, you'll see how the aside element is used for a sidebar and the article element is used for an article about a speaker.

Does this mean that you shouldn't ever use div elements? The quick answer is, no. In general, you should only use div elements as a last resort, but there will be times where it doesn't make sense to use section elements to define a quick grouping of elements. Just keep in mind that div elements should be used sparingly and only when an HTML5 semantic element doesn't apply.

In this book, we'll be using section elements whenever there isn't an appropriate HTML5 element for a grouping. The main point of HTML5 semantics, though, is to use the other HTML5 elements whenever they provide the appropriate meaning. That way, you'll get the benefits of HTML5.

The primary HTML5 semantic elements

Element	Contents
header	The header for a page.
section	A generic section of a document that doesn't indicate the type of content.
article	A composition like an article in the paper.
nav	A section of a page that contains links to other pages or placeholders.
aside	A section of a page like a sidebar that is related to the content that's near it.
footer	The footer for a page.

A page that's structured with header, section, and footer elements

```
<body>
    <header>
        <h1>San Joaquin Valley Town Hall</h1>
    </header>
    <section>
        <p>Welcome to San Joaquin Valley Town Hall. We have some
            fascinating speakers for you this season!</p>
    </section>
    <footer>
        <p>&copy; Copyright 2012 San Joaquin Valley Town Hall.</p>
    </footer>
</body>
```

The page displayed in a web browser

San Joaquin Valley Town Hall

Welcome to San Joaquin Valley Town Hall. We have some fascinating
speakers for you this season!

© Copyright 2012 San Joaquin Valley Town Hall.

Accessibility and SEO guideline

- Use the HTML5 semantic elements to indicate the structure of your pages.

Description

- HTML5 provides new *semantic elements* that you should use to structure the contents of a web page. Using these elements can be referred to as *HTML5 semantics*.

- All of the HTML5 elements in this figure are supported by the modern browsers.

Figure 3-9   How to structure a web page with the HTML5 semantic elements

How to use some of the other HTML5 semantic elements

Figure 3-10 presents some of the other HTML5 semantic elements that are currently supported by modern browsers. For instance, the hgroup element is used to group headings that should logically be treated as one. This is illustrated by the first example. Here, the h1 element provides the name of the organization and the h2 element provides a tag line or slogan for the site. By using the hgroup element to group them, they will be treated as one by search engines.

The second semantic element in this figure is the time element. It provides a date or date and time in a standard format that can be parsed by a browser. This is illustrated by the second example. Here, the <p> element says that next year's conference will be on May 31st. But the time element makes it clear that this is May 31st of 2012. If the time element is used within an article, you can also use the pubdate attribute to make it clear that the date is the publication date for the article.

The third and fourth semantic elements in this figure apply to the use of figures within web pages. A figure can be a block of text, an image, a diagram, or anything that is referred to from the text outside of the figure. Within the figure element that contains the figure, the figcaption element can be used to provide a caption for the figure. This is illustrated by the third example, which treats two lines of JavaScript code as a figure. Then, in chapters 8 and 9, you can see how these elements can be used to treat images and tables as figures.

Here again, these elements are designed to provide more meaning. That way, search engines can do a better job of ranking your pages and screen readers can do a better job of reading your pages. In addition, using these elements makes it easier for you to code and format your pages.

Other HTML5 semantic elements

Element	Contents
hgroup	Two or more headings that form a composite heading.
time	A date or date and time that can be parsed by a browser.
figure	An illustration, diagram, photo, code listing or the like that is referred to from the main content of the document.
figcaption	The caption that identifies a figure.

The attributes of the time element

Attribute	Description
datetime	A date and time in a standard format that can be parsed by a browser.
pubdate	A Boolean attribute that indicates that the date is the publication date for the article that contains the time element.

The hgroup element

```
<hgroup>
    <h1>San Joaquin Valley Town Hall</h1>
    <h2>Bringing cutting-edge speakers to the valley</h2>
</hgroup>
```

A time element

```
<p>Next year's conference will be on
    <time datetime="2012-05-31">May 31st</time>.</p>
```

The figure and figcaption elements

```
<figure>
    <code>
        var today = new Date();<br>
        document.writeln( today.getFullYear() );<br><br>
    </code>
    <figcaption>
        JavaScript code for getting the year
    </figcaption>
</figure>
```

The code displayed in a browser

```
var today = new Date();
document.writeln( today.getFullYear() );

JavaScript code for getting the year
```

Accessibility and SEO guideline

- Use the HTML5 semantic elements to indicate the structure of your pages.

Description

- Although there are other HTML5 semantic elements, these are the most useful ones that are currently supported by modern browsers.

Figure 3-10   How to use some of the other HTML5 semantic elements

How to code links, lists, and images

Because you'll use links, lists, and images in most of the web pages that you develop, the topics that follow introduce you to these elements. But first, you need to know how to code absolute and relative URLs so you can use them with your links and images.

How to code absolute and relative URLs

Figure 3-11 presents some examples of absolute and relative URLs. To help you understand how these examples work, the diagram at the top of this figure shows the folder structure for the web site used in the examples. As you can see, the folders for this web site are organized into three levels. The root folder for the site contains five subfolders, including the folders that contain the images and styles for the site. Then, the books folder contains subfolders of its own.

In chapter 1, you learned about the basic components of a URL. The URL you saw in that chapter was an *absolute URL*, which includes the domain name of the web site. This is illustrated by the first group of examples in this figure. Here, both URLs refer to pages at www.murach.com. The first URL points to the index.html file in the root folder of this web site, and the second URL points to the toc.html file in the root/books/php folder.

When used within the code for the web pages of a site, an absolute URL is used to refer to a file in another web site. In contrast, a *relative URL* is used to refer to a file within the same web site. As this figure shows, there are two types of relative URLs.

In a *root-relative path*, the path is relative to the root folder of the web site. This is illustrated by the second group of examples. Here, the leading slash indicates the root folder for the site. As a result, the first path refers to the login.html file in the root folder, and the second path refers to the logo.gif file in the images folder.

In a *document-relative path*, the path is relative to the current document. This is illustrated by the third group of examples. Here, the assumption is that the paths are coded in a file that is in the root folder for a web site. Then, the first path refers to a file in the images subfolder of the root folder, and the second path refers to a file in the php subfolder of the books subfolder. This illustrates paths that navigate down the levels of the folder structure.

But you can also navigate up the levels with a document-relative path. This is illustrated by the fourth group of examples. Here, the assumption is that the current document is in the root/books folder. Then, the first path goes up one level for the index.html file in the root folder. The second path also goes up one level to the root folder and then down one level for the logo.gif file in the images folder.

This shows that there's more than one way to code the path for a file. If, for example, you're coding an HTML file in the root/books folder, you can use

A simple web site folder structure

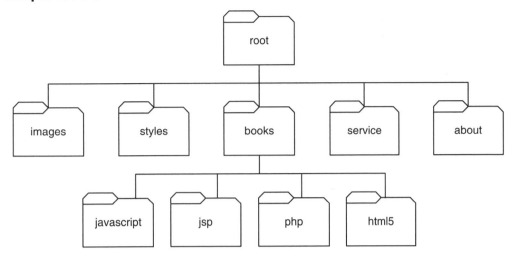

Examples of absolute and relative URLs

Absolute URLs

```
http://www.murach.com/index.html
http://www.murach.com/books/php/toc.html
```

Root-relative paths

```
/login.html              (refers to root/login.html)
/images/logo.gif         (refers to root/images/logo.gif)
```

Document-relative paths that navigate down from the root folder

```
images/logo.gif          (refers to root/images/logo.gif)
books/php/overview.html   (refers to root/books/php/overview.html)
```

Document-relative paths that navigate up from the root/books folder

```
../index.html            (refers to root/index.html)
../images/logo.gif       (refers to root/images/logo.gif)
```

Description

- When you code an *absolute URL*, you code the complete URL including the domain name for the site. Absolute URLs let you display pages at other web sites.

- When you code a *relative URL*, you base it on the current folder, which is the folder that contains the current page.

- A *root-relative path* is relative to the root folder of the web site. It always starts with a slash. Then, to go down one subfolder, you code the subfolder name and a slash. To go down two subfolders, you code a second subfolder name and another slash. And so on.

- A *document-relative path* is relative to the folder the current document is in. Then, to go down one subfolder, you code the subfolder name followed by a slash. To go down two subfolders, you code a second subfolder name followed by another slash. And so on.

- You can also go up in a document-relative path. To go up one level from the current folder, you code two periods and a slash. To go up two levels, you code two periods and a slash followed by two more periods and a slash. And so on.

Figure 3-11   How to code absolute and relative URLs

either a root-relative path or a document-relative path to get to the images subfolder. If this is a confusing right now, you'll quickly get used to it once you start coding your own pages.

How to code links

Most web pages contain *links* that go to other web pages or web resources. To code a link, you use the <a> element (or anchor element) as shown in figure 3-12. Because this element is an inline element, you usually code it within a block element like a <p> element.

In most cases, you'll code only the href attribute for the <a> element. This attribute specifies the URL for the resource you want to link to. The examples in this figure illustrate how this works.

The first example uses a relative URL to link to a page in the same folder as the current page. The second example uses a relative URL to link to a page in a subfolder of the parent folder. The third example uses a relative URL to link to a page based on the root folder. And the last example uses an absolute URL to link to a page at another web site.

By default, links are underlined when they're displayed in a browser to indicate that they're clickable. As a result, most web users have been conditioned to associate underlined text with links. Because of that, you should avoid underlining any other text.

When a link is displayed, it has a default color depending on its state. For instance, a link that hasn't been visited is displayed in blue, and a link that has been visited is displayed in purple. Note, however, that you can use CSS as described in the next chapter to change these settings.

When you create a link that contains text, the text should clearly indicate the function of the link. For example, you shouldn't use text like "click here" because it doesn't indicate what the link does. Instead, you should use text like that in the examples in this figure. In short, if you can't tell what a link does by reading its text, you should rewrite the text. This improves the accessibility of your site, and it helps search engines index your site.

Basic attribute of the <a> element

Attribute	Description
href	Specifies a relative or absolute URL for a link.

A link to a web page in the same folder

```
<p>Go view our <a href="products.html">product list</a>.</p>
```

A link to a web page in a subfolder of the parent folder

```
<p>Read about the <a href="../company/services.html">services we
provide</a>.</p>
```

A link to a web page based on the root folder

```
<p>View your <a href="/orders/cart.html">shopping cart</a>.</p>
```

A link to a web page at another web site

```
<p>To learn more about JavaScript, visit the
<a href="http://www.javascript.com/">official JavaScript web site</a>.</p>
```

The links in a web browser

SEO and accessibility guideline

- The content of a link should be text that clearly indicates where the link is going.

Description

- The <a> element is an inline element that creates a *link* that loads another web page. The href attribute of this element identifies the page to be loaded.
- The text content of a link is underlined by default to indicate that it's clickable.
- If a link hasn't been visited, it's displayed in blue. If it has been visited, it's displayed in purple. You can change these values using CSS.
- If the mouse hovers over a link, the cursor is changed to a hand with the finger pointed as shown above.
- See chapters 4 and 7 for more information on formatting and coding the <a> element.

Figure 3-12   How to code links

How to code lists

Figure 3-13 shows how to code the two basic types of lists: ordered lists and unordered lists. To create an *unordered list*, you use the ul element. Then, within this element, you code one li (list item) element for each item in the list. The content of each li element is the text that's displayed in the list. By default, when a list is displayed in a browser, each item in an unordered list is preceded by a bullet. However, you can change that bullet with CSS.

To create an *ordered list*, you use the ol element, along with one li element for each item in the list. This works like the ul element, except that the items are preceded by numbers rather than bullets when they're displayed in a browser. In this case, you can change the type of numbers that are used with CSS.

The two lists shown in this figure illustrate how this works. Here, the first list simply displays the names of several programming languages, so these items don't need to reflect any order. In contrast, the second list identifies three steps for completing an order. Because these steps must be completed in a prescribed sequence, they're displayed in an ordered list.

When you work with the li element, you should be aware that it can contain text, inline elements, or block elements. For example, an li element can contain an <a> element that defines a link. In fact, it's a best practice to code a series of links within an unordered list. You'll see an example of that later in this chapter, and you'll learn all about this in chapter 7.

Elements that create ordered and unordered lists

Element	Description
`<ul>`	Creates an unordered list.
`<ol>`	Creates an ordered list.
`<li>`	Creates a list item for an unordered or ordered list.

HTML that creates two lists

```
<p>We have books on a variety of languages, including</p>
<ul>
    <li>JavaScript</li>
    <li>PHP and MySQL</li>
    <li>Servlets and JSP</li>
    <li>ASP.NET</li>
</ul>

<p>You will need to complete the following steps:</p>
<ol>
    <li>Enter your billing information.</li>
    <li>Enter your shipping information.</li>
    <li>Confirm your order.</li>
</ol>
```

The lists in a web browser

We have books on a variety of languages, including

- JavaScript
- PHP and MySQL
- Servlets and JSP
- ASP.NET

You will need to complete the following steps:

1. Enter your billing information.
2. Enter your shipping information.
3. Confirm your order.

Description

- The two basic types of lists are *unordered lists* and *ordered lists*. By default, an unordered list is displayed as a bulleted list and an ordered list is displayed as a numbered list.
- See chapters 4 and 7 for more information on formatting and coding lists.

Figure 3-13   How to code lists

How to include images

Images are an important part of most web pages. To display an image, you use the img element shown in figure 3-14. This is an inline element that's coded as an empty tag. In the example in this figure, this tag is coded before an h1 element. The h1 element is displayed after it, though, because it's a block element that starts on a new line.

The src (source) attribute of an img element specifies the URL of the image you want to display, and it is required. For instance, the src attribute for the image in the example indicates that the image named murachlogo.gif can be found in the images subfolder of the current folder.

The alt attribute should also be coded for img elements. You typically use this attribute to provide information about the image in case it can't be displayed or the page is being accessed using a screen reader. This is essential for visually-impaired users.

For instance, because the image in this figure is our company's logo, the value of the alt attribute is set to "Murach Logo". If an image doesn't provide any meaning, however, you can code the value of the alt attribute as an empty string (""). You should do that, for example, when an image is only used for decoration.

The images that you include in a web page need to be in one of the formats that modern web browsers support. Currently, most web browsers support the JPEG, GIF, and PNG formats. Typically, a web designer uses imaging software such as Adobe Photoshop to create and maintain these files for a web site. In particular, you use imaging software to create images that are the right size for your web pages.

Then, you can use the height and width attributes of an img element to tell the browser what the size of an image is. That can help the browser lay out the page as the image is being loaded. Although you can also use the height and width attributes to render an image larger (known as "stretching") or smaller than the original image, it's better to use your image editor to make the image the right size. You'll learn more about working with images in chapter 8.

Attributes of the <img> element

Attribute	Description
src	Specifies the relative or absolute URL of the image to display. It is a required attribute.
alt	Specifies alternate text to display in place of the image. This text is read aloud by screen readers for users with disabilities. It is required.
height	Specifies the height of the image in pixels.
width	Specifies the width of the image in pixels.

An img element

```
<img src="images/murachlogo.gif" alt="Murach Logo" height="75">
<h1>Mike Murach &amp; Associates, Inc.</h1>
```

The image in a web browser

Mike Murach & Associates, Inc.

The image formats that are supported by most browsers

- JPEG (Joint Photographic Experts Group)
- GIF (Graphic Interchange Format)
- PNG (Portable Network Graphics)

Accessibility guidelines

- For images with useful content, always code an alt attribute that describes the image.
- For images that are used for decoration, code the alt attribute with no value ("").

Description

- The img element is an inline element that is used to display an image that's identified by the src attribute.
- The height and width attributes can be used to indicate the size of an image so the browser can allocate the correct amount of space on the page. These attributes can also be used to size an image, but it's usually better to use an image editor to do that.
- JPEG files commonly use the JPG extension and are typically used for photographs and scans. GIF files are typically used for small illustrations and logos. And PNG files combine aspects of JPEG and GIF files.
- See chapters 4 and 8 for more information on formatting and coding img elements.

Figure 3-14   How to include images

A structured web page

Now that you've seen the HTML elements for structuring a web page, you're ready to see a simple web page that uses these elements.

The page layout

The web page shown in figure 3-15 uses many of the HTML elements you learned about in this chapter. The purpose of this web page is to display information about a series of lectures being presented by a non-profit organization.

This figure shows the default formatting for the HTML that's used for this page. In other words, CSS hasn't been used to improve the formatting. In the next chapter, though, you'll learn how to use CSS to improve the formatting of this page.

A web page that uses some of the HTML presented in this chapter

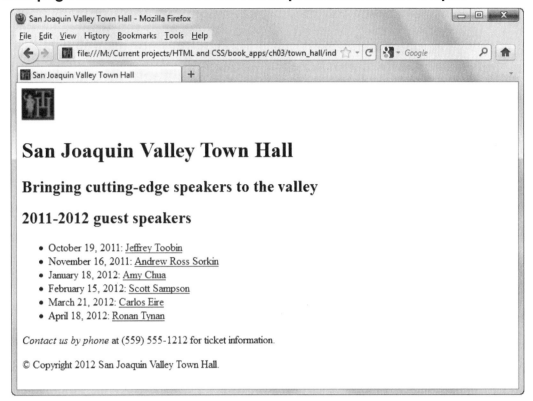

Description

- This web page provides information for a non-profit organization that arranges lectures by renowned speakers.
- This web page contains HTML5 semantic elements that define a header, a section, and a footer.
- The header element contains h1 and h2 elements that are treated as a group.
- The section element contains an h1 element, a nav element that contains an unordered list that contains <a> elements, and a <p> element.
- The footer element contains a <p> element that uses a character entity to include the copyright symbol.
- This page includes a favicon that's displayed to the left of the URL in the address bar and to the left of the page title in the tab.
- This illustrates the default formatting for the HTML elements. In the next chapter, you'll learn how to use CSS to format the HTML so it looks more appealing.

Figure 3-15   The page layout for a structured web page

The HTML file

Figure 3-16 presents the HTML file for the web page. To start, the DOCTYPE declaration, the html element, and the head element illustrate the way these items should be coded in every document that you create.

In the html element, you can see the use of the lang attribute. In the head element, you can see the coding for the charset meta element and the title element. Although the link element for the favicon is optional, most web sites use one. Beyond that, you should include meta elements for description and keywords in most web pages, although they aren't used in the examples in this book.

What's most important, though, is the use of the HTML5 semantic elements. Here, the header element contains an hgroup element that contains one h1 and one h2 element. That groups those elements so they're treated as one structural element. Then, the section element contains one h1 element, a nav element, and a <p> element. Last, the footer element contains one <p> element.

Within the nav element is an unordered list that contains six <a> elements. This is consistent with HTML5 semantics because a nav element should contain a series of links. It is also a best practice to code the <a> elements within an unordered list.

You can also see the use of an <em> element that italicizes the first four words in the second last paragraph and a character entity that inserts the copyright symbol into the last paragraph. But above all, the new HTML5 semantic elements make the structure of this page obvious.

The HTML file for the web page

```
<!DOCTYPE html>

<html lang="en">
    <head>
        <meta charset="utf-8">
        <title>San Joaquin Valley Town Hall</title>
        <link rel="shortcut icon" href="images/favicon.ico">
    </head>

    <body>
        <header>
            <img src="images/logo.jpg" alt="Town Hall Logo" width="50">
            <hgroup>
                <h1>San Joaquin Valley Town Hall</h1>
                <h2>Bringing cutting-edge speakers to the valley</h2>
            </hgroup>
        </header>

        <section>
            <h1>2011-2012 guest speakers</h1>
            <nav>
                <ul>
                    <li>October 19, 2011: <a href="speakers/toobin.html">
                        Jeffrey Toobin</a></li>
                    <li>November 16, 2011: <a href="speakers/sorkin.html">
                        Andrew Ross Sorkin</a></li>
                    <li>January 18, 2012: <a href="speakers/chua.html">
                        Amy Chua</a></li>
                    <li>February 15, 2012: <a href="speakers/sampson.html">
                        Scott Sampson</a></li>
                    <li>March 21, 2012: <a href="speakers/eire.html">
                        Carlos Eire</a></li>
                    <li>April 18, 2012: <a href="speakers/tynan.html">
                        Ronan Tynan</a></li>
                </ul>
            </nav>

            <p><em>Contact us by phone</em> at (559) 555-1212 for ticket
                information.</p>
        </section>

        <footer>
            <p>&copy; Copyright 2012 San Joaquin Valley Town Hall.</p>
        </footer>
    </body>
</html>
```

Figure 3-16   The HTML file for a structured web page

Perspective

This chapter has presented many of the HTML elements that you need for developing web pages. In particular, it has presented the main block and inline elements that you need for creating and identifying the content for a page. It has also presented the HTML5 elements that you need for structuring a page.

With these skills, you can create web pages with the default formatting of the browser. As I've mentioned throughout this chapter, though, the right way to format and lay out your web pages is to use CSS. That's why the next three chapters show you how to do that.

Terms

favicon
metadata
block element
inline element
character entity
semantic elements
HTML5 semantics
absolute URL
relative URL
root-relative path
document-relative path
link
ordered list
unordered list
JPEG (Joint Photographic Experts Group)
GIF (Graphic Interchange Format)
PNG (Portable Network Graphics)

Summary

- In the head section of an HTML document, the title element provides the text that's displayed in the browser's title bar. This is an important element for search engine optimization.

- One common use of the link element in the head section is to identify a custom icon called a *favicon* that appears in the browser's address bar. This icon may also appear in the browser tab for the document or as part of a bookmark.

- The meta elements in the head section provide *metadata* that is related to the page. Here, the charset metadata is required for HTML5 validation, and the description and keywords metadata should be coded because they can affect search engine optimization.

- *Block elements* are the primary content elements of a web site, and each block element starts on a new line when it is rendered by a browser. Headings and paragraphs are common block elements.

- *Inline elements* are coded within block elements, and they don't start on new lines when they are rendered. Some common inline elements like <i> (for italics) and b (for bold) can be used to format text without implying any meaning. Whenever possible, though, you should use the inline elements that imply meaning.

- *Character entities* are used to display special characters like the ampersand and copyright symbols in an HTML document. In code, character entities start with an ampersand and end with a semicolon as in   (a non-breaking space).

- The core attributes that are commonly used for HTML elements are the id, class, and title attributes. The id attribute uniquely identifies one element. The class attribute can be used to identify one or more elements. And the title attribute can provide other information about an element like its tooltip text.

- Historically, the div element has been used to divide the code for an HTML document into divisions, and the span element has been used to identify portions of text so formatting can be applied to them.

- The HTML5 *semantic elements* provide a new way to structure the content within an HTML document. This makes it easier to code and format elements. In the long run, it may also improve the way search engines rank your pages.

- When you code an *absolute URL*, you code the complete URL including the domain name. When you code a *relative URL*, you can use a *root-relative path* to start the path from the root folder for the web site or a *document-relative path* to start the path from the current document.

- The <a> element (or anchor element) is an inline element that creates a link that usually loads another page. By default, the text of an <a> element is underlined. Also, an unvisited link is displayed in blue and a visited link in purple.

- Lists are block elements that can be used to display both *unordered lists* and *ordered lists*. By default, these lists are indented with bullets before the items in an unordered list and numbers before the items in an ordered list.

- The img element is used to display an image file. The three common formats for images are *JPEG* (for photographs and scans), *GIF* (for small illustrations and logos), and *PNG*, which combines aspects of JPEG and GIF.

About the exercises

In the exercises for chapters 3 through 6, you'll develop a new version of the Town Hall web site. This version will be like the one in the text, but it will have different content, different formatting, and different page layouts. Developing this site will give you plenty of practice, and it will also show you how similar content can be presented in two different ways.

As you develop this site, you will use this folder structure:

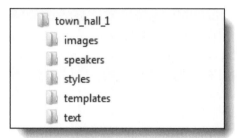

This is a realistic structure with images in the images folder, speaker HTML pages in the speakers folder, CSS files in the styles folder, and template files in the templates folder. In addition, the text folder contains text files that will provide all of the content you need for your pages. That too is realistic because a web developer often works with text that has been written by someone else.

Exercise 3-1   Enter the HTML for the home page

In this exercise, you'll code the HTML for the home page. When you're through, the page should look like the one on the facing page, but with three speakers.

Open the starting page and get the contents for it

1. Use your text editor to open this HTML file:

    `c:\html5_css3\exercises\town_hall_1\index.html`

    Note that it contains the head section for this web page as well as a body section that contains header, section, and footer tags.

2. Use your text editor to open this text file:

    `c:\html5_css3\exercises\town_hall_1\text\c3_content.txt`

    Note that it includes all of the text that you need for this web page.

Enter the header

3. Code the img element that gets the image at the top of the page from the images directory. To locate the image file use this document-relative path: images/town_hall_logo.gif. Be sure to include the alt attribute, and set the height attribute of the image to 100.

4. Copy the text for the first two headings from the txt file in the text folder into the header of the HTML file. Then, apply the h1, h2, and hgroup elements.

5. Test this page in Firefox. If necessary, correct the HTML and test again.

What the home page should look like

San Joaquin Valley Town Hall

Celebrating our 75th Year

Our Mission

San Joaquin Valley Town Hall is a non-profit organization that is run by an all-volunteer board of directors. Our mission is to bring nationally and internationally renowned, thought-provoking speakers who inform, educate, and entertain our audience! As one or our members told us:

> "Each year I give a ticket package to each of our family members. I think of it as the gift of knowledge...and that is priceless."

Our Ticket Packages

- Season Package: $95
- Patron Package: $200
- Single Speaker: $25

Our 2011-2012 Speakers

October 19, 2011
Jeffrey Toobin

© 2012, San Joaquin Valley Town Hall, Fresno, CA 93755

Enter the content for the section

6. Copy all of the content for the section from the txt file into the HTML file. Then, add h1 tags to these headings: "Our Mission," Our Ticket Packages," and "Our 2011-2012 Speakers".

7. Add <p> tags to the first block of text after the "Our Mission" heading, and add blockquote tags to the second block of text as shown above.

8. Add the ul and li tags that are needed for the three items after the "Our Ticket Packages" heading. Then, test these changes and make any adjustments.

9. Format the name and date for the first speaker after the "Our 2011-2012 Speakers" heading as one h2 element with a <br> in the middle that rolls the speaker's name over to a second line. Then, test and adjust.

10. When that works, do the same for the next two speakers.

11. Enclose the name for each speaker in an <a> tag. The href attribute for each tag should refer to a file in the speakers subfolder that has the speaker's last name as the filename and html as the file extension. In other words, the reference for the first speaker should be:

`speakers/toobin.html`

12. After the h2 element for each speaker, code an img element that displays the image for the speaker, and be sure to include the alt attribute. The images are in the images subfolder, and the filename for each is the speaker's last name, followed by 75 (to indicate the image size), with jpg as the extension. So to refer to the first speaker's file, you need to use a document-relative path like this: images/toobin75.jpg. Now, test and adjust.

Enter the footer

13. Copy the last paragraph in the txt file into the footer of the HTML file. Then, enclose the text in a <p> element.

Add character entities and formatting tags

14. Use character entities to add the quotation marks at the start and end of the text in the blockquote element.

15. Use a character entity to add the copyright symbol to the start of the footer.

16. Add the sup tags that you need for raising the *th* in the second line of the header (as in 75th). Then, test these enhancements.

Test the links, validate the HTML, and test in IE

17. Click on the link for the first speaker. This should display a page that gives the speaker's name and says "This page is under construction". If this doesn't work, fix the href attribute in the link and test again. To return to the first page, you can click the browser's Back button.

18. Open the toobin.html file that's in the speakers subfolder. Then, add a link within a <p> element that says "Return to index page." To refer to the index.html file, you'll have to go up one level in the folder structure with a document-relative path like this: (../index.html). Now, test this link.

19. Validate the HTML for the index page as shown in figure 2-15 of chapter 2. This should indicate two warnings but no errors. If any errors are detected, fix them and validate the HTML again.

20. Test the index page in the IE browser. If necessary, fix any problems and test again in both Firefox and IE.

4

How to use CSS to format the elements of a web page

After you code the HTML that defines the structure of a web page, you're ready to code the CSS rule sets that determine how the page is formatted. To do that, you need to learn how to code selectors, and you need to learn how to code the properties and values for rule sets.

In this chapter, you'll learn how to code all types of selectors, and you'll learn how to apply the CSS properties for formatting text. Then, in the next chapter, you'll learn how to use the CSS box model for doing other types of formatting.

An introduction to CSS

Before you code the CSS for a web page, you need to know how to provide the CSS for a web page. You also need to know how to provide the workarounds for using CSS to format the HTML5 semantic elements in older browsers.

Three ways to provide CSS styles for a web page

Figure 4-1 shows three ways to provide CSS styles for a web page. First, you can code a link element that refers to an *external style sheet*. That's a separate file that contains the CSS for the page. This separates the content from the formatting and makes it easy to use the same styles for more than one page.

The attributes for a link element that links to an external file are the rel (relationship) attribute with a value of "stylesheet", and the href attribute that locates the file. As you learned in the last chapter, href attributes are usually coded with a URL that is relative to the current file. As a result, the relative URL in the first example goes down one folder to the styles folder and locates a file named main.css.

Second, you can embed a CSS style sheet in the HTML for a page. This is referred to as an *embedded style sheet*. When you embed a style sheet, the CSS rule sets are coded in a style element in the head section of the HTML. For instance, the embedded style sheet in the first example in this group contains one rule set for the body element and another for the h1 element. This works okay if the styles are only going to be used for that one document, but otherwise it's better to use an external style sheet.

Third, you can use *inline styles* within an HTML document as shown by the third example. When you use an inline style, you code a style attribute for the HTML element with a value that contains all the CSS rules that apply to the element. For instance, the inline style in this example applies two CSS rules to the h1 element. Unfortunately, this type of formatting means that the content and formatting are tightly linked, so this can quickly get out of control.

If you use more than one way to provide styles for a page, the styles that are applied last override the styles that are applied earlier. This is illustrated by the example in this figure. Here, an inline style sets the font size for h1 elements, and that will override the embedded style that sets the font size for h1 elements.

The next example in this figure shows that you can include more than one style sheet in a single document. Then, the styles are applied from the first external style sheet to the last. Here again, a style in the last style sheet will override a style for the same element in an earlier style sheet.

The last example shows how you can use the media attribute in a link element to specify that a style sheet should be used for a specific medium. In this case, the print medium is specified, which means that its styles will be applied to the page when it is printed. You'll learn more about this in chapter 12. Since the default for this attribute is "screen", you don't need to use this attribute for normal browsers.

Three ways to provide styles

Use an external style sheet by coding a link element in the head section

```
<link rel="stylesheet" href="styles/main.css">
```

Embed the styles in the head section

```
<style>
    body {
        font-family: Arial, Helvetica, sans-serif;
        font-size: 87.5%; }
    h1 { font-size: 250%; }
</style>
```

Use the style attribute to apply styles to a single element

```
<h1 style="font-size: 500%; color: red;">Valley Town Hall</h1>
```

The sequence in which styles are applied

- Styles from an external style sheet
- Embedded styles
- Inline styles

A head element that includes two style sheets

```
<head>
    <title>San Joaquin Valley Town Hall</title>
    <link rel="stylesheet" href="../styles/main.css">
    <link rel="stylesheet" href="../styles/speaker.css">
</head>
```

The sequence in which styles are applied

- From the first external style sheet to the last

How to specify the medium that an external style is for

```
<link rel="stylesheet" href="../styles/print.css" media="print">
```

Description

- When you use *external style sheets,* you separate content (HTML) from formatting (CSS). That makes it easy to use the same styles for two or more documents.

- If you use *embedded styles*, you have to copy the styles to other documents before you can use them a second time.

- If you use *inline styles* to apply styles, the formatting is likely to get out of control.

- If more than one rule for the same property is applied to the same element, the last rule overrides the earlier rules.

- When you specify a relative URL for an external CSS file, the URL is relative to the current file.

- You can use the media attribute of a link element to specify the medium that the style sheet is for. This lets you use different style sheets for different media. Since the default is screen, you don't have to use this attribute for a normal page. You'll see how this works for print in chapter 12.

Figure 4-1   Three ways to provide CSS styles for a web page

How to use CSS with the HTML5 semantic elements in older browsers

For cross-browser compatibility, you need to make sure that the HTML5 semantic elements will work in older browsers. Since these elements are just ignored by older browsers, you don't need to do anything to have a page displayed with its default formatting. But you do need to provide for this if you want to use CSS to format the new HTML5 elements. Figure 4-2 shows how.

To start, you need to make sure that the new elements are added to the Document Object Model, or DOM. To do that, you can code a script element in the head section of a document to load a JavaScript file known as a *shiv* (or *shim*). This is illustrated by the first example in this figure, which gets the file from a web site. Then, when the web page is loaded, the JavaScript file is loaded and executed, which adds the HTML5 elements to the DOM.

The second example in this figure gives you an idea of what the shiv actually does. Here, the script element in the HTML provides JavaScript code that uses the createElement method of the document to add HTML5 elements to the DOM. Although only seven of the new elements are added to the DOM by this code, you can expand this code so it includes any other new elements that you use in the HTML. In contrast, the JavaScript file that's loaded by the first example adds all of the HTML5 elements to the DOM, which makes doing this a lot easier.

The result of using the shiv is that the browser doesn't ignore the new elements when it encounters them. As a result, CSS formatting can be applied to these elements.

However, before you start using CSS to apply formatting to these elements, you need to code a CSS rule set for these elements that tells the older browsers that they are block elements. To do that, you use a rule set like the one in the last example in this figure. Otherwise, the older browsers assume that the HTML5 elements are inline elements.

In the application at the end of this chapter, you'll see how both the shiv and the CSS rule set are used. All you need to do is include the shiv in the head section of the HTML document and the rule set at the start of the external style sheet. You can do that even if you don't understand exactly how this works.

The JavaScript shiv for using CSS with the HTML5 structural tags

```
<head>
    <script src="http://html5shiv.googlecode.com/svn/trunk/html5.js">
    </script>
</head>
```

An alternative to using the shiv

```
<head>
    <script>
        document.createElement(article);
        document.createElement(aside);
        document.createElement(figure);
        document.createElement(footer);
        document.createElement(header);
        document.createElement(nav);
        document.createElement(section);
    </script>
</head>
```

CSS for using the HTML5 structural tags in older browsers

```
article, aside, figure, footer, header, nav, section {
    display: block;
}
```

Description

- To help the older browsers recognize the HTML5 structural tags so they can apply CSS to them, you need to use a JavaScript workaround known as a *shiv* (or *shim*). This shiv is shown above.

- The JavaScript shiv uses the createElement method of the DOM to create the tags that the older browsers don't understand.

- You also need to use the CSS rule set shown above to tell the browser that the HTML5 elements are block elements, not inline elements.

Figure 4-2   How to use CSS with the HTML5 semantic elements in older browsers

How to specify measurements and colors

For many of the properties of a rule set, you will need to know how to specify measurements and colors. So let's start there.

How to specify measurements

Figure 4-3 shows the four units of measure that are commonly used with CSS: pixels, points, ems, and percent. Here, the first two are *absolute units of measure*, and the second two are *relative units of measure*. Other absolute units are inches and picas, but they aren't used as often.

When you use relative units of measure like ems or a percent, the measurement will change if the user changes the browser's font size. If, for example, you set the size of a font to 80 percent of the browser's default font size, that element will change if the user changes the font size in the browser. Because this lets the users adjust the font sizes to their own preferences, we recommend that you use relative measurements for font sizes.

In contrast, when you use an absolute unit of measure like pixels or points, the measurement won't change even if the user changes the font size in the browser. If, for example, you set the width of an element in pixels and the font size in points, the width and font size won't change.

When you use pixels, though, the size will change if the screen resolution changes. That's because the screen resolution determines the number of pixels that are displayed on the monitor. For instance, the pixels on a monitor with a screen resolution of 1280 x 1024 are closer together than the pixels on the same monitor with a screen resolution of 1152 x 864. That means that a measurement of 10 pixels will be smaller on the screen with the higher resolution. In contrast, a point is 1/72nd of an inch no matter what the screen resolution is.

The examples in this figure show how you can use pixels and relative measurements in your CSS. Here, the bottom border for the header is set to 3 pixels. In contrast, the font sizes are set as percentages, and the margins and padding are set as ems. This is a typical way to use these measurements.

To start, a font size of 87.5% is applied to the body element. This means that the font will be set to 87.5% of the default font size for the browser, which is usually 16 pixels, so the font size for the body element will be 14 pixels. A left margin of 2 ems is also applied to the body element. Because an em is equal to the current font size, the body element is indented 28 pixels (2 times 14 pixels).

Next, the padding below the header element is set to .75 em, or 10.5 pixels (14 times .75). Then, a solid black border that's 3 pixels wide is added below the padding, and the margin below the border is set to 0. For the margin bottom, no unit of measure is specified because it doesn't matter what the unit of measure is when the value is zero.

The last rule set indicates that the h1 element should be 200% of the base font, which was set in the rule set for the body element. Also, the margin below the heading should be zero.

Common units of measure

Symbol	Name	Type	Description
px	pixels	absolute	A pixel represents a single dot on a monitor. The number of dots per inch depends on the resolution of the monitor.
pt	points	absolute	A point is 1/72 of an inch.
em	ems	relative	One em is equal to the font size for the current font.
%	percent	relative	A percent specifies a value relative to the current value.

The HTML for a web page

```
<body>
    <header>
        <h1>San Joaquin Valley Town Hall</h1>
    </header>
    <section>
        <p>Welcome to San Joaquin Valley Town Hall. We have some
            fascinating speakers for you this season!</p>
    </section>
</body>
```

CSS that uses relative units of measure with a fixed border

```
body {
    font-size: 87.5%;
    margin-left: 2em; }
header {
    padding-bottom: .75em;
    border-bottom: 3px solid black;
    margin-bottom: 0; }
h1 {
    font-size: 200%;
    margin-bottom: 0; }
```

The web page in a web browser

San Joaquin Valley Town Hall

Welcome to San Joaquin Valley Town Hall. We have some fascinating speakers for you this season!

Description

- You use the units of measure to specify a variety of CSS properties, including font-size, line-height, width, height, margin, and padding.
- To specify an *absolute measurement*, you can use pixels or points.
- To specify a *relative measurement*, you can use ems or percents. This type of measurement is relative to the size of another element.

Figure 4-3   How to specify measurements

How to specify colors

Figure 4-4 shows three ways to specify colors. The easiest way is to specify a color name, and this figure lists the names for 16 colors that are supported by all browsers. In addition to these names, though, most browsers support the color names in the draft CSS3 Color specification. To find a complete list of these color names, you can go to the web site listed in this figure.

Another way to specify a color is to use an *RGB* (red, green, blue) *value*. One way to do that is to specify the percent of red, green, and blue that make up the color. For instance, the example in this figure specifies 100% red, 40% green, and 20% blue. When you use this method, you can also use any values from 0 through 255 instead of percents. Then, 0 is equivalent to 0% and 255 is equivalent to 100%. This gives you more precision over the resulting colors.

The third way to specify a color is to use *hexadecimal*, or *hex*, *values* for the red, green, and blue values, and this is the method that has been preferred by most web designers. In hex, a value of "000000" results in black, and a value of "FFFFFF" results in white. The simple conversion of percentages to hex is 0% is 00, 20% is 33, 40% is 66, 60% is 99, 80% is CC, and 100% is FF. When you use this technique, the entire value must be preceded by the pound sign (#).

When you use hex values for colors, you usually get the hex value that you want from a chart or palette that shows all of the colors along with their hex values. For instance, you can get a complete list of the hex values for colors by going to the web site listed in this figure. Or, if you're using an IDE like Dreamweaver, you may also be able to choose a color from a palette and then have the IDE insert the hex value for that color into your code. A third alternative is to get the right hex values from printed color charts, which are commonly found in graphics design books.

Before I go on, you should realize that the color property determines the foreground color, which is the color of the text. In the CSS in this figure, for example, the color of the h1 element is set to blue (#00F or #0000FF), and the background color of the body is set to a light yellow (#FFFFCC or #FFC). You'll learn more about setting background colors in the next chapter.

You should also realize that the color property for an element is *inherited* by any child elements. If, for example, you set the color property of the body element to navy, that color will be inherited by all of the elements in the body of the document. However, you can override an inherited property by coding a rule set with a different value for that property. Throughout this chapter and book, I'll point out the properties that are inherited as well as those that aren't.

Whenever you're using colors, please keep the visually-impaired in mind. For anyone, dark text on a light background is easier to read, and black on white is easiest to read. In general, if your pages are hard to read when they're displayed or printed in black and white, they aren't good for the visually-impaired. On that basis, the example in this figure could be improved.

16 descriptive color names

black	silver	white	aqua
red	lime	green	maroon
yellow	olive	purple	teal
gray	blue	fuchsia	navy

Three ways to specify colors

With a color name
```
color: silver;
```

With an RGB (red-green-blue) value
```
color: rgb(100%, 40%, 20%);
color: rgb(255, 102, 51);    /* Using multiples of 51 from 0 to 255 */
```

With an RGB value that uses hexadecimal numbers
```
color: #ffffff;              /* This color is white */
color: #000000;              /* This color is black */
color: #ff0000;              /* This color is red */
```

CSS that uses hexadecimal values to specify colors
```
body {
    font-size: 87.5%;
    margin-left: 2em;
    background-color: #FFFFCC; }   /* This could also be coded as #FFC */
h1 {
    font-size: 200%;
    color: #00F; }                 /* This could also be coded as #0000FF */
```

The HTML in a web browser

San Joaquin Valley Town Hall

Welcome to San Joaquin Valley Town Hall. We have some fascinating speakers for you this season!

Accessibility guideline
- Remember the visually-impaired. Dark text on a light background is easier to read, and black type on a white background is easiest to read.

Description
- All browsers support the 16 color names shown above, and most browsers support many more. These are okay for getting started with the use of colors.
- Most graphic designers use *hexadecimal*, or *hex*, values to specify an *RGB value* because that lets them choose from over 16 million colors. You can find a list of color names and their corresponding hex values at http://www.w3.org/TR/css3-color.
- With IDEs like Dreamweaver, you can select a color from a palette of colors and let the IDE insert the right color codes into your rule sets in either RGB or hex format.

Figure 4-4   How to specify colors

How to use the CSS3 color specifications

To provide even more color options for web designers, CSS3 lets you code color specifications in three more ways. These are summarized in figure 4-5.

First, you can use *RGBA values*. This works like RGB values, but with a fourth parameter that provides an opacity value. If, for example, you set this value to 0, the color is fully transparent so anything behind it will show through. Or, if you sent this value to 1, nothing will show through.

Second, you can use *HSL values*. To do that, you provide a number from 1 through 359 that represents the hue that you want. The hue is one of the main properties of a color. Then, you can provide a number from 0 through 100 that represents the saturation percent with 100 being the full hue. Last, you can provide a number from 0 through 100 that represents the lightness percent with 50 being normal, 100 being white, and 0 being black.

Third, you can use *HSLA values*. This is just like HSL values, but with a fourth parameter that provides an opacity value between 0 and 1.

The examples in this figure give you some idea of how these values work, especially if you see them in color in the eBook. Note here that the second and third examples are the same hue, but the saturation and lightness percents make them look quite different. This should give you some idea of the many color variations that CSS3 offers. But here again, please keep accessibility in mind whenever you're using colors.

Besides providing for RGBA, HSL, and HSLA values, CSS3 also provides 147 more keywords for colors that are generally supported by modern browsers. For a complete listing, you can go to the URL in this figure.

Three ways to code CSS3 colors

The syntax for RGBA colors

```
rgba(red%, green%, blue%, opacity-value)
```

The syntax for HSL and HSLA colors

```
hsl(hue-degrees, saturation%, lightness%)
hsla(hue-degrees, saturation%, ligntness%, opacity-value)
```

Values	Description
`opacity-value`	A number from 0 to 1 with 0 being fully transparent and 1 being fully opaque.
`hue-degrees`	A number of degrees ranging from 0 to 359 that represents the color.
`saturation%`	A percentage from 0 to 100 with 0 causing the hue to be ignored and 100 being the full hue.
`lightness%`	A percentage from 0 to 100 with 50 being normal lightness, 0 being black, and 100 being white.

Examples

```
h1 { color: rgba(0, 0, 255, .2)       /* transparent blue */ }
h1 { color: hsl(120, 100%, 25%)       /* dark green */ }
h1 { color: hsl(120, 75%, 75%)        /* pastel green */ }
h1 { color: hsla(240, 100%, 50%, 0.5) /* semi-transparent solid blue */ }
```

The colors in a browser

San Joaquin Valley Town Hall

San Joaquin Valley Town Hall

San Joaquin Valley Town Hall

San Joaquin Valley Town Hall

Description

- *RGBA* enhances the RGB specification by providing a fourth value for opacity.
- With *HSL* (Hue, Saturation, and Lightness) and *HSLA,* you specify the number of hue degrees for a color. Then, you can enhance the hue by providing for both saturation and lightness percentages.
- HLSA also offers a fourth value for opacity.
- CSS3 also provides 147 more keywords for colors that are generally supported by modern browsers. For a complete listing, go to:
  `http://www.w3.org/TR/SVG/types.html#ColorKeywords`
- With an IDE like Dreamweaver, you can select the type of color specification you want to use (RGBA, HSL, or HSLA). Then, you can select the color or hue, saturation, lightness, and opacity.

Figure 4-5   How to use the CSS3 color specifications

How to code selectors

Now, you're ready to learn how to code selectors. Once you understand that, you will be able to apply CSS formatting to any elements in a web page.

How to code selectors for all elements, element types, ids, and classes

Figure 4-6 presents the four types of selectors that you'll use the most. To start, this figure shows the body of an HTML document that contains a section and a footer element. Here, the section element is assigned an id of "main", and the two <p> elements in this section have class attributes with the value "blue". Also, the <p> element in the footer has a class attribute with two values: "blue" and "right". This means that this element is assigned to two classes.

Next, this figure shows the CSS rule sets that are used to format the HTML. Here, the rule set in the first example uses the *universal selector* (*) so it applies to all HTML elements. This sets the top and bottom margins for all elements to .5em and the left and right margins to 1em.

The two rule sets in the second group of examples select elements by type. These are referred to as *type selectors*. To code a type selector, you just code the name of the element. As a result, the first rule set in this group selects all h1 elements. The second rule set selects all p elements. These rule sets set the font family for the h1 elements and set the left margin for all <p> elements.

The rule set in the third group of examples selects an element by its id. To do that, the selector is a pound sign (#) followed by an id value that uniquely identifies an element. As a result, this rule set selects the section element that has an id of "main". Then, its rule set adds a border to the section and sets the padding for the section to 1em.

The two rule sets in the last group of examples select HTML elements by class. To do that, the selector is a period (.) followed by the class name. As a result, the first rule set selects all elements that have been assigned to the "blue" class, which are all three <p> elements. The second rule set selects any elements that have been assigned to the "right" class. That is the paragraph in the footer division. Then, the first rule set sets the color of the font to blue and the second rule set aligns the paragraph on the right.

One of the key points here is that a class attribute can have the same value for more than one element on a page. Then, if you code a selector for that class, it will be used to format all the elements in that class. In contrast, since the id for an element must be unique, an id selector can only be used to format a single element.

Incidentally, since there is only one section element in the example in this figure, you don't need to use an id to select it. Instead, you could select it by using a type selector for "section". Also, the margin-left property for the <p> elements overrides the margin setting for all elements, which of course includes all <p> elements. That's why the two paragraphs in the section are indented.

HTML that can be selected by element type, id, or class

```
<section id="main">
    <h1>The 2011-2012 Speaker Lineup</h1>
    <p class="blue">October 19, 2011: Jeffrey Toobin</p>
    <p class="blue">November 16, 2011: Andrew Ross Sorkin</p>
</section>
<footer>
    <p class="blue right">Copyright 2012</p>
</footer>
```

CSS rule sets that select by element type, id, and class

All elements

```
* { margin: .5em 1em; }
```

Elements by type

```
h1 { font-family: Arial, sans-serif; }
p { margin-left: 3em; }
```

One element by ID

```
#main {
    border: 2px solid black;
    padding: 1em; }
```

Elements by class

```
.blue { color: blue; }
.right { text-align: right; }
```

The elements displayed in a browser

The 2011-2012 Speaker Lineup

October 19, 2011: Jeffrey Toobin

November 16, 2011: Andrew Ross Sorkin

Copyright 2012

Description

- You code a selector for all elements by coding the *universal selector* (*).
- You code a selector for all elements of a specific type by naming the element. This is referred to as a *type selector*.
- You code a selector for an element with an id attribute by coding a pound sign (#) followed by the id value.
- You code a selector for an element with a class attribute by coding a period followed by the class name. Then, the rule set applies to all elements with that class name.

Figure 4-6   How to code selectors for all elements, element types, ids, and classes

How to code relational selectors

Figure 4-7 shows how to code *relational selectors*. As you read about these selectors, keep in mind that terms like *parent*, *child*, *sibling*, and *descendent* are used in the same way that they are in a family tree. Child elements are at the first level below a parent element. Sibling elements are at the same level. And descendent elements can be one or more levels below a parent element.

That means a *descendant selector* selects all the elements that are contained within another element. For instance, all of the elements in the HTML in this figure are descendents of the section element, the li elements are also descendents of the ul element, and the <a> elements are descendents of the li, ul, and section elements.

To code a descendant selector, you code a selector for the parent element, followed by a space and a selector for the descendent element. This is illustrated by the first group of examples. Here, the first selector selects all li elements in the section with the id "main". Then, the second descendant selector selects all the <a> elements that are descendants of the ul element.

The next group of examples shows how to use an *adjacent sibling selector* to select an element that's coded at the same level as another element and is also coded right next to it. For instance, the h1, ul, h2, and <p> elements in the HTML are all siblings, and the h1 and ul elements are adjacent siblings. In contrast, the h1 element and the <p> elements aren't adjacent siblings, but the h2 element and the first <p> element are adjacent siblings.

To code an adjacent sibling selector, you code a selector for the first element, followed by a plus sign and a selector for the sibling element. In the example in this group, the selector will select any <p> elements that are adjacent to h2 elements. That means it will select the first <p> element that follows the h2 element.

If you want to select elements only when they're child elements of a parent element, you can code a *child selector*. To do that, you separate the parent and child selector with a greater than (>) sign. In this figure, for example, the first child selector selects the <p> elements that are children of the section with the "main" id, and the second selector selects the <a> elements that are children of the li elements.

Unlike the adjacent sibling selector, a *general sibling selector* selects any sibling element whether or not the elements are adjacent. To code this type of selector, you separate the selector for the first element and the selector for the sibling element by a tilde (~). In this figure, the general sibling selector selects all the <p> elements that follow any h2 element.

HTML that can be selected by relationships

```
<section id="main">
    <h1>Winter 2012 Town Hall speakers</h1>
    <ul class="speakers">
        <li>January 20, 2012: <a href="speakers/brancaccio.html">
            David Brancaccio</a></li>
        <li>February 17, 2012: <a href="speakers/fitzpatrick.html">
            Robert Fitzpatrick</a></li>
        <li>March 17, 2012: <a href="speakers/williams.html">
            Juan Williams</a></li>
    </ul>
    <h2>Post-lecture luncheons</h2>
    <p>Extend the excitement by going to the luncheon</p>
    <p>A limited number of tickets are available.</p>
    <p><em>Contact us by phone</em> at (559) 555-1212.</p>
</section>
```

CSS rule sets with relational selectors

Descendant

```
#main li { font-size: 14pt; }
ul a { color: green; }
```

Adjacent sibling

```
h2+p { margin-top: .5em; }
```

Child (not supported by some older browsers like IE6)

```
#main>p { font-size: 11pt; }
li>a { color: green; }
```

General sibling (a new feature of CSS3)

```
h2~p { margin-left: 2em; }
```

Description

- When you use relational selectors, you can often avoid the need for id or class attributes.

- To select elements only when they are descendants of a higher-level element, use a *descendant selector* that consists of the higher element, a space, and the descendent element.

- To select a sibling element that's adjacent to another element, use an *adjacent sibling selector* that consists of the first element, a plus sign (+), and the sibling element.

- To select elements only when they are child elements of the parent element, you can use a *child selector* that consists of the parent element, the greater than sign (>), and the child element, but this isn't supported by some of the older browsers.

- To select any elements that are siblings to another element, you can use a *general sibling selector* that consists of the first element, a tilde (~), and the sibling element, but this can only be used by browsers that support CSS3.

Figure 4-7   How to code relational selectors

How to code combinations of selectors

The first group of examples in figure 4-8 shows how to code selector combinations. To select an element type by class name, for example, you code the element name, followed by a period and the class name. Here, the first rule set selects ul elements that have a class of "speakers".

You can also code multiple selectors for the same rule set. To do that, you separate the selectors with commas as shown in the next group of examples. Here, the first rule set uses multiple selectors to apply its rules to all h1, h2, and h3 elements. Then, the second rule set uses multiple selectors to apply its rules to all <p> elements and to li elements that are descendents of the ul elements that are assigned to the speakers class.

How to code attribute selectors

An *attribute selector* selects elements based on an attribute or attribute value. This is illustrated by the second group of examples in this figure. Although you may never need to code attribute selectors for your HTML code, these selectors are often used by JavaScript.

To code an attribute selector that selects elements that have an attribute, you code an element selector followed by the name of the attribute in brackets [ ]. For instance, the first attribute example uses the universal selector to select all elements that have an href attribute. Note, however, that you can also omit the universal selector and code just the attribute in brackets to select all elements with that attribute. In contrast, the second attribute selector selects all of the <a> elements that have an href attribute.

To code an attribute selector that selects elements with the specified attribute value, you follow the attribute name with an equals sign and the value enclosed in quotation marks. This is illustrated in the third example. This selector will select all input elements with a type attribute whose value is set to "submit".

Combinations of selectors

A selector for a class within an element
```
ul.speakers { list-style-type: square; }
```

Multiple selectors
```
h1, h2, h3 { color: blue; }
p, ul.speakers li { font-family: "Times New Roman", serif; }
```

Attribute selectors (not supported by older browsers like IE6)

All elements with href attributes
```
*[href] { font-size: 95%; }
```

All <a> elements with href attributes
```
a[href] { font-family: Arial, sans-serif; }
```

All input elements with type attributes that have a value of "submit"
```
input[type="submit"] {
    border: 1px solid black;
    color: #ef9c00;
    background-color: #facd8a; }
```

Description

- To code a selector for an element and class, code the element name, a period, and the class name.

- To code multiple selectors for the same rule set, use commas to separate the selectors.

- To select all elements with a specific attribute, you can use an *attribute selector* that consists of the universal selector followed by the attribute name in brackets. You can also omit the universal selector when you code this type of selector.

- To select elements with a specific attribute, you can use an attribute selector that consists of the element followed by the attribute name within brackets, but this isn't supported by some of the older browsers.

- To select an element with a specific attribute value, you can use an attribute selector that consists of the element followed by the attribute name, an equals sign, and a value within quotation marks.

- When you're coding the CSS for an HTML page, you usually don't need attribute selectors. They're more useful when you're using JavaScript.

Figure 4-8   How to code combinations and attribute selectors

How to code pseudo-class and pseudo-element selectors

Figure 4-9 shows how to code *pseudo-class* and *pseudo-element selectors*. To code pseudo-class selectors, you use the classes in the first two tables of this figure. These classes represent conditions that apply to the elements on a page. For example, you can use the :link pseudo-class to refer to a link that hasn't been visited, the :hover pseudo-class to refer to the element that has the mouse hovering over it, and the :focus pseudo-class to refer to the element that has the focus.

You can also use the CSS3 pseudo-classes to refer to specific relationships. For example, the :first-child class refers to the first child of an element, and the :only-child class refers to the only child for an element that has only one. Although some older browsers don't support these classes, that's okay if these selectors are only used for graphics.

The third table in this figure presents *pseudo-elements* that you can use to select portions of text. For instance, you can use the :first-line element to refer to the first line in a paragraph that consists of more than one line. In CSS3, these elements have been redefined so they're supposed to be coded with two colons (like ::first-letter). However, older browsers like IE6, IE7, and IE8 support these elements only when coded with a single colon. That's why the fourth example in this figure uses a single colon for the first-letter pseudo-element.

In the examples, the first pseudo-class selector causes all links to be displayed in green. Then, the second selector is a combination selector that applies to any link that has the mouse hovering over it or the focus on it. As the accessibility guideline in this figure indicates, you should always code the hover and focus pseudo-classes for links in combination so the formatting is the same whether the user hovers the mouse over a link or tabs to it.

The third example uses a pseudo-class selector that causes the text in the first <p> element in the section to be boldfaced. You can see how this works in the browser display. Note here that the second <p> element in the main division isn't boldfaced because it isn't the first child in the section.

The fourth example takes this one step further by combining a pseudo-class and a pseudo-element in a selector. As a result, the first letter of the first child in the section is larger than the other letters in the paragraph.

Although the pseudo-class and pseudo-element selectors in this figure are the ones you'll use most often, there are others that can be useful. In chapter 9, for example, you'll be introduced to some CSS3 pseudo-classes that apply to tables. For a complete list of these classes and elements, you can go to the W3C documentation on the web.

Common CSS pseudo-classes

:link	A link that hasn't been visited. By default, blue, underlined text.
:visited	A link that has been visited. By default, purple, underlined text.
:active	The active link (mouse button down but not released). By default, red, underlined text.
:hover	An element with the mouse hovering over it. Code this after :link and :visited.
:focus	An element like a link or form control that has the focus.

Common CSS3 pseudo-classes

:first-child	The first child of an element.
:last-child	The last child of an element.
:only-child	The only child of an element.

Common pseudo-elements

:first-letter	The first letter of an element.
:first-line	The first line of an element.

HTML that can be used by pseudo-class selectors

```
<section>
    <p>Welcome to San Joaquin Valley Town Hall.</p>
    <p>We have some fascinating speakers for you this season!</p>
    <ul>
        <li><a href="toobin.html">Jeffrey Toobin</a></li>
        <li><a href="sorkin.html">Andrew Ross Sorkin</a></li>
        <li><a href="chua.html">Amy Chua</a></li>
</section>
```

The CSS for pseudo-class and pseudo-element selectors

```
a:link { color: green; }
a:hover, a:focus { color: fuchsia }
section p:first-child { font-weight: bold; }
section p:first-child:first-letter { font-size: 150% }
```

The pseudo-class and pseudo-element selectors in a browser

Welcome to San Joaquin Valley Town Hall.

We have some fascinating speakers for you this season!

- Jeffrey Toobin
- Andrew Ross Sorkin
- Amy Chua

Accessibility guideline

- Apply the same formatting to the :hover and :focus pseudo-classes for an element. That way, those who can't use the mouse will have the same experience as those who can.

Description

- *Pseudo-classes* are predefined classes that apply to specific conditions. In contrast, *pseudo-elements* let you select a portion of text.

Figure 4-9   How to code pseudo-class and pseudo-element selectors

How the cascade rules work

The term *Cascading Style Sheets* refers to the fact that more than one style sheet can be applied to a single web page. Then, if two or more rules for the same property are applied to the same element, the cascade order and other rules in figure 4-10 determine which rule takes precedence.

Before you can understand the cascade rules, though, you need to know that a user can create a *user style sheet* that provides default rule sets for web pages. Because most users don't create user style sheets, this usually isn't an issue. But some users do. For instance, users with poor vision often create user style sheets that provide for large font sizes. In that case, you need to consider how the user style sheets could affect your web pages.

You should also know how to identify one of your rules as important so it has precedence over other rules. To do that, you code "!important" as part of the rule. This is shown by the example in this figure.

With that as background, this figure lists the five levels of the *cascade order* from highest to lowest. As you can see, the important rules in a user style sheet override the important rules in a web page, but the normal rules in a web page override the normal rules in a user style sheet. Below these rules are the default rules in the web browser.

What happens if an element has more than one rule applied to it at the same level? To start, the rule with the highest specificity takes precedence, and this figure shows you which parts of a selector are more specific. For instance, the #main selector is more specific than the .speakers selector because an id is more specific than a class.

If a selector contains multiple parts, the additional parts add to that selector's specificity. This means that a selector with a class and an element is more specific than a selector with just a class. For instance, the p.highlight selector is more specific than the .highlight selector. As a result, p.highlight takes precedence.

If that doesn't settle the conflict, the rule that's specified last is applied. Earlier in this chapter, for example, you learned that if you provide two or more external style sheets for a document, the rule sets in each style sheet will override the rule sets in the preceding style sheets. This notion also applies if you accidentally code two rule sets for the same element in a single style sheet. Then, the one that is last takes precedence. In addition, inline styles take precedence over the styles in an embedded style sheet, and embedded styles take precedence over the styles in an external style sheet.

If this sounds complicated, it usually isn't a problem if you do a good job of organizing your style sheets. Then, if one or your styles isn't applied, you can usually solve the problem by making your selector more specific.

How to identify a rule as important

```
.highlight {
    font-weight: bold !important;
}
```

The cascade order for applying CSS rule sets

Search for the rule sets that apply to an element in the sequence that follows and apply the rule set from the first group in which it's found:

- !important rules in a user style sheet
- !important rules in a web page
- Normal rules in a web page
- Normal rules in a user style sheet
- Default rules in the web browser

If more than one rule set at a cascade level is applied to an element...

- Use the rule set with the highest specificity. For example, the p.highlight selector is more specific than the .highlight selector.
- If the specificity is the same for two or more rule sets in a group, use the rule set that's specified last.

How to determine the specificity of a selector

- An id is the most specific.
- A class, attribute selector, or pseudo-class selector is less specific.
- An element or pseudo-element selector is least specific.

Description

- When two or more rule sets are applied to an HTML element, CSS uses the *cascade order* and rules shown above to determine which rule set to apply.
- A user can create a *user style sheet* that provides a default set of rules for web pages. Users with poor vision often do this so the type for a page is displayed in a large font.
- Since most users don't create user style sheets, you usually can control the way the rules are applied for your web applications. But you should keep in mind how your web pages could be affected by user style sheets.
- If you want to create or remove a user style sheet, you can search the Internet for the procedures that your browser requires.

Figure 4-10   How the cascade rules work

How to work with text

Now that you know how to select the elements that you want to format, you're ready to learn how to use CSS to apply that formatting. To start, you'll learn how to style fonts and format text.

How to set the font family and font size

Figure 4-11 shows how to set the *font family* and font size for text elements. The table at the top of this figure lists the five generic font families, and the examples below that table show what typical fonts in these families look like.

When you develop a web site, your primary font family should be a sans-serif font family. That's because sans-serif fonts are easier to read in a browser than the other types of fonts, including serif fonts, even though serif fonts have long been considered the best for printed text. You can also use serif and monospace fonts for special purposes, but you should avoid the use of cursive and fantasy fonts.

When you code the values for the font-family property, you code a list of the fonts that you want to use. For instance, the first example in this figure lists Arial, Helvetica, and sans-serif as the fonts, and sans-serif is a generic font name. Then, the browser will use the first font in the list that is available to it. But if none of the fonts are available, the browser will substitute its default font for the generic font that's coded last in the list.

If the name of a font family contains spaces, like "Times New Roman", you need to enclose the name in quotation marks when you code the list. This is illustrated by the second and third examples in the first group.

To set the font size for a font, you use the font-size property as illustrated by the second group of examples. For this property, we recommend relative measurements so the users will be able to change the font sizes in their browsers.

When you use a relative measurement, it's relative to the parent element. For example, the second rule in the second set of examples will cause the font to be 150% larger than its parent element. So if the parent element is 12 points, this element will be 18 points. Similarly, the third rule specifies 1.5 ems so it will also be 150% of the parent font.

The next example shows how the font family and font size can be set in the body element. Here, the default font family for the browser is changed to a sans-serif font, and the default font size is changed to 87.5 percent of the browser's default size. Remember that most browsers use Times New Roman and 16 pixels as the defaults, and these defaults are typically changed by CSS.

Like colors, the font properties that you set in an element are inherited by all of its descendents. Note, however, that it's not the relative value that's inherited when you use a relative measurement for the font size. Instead, it's the actual size that's calculated for the font. If, for example, the default font size is 16 pixels and you set the font-size property to 125%, the size of the element and any descendents will be 20 pixels.

The five generic font families

Name	Description
`serif`	Fonts with tapered, flared, or slab stroke ends.
`sans-serif`	Fonts with plain stroke ends.
`monospace`	Fonts that use the same width for each character.
`cursive`	Fonts with connected, flowing letters that look like handwriting.
`fantasy`	Fonts with decorative styling.

Examples of the five generic font families

Times New Roman is a serif font. It is the default for most web browsers.

Arial is a sans-serif font that is widely used, and sans-serif fonts are best for web pages.

Courier New is a monospace font that is used for code examples.

Lucida Handwriting is a cursive font that is not frequently used.

Impact is a fantasy font that is rarely used.

How to specify a font family

```
font-family: Arial, Helvetica, sans-serif;
font-family: "Times New Roman", Times, serif;
font-family: "Courier New", Courier, monospace;
```

How to specify the font size

```
font-size: 12pt;          /* in points */
font-size: 150%;          /* as a percent of the parent element */
font-size: 1.5em;         /* same as 150% */
```

A font-family rule in the body element that is inherited by all descendents

```
body {
    font-family: Arial, Helvetica, sans-serif;
    font-size: 87.5%; }
```

A font-family rule in a descendent that overrides the inherited font family

```
p { font-family: "Times New Roman", Times, serif; }
```

Description

- The fonts specified for the font-family property are searched in the order listed. If you include a font name that contains spaces, the name must be enclosed in quotes.

- If you specify a generic font last and the web browser can't find any of the other fonts in the list, it will use its default font for the generic font that you specified.

- The font properties that you set for an element are inherited by all of its descendents.

- If you use relative font sizes, the users will be able to vary the sizes by using their browsers. If you use pixels, the font size will vary based on the screen resolution.

Figure 4-11   How to set the font family and font size

How to set the other properties for styling fonts

The table in figure 4-12 summarizes the other properties that you can use for styling a font. Like the font-family and font-size properties, these properties are also inherited by their descendants.

In this figure, the first group of examples shows how italics and small caps can be applied to a font by using the font-style and font-variant properties. Then, the second group of examples shows how font weights can be applied to a font. In most cases, you'll use the bold keyword to boldface a font. But if you want to use varying degrees of boldness, you can use multiples of 100. You can also specify the boldness of a font relative to the boldness of the parent font by using the lighter or bolder keyword as shown in the last example.

The third group of examples shows how to set the line height for a font. This property lets you increase or decrease the amount of vertical space that's used for a font. If, for example, you set the line height to 14 points for a font that is set to 12 points, there will be two extra points of space for the font. This space will be divided equally above and below the font. This provides extra spacing for block elements that are displayed on more than one line.

Like the font-size property, it's usually better to set the line-height property with a relative measurement like a percent or ems. That way, all modern browsers will be able to adjust the line height relative to the font size. The first three examples illustrate that. The fourth example is similar, but it specifies a number that is used to calculate the line height.

Note that when you use a percent or ems as in the second and third examples, the actual line height will be inherited by descendent elements. When you use a number, however, the number itself will be inherited. If a descendent element has a smaller font size, then, the line height will also be smaller, which is usually what you want.

Often, you code each of the font properties that you've just learned about in a separate rule. However, you can also use the *shorthand property* for fonts that's shown in this figure. If you look at the syntax for this property, you can see that it provides for all six font properties. In this syntax summary, the properties in brackets [ ] are optional, which means that only the font-size and font-family are required.

When you use this property, you code the font properties separated by spaces without coding the property names. You combine the font-size and line-height properties separated by a slash. And you separate the list of fonts for the font-family property with commas. This is illustrated by the three examples after the syntax summary.

Here, the first rule includes all the font properties except for font-variant. The second rule includes the font-variant, font-size, and font-family properties. And the third rule includes the font-size, line-height, and font-family properties.

Other properties for styling fonts

Property	Description
font-style	A keyword that determines how the font is slanted: normal, italic, and oblique.
font-weight	A keyword or number that determines the boldness of the font: normal, bold, bolder, lighter, or multiples of 100 from 100 through 900, with 400 equivalent to normal. Bolder and lighter are relative to the parent element.
font-variant	A keyword that specifies whether small caps will be used: normal and small-caps.
line-height	A relative or absolute value or a number that specifies the amount of vertical space for each line. The excess space is divided equally above and below the font.

How to specify font styles and variants

```
font-style: italic;
font-style: normal;          /* remove style */
font-variant: small-caps;
```

How to specify font weights;

```
font-weight: 700;
font-weight: bold;           /* same as 700 */
font-weight: normal;         /* same as 400 */
font-weight: lighter;        /* relative to the parent element */
```

How to specify line height

```
line-height: 14pt;
line-height: 140%;
line-height: 1.4em;          /* same as 140% */
line-height: 1.4;            /* same as 140% and 1.4em */
```

The syntax for the shorthand font property

```
font: [style] [weight] [variant] size[/line-height] family;
```

How to use the shorthand font property

```
font: italic bold 14px/19px Arial, sans-serif;
font: small-caps 150% "Times New Roman", Times, serif;
font: 90%/120% "Comic Sans MS", Impact, sans-serif;
```

Description

- You can set the font-style, font-weight, and font-variant properties to a value of "normal" to remove any formatting that has been applied to these properties.

- The line-height property determines the spacing between lines within a block element.

- If you specify just a number for the line-height property, the font size is multiplied by that value to determine the line height, and the multiplier is inherited by child elements. If you specify an absolute or relative size for the line-height property, the actual line height is inherited by child elements.

- You can use the *shorthand property* for a font to set all six font properties with a single rule. When you use this property, the font-size and font-family properties are required.

Figure 4-12   How to set the other properties for styling fonts

How to indent and align text

Figure 4-13 presents the properties for indenting and aligning text. You can use the text-indent property to indent the first line of text in a paragraph. When you set this property, it usually makes sense to use a relative unit of measure such as ems. That way, if the size of the current font changes, the indentation will also change.

To align text horizontally, you can use the text-align property. By default, most elements are left-aligned, but you can use the "center", "right", or "justify" values to change that. Note, however, that when you justify text, the spacing between words is adjusted so the text is aligned on both the left and right sides. Since this makes the text more difficult to read, justified text should be avoided.

You can also align inline elements vertically. To illustrate, suppose that you code a span element within a paragraph, and you code a style rule that sets the font size for the text in the span element so it's smaller than the text in the paragraph. Then, the vertical-align property determines how the span element is aligned relative to its parent element. If, for example, you set the vertical-align property to "text-bottom", the bottom of the text in the span element will be aligned with the bottom of the text in the paragraph. Another alternative is to specify a relative or absolute value for this property to determine how far above or below its normal position the element should be displayed.

The example in this figure shows how to use the text-indent and text-align properties. Here, the paragraph below the heading is indented by 2 ems, and the paragraph that contains the copyright information is right-aligned.

Properties for indenting and aligning text

Property	Description
text-indent	A relative or absolute value that determines the indentation for the first line of text. This property is inherited.
text-align	A keyword that determines the horizontal alignment of text. Possible values are left, center, right, and justify. This property is inherited.
vertical-align	A relative or absolute value or a keyword that determines the vertical alignment of text. Possible keywords are baseline, bottom, middle, top, text-bottom, text-top, sub, and super. If you use pixels, points, or ems to specify the value for the vertical-align property, the text is raised if the value is positive and lowered if it's negative. If you specify a percent, the text is raised or lowered based on the percentage of the line height.

The HTML for a web page

```
<header>
    <h1>San Joaquin Valley Town Hall</h1>
</header>
<section id="main">
    <p>Welcome to San Joaquin Valley Town Hall. We have some
        fascinating speakers for you this season!</p>
</section>
<footer>
    <p>&copy; Copyright 2012 San Joaquin Valley Town Hall.</p>
</footer>
```

CSS that specifies a text indent and horizontal alignment

```
body {
    font-size: 87.5%;
    margin: 2em; }
h1 {
    font-size: 180%; }
#main p { text-indent: 2em; }
footer p {
    font-size: 80%;
    text-align: right; }
```

The HTML in a web browser

San Joaquin Valley Town Hall

Welcome to San Joaquin Valley Town Hall. We have some fascinating speakers for you this season!

© Copyright 2012 San Joaquin Valley Town Hall.

Description

* The text-indent and text-align properties are often used with text, and the vertical-align property is often used with tables.

Figure 4-13   How to indent and align text

How to transform and decorate text

Figure 4-14 shows two more properties for formatting text. To start, you can use the text-transform property to display text in all uppercase letters, all lowercase letters, or with the first letter of each word capitalized.

You can use the text-decoration property to display a line under, over, or through text. You can also use this property to blink the text. However, this property has limited value for three reasons. First, blinking text is discouraged in modern web sites. Second, you usually shouldn't underline words that aren't links. Third, you can use borders as shown in the next chapter to put lines over and under a block element, and that gives you more control over the lines.

The example in this figure illustrates how the text-transform and text-decoration properties work. Here, the text-transform property for the h1 element is set so the text is displayed in all uppercase letters. In addition, the text-decoration property is set so a line is drawn both above and below the heading. Notice that the heading is also centered using the text-align property.

If you want to remove any text decorations and transformations that have been applied to an element, you can specify a value of "none" for these properties. For example, the text-decoration property of an <a> element is set to "underline" by default. If that's not what you want, you can set this property to "none".

Properties for transforming and decorating text

Property	Description
text-transform	A keyword that determines how text is capitalized. Possible values are uppercase, lowercase, capitalize, and none. This property is inherited.
text-decoration	A keyword that determines special decorations that are applied to text. Possible values are underline, overline, line-through, blink, and none.

The HTML for a web page

```
<header>
    <h1>San Joaquin Valley Town Hall</h1>
</header>
<section>
    <p>Welcome to San Joaquin Valley Town Hall. We have some fascinating
        speakers for you this season!</p>
</section>
```

CSS that specifies transforms and decorations

```
h1 {
    font-size: 150%;
    text-align: center;
    text-transform: uppercase;
    text-decoration: underline overline;
}
```

The HTML in a browser

SAN JOAQUIN VALLEY TOWN HALL

Welcome to San Joaquin Valley Town Hall. We have some fascinating speakers for you this season!

Description

- Although the text-decoration property isn't technically inherited if it is specified for a block element, its value is applied to inline children elements and block descendant elements.

- Internet Explorer doesn't support the blink keyword for the text-decoration property, and blinking is discouraged.

Figure 4-14   How to transform and decorate text

How to use CSS3 to add shadows to text

Before CSS3, you had to use an image to display text with shadows. But now, CSS3 offers the text-shadow property for this purpose. That makes it much easier to provide shadows.

Figure 4-15 shows how to use this property. As the syntax shows, you can set four parameters for it. The first one specifies how much the shadow should be offset to the right (a positive value) or left (a negative value). The second one specifies how much the shadow should be offset down (a positive value) or up (a negative value). The third one specifies how big the blur radius for the shadow should be. And the fourth one specifies the color for the shadow.

The first example shows text with a shadow that is 4 pixels to the right and down, with no blur and with the shadow the same color as the text. The result is shown in the browser.

In contrast, the shadow for the heading in the second example is offset to the left and up by 2 pixels, with a blur radius of 4 pixels and with the shadow in red. Since the heading is in blue, this provides an interesting effect.

As this figure shows, this property is supported by all modern browsers. But if a browser doesn't support this property, it is simply ignored so no harm is done: the heading is just displayed without the shadow. That's why you can start using this property right away.

When you use this property, though, remember the visually-impaired. If the offsets or blur are too large, the shadow can make the text more difficult to read. On that basis, both examples in this figure should probably be toned down so they're easier to read.

The syntax of the text-shadow property

```
text-shadow: horizontalOffset, verticalOffset, blurRadius, shadowColor;
```

Two examples

The h1 element

```
<h1>San Joaquin Valley Town Hall</h1>
```

The CSS

```
h1 {
    color: #ef9c00;
    text-shadow: 4px 4px; }
```

The heading in a browser

San Joaquin Valley Town Hall

Different CSS for the same h1 element

```
h1 {
    color: blue;
    text-shadow: -2px -2px 4px red; }
```

The heading in a browser

San Joaquin Valley Town Hall

Accessibility guideline

- Remember the visually-impaired. Too much shadow or blur makes text harder to read.

Description

- Positive values offset the shadow to the right or down. Negative values offset the shadow to the left or up.
- The blur radius determines how much the shadow is blurred.
- The text-shadow property is supported by all modern browsers.
- If this property isn't supported by a browser, it is ignored so there's no shadow, which is usually okay.

Figure 4-15   How to use CSS3 to add shadows to text

How to float an image so text flows around it

In chapters 5 and 6, you'll learn everything you need to know about setting margins and floating an image so the text flows around it. But just to get you started with this, figure 4-16 shows how you can float the logo for a header to the left so the headings flow to its right.

In the HTML for the example, you can see an img element, an h1 element, and an h2 element. Then, in the CSS for the img element, the float property is set to left and the right-margin property is set to 1em. The result is that the two headings flow to the right of the img as shown in the first browser example.

You should know, however, that this depends on the size of the image. Because the width of the image is set to 100 pixels for the first example, both headings flow to its right. But if the width is reduced to 60 pixels as in the second example, the second heading is under the image because the image is too short for the heading to flow to its right.

This shows that you're going to have to fiddle with the image size to get this to work right for the time being. But in the next two chapters, you'll learn the right ways to get this result.

If you want to stop elements from flowing to the right of a floated element, you can use the clear property that's shown in this figure. Here, the clear property is used for the section element, and it stops the flow around an element that has been floated to its left. If this section follows a header, the flow of the text will stop before any of the elements in the section are displayed.

An image that has been floated to the left of the headings that follow

San Joaquin Valley Town Hall

Bringing cutting-edge speakers to the valley

The HTML

```
<img src="images/logo.jpg" alt="Town Hall Logo" width="100">
<h1>San Joaquin Valley Town Hall</h1>
<h2>Bringing cutting-edge speakers to the valley</h2>
```

The CSS

```
img {
    float: left;
    margin-right: 1em;
}
```

The page if the width of the image is reduced to 60

San Joaquin Valley Town Hall

Bringing cutting-edge speakers to the valley

The property that will stop the floating before a subsequent element

```
section { clear: left; }
```

Description

- To float an image, you use the float property, and to set the margins around it, you use the margin property.

- In chapters 5 and 6, you'll learn how to set margins and float elements, but this will give you an idea of how you can use an image in a header.

- When you float an image to the left, the block elements that follow it fill the space to the right of it. When the elements that follow get past the height of the image and its top and bottom margins, they flow into the space below the element.

- You can use the clear property to stop an element from flowing into the space alongside a floated element.

- For now, you can experiment with the size of the image to get the effect that you want, but in the next two chapters you'll learn the right ways to get the same results.

Figure 4-16   How to float an image so text flows around it

A web page that uses an external style sheet

Now that you've learned how to code selectors and how to format text, you're ready to see a web page that uses these skills.

The page layout

Figure 4-17 presents a web page that uses an external style sheet. If you study this web page, you can see that the CSS in the style sheet has been used to change the default font to a sans-serif font, to apply colors to some of the headings and text, to center the headings in the header, to apply shadows to the text in the first heading, to add line height to the items in the unordered list, to apply boldfacing to portions of text, and to right-align the footer. Overall, this formatting makes the page look pretty good.

In terms of typography, though, this web page needs to be improved. For instance, there should be less space after "2011-2012 guest speakers", less space after "Looking for a unique gift?", and less space between the first three paragraphs. To make these adjustments, though, you need to know how to use the margin and padding properties that are part of the CSS box model. So that's what you'll learn first in the next chapter. Once you learn how to use those properties, you'll be able to get the typography just the way you want it.

A web page that uses some of the styles presented in this chapter

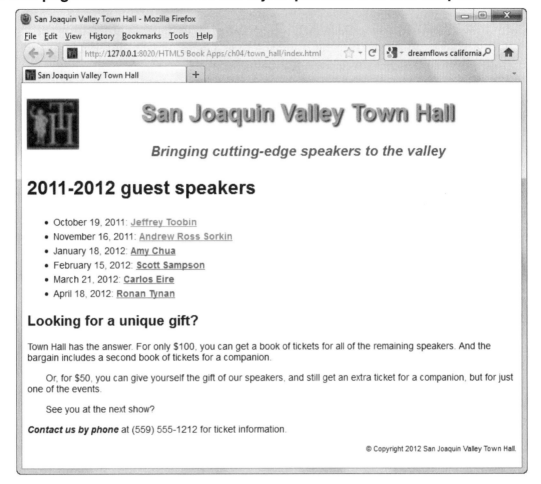

Description

- This web page uses an external style sheet to apply the styles that are illustrated.
- A sans-serif font has been applied to all of the text in this document because that's the most readable type of font for web pages. Also, relative font sizes have been applied to the elements on the page.
- Italics and boldfacing have been applied to portions of the text, the copyright information has been right-aligned, and colors have been applied to two of the headings.
- Colors have also been applied to the <a> tags in the unordered list. Because the first two lectures have passed, the first two links in the list have the color gray applied to them.

What's wrong with the typography in this web page

- The spacing above and below the block elements should be improved. In the next chapter, you'll learn how to do that by using the margin and padding properties.

Figure 4-17   The page layout for a web page that uses an external style sheet

The HTML file

Figure 4-18 presents the HTML for the web page in figure 4-17. In the head section, you can see the link element that refers to the external style sheet that is used for formatting this web page. It is in the styles folder.

You can also see the script element that loads the shiv that lets older browsers apply CSS to the HTML5 semantic elements. Although you should include this shiv on every page as long as older browsers are in use, we won't show this code in the rest of the examples in this book. Just assume that it's there.

In the body section, the header and first part of the section is the same as it was in the example at the end of the last chapter. But after the nav element, this HTML includes another h2 element and three new <p> elements.

If you look at the <a> elements in the first and second <li> elements, you can see that they have class attributes that assign them to the "date_passed" class. This class name will be used to apply the color gray to those items because this example assumes that the dates for those events have already passed, and the gray color is intended to indicate that to the user.

Similarly, the second and third <p> elements have their class attributes set to "indent". Then, this class will be used as the CSS selector for indenting these paragraphs.

The HTML file for the web page

```
<!DOCTYPE HTML>

<html lang="en">
<head>
    <meta charset="utf-8">
    <title>San Joaquin Valley Town Hall</title>
    <link rel="shortcut icon" href="images/favicon.ico">
    <link rel="stylesheet" href="styles/main.css">
    <script src="http://html5shiv.googlecode.com/svn/trunk/html5.js"></script>
</head>

<body>
    <header>
        <img src="images/logo.jpg" alt="Town Hall Logo" width="80">
        <hgroup>
            <h1>San Joaquin Valley Town Hall</h1>
            <h2>Bringing cutting-edge speakers to the valley</h2>
        </hgroup>
    </header>
    <section>
        <h1>2011-2012 guest speakers</h1>
        <nav>
            <ul>
                <li>October 19, 2011: <a class="date_passed"
                    href="speakers/toobin.html">Jeffrey Toobin</a></li>
                <li>November 16, 2011: <a class="date_passed"
                    href="speakers/sorkin.html">Andrew Ross Sorkin</a></li>
                <li>January 18, 2012: <a href="speakers/chua.html">
                    Amy Chua</a></li>
                <li>February 15, 2012: <a href="speakers/sampson.html">
                    Scott Sampson</a></li>
                <li>March 21, 2012: <a href="speakers/eire.html">
                    Carlos Eire</a></li>
                <li>April 18, 2012: <a href="speakers/tynan.html">
                    Ronan Tynan</a></li>
            </ul>
        </nav>

        <h2>Looking for a unique gift?</h2>
        <p>Town Hall has the answer. For only $100, you can get a book of
            tickets for all of the remaining speakers. And the bargain includes
            a second book of tickets for a companion.</p>
        <p class="indent">Or, for $50, you can give yourself the gift of our
            speakers, and still get an extra ticket for a companion, but for
            just one of the events.</p>
        <p class="indent">See you at the next show?</p>

        <p><em>Contact us by phone</em> at (559) 555-1212 for ticket
            information.</p>
    </section>
    <footer>
        <p>&copy; Copyright 2012 San Joaquin Valley Town Hall.</p>
    </footer>
</body>
</html>
```

Figure 4-18   The HTML file for the web page

The CSS file

Figure 4-19 shows the CSS file for the web page. To start, note the first rule set. It tells older browsers that the HTML5 semantic elements are block elements. That way, the CSS code will work correctly in those browsers. Here again, you should include this rule set as long as older browsers are in use, but we won't show it in the rest of the examples in this book. Just assume that it's there.

Next, notice the way that the code that follows is structured. First, the rule sets for specific elements are presented. In effect, this sets the default formatting for these elements. Then, these rule sets are followed by rule sets that are specific to the header, section, and footer elements. The rules in these rule sets override the ones for the elements because they're more specific. For instance, the font size for the section h1 selector overrides the font size for the h1 selector.

You might also note that many of the rule sets that contain a single rule are coded on a single line. This of course is a valid way to code these rule sets because white space is ignored. For rule sets that require more than one rule, though, each rule is coded on a single line to make the rules easier to read.

In the rule set for the body element, the two properties specify the font-family and font-size. Because these properties are inherited, they become the defaults for the document. Notice too that the font size is specified as a percent. That means it will be determined by the default font size for the browser. The font sizes for the headings are also specified as percents, so they will be based on the size that's calculated for the body element.

In the rule sets for the <a> element, the hover and focus pseudo-classes are set to the same color. Then, in the rule set for the unordered list, the line-height property is specified to increase the spacing between the items. Similarly, the font weight is specified for the em element so it is boldfaced. However, this element will also be italicized because that's its normal behavior. To remove the italics, you would have to code a font-style property with normal as its value.

In the rule sets for the header, you can see that the image is floated to the left and that the h1 and h2 elements are centered. You can also see that the h1 heading has a 2 pixel, black shadow to its right and down with 2 pixels of blur.

In the rule sets for the section, you can see that the clear property is used to stop the flow of the text around the image that has been floated left. You can also see that the elements in the "indent" class will be indented 2 ems, and the elements in the "date_passed" class will be gray.

Of course, you can code the CSS in other ways and get the same results. For instance, you could code this rule set for the h1 and h2 elements in the header:

```
header h1, header h2 { text-align: center; }
```

Then, you could drop the text-align properties from the header h1 and header h2 rule sets that follow. Or, you could replace the selectors in the example above with the hgroup selector. That would align both of the headings that the hgroup element contains. You could also code the selectors for the date_passed and indent classes so they're less specific since they aren't used outside the section. If you code the selectors so they're more specific, though, they're less likely to cause problems if you add rule sets later on.

The CSS file for the web page

```
/* So the HTML5 semantic elements can be formatted correctly */
article, aside, figure, footer, header, nav, section {
    display: block;
}

/* the styles for the elements */
body {
    font-family: Arial, Helvetica, sans-serif;
    font-size: 87.5%;
}

h1 { font-size: 250%; }
h2 { font-size: 150%; }

a { font-weight: bold; }
a:link { color: green; }
a:hover, a:focus { color: blue; }

ul { line-height: 1.5; }

em { font-weight: bold; }

/* the styles for the header */
header img { float: left; }
header h1 {
    color: #ef9c00;
    text-align: center;
    text-shadow: 2px 2px 2px black;
}
header h2 {
    color: green;
    font-style: italic;
    text-align: center;
}

/* the styles for the section */
section { clear: left; }
section h1 { font-size: 200%; }

section a.date_passed  { color: gray; }
section .indent { text-indent: 2em; }

/* the styles for the footer */
footer p {
    font-size: 80%;
    text-align: right;
}
```

Figure 4-19   The CSS file for the web page

Perspective

At this point, you should know how to code all types of selectors, and you should know how to code the CSS properties for formatting text. That gets you off to a good start with CSS, but there's still a lot to learn.

So, in the next chapter, you'll learn how to use the CSS box model. You use that model to set the margins, padding, and borders for the elements in your pages so your typography looks the way you want it to. Then, in chapter 6, you'll learn how to use CSS for page layout. When you finish those chapters, you'll have all the skills you need for using CSS at a professional level.

Terms

external style sheet	type selector
embedded style sheet	id selector
inline style	class selector
shiv	relational selector
shim	descendant selector
absolute unit of measure	adjacent sibling selector
relative unit of measure	child selector
absolute measurement	general sibling selector
relative measurement	attribute selector
RGB value	pseudo-class selector
hexadecimal (hex) value	pseudo-element selector
inherited property	cascade order
RGBA value	user style sheet
HSL value	font family
HSLA value	shorthand property
universal selector	

Summary

- If you're going to use a style sheet for more than one HTML document, it's usually best to use an *external style sheet*. However, you can also apply CSS by embedding a style sheet in the HTML or by using the style attribute of an inline element.

- To format the HTML5 semantic elements with CSS, you need to use a JavaScript *shiv* in the head section and a CSS rule set that specifies that these elements are block elements.

- You can use *absolute measurements* like pixels or *relative measurements* like ems or percents to specify the CSS properties for sizes. For fonts, it's better to use relative measurements so the user can change the font sizes by changing the browser's default font size.

- Most graphic designers use *hex* for the *RGB values* that represent the colors that they want because that gives them the most control. However, most browsers also support 16 standard color names like red and blue.

- CSS3 lets you use *RGBA*, *HSL*, and *HLSA* values to specify colors. This gives the web designer more control over colors and transparency. CSS also provides 147 more keywords for colors.

- You can code CSS selectors for element types, ids, classes, relations, and attributes. You can also code selectors for combinations of these items.

- A *pseudo-class selector* can be used to apply CSS formatting when certain conditions occur or have occurred, like when the mouse hovers over an element or the focus is on an element. A *pseudo-element selector* lets you select a portion of text.

- If more than one style sheet is applied to an HTML document and two or more rule sets apply to the same element, the *cascade order* determines which rule set takes precedence. The first four levels of this order are: the important rules in a *user style sheet* for the browser; the important rules in a web page; the normal rules in a web page; and the normal rules in a user style sheet.

- If more than one rule set in a cascade level is applied to an element, the rule set with the highest specificity is used. But if the specificity is the same for two or more rule sets in a cascade level, the rule set that's specified last is used.

- The default font for most browsers is a 16-pixel, serif font. However, because sans-serif fonts are easier to read in a browser, you normally change the font family. It's also good to change the font size to a relative measurement like a percent of the default font size.

- The colors and font properties of a parent element are *inherited* by the child elements. But those properties can be overridden by the rule sets for the children.

- The *shorthand property* for fonts can be used to apply all six of the font properties to an element: font-family, font-size, font-style, font-weight, font-variant, and line-height.

- Text properties can be used to indent, align, transform, and decorate the text in a block element like a heading or paragraph. CSS3 also provides for adding shadows to text.

- You can use the float property of an image to float the image to the left. Then, the block elements that follow in the HTML flow to its right. To stop the flow, you can code the clear property for an element.

Exercise 4-1   Format the Town Hall home page

In this exercise, you'll format the home page that you built in exercise 3-1 by using the skills that you've learned in this chapter. When you're through, the page should look like this.

San Joaquin Valley Town Hall

Celebrating our 75th Year

Our Mission

San Joaquin Valley Town Hall is a non-profit organization that is run by an all-volunteer board of directors. Our mission is to bring nationally and internationally renowned, thought-provoking speakers who inform, educate, and entertain our audience! As one or our members told us:

"Each year I give a ticket package to each of our family members. I think of it as the gift of knowledge...and that is priceless."

Our Ticket Packages

- Season Package: $95
- Patron Package: $200
- Single Speaker: $25

Our 2011-2012 speakers

October 19, 2011
Jeffrey Toobin

November 16, 2011
Andrew Ross Sorkin

January 18, 2012
Amy Chua

© 2012, San Joaquin Valley Town Hall, Fresno, CA 93755

Open the index.html page and update the head section

1. Use your text editor to open the HTML file that you created for exercise 3-1:

   `c:\html5_css3\exercises\town_hall_1\index.html`

2. Use your text editor to open this HTML template file:

   `c:\html5_css3\exercises\town_hall_1\templates\basic.html`

   Then, copy the second link element and the script element from the head section to the clipboard, switch to the index.html file, and paste these elements at the end of the head section. The script element is the one that you need for using the new semantic elements with older browsers.

3. Complete the href attribute in the link element that you just copied into the head section so it refers to the main.css file in the styles subfolder. Then, close the template.

Open the main.css file and format the header

4. Use your text editor to open this CSS file:

   `c:\html5_css3\exercises\town_hall_1\styles\main.css`

   Note that this file contains some of the CSS code that you'll need, including the rule set that you need for compatibility with older browsers, the rule set that specifies the font family and font size for the body, the rule set that floats the image in the header, and the rule set that clears the floating in the section.

5. Add two rule sets for the header to the style sheet. The first one should set the color for the h1 element in the header to #800000 and indent it 30 pixels. The second one should set the font style for the h2 element in the header to italic and indent it 30 pixels.

6. Test the HTML page in Firefox to make sure that the style sheet has been linked properly, the image has been floated, and the headings have been formatted correctly. If necessary, make corrections and test again.

Format the section and the footer

From now on, test each change right after you make it.

7. Add a rule set for the h1 elements in the section that sets the font size to 150% and the color to #800000.

8. Add a rule set for the h2 elements in the section that sets the font size to 120%.

9. Add a rule set for just the heading that says: "Our 2011-2012 Speakers". To do that, first add an id attribute to this heading in the HTML file with the value "speakers". Then, create a rule set that uses an id selector (#speakers) for that id, and set the font size to 175% and the color to black.

10. Add a rule set that italicizes any link that has the focus or has the mouse hovering over it.

11. Add a rule set that centers the <p> tag in the footer.

Add the finishing touches and test in IE

12. Add text shadow to the *75ᵗʰ* in the second heading in the header. To do that, enclose the *75ᵗʰ* in the HTML in an em or span element and give that element a class attribute with a value of "shadow". Then, create a rule set that uses a class selector (.shadow) for that class, and code a rule that adds shadow to the text with #800000 as the color of the shadow.

13. Experiment on your own to see if you can improve the formatting. For instance, you may want to enhance the formatting for the <a> elements.

14. When you're through experimenting, test the page in IE. There the text shadow may not work because it isn't supported. But if you see any other formatting problems, make the corrections and test again in both Firefox and IE.

5

How to use the CSS box model for spacing, borders, and backgrounds

In the last chapter, you learned some basic CSS properties for formatting text. Now, you'll learn the properties for controlling the spacing between elements and for displaying borders and backgrounds. Specifically, you'll learn how to use the CSS box model for those purposes.

An introduction to the box model

When a browser displays a web page, it places each HTML block element in a box. That makes it easy to control the spacing, borders, and other formatting for elements like headers, sections, footers, headings, and paragraphs. Some inline elements like images are placed in a box as well. To work with boxes, you use the CSS *box model*.

How the box model works

Figure 5-1 presents a diagram that shows how the box model works. By default, the box for a block element is as wide as the block that contains it and as tall as it needs to be based on its content. However, you can explicitly specify the size of the content area for a block element by using the height and width properties. You can also use other properties to set the borders, margins, and padding for a block element.

If you look at the diagram in this figure, you can see that *padding* is the space between the content area and a border. Similarly, a *margin* is the space between the border and the outside of the box.

If you need to calculate the overall height of a box, you can use the formula in this figure. Here, you start by adding the values for the margin, border width, and padding for the top of the box. Then, you add the height of the content area. Last, you add the values for the padding, border width, and margin for the bottom of the box. The formula for calculating the overall width of a box is similar.

When you set the height and width properties for a block element, you can use any of the units that you learned about in the last chapter. In most cases, though, you'll use pixels so the sizes are fixed. That way, the size of the page won't change if the user changes the size of the browser window. This is referred to as a *fixed layout*.

When you use a fixed layout, you can use either absolute or relative units of measure for margins and padding. If you use a relative unit such as ems, the margins and padding will be adjusted if the font size changes. If you use an absolute unit, the margins and padding will stay the same.

The CSS box model

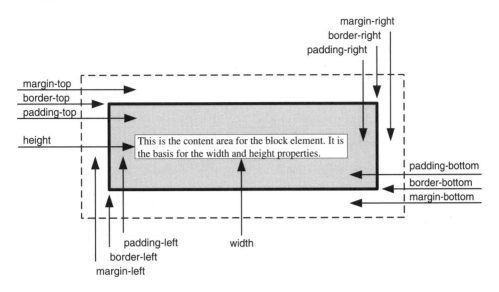

The formula for calculating the height of a box

```
top margin + top border + top padding +
height +
bottom padding + bottom border + bottom margin
```

The formula for calculating the width of a box

```
left margin + left border + left padding +
width +
right padding + right border + right margin
```

Description

- The CSS *box model* lets you work with the boxes that a browser places around each block element as well as some inline elements. This lets you add formatting such as margins, padding, and borders.

- By default, the box for a block element is as wide as the block that contains it and as tall as it needs to be based on its content.

- You can use the height and width properties to specify the size of the content area for a block element explicitly.

- You can use other properties to control the margins, padding, and borders for a block element. Then, these properties are added to the height and width of the content area to determine the height and width of the box.

Figure 5-1   How the box model works

A web page that illustrates the box model

To help you understand how the box model works, figure 5-2 presents the HTML for a simple web page. Then, the CSS adds borders to the four types of elements in the HTML: a dotted 3-pixel border to the body, a solid 2-pixel border to the section, and dashed 1-pixel borders to the h1 and <p> elements. If you look at the web page in the browser, you can see how these four borders are rendered. You can also see how the margins and padding for these boxes work.

For the body, the margin on all four sides is set to 10 pixels. You can see that margin on the left, top, and right of the body border, but not on the bottom. That's because the bottom margin for the body is determined by the size of the window.

For the section, the width is set to 500 pixels, and the margins on all four sides of the box are set to 20 pixels. You can see these margins on the left, top, and bottom of the section box, but not on the right because the width of the section is set to 500 pixels.

The next rule set sets properties for both the h1 and <p> elements. In this case, the properties set the border and the padding for these elements. Then, the next two rule sets set additional properties for each of these elements.

The rule set for the h1 element sets the top margin to .5em, the right and left margins to 0, and the bottom margin to .25em. As a result, there is more space above the h1 element than below it. This rule set also sets the padding on the left side of the element to 15 pixels so space is added between the border of the box and the text.

The rule set for the <p> element starts by setting all the margins to 0. As a result, all of the space between the h1 and <p> elements is due to the bottom margin of the h1 element. In addition, the padding on the left side of the element is set to 15 pixels so the text for the h1 and <p> elements is aligned.

Please note that if I had used relative measures for the padding on the left of the h1 and <p> elements, they wouldn't be aligned because the font sizes for these elements are different. One more thing to notice is that the padding-left properties in the rule sets for the h1 and <p> elements override the left padding specified by the rule set for both of these elements.

This should help you understand how the box model works. Now, it's on to the details for setting the properties for the box model.

The HTML for a page that uses the box model

```
<body>
    <section>
        <h1>San Joaquin Valley Town Hall</h1>
        <p>Welcome to San Joaquin Valley Town Hall.
        We have some fascinating speakers for you this season!</p>
    </section>
</body>
```

The CSS for the page

```
body {
    border: 3px dotted black;
    margin: 10px;
}
section {
    border:  2px solid black;
    width:   500px;
    margin:  20px;          /* all four sides */
    padding: 10px;          /* all four sides */
}
h1, p {
    border: 1px dashed black;
    padding: 10px;
}
h1 {
    margin: .5em 0 .25em;    /* .5em top, 0 right and left, .25em bottom */
    padding-left: 15px;
}
p {
    margin: 0;               /* all four sides */
    padding-left: 15px;
}
```

The web page in a browser

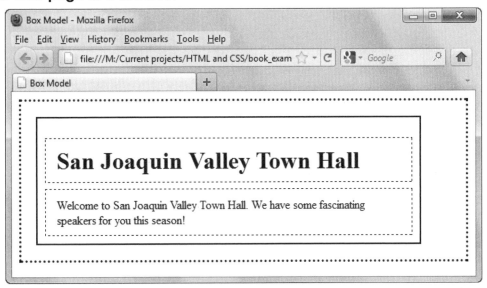

Figure 5-2   A web page that illustrates the box model

How to size and space elements

As you saw in the last figure, you can use several different properties to determine the size of an element and the spacing between the elements on a page. In the topics that follow, you'll learn the details of coding these properties.

How to set heights and widths

Figure 5-3 presents the properties for setting heights and widths. The two properties you'll use most often are width and height. By default, these properties are set to a value of "auto". As a result, the size of the content area for the element is automatically adjusted so it's as wide as the element that contains it and as tall as the content it contains. To change that, you can use the height and width properties.

The first two sets of examples in this figure illustrate how this works. Here, the first example in each set specifies an absolute value using pixels. Then, the second example specifies a relative value using percents. As a result, the width is set to 75% of the *containing block*.

Finally, the third example in each set uses the keyword "auto". That sets the width based on the size of the containing element and the height based on the content of the element. Because the default width and height is "auto", you usually won't need to use that value.

In addition to the width and height properties, you can use the min-width, max-width, min-height, and max-height properties to specify the minimum and maximum width and height of the content area. Like the width and height properties, you can specify either a relative or an absolute value for these properties. For instance, the last set of examples in this figure sets the values of these properties using pixels.

Properties for setting heights and widths

Property	Description
width	A relative or absolute value that specifies the width of the content area for a block element. You can also specify auto if you want the width of the box calculated for you based on the width of its containing block. This is the default.
height	A relative or absolute value that specifies the height of the content area for a block element. You can also specify auto if you want the height of the area calculated for you based on its content. This is the default.
min-width	A relative or absolute value that specifies the minimum width of the content area for a block element. The area will always be at least this wide regardless of its content.
max-width	A relative or absolute value that specifies the maximum width of the content area for a block element. You can also specify none to indicate that there is no maximum width.
min-height	A relative or absolute value that specifies the minimum height of the content area for a block element. The area will always be at least this tall regardless of its content.
max-height	A relative or absolute value that specifies the maximum height of the content area for a block element. You can also specify none to indicate that there is no maximum height.

How to set the width of the content area

```
width: 450px;       /* an absolute width */
width: 75%;         /* a relative width */
width: auto;        /* width based on its containing block (the default) */
```

How to set the height of the content area

```
height: 125px;
height: 50%;
height: auto;       /* height based on its content (the default) */
```

How to set the minimum and maximum width and height

```
min-width: 450px;
max-width: 600px;
min-height: 120px;
max-height: 160px;
```

Description

- If you specify a percent for the width property, the width of the content area for the block element is based on the width of the block that contains it, called the *containing block*. In that case, the width of the containing block must be specified explicitly.

- If you specify a percent for the height property, the height of the content area for the block element is based on the height of the containing block. In that case, the height of the containing block must be specified explicitly. Otherwise, "auto" is substituted for the percent.

- The min-width, max-width, min-height, and max-height properties are typically used to accommodate a change in font size.

Figure 5-3   How to set heights and widths

How to set margins

Figure 5-4 presents the properties for setting margins. As you can see, you can use individual properties like margin-top or margin-left to set individual margins. This is illustrated in the first set of examples in this figure.

Instead of setting individual margins, though, you can use the margin property to set the margins for all four sides of a box. When you use a *short-hand property* like this, you can specify one, two, three, or four values. If you specify all four values, they are applied to the sides of the box in a clockwise order: top, right, bottom, and left. To remember this order, you can think of the word *trouble*.

If you specify fewer than four values, this property still sets the margins for all four sides of the box. If, for example, you only specify one value, each margin is set to that value. If you specify two values, the top and bottom margins are set to the first value, and the left and right margins are set to the second value. And if you specify three values, the top margin is set to the first value, the left and right margins are set to the second value, and the bottom margin is set to the third value. This is illustrated in the second set of examples in this figure.

Although it isn't shown here, you can also specify the keyword "auto" for any margin. In most cases, you'll use this keyword to center a page in the browser window or a block element within its containing block. To do that, you specify auto for both the left and right margins. For this to work, you must also set the width of the element. You'll see an example of how this works in figure 5-6.

One more thing you should know about margins is that different browsers have different default margins for the block elements. Because of that, it's a good practice to explicitly set the top and bottom margins of the elements that you're using. That way, you can control the space between elements like headings and paragraphs.

Finally, if you specify a bottom margin for one element and a top margin for the element that follows it, the margins are *collapsed*. That means the smaller margin is ignored, and only the larger margin is applied. In that case, there may not be as much space between the two elements as you expected. One solution to this problem is to set the margins to zero and use padding for the spacing.

Properties for setting margins

Property	Description
margin	One to four relative or absolute values that specify the size of the margins for a box. One value is applied to all four margins. Two values are applied to the top and bottom and right and left margins. Three values are applied to the top, right and left, and bottom margins. And four values are applied to the top, right, bottom, and left margins (think *trouble*).
margin-top	A relative or absolute value that defines the space between the top border of an element and the top of the containing block or the bottom of the element above it.
margin-right	A relative or absolute value that defines the space between the right border of an element and the right side of the containing block or the left side of the element to its right.
margin-bottom	A relative or absolute value that defines the space between the bottom border of an element and the bottom of the containing block or the top of the element below it.
margin-left	A relative or absolute value that defines the space between the left border of an element and the left side of the containing block or the right side of the element to its left.

How to set the margin on a single side of an element

```
margin-top: .5em;
margin-right: 1em;
margin-bottom: 2em;
margin-left: 1em;
```

How to set the margins on multiple sides of an element

```
margin: 1em;            /* all four sides */
margin: 0 1em;          /* top and bottom 0, right and left 1em */
margin: .5em 1em 2em;   /* top .5em, right and left 1em, bottom 2em */
margin: .5em 1em 2em 1em; /* top .5em, right 1em, bottom 2em, left 1em */
```

Description

- If you specify a bottom margin for one element and a top margin for the element that follows in the HTML, the margins are *collapsed*, which means that only the larger margin is applied.

- You typically use the "auto" keyword to center an element in its *containing block*. To do that, you must also specify the width of the element.

- Because different browsers have different default margins for block elements, you often need to set these margins explicitly.

Figure 5-4   How to set margins

How to set padding

The properties for setting padding are similar to the properties for setting margins. These properties are presented in figure 5-5. As you can see, you can set the padding for the sides of a box individually, or you can set the padding for all four sides of a box at once using a shorthand property.

Properties for setting padding

Property	Description
padding-top	A relative or absolute value that defines the space between the top of an element and its top border.
padding-right	A relative or absolute value that defines the space between the right side of an element and its right border.
padding-bottom	A relative or absolute value that defines the space between the bottom of an element and its bottom border.
padding-left	A relative or absolute value that defines the space between the left side of an element and its left border.
padding	One to four relative or absolute values that specify the padding on multiple sides of an element. One value is applied to all four sides. Two values are applied to the top and bottom and right and left. Three values are applied to the top, right and left, and bottom. And four values are applied to the top, right, bottom, and left (think *trouble*).

How to set the padding on a single side of an element

```
padding-top: 0;
padding-right: 1em;
padding-bottom: .5em;
padding-left: 1em;
```

How to set the padding on multiple sides of an element

```
padding: 1em;            /* all four sides */
padding: 0 1em;          /* top and bottom 0, right and left 1em */
padding: 0 1em .5em;     /* top 0em, right and left 1em, bottom .5em */
padding: 0 1em .5em 1em; /* top 0em, right 1em, bottom .5em, left 1em */
```

Description

* If you set the top and bottom margins for elements to zero, you can use padding to set the spacing between the elements.

Figure 5-5   How to set padding

A web page that illustrates sizing and spacing

To illustrate the use of the properties for sizing and spacing, figure 5-6 presents a web page that uses many of these properties. This web page is similar to the one at the end of the last chapter. However, the page has been centered in the browser window, the spacing between the elements has been improved, and the second and third paragraphs aren't indented.

The HTML for the web page

The HTML for this web page is the same as in the application at the end of the last chapter, with two exceptions. First, the last paragraph in the section has an id attribute of "contact_us". Second, the second and third paragraphs in the section don't have a class attribute that's used to indent them.

If you want to review this HTML before you look at the CSS for this page, you can refer back to the last chapter. Or, you can open this page in your text editor. You shouldn't need to do that, though, because the focus here is on margins, padding, and the use of the box model.

A web page that uses widths, margins, and padding

Description

- This page is centered in the browser window and uses margins and padding to improve the spacing before and after headings, between list items, and between paragraphs.

Figure 5-6   A web page that illustrates the use of margins and padding

The CSS for the web page

Figure 5-7 presents the CSS for the web page. Here, I've highlighted all the style rules that affect the size and spacing of the elements on the page.

To start, the rule set for the body sets the width of the page to 600 pixels. Then, the top and bottom margins are set to 1em so there's space between the body and the top of the browser window. In addition, the left and right margins are set to "auto". Because a width is specified for the body, this causes the left and right margins to be calculated automatically so the page is centered in the browser window.

The next highlighted rule set is for the h1, h2, and <p> elements. This sets the margins and padding for these elements to 0. This prevents margin collapse when these items are next to each other. Then, the rule sets that follow can provide the right margins and padding for these elements.

For instance, the rule set for the <p> element sets the top and bottom padding to .25em, which provides the spacing between the paragraphs. Also, the rule set for the h1 element in the header sets the margin bottom to .25em, and the rule set for the h1 element in the section sets the margin top to 1em and the margin bottom to .35em. This provides the proper spacing before and after the headings.

In the rule set for the ul element, you can see that the bottom margin is set to 1.5em, and the other margins are set to zero. This reduces the space before the unordered list and increases the space after. Similarly, the bottom padding for the li elements is set to .35em. That provides the spacing after the list items, which means that you don't have to set the line height for the list.

Last, in the rule set for the element with "contact_us" as its id, you can see that the top margin is set to 1em, which provides the spacing before it. And the rule set for the footer sets the top margin to 1em which provides more space between it and the last paragraph in the section.

If you study all of this code, you can see that it avoids the problems of collapsing margins. It does that by first setting the margins for the elements to zero and then overriding those margins or using padding to provide the spacing before and after elements.

The CSS for the web page

```
/* So the HTML5 semantic elements are formatted in older browsers */
article, aside, figure, footer, header, nav, section {
    display: block;
}
/* the styles for the elements */
body {
    font-family: Arial, Helvetica, sans-serif;
    font-size: 87.5%;
    width: 600px;
    margin: 1em auto; }          /* centers the page in the browser window */

h1 { font-size: 250%; }
h2 { font-size: 150%; }

h1, h2, p {                      /* sets the margins and padding to zero */
    margin: 0;
    padding: 0; }

a { font-weight: bold; }
a:link { color: green; }
a:hover, a:focus { color: blue; }

ul { margin: 0 0 1.5em; }
li { padding-bottom: .35em; }

p { padding: .25em 0; }
em { font-weight: bold; }

/* the styles for the header */
header img { float: left; }
header h1 {
    color: #ef9c00;
    text-align: center;
    text-shadow: 2px 2px 0 black;
    margin-bottom: .25em; }
header h2 {
    color: green;
    font-style: italic;
    text-align: center; }

/* the styles for the section */
section { clear: left; }
section h1 {
    font-size: 200%;
    margin: 1em 0 .35em; }
section a.date_passed  { color: gray; }
#contact_us { margin-top: 1em; }   /* adds space before the paragraph */

/* the styles for the footer */
footer { margin-top: 1em; }
footer p {
    font-size: 80%;
    text-align: right; }
```

Figure 5-7   The CSS for the web page

A version of the CSS that uses a reset selector

In figure 5-8, you can see another version of the CSS for this application. This time, the CSS uses a *reset selector*. That refers to the use of a universal selector that sets the margins and padding for all of the elements to zero. After you code the reset selector, you can get the spacing that you want by applying margins and padding to specific elements, which overrides the settings of the reset selector. This is an approach that's used by many professionals.

In the CSS for this figure, only the rule sets that provide margins or padding are listed. This works pretty much the way the code in the previous figure works, except for the ul and li elements. Because the reset selector set the margins and padding for these elements to zero, you need to provide margins and padding for these elements.

To bring the ul element in line with the heading above it, you need to set its left margin. In this example, the left margin is set to 1.25em. You also need to provide left padding for the li elements to provide space between the bullets and the text. In this example, that space is set to .25em.

Because of these CSS differences, the formatting of the web page in this figure is slightly different than the formatting in figure 5-6. Specifically, the bulleted list isn't indented, and there's more space between the bullets and text in the list items. Of course, you could make them the same by changing the settings for the ul and li elements, but this shows the options that you have when you use a reset selector. In chapter 7, you'll learn more about formatting lists.

A slightly modified version of the page that uses a reset selector

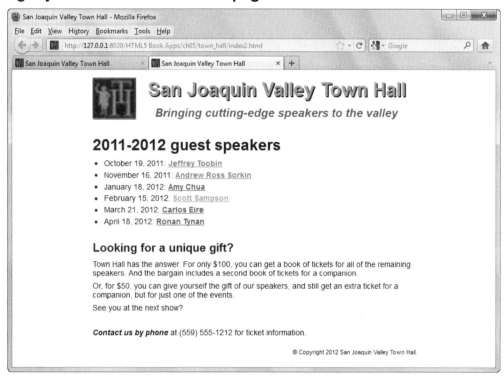

The CSS for this version of the page

```css
/* the reset selector */
* {
    margin: 0;
    padding: 0; }

/* just the styles for the elements that provide margins or padding */
body {
    font-family: Arial, Helvetica, sans-serif;
    font-size: 87.5%;
    width: 600px;
    margin: 1em auto; }

h1, h2 { margin-bottom: .25em; }

ul { margin: 0 0 1.5em 1.25em; }
li {
    padding-bottom: .35em;
    padding-left: .25em; }
p { padding: .25em 0; }

section h1 {
    font-size: 200%;
    margin-top: 1em; }
#contact_us { margin-top: 1.5em; }
footer { margin-top: 1em; }
```

Figure 5-8   A version of the CSS that uses a reset selector

How to set borders and backgrounds

Now that you know how to size and space elements using the box model, you're ready to learn how to apply other formatting to boxes. That includes adding borders and setting background colors and images.

How to set borders

Figure 5-9 presents the properties for setting *borders* and illustrates how they work. To start, if you want the same border on all four sides of a box, you can use the shorthand border property. This property lets you set the width, style, and color for the borders. This is illustrated in the first set of examples in this figure.

Here, the first rule creates a thin, solid, green border. Note that different browsers interpret the thin keyword, as well as the other keywords for width, differently. Because of that, you'll typically set the width of a border to an absolute value as shown in the second and third rules. Notice that the third rule doesn't specify a color. In that case, the border will be the same color as the element's text.

To set the border for just one side of a box, you can use the shorthand property for a border side. This is illustrated by the second set of examples. Here, the first rule sets the top border and the second rule sets the right border.

Most of the time, you'll use the shorthand properties to set all four borders or just one border of a box. However, you can use the other properties in this figure to set the width, styles, and colors of the sides of a border. This is illustrated by the last four groups of examples in this figure. You may want to use these properties to override another border setting for an element.

For instance, to set the width for each side of a border, you can use the border-width property as shown in the third set of examples. Here, you can specify one, two, three, or four values. This works just like the shorthand margin and padding properties you learned about earlier in this chapter. That means that the values are applied to the top, right, bottom, and left sides of the border.

The border-style and border-color properties are similar. You can use them to set the style and color for each side of a border by specifying one to four values. This is illustrated in the fourth and fifth sets of examples in this figure. Notice in the last example for the border-style property that the left and right borders are set to "none". That way, only the top and bottom borders will be displayed.

Properties for setting borders

Property	Description
`border`	A border width, border style, and border color. The values are applied to all sides of the border.
`border-side`	Border width, style, and color values for the specified side of a border.
`border-width`	One to four relative or absolute values (excluding a percent) or keywords that specify the widths for each side of a border. Possible keywords are thin, medium, and thick.
`border-style`	One to four keywords that specify the styles for each side of a border. Possible values are dotted, dashed, solid, double, groove, ridge, inset, outset, and none. The default is none.
`border-color`	One to four color values or keywords that specify the color for each side of a border. The default is the color of the element.
`border-side-width`	A relative or absolute value (excluding a percent) or a keyword that specifies the width of the indicated side of a border.
`border-side-style`	A keyword that specifies the style for the indicated side of a border.
`border-side-color`	A color value or keyword that specifies the color of the indicated side of a border.

The syntax for the shorthand border and border-*side* properties

```
border: [width] [style] [color];
border-side: [width] [style] [color];
```

How to set border properties

```
border: thin solid green;
border: 2px dashed #808080;
border: 1px inset;            /* uses the element's color property */
```

How to set side borders

```
border-top: 2px solid black;
border-right: 4px double blue;
```

How to set the widths of borders

```
border-width: 1px;              /* all four sides */
border-width: 1px 2px;          /* top and bottom 1px, right and left 2px */
border-width: 1px 2px 2px;      /* top 1px, right and left 2px, bottom 2px */
border-width: 1px 2px 2px 3px;  /* top 1px, right 2px, bottom 2px, left 3px */
```

How to set the style of borders

```
border-style: dashed;     /* dashed line all sides */
border-style: solid none; /* solid top and bottom, no border right and left */
```

How to set the color of borders

```
border-color: #808080;
border-color: black gray; /* black top and bottom, gray right and left */
```

How to set the width, style, and color of border sides

```
border-bottom-width: 4px;
border-right-style: dashed;
border-left-color: gray;
```

Figure 5-9   How to set borders

How to use CSS3 to add rounded corners and shadows to borders

Figure 5-10 shows how to use the CSS3 features for adding *rounded corners* and *shadows* to borders. This lets you supply these graphic effects without using images. These features are currently supported by all modern browsers. But if an older browser doesn't support them, it just ignores them, which is usually okay. That's why you can start using these features right away.

To round the corners, you use the border-radius property that's summarized in this figure. If you supply one value for it, it applies to all four corners of the border. But if you supply four values as in the example, you can apply specific rounding to each corner. Here, the upper-left corner has a 10 pixel radius, the upper-right corner has a 20 pixel radius, the lower-right corner has a zero radius so it isn't rounded, and the lower-left corner has a 20 pixel radius.

To add shadows to a border, you use the box-shadow property. This works much like the text-shadow property that you learned about in the last chapter. With the first two values, you specify the offset for the shadow. With the third value, you can specify the blur radius. With the fourth value, you specify how far the blur is spread. And with the fifth value, you can specify a different color for the shadow than the one for the border. To get the effects that you want, you usually need to experiment with these values, but this is easier than using an image to get those effects.

Although all modern browsers support these features, you can also provide backward compatibility for older browsers by using the properties that are summarized in the compatibility guidelines in this figure. For instance, you can get these features to work in older Firefox browsers by using the border-radius and box-shadow properties with -moz- as the prefix. And you can get the box-shadow property to work in older Safari and Chrome browsers by using -webkit- as the prefix.

Incidentally, there are some options for these features that aren't presented in this figure. For instance, you can use a separate property like border-top-left-radius for each corner. You can also set the curvature of a corner by supplying two values for a single corner like this:

```
border-top-left-radius: 50px 20px;
```

So, if you want to go beyond what this figure offers, please refer to the W3C documentation.

The syntax for the border-radius and box-shadow properties

```
border-radius: radius;  /* applies to all four corners */
border-radius: topLeft topRight lowerRight lowerLeft;
box-shadow: horizontalOffset verticalOffset blurRadius spread color;
```

The HTML for a section

```
<section>
    <a href="ebooks_index.html">$10 Ebooks!</a>
</section>
```

The CSS for the section

```
section {
    padding: 20px;
    width: 160px;
    border: 5px double blue;
    color: blue;
    font-size: 200%;
    text-align: center;
    font-weight: bold;
    border-radius: 10px 20px 0 20px;
    box-shadow: 3px 3px 4px 4px red;
}
```

The section in a browser

Guidelines for backward compatibility

- To round corners and add shadows in older versions of Firefox, you can use the -moz-border-radius and -moz-box-shadow properties.
- To add shadows in older versions of Safari and Chrome, you can use the -webkit-box-shadow property.

Discussion

- When you code the border-radius property, you can assign one rounding radius to all four corners or a different radius to each corner.
- When you code the box-shadow property, positive values offset the shadow to the right or down, and negative values offset the shadow to the left or up.
- The third value in the box-shadow property determines how much the shadow is blurred, and the fourth value determines how far the blur is spread.
- The fifth value in the box-shadow property specifies the color of the shadow. If this is omitted, it is the same color as the border.
- These properties are supported by all modern browsers. If they aren't supported by a browser, they are ignored, which is usually okay.

Figure 5-10   How to use CSS3 to add rounded corners and shadows to borders

How to set background colors and images

Figure 5-11 presents the properties you can use to set the *background* for a box. When you set a background, it's displayed behind the content, padding, and border for the box, but it isn't displayed behind the margin.

When you specify a background, you can set a background color, a background image, or both. If you set both, the browser displays the background color behind the image. As a result, you can only see the background color if the image has areas that are transparent or the image doesn't repeat.

As this figure shows, you can set all five properties of a background by using the shorthand background property. When you use this property, you don't have to specify the individual properties in a specific order, but it usually makes sense to use the order that's shown. If you omit one or more properties, the browser uses their default values.

The first set of examples illustrates how this works. Here, the first rule sets the background color to blue, the second rule sets the background color and specifies the URL for an image, and the third rule specifies all five background properties. You can also code each of these properties individually.

By default, the background color for a box is transparent. As a result, you can see through the box to the color that's behind it, which is usually what you want. Otherwise, you need to set the color. The first rule in the second set of examples shows how to do that using the background-color property.

If you want to display a background image, you need to specify a URL that points to the file for the image. You can do that using the background-image property as shown in the second rule in the second set of examples.

If you add a background image to a box, it will repeat horizontally and vertically to fill the box by default. This works well for small images that are intended to be tiled across or down a box. If you want to change this behavior, you can set the background-repeat property so the image is only repeated horizontally, so it's only repeated vertically, or so it isn't repeated at all. This is illustrated by the first four rules in the last set of examples.

If an image doesn't repeat horizontally and vertically, you may need to set additional properties to determine where the image is positioned and whether it scrolls with the page. By default, an image is positioned in the top left corner of the box. To change that, you use the background-position property. This property lets you specify both a horizontal and a vertical position.

The next three rules illustrate how this works. The first rule positions the image at the top left corner of the box, which is the default. The second rule centers the image at the top of the box. And the third rule positions the image starting 90% of the way from the left side to the right side of the box and 90% of the way from the top to the bottom of the box.

In most cases, you'll want a background image to scroll as you scroll the box that contains it. For example, if you use a background image for an entire page and the page is larger than the browser window, you'll usually want the image to scroll as you scroll through the page. If not, you can set the background-attachment property to "fixed".

The properties for setting the background color and image

Property	Description
`background`	Background color, image, repeat, attachment, and position values.
`background-color`	A color value or keyword that specifies the color of an element's background. You can also specify the transparent keyword if you want elements behind the element to be visible. This is the default.
`background-image`	A relative or absolute URL that points to the image. You can also specify the keyword none if you don't want to display an image. This is the default.
`background-repeat`	A keyword that specifies if and how an image is repeated. Possible values are repeat, repeat-x, repeat-y, no-repeat. The default is repeat, which causes the image to be repeated both horizontally and vertically to fill the background.
`background-attachment`	A keyword that specifies whether an image scrolls with the document or remains in a fixed position. Possible values are scroll and fixed. The default is scroll.
`background-position`	One or two relative or absolute values or keywords that specify the initial horizontal and vertical positions of an image. Keywords are left, center, and right; top, center, and bottom. If a vertical position isn't specified, center is the default. If no position is specified, the default is to place the image at the top-left corner of the element.

The syntax for the shorthand background property

```
background: [color] [image] [repeat] [attachment] [position];
```

How to use the shorthand property

```
background: blue;
background: blue url("../images/texture.gif");
background: #808080 url("../images/header.jpg") repeat-y scroll center top;
```

How to set the background color and image with separate properties

```
background-color: blue;
background-image: url("../images/texture.gif");
```

How to control image repetition, position, and scrolling

```
background-repeat: repeat;        /* repeats both directions */
background-repeat: repeat-x;      /* repeats horizontally */
background-repeat: repeat-y;      /* repeats vertically */
background-repeat: no-repeat;     /* doesn't repeat */

background-position: left top;    /* 0% from left, 0% from top */
background-position: center top;  /* centered horizontally, 0% from top */
background-position: 90% 90%;     /* 90% from left, 90% from top */

background-attachment: scroll;    /* image moves as you scroll */
background-attachment: fixed;     /* image does not move as you scroll */
```

Accessibility guideline

- Don't use a background color or image that makes the text that's over it difficult to read.

Figure 5-11   How to set background colors and images

How to use CSS3 to set background gradients

Figure 5-12 shows the basics of how to use the new CSS3 feature for *linear gradients*. Here again, this feature lets you provide interesting backgrounds without using images. And if a browser doesn't support this feature, it just ignores it, which is usually okay.

At present, all modern browsers support this feature except IE9. However, the browsers support this feature with properties that are prefixed by -moz- for Firefox, -webkit- for Safari and Chrome, and -o- for Opera. Eventually, though, these prefixes will be dropped. For simplicity, the examples in this figure only use the –moz- prefix, but all of the prefixes are used in figure 5-15.

If you study the examples in this figure, you'll start to see how this feature works. In the first example, the color goes from left to right; the first color is white starting at the far left (0%), and the second color is red ending at the far right (100%). Then, CSS provides the gradient from left to right when the page is rendered.

In the second example, the direction is 45 degrees and there are three color groups. Red starts at the far left (0%). White is in the middle (50%). And blue is on the right (100%). Then, CSS provides the gradients when the page is rendered.

In the third coding example, after the browser display, you can see how to code solid stripes. Here, both a starting and ending point is given for each color. The result is three solid stripes of red, white, and blue at a 45 degree angle.

If you experiment with this feature, you'll see the interesting effects that you can get with it. But you can take this feature even further. For complete details, please refer to the W3C documentation.

The syntax for using a linear gradient in the background-image property

```
background-image:
    linear-gradient(direction, color %, color %, ... );
```

The HTML for two divisions

```
<div id="eg1"></div>
<div id="eg2"></div>
```

The CSS for the two divisions using Mozilla prefixes (-moz-)

```
#eg1 {
    background-image: -moz-linear-gradient(left, white 0%, red 100%); }
#eg2 {
    background-image: -moz-linear-gradient(
        45deg, red 0%, white 50%, blue 100%); }
```

The linear gradients in a browser

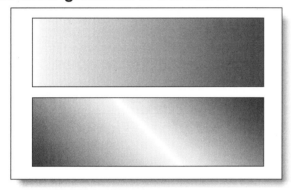

A background-image property that creates red, white, and blue stripes

```
background-image:
    -moz-linear-gradient(45deg, red 0%, red 33%, white 33%, white 66%,
                         blue 66%, blue 100%)
```

Discussion

*   The CSS3 for *linear gradients* lets you create gradients for backgrounds without using images. That's why this feature will be useful when it's fully implemented.

*   Today, all of the current browsers except IE9 support linear gradients. However, they implement them with their own prefixes: -moz- for Mozilla Firefox, -webkit- for WebKit browsers like Safari and Chrome, and -o- for Opera. Later, when the final CSS3 specification is set, these prefixes will be removed.

*   The first parameter of a linear gradient indicates the direction the gradient will go: left for left to right, top for top to bottom, right for right to left, bottom for bottom to top, and a number of degrees if the gradient should be on an angle.

*   The direction is followed by two or more parameters that consist of a color and a percent. The first percent indicates where the first color should start, the last percent indicates where the last color should end, and the percents in between indicate the points at which one gradient stops and the next one starts.

Figure 5-12   How to use CSS3 to set background gradients

A web page that uses borders and backgrounds

Figure 5-13 presents a web page that's similar to the one in figure 5-6. In fact, the HTML for these two pages is identical. However, the page in this figure has some additional formatting.

First, this page uses a gradient for the background behind the body. It also uses white as the background color for the body. That way, the gradient doesn't show behind the body content.

Second, this page has a border around the body with rounded corners and shadows. Also, the header has a border below it, and the footer has a border above it.

Third, the shadow for the text in the h1 element of the heading has been adjusted so the shadow is black and there is no blur. This makes this heading easier to read.

The HTML for the web page

The HTML is identical to the HTML for the page shown in figure 5-6. If you want to review this HTML, you can open the HTML for this application in your text editor.

A web page that uses borders and a background gradient

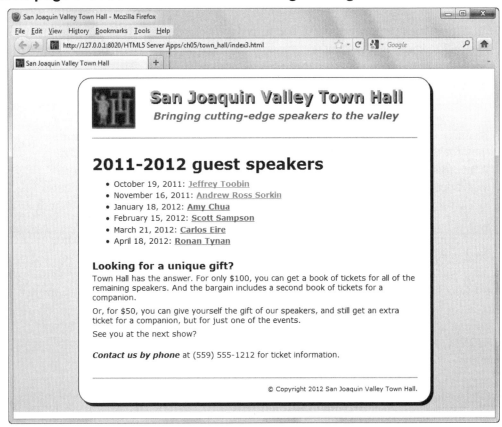

Description

- The HTML for this web page is the same as for figure 5-6.
- The styles for this web page include a border around the page content, a border below the header, and a border above the footer.
- The border around the body of the page has rounded corners and a drop shadow, and the background behind the body is a linear gradient. If you use a browser that doesn't support these CSS3 features, they will be ignored.

Figure 5-13   A web page that uses borders and a linear gradient for the background

The CSS for the web page

Figure 5-14 presents the CSS for the web page in figure 5-13. In this case, I've highlighted the rules that are different from the ones in figure 5-7. Although you should be able to understand this code without any help, here are some points that you should note.

First, a gradient is used for the background image of the html element. This is the gradient that you see on the top, bottom, and sides of the body element. To make this work in all browsers, the gradient is coded four times: one time each for the -moz-, -webkit-, and -o- prefixes, and one time without a prefix. When this rule set is rendered by a browser, the browser will ignore any rules that it doesn't recognize and render the first rule that it does recognize. When all of the browsers drop their prefixes, the last rule is the one that the browsers will execute.

Second, the background color of the body of the document is set to white. That way, the contents of the page will be displayed on a white background. Also, the top and bottom margins for the body are set to 15px, which lets the gradient show above and below the body, and the right and left margins are set to auto, which centers the body in the browser window. Next, the top and bottom padding for the body is set to 15px and the left and right padding is set to 25px. Then, a border with rounded corners and a shadow is added to the body.

Third, a border has been added below the header and above the footer. For the footer, the top margin is 2 ems, which is the space above the border, and top padding is .7 ems, which is the space between the border and the paragraph below it.

Last, the text-shadow property for the header h1 selector has been changed so there is no blur and the shadow is black. If you compare this heading in figure 5-13 with the one in figure 5-6, I think you'll agree that it's easier to read.

If you want the rounded corners and shadows to work in older browsers, you could add the prefixed properties that are described in the compatibility guidelines in figure 5-10. But if the body corners aren't rounded and shadowed, there will be little effect on the user experience. Also, the percentage of older browsers goes down every year so this is less of an issue each year. As a result, there is little to be gained by adding these properties to the code.

The CSS for the web page

```css
/* the styles that provide the background behind the body */
html {
    background-image: -moz-linear-gradient(top, white 0%, #facd8a 100%);
    background-image: -webkit-linear-gradient(top, white 0%, #facd8a 100%);
    background-image: -o-linear-gradient(top, white 0%, #facd8a 100%);
    background-image: linear-gradient(top, white 0%, #facd8a 100%);
}
/* the styles for the body that is centered and bordered */
body {
    font-family: Verdana, Arial, Helvetica, sans-serif;
    font-size: 87.5%;
    width: 600px;
    background-color: white;
    margin: 15px auto;
    padding: 15px 25px;
    border: 1px solid black;
    border-radius: 25px;
    box-shadow: 5px 5px 0 0;
}

/* the styles for the other type selectors are the same as in figure 5-7 */

/* the styles for the header */
header {
      padding-bottom: 2em;
    border-bottom: 2px solid #ef9c00; }
header img { float: left; }
header h1 {
    color: #ef9c00;
    text-align: center;
    text-shadow: 2px 3px 0 black;
    margin-bottom: .25em; }
header h2 {
    color: green;
    font-style: italic;
    text-align: center; }

/* the styles for the section */
section { clear: left; }
section h1 {
      font-size: 200%;
      margin: 1em 0 .35em; }
section a.date_passed  { color: gray; }
#contact_us { margin-top: 1em; }

/* the styles for the footer */
footer {
    margin-top: 2em;
    border-top: 2px solid #ef9c00;
    padding-top: .7em; }
footer p {
      font-size: 80%;
      text-align: right; }
```

Figure 5-14   The CSS for the web page

Perspective

Now that you've completed this chapter, you should understand how the box model is used for margins, padding, borders, backgrounds, and background images. As a result, you should be able to get the spacing, borders, and backgrounds for your web pages just the way you want them.

In the next chapter, though, you'll learn how to use CSS for laying out the elements on a page in two- and three-column arrangements with both headers and footers. That will complete your crash course in HTML and CSS.

Terms

box model	reset selector
padding	border
margin	background
fixed layout	rounded corners
containing block	shadows
shorthand property	linear gradient
collapsed margins	

Summary

- The CSS *box model* refers to the box that a browser places around each block element as well as some inline elements. Each box includes the content of the element, plus optional padding, borders, and margins.

- To set the height and width of a content area, you can use absolute measurements like pixels or relative measurements like percents. If you use a percent, the percent applies to the block that contains the box you're formatting.

- You can set the *margins* for all four sides of a box. Because different browsers have different default values for margins, it's good to set the margins explicitly.

- If you specify a bottom margin for one element and a top margin for the element that follows, the margins are *collapsed* to the size of the largest margin.

- Like margins, you can set the *padding* for all four sides of a box. One way to avoid margin collapse is to set the margins to zero and use padding for the spacing.

- A *border* can be placed on any of the sides of a box. That border goes on the outside of the padding for the box and inside any margins, and you can set the width, style, and color for a border.

- When you set the *background* for a box, it is displayed behind the content, padding, and border for the box, but not behind the margins. The background can consist of a color, an image, or both.

- You can use CSS3 to *round corners* and add *shadows* to borders. You can also use CSS3 to provide *linear gradients* as backgrounds.

Exercise 5-1   Enhance the Town Hall home page

In this exercise, you'll enhance the formatting of the Town Hall home page that you formatted in exercise 4-1. When you're through, the page should look like this:

San Joaquin Valley Town Hall
Celebrating our 75th Year

Our Mission

San Joaquin Valley Town Hall is a non-profit organization that is run by an all-volunteer board of directors. Our mission is to bring nationally and internationally renowned, thought-provoking speakers who inform, educate, and entertain our audience! As one or our members told us:

> *"Each year I give a ticket package to each of our family members. I think of it as the gift of knowledge...and that is priceless."*

Our Ticket Package

- Season Package: $95
- Patron Package: $200
- Single Speaker: $25

Our 2011-2012 Speakers

October 19, 2011
Jeffrey Toobin

November 16, 2011
Andrew Ross Sorkin

January 18, 2012
Amy Chua

© 2012, San Joaquin Valley Town Hall, Fresno, CA 93755

Open the HTML and CSS files and start enhancing the CSS

1. Use your text editor to open the HTML and CSS files that you created for exercise 4-1:

   ```
   c:\html5_css3\exercises\town_hall_1\index.html
   c:\html5_css3\exercises\town_hall_1\styles\main.css
   ```

2. Enhance the rule set for the body, by setting the width to 600 pixels, setting the top and bottom margins to 0 and the right and left margins to auto, and adding a 3-pixel, solid border with #800000 as its color. Then, test this change in Firefox. If the page isn't centered with a border, make the required corrections.

3. Add one more rule to the body that sets the background color to #fffded. Then, test this change, and note that the entire window is set to the background color, not just the body.

4. To fix this, code a rule set for the html element that sets the background color to white. Then, test to make sure that worked.

Add the other borders

From this point on, test each change in Firefox right after you make it.

5. Add a bottom border to the header and a top border to the footer. Both borders should be the same as the border around the body.

6. You should already have a rule set that uses an id selector to select this heading: "Our 2011-2012 Speakers". Find it, and delete any rules that it contains. Then, code rules that add top and bottom borders to this heading. Both borders should be the same as the borders for the header and footer.

Get the padding right for the header, section, and footer

At this point, you have all of the borders and colors the way they should be, so you just need to set the margins and padding. In the steps that follow, you'll start by adding a reset selector to the CSS file. Then, with one exception, you'll use padding to get the spacing right.

7. Add a reset selector like the one in figure 5-8 to the CSS file. When you test this change, the page won't look good at all because the default margins and padding for all of the elements have been removed.

8. For the header, add 1.5 ems of padding at the top and bottom. Then, delete the text-indent rules for the h1 and h2 elements in the header, and add 30 pixels of padding to the right and left of the image in the header. When you test these changes, and you'll see that the heading looks much better.

9. For the section, add 2 ems of padding to the right and left.

Get the padding right for the headings and text

10. In the section, set the padding for the headings and text as follows:

Element	Padding
h1	.5em top, .25em bottom
h2	.25em bottom
img	1em bottom
p	.5em bottom
blockquote	2em right and left
ul	1.5em bottom, 1.25em left
li	.35em bottom

11. Set the padding for the top and bottom of the footer to 1em.

12. Test these changes in Firefox. At this point, everything should look right except that there isn't enough space between the bottom border of the 2011-2012 Speakers heading and the date that follows it. One way to fix this is to add a .75em bottom margin to the Speakers heading, which will add space below the bottom border. Try that.

Add the finishing touches and test in IE

13. Italicize the blockquote element to make it stand out.

14. Add a linear gradient as the background for the header. The one that's shown uses #800000, #fffded, white, #ffded, and #800000 as its five colors at a 30 degree angle. But experiment with this until you get it the way you want it.

15. Do one final test to make sure that the page looks like the one at the start of this exercise. Then, experiment on your own to see if you can improve the formatting. For instance, you may want to add some space between the author names and their images.

16. When you're through experimenting, test the page in IE. There the text shadow and the linear gradient may not work because they still aren't supported. But if you see any other problems, fix them and test again in both Firefox and IE.

Exercise 5-2   Add rounded corners and box shadows to the Speakers heading

Use CSS to add a double border with rounded corners and box shadows to the Speakers heading so it looks like this:

This should work in both Firefox and IE.

6

How to use CSS for page layout

In this chapter, you'll learn how to use CSS to control the layout of a page. That means that you can control where each of the HTML elements appear on the page. When you finish this chapter, you should be able to implement sophisticated 2- and 3-column page layouts.

How to float elements in 2- and 3-column layouts

To create a page layout with two or three columns, you usually float the elements that make up the columns of the page. You'll learn how to do that in the topics that follow.

How to float and clear elements

By default, the block elements defined in an HTML document flow from the top of the page to the bottom of the page, and inline elements flow from the left side of the block elements that contain them to the right side. When you *float* an element, though, it's taken out of the flow of the document. Because of that, any elements that follow the floated element flow into the space that's left by the floated element.

Figure 6-1 presents the basic skills for floating an element on a web page. To do that, you use the float property to specify whether you want the element floated to the left or to the right. You also have to set the width of the floated element. In the example, the aside is 150 pixels wide, and it is floated to the right. As a result, the section that follows flows into the space to the left of the aside.

Although you can use the float property with any block element, you can also use it with some inline elements. In chapter 4, for example, you learned how to float an image in the header of a document. When you float an img element, you don't have to set the width property because an image always has a default size.

By default, any content that follows a floated element in an HTML document will fill in the space to the side of the floated element. That includes block elements as well as inline elements.

However, if you want to stop the flow of elements into the space beside a floated element, you can use the clear property. In this example, this property is used to stop the footer from flowing into the space next to the aside. The value for this property can be left, right, or both, and either right or both will work if the element ahead of it is floated to the right. Similarly, left or both will work if the element ahead of it is floated to the left.

The properties for floating and clearing elements

Property	Description
float	A keyword that determines how an element is floated. Possible values are left, right, and none. None is the default.
clear	Determines whether an element is cleared from flowing into the space left by a floated element. Possible values are left, right, both, and none (the default).

The HTML for a web page with a sidebar

```
<body>
    <aside>
        <p>The luncheon starts 15 minutes after the lecture ends</p>
    </aside>
    <section>
        <p>Welcome to San Joaquin Valley Town Hall. We have some fascinating
            speakers for you this season!</p>
    </section>
    <footer>
        <p>Please call today at (559) 555-1212 to get your tickets!</p>
    </footer>
</body>
```

The CSS for the web page for floating the sidebar

```
body { width: 500px; }
section, aside, footer {
    margin: 0;
    padding: 0px 20px; }
aside {
    margin: 0 20px 10px;
    width: 150px;
    float: right;
    border: 1px solid black; }
footer { clear: both; }
```

The web page in a browser

Welcome to San Joaquin Valley Town Hall. We have some fascinating speakers for you this season!

The luncheon starts 15 minutes after the lecture ends

Please call today at (559) 555-1212 to get your tickets!

Description

- When you *float* an element to the right or left, the content that follows flows around it.
- When you use the float property for an element, you also need to set its width.
- To stop the floating before an element, use the clear property.
- In the example above, if the clear property for the footer isn't set, its content will flow into the space beside the floated element.

Figure 6-1   How to float and clear elements

How to use floating
in a 2-column, fixed-width layout

Figure 6-2 shows how floating can be used to create a 2-column, fixed-width page layout. Here, the HTML consists of four elements: header, section, aside, and footer.

In the CSS, you can see that the width is set for the body, section, and aside. Here, the width of the body must be the sum of the widths of the section and aside, plus the widths of any margins, padding, or borders for the section and aside. Since the right border for the section is 2 pixels and neither the section nor aside have margins or padding, the width of the body is 962 pixels (360 + 600 + 2).

After you set up the widths for the body and columns, you create the columns by floating the section to the left and the aside to the right. This will work whether the section or aside is coded first in the HTML.

Another alternative is to float both the section and aside to the left. But then, the section must come first in the HTML. In that case, though, the aside doesn't need to be floated at all. That's because the natural behavior of the aside is to flow into the space left by the floated section that's ahead of it in the HTML.

A 2-column web page with fixed-width columns

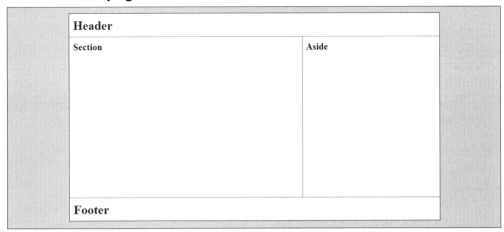

The HTML for the page

```
<body>
    <header><h1>Header</h1></header>
    <section><h1>Section</h1></section>
    <aside><h1>Aside</h1></aside>
    <footer><h1>Footer</h1></footer>
</body>
```

The CSS for the page

```
* { margin: 0; padding: 0; }
body {
    width: 962px;
    background-color: white;
    margin: 15px auto;
    border: 1px solid black; }
h1 { padding: 10px; }

header { border-bottom: 2px solid #ef9c00; }
section {
    height: 400px;      /* to give the sidebar some height for its border */
    width: 600px;
    float: left;
    border-right: 2px solid #ef9c00;
    float: left; }
aside {
    width: 360px;
    float: right; }
footer {
    clear: both;
    border-top: 2px solid #ef9c00; }
```

Description

- The section is floated to the left and the aside is floated to the right. Then, it doesn't matter whether the aside comes before or after the section in the HTML.

- Another alternative is to float both the section and the aside to the left, but then the section has to be coded before the aside in the HTML.

Figure 6-2   How to use floating in a 2-column, fixed-width layout

How to use floating in a 2-column, liquid layout

Instead of creating a *fixed layout* like the one in figure 6-2, you can create a *liquid layout*. With a liquid layout, the width of the page changes as the user changes the width of the browser window. Also, the width of one or more columns within the page changes.

The key to creating a liquid layout is using percents to specify the widths of one or more elements. This is illustrated by figure 6-3. In both of these examples, the width of the page is set to 90%. That means that the page will always occupy 90% of the browser window, no matter how wide the window is. Of course, you can omit the width property entirely if you want the page to occupy 100% of the browser window.

In the first example, the widths of the section and aside are set to percents. This means that the widths of both columns will change if the user changes the width of the browser window. In this case, since the section has a 2-pixel right border, the sum of the widths of the section and aside is 99%, not 100%. However, if there wasn't a border, the sum could be 100%.

In the second example, the width of the aside is set to 360 pixels and no width is specified for the section. That way, if the user changes the width of the browser window, the width of the section will change so it occupies the width of the page minus the width of the aside. In this case, the border is applied to the left of the aside rather than to the right of the section because it's the width of the aside that's fixed.

As you decide whether to use a fixed or a liquid layout, your main consideration should be the content of the page. If the page consists of a lot of text, you probably won't want to use a liquid layout. That's because a page becomes more difficult to read as the length of a line of text gets longer. On the other hand, if you want the users to be able to use their browsers to increase the size of the text on a page, you might want to use a liquid layout. Then, the users can adjust the size of their browser windows to get the optimal line length for reading.

A 2-column web page with liquid widths for both columns

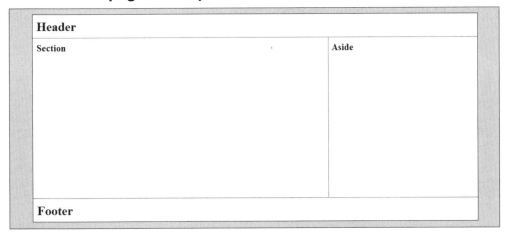

The CSS for the page when both columns are liquid

```
body {
    width: 90%;
    background-color: white;
    margin: 15px auto;
    border: 1px solid black; }
section {
    width: 66%;
    height: 400px;          /* to give this section some height */
    border-right: 2px solid #ef9c00;
    float: left; }
aside {
    width: 33%;
    float: right; }
```

The CSS for the page when the aside is fixed and the section is liquid

```
body {
    width: 90%;
    background-color: white;
    margin: 15px auto;
    border: 1px solid black; }
section {
    float: left; }
aside {
    height: 400px;          /* to give this aside some height */
    width: 360px;
    border-left: 2px solid #ef9c00;
    float: right; }
```

Description

- The benefit of using liquid column sizes is that the size of the page is adjusted to the resolution of the browser.

- The disadvantage is that changing the size of the columns may affect the typography or the appearance of the page.

Figure 6-3   How to use floating in a 2-column liquid layout

How to use floating
in a 3-column, fixed-width layout

Figure 6-4 shows how to take floating to one more level and thus create a 3-column, fixed-width page layout. Here, the width of the body is 964 pixels, which is the sum of the two sidebars, the section, and the two sidebar borders. Once those widths are set up, the first sidebar is floated to the left. The section is floated to the left. And the second sidebar is floated to the right.

One of the keys here is getting the widths right. If, for example, you set the body width to 960 pixels instead of 964 pixels, the two sidebars and the section won't fit into the width of the body. In that case, the section will flow beneath the left sidebar.

A 3-column web page with fixed-width columns

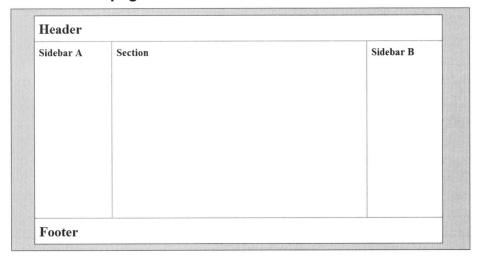

The HTML for the page

```
<body>
    <header><h1>Header</h1></header>
    <aside id="sidebarA"><h1>Sidebar A</h1></aside>
    <section><h1>Section</h1></section>
    <aside id="sidebarB"><h1>Sidebar B</h1></aside>
    <footer><h1>Footer</h1></footer>
</body>
```

The critical CSS for the page

```
body {
    width: 964px;
    background-color: white;
    margin: 15px auto;
    border: 1px solid black; }
#sidebarA {
    width: 180px;
    height: 400px;        /* to give the sidebar some height for its border */
    float: left;
    border-right: 2px solid #ef9c00; }
section {
    width: 600px;
    float: left; }
#sidebarB {
    width: 180px;
    height: 400px;        /* to give the sidebar some height for its border */
    float: right;
    border-left: 2px solid #ef9c00; }
```

Description

- The first aside is floated to the left; the section is floated to the left; and the second aside is floated to the right.

- You could get the same result by floating both asides and the section to the left.

Figure 6-4   How to use floating in a 3-column, fixed-width layout

Two web pages that use a 2-column, fixed-width layout

To show how floating works in a more realistic application, the next topics present two pages of a web site along with their HTML and CSS.

The home page

Figure 6-5 shows the home page for the Town Hall web site. It uses a 2-column, fixed-width layout. Except for the aside, this is the same content that you saw in the page at the end of the last chapter. It's just formatted a little differently.

A home page with a sidebar floated to the right of a section

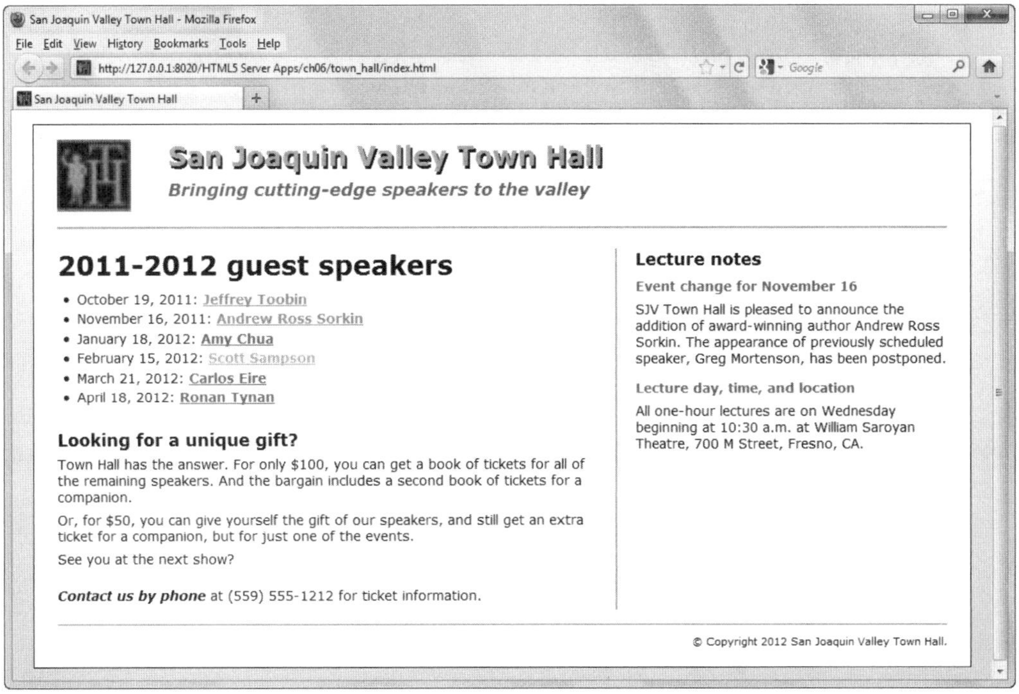

Description

- This web page illustrates a common page layout that includes a header, two columns, and a footer.
- The columns for this page are coded as a section element and an aside element.
- The columns are created by floating the aside element to the right so the section element that follows it in the HTML flows to its left.
- The image in the heading is floated to the left so it appears to the left of the h1 and h2 elements that follow it.
- A bottom border is applied to the header, and a top border is applied to the footer.
- A right border is applied to the section, not the aside, because the section content is longer than the aside content.
- If a left border was applied to the aside element, it would only be as long as the content in the aside.

Figure 6-5 A 2-column, fixed-width home page

The HTML for the home page

Figure 6-6 presents the HTML for this web page. Here, the only new content is in the aside. Note that the aside is coded before the section. Then, if the aside is floated to the right, the section will flow beside it.

Before looking at the CSS, take a minute to note the use of the HTML5 semantic elements. The header and footer start and end the HTML. The aside and section provide the content for the two columns. And the nav element within the section marks the navigation list. That helps make this code easy to understand.

The HTML for the home page (index.html)

```
<head>
    .
    <link rel="stylesheet" href="styles/main.css">
</head>
<body>
    <header>
        <img src="images/logo.jpg" alt="Town Hall Logo" width="80">
        <hgroup>
            <h1>San Joaquin Valley Town Hall</h1>
            <h2>Bringing cutting-edge speakers to the valley</h2>
        </hgroup>
    </header>
    <aside>
        <h1>Lecture notes</h1>
        <h2>Event change for November 16</h2>
        <p>SJV Town Hall is pleased to announce the addition of award-winning
            author Andrew Ross Sorkin. The appearance of previously scheduled
            speaker, Greg Mortenson, has been postponed.</p>
        <h2>Lecture day, time, and location</h2>
        <p>All one-hour lectures are on Wednesday beginning at 10:30 a.m. at
            William Saroyan Theatre, 700 M Street, Fresno, CA.</p>
    </aside>
    <section>
        <h1>2011-2012 guest speakers</h1>
        <nav>
            <ul>
                <li>October 19, 2011: <a class="date_passed"
                    href="speakers/toobin.html">Jeffrey Toobin</a></li>
                    .
                    .
                <li>February 15, 2012: <a href="sampson.html">
                    Scott Sampson</a></li>
                <li>March 21, 2012: <a href="speakers/eire.html">
                    Carlos Eire</a></li>
                <li>April 18, 2012: <a href="speakers/tynan.html">
                    Ronan Tynan</a></li>
            </ul>
        </nav>
        <h2>Looking for a unique gift?</h2>
        <p>Town Hall has the answer. For only $100, you can get
            a book of tickets for all of the remaining speakers. And the
            bargain includes a second book of tickets for a companion.</p>
        <p>Or, for $50, you can give yourself the gift of our speakers, and
            still get an extra ticket for a companion, but for just one of the
            events.</p>
        <p>See you at the next show?</p>
        <p id="contact_us"><em>Contact us by phone</em> at (559) 555-1212 for
            ticket information.</p>
    </section>
    <footer>
        <p>&copy; Copyright 2012 San Joaquin Valley Town Hall.</p>
    </footer>
</body>
</html>
```

Figure 6-6   The HTML for the home page

The CSS for the home page

Figure 6-7 presents the CSS for this web page. Since you've already seen most of this code in the earlier figures, you shouldn't have much trouble following it. But here are a few highlights.

First, the width of the body is set to 962 pixels, but the width of the section is set to 580 pixels and the width of the aside is set to 340 pixels, or a total of 920 pixels. The other 42 pixels come from right padding for the section (20 pixels), the left padding for the aside (20 pixels), and the 2 pixels for the right section border.

Second, the left margins of the h1 and h2 elements in the header are set to 120 pixels instead of being centered as they were in previous examples. This sets them to the right of the image in the header, which has been floated to the left.

Third, both the aside and section are floated to the right, but you could float the section to the left. This would also work if you didn't float the section at all since the aside comes first in the HTML.

The CSS for the home page (main.css)

```
section, aside, h1, h2, p, ul {
    margin: 0;
    padding: 0; }
section, aside {
    margin-top: 1.5em;
    margin-bottom: 1em; }

/* the changes to the body element in figure 5-14 */
body {
    width: 962px;
    /* no border radius or box shadow */
}

/* the changes to the header styles in figure 5-14 */
header h1 {
    color: #ef9c00;
    text-shadow: 2px 3px 0 black;
    margin-left: 120px;
    margin-bottom: .25em; }
header h2 {
    color: green;
    font-style: italic;
    margin-left: 120px; }
header img { float: left; }

/* the styles for the section */
section {
    width: 580px;
    border-right: 2px solid #ef9c00;
    padding-right: 20px;
    float: right; }
section h1 { margin-bottom: .35em; }
section h2 { margin-bottom: .35em; }
#contact_us { margin-top: 1em; }
a.date_passed  { color: gray; }

/* the styles for the sidebar */
aside {
    width: 340px;
    float: right;
    padding-left: 20px; }
aside h1 {
    font-size: 125%;
    padding-bottom: .5em; }
aside h2 {
    font-size: 100%;
    color: green;
    padding-bottom: .5em; }
aside p {
    margin-bottom: .5em; }

/* the styles for the footer that have been added or changed */
footer {
    clear: both;
    margin-top: 1em;
    border-top: 2px solid #ef9c00; }
```

Figure 6-7   The CSS for the home page

The speaker page

Figure 6-8 shows the page that's displayed if you click on the fourth link of the home page. This page has the same header and footer as the home page, and it has a 2-column, fixed-width page layout like the one for the home page.

Unlike the home page, though, this page uses an article for its main content instead of a section. This is consistent with HTML5 semantics since the content is an article about the speaker. Within the article, an image of the speaker is floated to the left of the text.

A speaker page with a sidebar floated to the right of an article

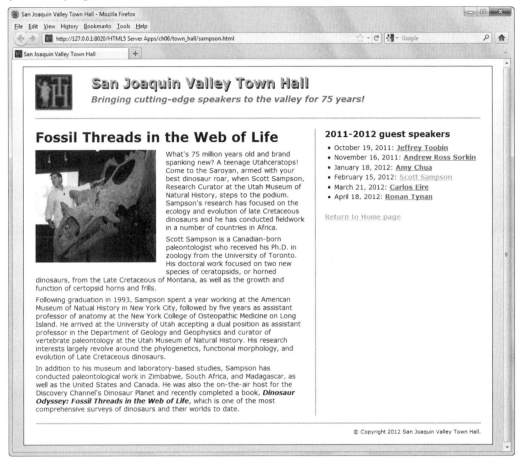

Description

- The columns for this page are coded as an article element and an aside element.
- The columns are created by floating the aside element to the right so the article element that follows it in the HTML flows to its left.
- The image in the article is floated to the left. In the HTML, the image is coded after the h1 element and before the <p> elements that make up the article.
- A right border is applied to the article, not the aside, because the article content is longer than the aside content.

Figure 6-8   A 2-column, fixed-width speaker page

The HTML for the speaker page

Figure 6-9 presents just the HTML changes for the speaker page. For instance, it doesn't include the header and footer elements because they are the same for the home page and the speaker pages.

To start, the link element refers to a different style sheet named speaker.css. This style sheet can be used for all of the speaker pages.

After that, you can see the contents for the aside, which includes a nav element. You can also see the contents for the article, which includes an h1 element, an img element, and several <p> elements.

The CSS for the speaker page

Figure 6-9 also presents the CSS changes for the speaker page. Otherwise, the CSS is the same as the CSS for the home page.

First, the margins and padding are set up for the article and the aside, just as they were for the section and aside of the home page. Then, the article is formatted just like the section of the home page. In addition, though, the img element within the article is floated to the left.

Like the home page, both the aside and article are floated to the right, but you could float the article to the left. This would also work if you didn't float the article at all.

Because the CSS for the home page (main.css) and the CSS for the speaker pages (speaker.css) are so much alike, you could combine the CSS into a single file. Often, though, it's easier to manage the CSS if you keep it in separate files. Then, if you want to modify the CSS for the speaker pages, you don't have to worry about affecting the home page.

The HTML changes for the speaker page (sampson.html)

```
<head>
    .
    <link rel="stylesheet" href="styles/speaker.css">
</head>
<aside>
    <h1>2011-2012 guest speakers</h1>
    <nav>
        <ul>
            <li>October 19, 2011: <a class="date_passed"
                href="speakers/toobin.html">Jeffrey Toobin</a></li>
            .
            .
            <li>April 18, 2012: <a href="speakers/tynan.html">
                Ronan Tynan</a></li>
        </ul>
        <p><a href="index.html">Return to Home page</a></p>
    </nav>
</aside>
<article>
    <h1>Fossil Threads in the Web of Life</h1>
    <img src="images/sampson_dinosaur.jpg" alt="Scott Sampson" width="260">
    <p>What's 75 million years old and brand spanking new? A teenage
        ...
        ...</p>
    <p>Scott Sampson is a Canadian-born paleontologist who received his
        ...
        ...</p>
    <p>Following graduation in 1993, Sampson spent a year working at the
        ...
        ...</p>
    <p>In addition to his museum and laboratory-based studies, Sampson has
        ...
        ...</p>
</article>
```

The CSS changes for the speaker page (speaker.css)

```
article, aside, h1, h2, p, ul {
    margin: 0;
    padding: 0; }
article, aside {
    margin-top: 1.5em;
    margin-bottom: 1em; }

/* the styles for the article */
article {
    width: 580px;
    border-right: 2px solid #ef9c00;
    padding-right: 20px;
    float: right; }
article h1 {
    margin-bottom: .35em; }
article img {
    float: left;
    margin: 0 1.5em 1em 0; }
```

Figure 6-9   The HTML and CSS for the speaker page

How to use CSS3 to create text columns

So far, we've been talking about the columns in a page layout. But CSS3 provides a new feature that makes it easy to create text columns. For instance, you can easily format an article into two or more text columns within a 2- or 3-column page layout.

The CSS3 properties for creating text columns

Figure 6-10 summarizes the properties for creating text columns. For instance, the column-count property automatically formats the text within an article into the number of columns specified. You can use the column-gap property to set the width of the gaps between columns. You can use the column-rule property to set borders within the columns. And you can use the column-span property to cause an element to span the columns.

Three of these properties are illustrated by the example in this figure. Here, an article is formatted into 3 columns with 25 pixel gaps, and 2 pixel rules between the columns. To fit this into this figure, the bottom of the article is truncated, but the entire article is formatted correctly.

The problem with this feature is that only Opera supports it in its native form, IE doesn't support it at all, and the other browsers require prefixes. That's why the code in this example uses the required prefixes. Nevertheless, this is a powerful feature that can easily improve the readability of an article by shortening the line length.

When using this feature, though, you don't want to make the columns too narrow because that can make the text more difficult to read. Also, you don't want to justify the text because that can cause gaps between the words.

The primary CSS3 properties for creating text columns

Property	Description
column-count	The number of columns that the text should be divided into.
column-gap	The width between the columns. Otherwise, this is set by default.
column-rule	Defines a border between columns.
column-span	With the value "all", this property can be used to have everything that precedes the element span all of the columns, but at present this is only supported by Chrome and Safari, not Opera.

3 columns with default-sized gaps

```
article {
    -moz-column-count: 3;
    -webkit-column-count: 3;
    column-count: 3; }
```

3 columns with 25px gaps and 2px rules between the columns

```
article {
    -moz-column-count: 3;
    -webkit-column-count: 3;
    column-count: 3;
    -moz-column-gap: 25px;
    -webkit-column-gap: 25px;
    column-count-gap: 25px;
    -moz-column-rule: 2px solid black;
    -webkit-column-rule: 2px solid black;
    column-rule: 2px solid black; }
```

3 columns with 25px gaps and 2px rules in a browser window

Fossil Threads in the Web of Life

What's 75 million years old and brand spanking new? A teenage Utahceratops! Come to the Saroyan, armed with your best dinosaur roar, when Scott Sampson, Research Curator at the Utah Museum of Natural

doctoral work focused on two new species of ceratopsids, or horned dinosaurs, from the Late Cretaceous of Montana, as well as the growth and function of certopsid horns and frills.

Following graduation in 1993, Sampson spent a year working at the American

History. His research interests largely revolve around the phylogenetics, functional morphology, and evolution of Late Cretaceous dinosaurs.

In addition to his museum and laboratory-based studies, Sampson has conducted paleontological work in Zimbabwe, South

Description

- At this writing, only Opera supports these properties in their native form. Firefox requires the -moz- prefix, Chrome and Safari require the -webkit- prefix, and IE provides no support for these properties.

- If you want the heading of an article to span the columns, you can code the HTML for the heading before the article. Then, you don't have to use the column-span property.

- If the columns are too narrow, an article becomes harder to read.

Figure 6-10   The properties for creating text columns

A 2-column web page with a 2-column article

Figure 6-11 shows how easily this feature can add columns to the article in the speaker page of figure 6-8. It just takes one column-count property, plus the two prefixed versions of it. Then, if a browser doesn't support this property, it just ignores it, so there's no harm done.

If you want the heading to span the columns, you have to do some other work because the column-span property is currently supported only by Safari and Chrome. But this is still an excellent feature that you can start using right away.

Incidentally, if you want to float the image that's coded at the start of the text to the right when you use two or more columns, it won't work the way you want. Instead of floating the image in the rightmost column, the browser will float the image in the first column. Although there are ways around this, it's usually best to float the image to the left when you use this feature.

A web page with a two-column article

The CSS for creating the columns

```
article {
    -moz-column-count: 2;
    -webkit-column-count: 2;
    column-count: 2;
}
```

Description

- This shows how easy it is to divide an article in columns.

- If you compare this page with the one in figure 6-8, you can see that this page is easier to read because the lines are shorter, but not too short.

- If a browser doesn't support this feature, the page is displayed as in figure 6-8, which is acceptable.

- If you want the heading in the article to span the columns without using the CSS3 column-span property, you have to code the heading before the article in the HTML.

- In general, it's best to float an image within the columns area to the left so it will be in the leftmost column. If you float it to the right, the browser will float the image to the right, but in the first column, which usually isn't what you want.

Figure 6-11   A 2-column web page with a 2-column article

How to position elements

Although floating provides an easy way to create pages with two or more columns, you may occasionally need to use other positioning techniques. You'll learn about those techniques in the topics that follow.

Four ways to position an element

To position the elements on a page, you use the properties shown in the first table in figure 6-12. The first property, position, determines the type of positioning that will be used. This property can have four different values as shown in the second table.

The first value, static, is the default. This causes elements to be placed in the normal flow.

The second value, absolute, removes the element from the normal flow and positions it based on the top, bottom, right, and left properties you specify. When you use *absolute positioning*, the element is positioned relative to the closest containing block. If no containing block is positioned, the element is positioned relative to the browser window.

The third value, fixed, works like absolute in that the position of the element is specified using the top, bottom, left, and right properties. Instead of being positioned relative to a containing block, however, an element that uses *fixed positioning* is positioned relative to the browser window. That means that the element doesn't move when you scroll through the window.

The fourth value, relative, causes an element to be positioned relative to its normal position in the flow. When you use the top, bottom, left, and right properties with *relative positioning*, they specify the element's offset from its normal position.

One more property you can use to position elements is z-index. This property is useful if an element that you position overlaps another element. In that case, you can use the z-index property to determine which element is on top.

Properties for positioning elements

Property	Description
`position`	A keyword that determines how an element is positioned. See the table below for possible values.
`top, bottom, left, right`	For absolute or fixed positioning, a relative or absolute value that specifies the top, bottom, left, or right position of an element's box. For relative positioning, the top, bottom, left, or right offset of an element's box.
`z-index`	An integer that determines the stack level of an element whose position property is set to absolute, relative, or fixed.

Possible values for the position property

Value	Description
`static`	The element is placed in the normal flow. This is the default.
`absolute`	The element is removed from the flow and is positioned relative to the closest containing block that is also positioned. The position is determined by the top, bottom, left, and right properties.
`fixed`	The element is positioned absolutely relative to the browser window. The position is determined by the top, bottom, left, and right properties.
`relative`	The element is positioned relative to its position in the normal flow. The position is determined by the top, bottom, left, and right properties.

Description

- By default, static positioning is used to position block elements from top to bottom and inline elements from left to right.

- To change the positioning of an element, you can code the position property. In most cases, you also code one or more of the top, bottom, left, and right properties.

- When you use absolute, relative, or fixed positioning for an element, the element can overlap other elements. Then, you can use the z-index property to specify a value that determines the level at which the element is displayed. An element with a higher z-index value is displayed on top of an element with a lower z-index value.

Figure 6-12   Four ways to position an element

How to use absolute positioning

To give you a better idea of how positioning works, figure 6-13 presents an example of absolute positioning. Here, the aside element is positioned absolutely within its containing element, which is the body of the HTML document.

For this to work, the containing element must also be positioned. However, the positioning can be either relative or absolute, and the top, bottom, left, and right properties don't have to be set. Since they aren't set in this example, the body is positioned where it is in the natural flow. In other words, nothing changes. However, because the body is positioned, the elements that it contains can be absolutely positioned within it. In this case, the aside element is positioned 30 pixels from the right side of the body and 50 pixels from the top.

When you use absolute positioning, you typically specify the top or bottom and left or right properties. You also are likely to specify the width or height of the element. However, you can also specify all four of the top, bottom, left, and right properties. Then, the height and width are determined by the difference between the top and bottom and left and right properties.

How to use fixed positioning

Fixed positioning is like absolute positioning except that it's positioning is relative to the browser window. So, to change the example in figure 6-13 from absolute positioning to fixed positioning requires just two changes. First, you delete the position property for the body since fixed positioning is relative to the browser window. Second, you change the position property for the aside to fixed.

The benefit of fixed positioning is that the element that's fixed stays there when you scroll down the page. If, for example, the section in this figure was so long that it required scrolling, the aside would stay where it is while the user scrolls.

The HTML for a web page

```
<body>
    <section>
        <h1>Our speakers for 2011-2012</h1>
        <ul>
            <li>October 19, 2011: <a href="speakers/toobin.html">
                Jeffrey Toobin</a></li>
            <li>November 16, 2011: <a href="speakers/sorkin.html">
                Andrew Ross Sorkin</a></li>
            <li>January 18, 2012: <a href="speakers/chua.html">
                Amy Chua</a></li>
        </ul>
        <p>Please contact us for tickets.</p>
    </section>
    <aside>
        <p><a href="raffle.html">Enter to win a free ticket!</a></p>
    </aside>
</body>
```

The CSS for the web page with absolute positioning

```
p { margin: 0; }
body {
    width: 500px;
    margin: 0 25px 20px;
    border: 1px solid black;
    position: relative; }  /* not needed for fixed positioning */
aside {
    width: 80px;
    padding: 1em;
    border: 1px solid black;
    position: absolute;     /* change to fixed for fixed positioning */
    right: 30px;
    top: 50px; }
```

The web page with absolute positioning in a browser

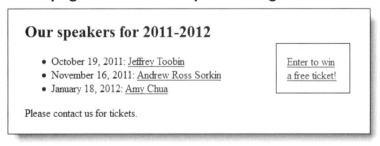

Description

- When you use *absolute positioning*, the remaining elements on the page are positioned as if the element weren't there. As a result, you may need to make room for the positioned element by setting the margins or padding for other elements.

- When you use *fixed positioning* for an element, the positioning applies to the browser window and the element doesn't move even when you scroll.

Figure 6-13   How to use absolute and fixed positioning

A table of contents that uses positioning

Because floating works so well, you won't need to use positioning much. Occasionally, though, it comes in handy.

In figure 6-14, for example, you can see the table of contents for a book that makes good use of positioning. If positioning weren't used, you would have to use a table to display a table of contents like this, which would take more code and be more difficult.

In the HTML for the table of contents, a section element is used as the container for the table of contents. Within this container, h2 elements are used for the sections of the table of contents and h3 elements are used for the chapters. Within the h2 and h3 elements, span elements with "title" as the class name are used to specify the titles of the sections and chapters. And within the h3 elements, span elements with "number" as the class name are used to specify the page numbers of the chapters.

In the CSS for the table of contents, you can see that the h2 and h3 elements are given relative positioning. However, the top, bottom, left, and right properties have been omitted. Because of that, the elements aren't actually offset, but they can be used as containers for absolute positioning. Then, the title and number classes are positioned absolutely within those elements. This indents the titles as shown in the browser display and right aligns the page numbers.

A table of contents that uses absolute positioning

Murach's JavaScript and DOM Scripting

Section 1	**Introduction to JavaScript programming**	
Chapter 1	Introduction to web development and JavaScript	3
Chapter 2	How to code a JavaScript application	43
Chapter 3	How to test and debug a JavaScript application	89
Chapter 4	A crash course in HTML	121
Chapter 5	A crash course in CSS	169
Section 2	**JavaScript essentials**	
Chapter 6	How to get input and display output	223

The HTML for the positioned elements

```
<section>
    <h1><i>Murach&rsquo;s JavaScript and DOM Scripting</i></h1>
    <h2>Section 1<span class="title">Introduction to JavaScript
        programming</span></h2>
    <h3>Chapter 1<span class="title">Introduction to web development and
        JavaScript</span><span class="number">3</span></h3>
    <h3>Chapter 2<span class="title">How to code a JavaScript
        application</span><span class="number">43</span></h3>
    ...
    <h2>Section 2<span class="title">JavaScript essentials</span></h2>
    <h3>Chapter 6<span class="title">How to get input and display
        output</span><span class="number">223</span></h3>
    ...
</section>
```

The CSS for the positioned elements

```
section h2 {
    margin: .6em 0 0;
    position: relative; }
section h3 {
    font-weight: normal;
    margin: .3em 0 0;
    position: relative; }
.title {
    position: absolute;
    left: 90px; }
.number {
    position: absolute;
    right: 0; }
```

Description

- To implement absolute positioning, span elements with class names are used to identify the text to be positioned at the left and the page numbers to be positioned at the right.

- The h2 and h3 elements use relative positioning, but no positions are specified. That way, the .title and .number elements that they contain can be positioned relative to the headings.

Figure 6-14   A table of contents that uses positioning

Perspective

Now that you've completed this chapter, you should be able to develop web pages that have headers, footers, and 2- or 3-column layouts. Better yet, you'll be using CSS to do these layouts, which makes these pages easier to create and maintain. In contrast, if you look at the source code for many web sites today, you'll find that they're still using HTML tables to implement page layouts.

This completes the first section of this book, which we think of as a crash course in HTML and CSS. With these skills, you should be able to develop web pages at a professional level. Then, to add to these skills, you can read any of the chapters in the rest of this book in whatever sequence you prefer. In other words, you can learn those skills whenever you need them.

Terms

float
fixed layout
liquid layout
absolute positioning
relative positioning
fixed positioning

Summary

- When you use the float property to *float* an element, any elements after the floated element will flow into the space left vacant. To make this work, the floated element has to have a width that's either specified or implied.

- To stop an element from flowing into the space left vacant by a floated element, you can use the clear property.

- In a *fixed layout*, the widths of the columns are set. In a *liquid layout*, the width of the page and the width of at least one column change as the user changes the width of the browser window.

- When you use *absolute positioning* for an element, the remaining elements on the page are positioned as if the element weren't there. Because of that, you may need to make room for positioned elements by adjusting other elements.

- When you use *relative positioning* for an element, the remaining elements leave space for the moved element as if it were still there.

- When you use *fixed positioning* for an element, the element doesn't move in the browser window, even when you scroll.

Exercise 6-1   Enhance the Town Hall home page

In this exercise, you'll enhance the formatting of the Town Hall home page that you formatted in exercise 5-1. When you're through, the page should look like this, but without the Speaker of the Month content:

San Joaquin Valley Town Hall
Celebrating our 75ᵗʰ Year

2011-2012 Speakers

October 19, 2011
Jeffrey Toobin

November 16, 2011
Andrew Ross Sorkin

January 18, 2012
Amy Chua

February 15, 2012
Scott Sampson

Our Mission

San Joaquin Valley Town Hall is a non-profit organization that is run by an all-volunteer board of directors. Our mission is to bring nationally and internationally renowned, thought-provoking speakers who inform, educate, and entertain our audience! As one or our members told us:

> *"Each year I give a ticket package to each of our family members. I think of it as the gift of knowledge...and that is priceless."*

Speaker of the Month

Fossil Threads in the Web of Life

February 15, 2012
Scott Sampson

What's 75 million years old and brand spanking new? A teenage Utahceratops! Come to the Saroyan, armed with your best dinosaur roar, when Scott Sampson, Research Curator at the Utah Museum of Natural History, steps to the podium. Sampson's research has focused on the ecology and evolution of late Cretaceous dinosaurs and he has conducted fieldwork in a number of countries in Africa.

Read more. **Or meet us there!**

Our Ticket Package

- Season Package: $95
- Patron Package: $200
- Single Speaker: $25

© 2012, San Joaquin Valley Town Hall, Fresno, CA 93755

Open the HTML and CSS files

1. Use your text editor to open the HTML and CSS files that you created for exercise 5-1 or 5-2:

   ```
   c:\html5_css3\exercises\town_hall_1\index.html
   c:\html5_css3\exercises\town_hall_1\styles\main.css
   ```

Enhance the HTML and CSS to provide for the two columns

2. In the HTML file, add aside tags so the "Our 2011-2012 Speakers" heading and the headings and images that follow it are within the aside element, and not within the section element. Also, delete the word "Our" from the "Our 2011-2012 Speakers" heading.

3. Still in the HTML file, add the heading and image for the fourth speaker.

4. In the CSS file, enhance the rule set for the body so the width is 800 pixels. Next, set the width of the section to 525 pixels and float it to the right, and set the width of the aside to 215 pixels and float it to the right. Then, use the clear property in the footer to clear the floating. Last, delete the rule set for the Speakers heading. Now, test this. The columns should be starting to take shape.

5. To make this look better, delete the rule set for the Speakers heading. Then, set the left padding for the aside to 20 pixels, and change the right and left padding for the section to 20 pixels. Now, test again.

Get the headings right

6. Add rule sets for the h1 and h2 elements in the aside. They should have the same rules as the h1 and h2 elements in the section.

7. Add a rule set for the img elements in the aside so the bottom padding is set to 1em. Then, test this change.

8. At this point, the page should look good, but it won't include the Speaker of the Month content. Now, make any adjustments, test them in both Firefox and IE, and then go on to the next exercise.

Exercise 6-2   Add the Speaker of the Month

In this exercise, you'll add the Speaker of the Month to the home page. Whenever appropriate, test the changes in Firefox.

Enhance the HTML page

1. Copy the content for the speaker of the month from the file named c6_content.txt in the text folder into the HTML file right before the heading for "Our Ticket Packages".

2. Enclose the Speaker of the Month heading in h1 tags, and enclose the rest of the content in an article element.

3. Within the article, enclose the first heading in h1 tags; enclose the second heading (the date and speaker's name) in h2 tags with a <br> tag to provide the line break; and enclose the rest of the text in <p> tags.

4. Add an <a> element within the last paragraph that goes to the sampson.html page in the speakers folder when the user clicks on "Read more." Also, add a non-breaking space and <b> tags so the rest of the line looks right.

5. Add an image element between the h1 and h2 elements in the article, and display the image named sampson_dinosaur.jpg from the images folder.

Enhance the CSS for the home page

6.   Add 2 pixel top and bottom borders to the article with #800000 as the color.

7.   Float the image in the article to the right, and set its top, bottom, and left margins so there's adequate space around it. Then, add a 1 pixel, black border to the image so the white in the image doesn't fade into the background. Also, delete the rule set for images in the section to get rid of the bottom padding.

8.   Change the font color of the h1 elements in the article to to black.

9.   Make any final adjustments to the margins or padding, validate the HTML page, and test in IE.

Exercise 6-3   Add one speaker page

In this exercise, you'll add the page for one speaker. This page will be like the home page, but the speaker information will be in the second column as shown below. As you develop this page, test it in Firefox whenever appropriate.

San Joaquin Valley Town Hall
Celebrating our 75th Year

2011-2012 Speakers

October 19, 2011
Jeffrey Toobin

November 16, 2011
Andrew Ross Sorkin

January 18, 2012
Amy Chua

February 15, 2012
Scott Sampson

Return to Home page

Fossil Threads in the Web of Life

February 15, 2012
Scott Sampson

What's 75 million years old and brand spanking new? A teenage Utahceratops! Come to the Saroyan, armed with your best dinosaur roar, when Scott Sampson, Research Curator at the Utah Museum of Natural History, steps to the podium. Sampson's research has focused on the ecology and evolution of late Cretaceous dinosaurs and he has conducted fieldwork in a number of countries in Africa.

Scott Sampson is a Canadian-born paleontologist who received his Ph.D. in zoology from the University of Toronto. His doctoral work focused on two new species of ceratopsids, or horned dinosaurs, from the Late Cretaceous of Montana, as well as the growth and function of certopsid horns and frills.

Following graduation in 1993, Sampson spent a year working at the American Museum of Natual History in New York City, followed by five years as assistant professor of anatomy at the New York College of Osteopathic Medicine on Long Island. He arrived at the University of Utah accepting a dual position as assistant professor in the Department of Geology and Geophysics and curator of vertebrate paleontology at the Utah Museum of Natural History. His research interests largely revolve around the phylogenetics, functional morphology, and evolution of Late Cretaceous dinosaurs.

In addition to his museum and laboratory-based studies, Sampson has conducted paleontological work in Zimbabwe, South Africa, and Madagascar, as well as the United States and Canada. He was also the on-the-air host for the Discovery Channel's Dinosaur Planet and recently completed a book, *Dinosaur Odyssey: Fossil Threads in the Web of Life*, which is one of the most comprehensive surveys of dinosaurs and their worlds to date.

© 2012, San Joaquin Valley Town Hall, Fresno, CA 93755

Create the CSS and HTML files for the speaker

1. Copy the index.html file that you've been working with into the speakers folder and name it sampson.html. (With Aptana, you can use the Save As command to save the index file with the new name.)

2. Copy the main.css file that you've been working with into the styles folder and name it speaker.css. (With Aptana, you can the Save As command to do this.)

3. In the head section of the sampson.html file, change the link element so it refers to the speaker.css file in the styles folder. To do that, you can code a document-relative path like this:

```
../styles/speaker.css
```

Modify the HTML file

4. Update all the image and link references to document-relative paths. Then, at the bottom of the HTML aside element, add a link back to the home page within an h2 element.

5. Delete all of the content from the section in the sampson.html file, but not the section tags. Then, copy the text for the speaker from the c6.sampson.txt file in the text folder into the section of the sampson.html file.

6. Enclose the first heading ("Fossil Threads in the Web of Life") within an h1 element. Then, code an image element after the first heading that displays the sampson_dinosaur.jpg file that's in the images folder.

7. Enclose the rest of the content for the speaker in an article element. Within the article, enclose the first heading (the date and speaker's name) in h2 tags with a <br> tag to provide the line break, and enclose the rest of the text in <p> tags.

8. Validate the file, and fix any errors.

Modify the CSS file

9. If you test the page right now, it should look pretty good. Then, you just need to adjust the styles to get the page to look the way you want it. For instance, you should delete the borders from the rule set for the article, and add some spacing above the footer.

10. Test all the links to make sure they work correctly. Also, make sure the favicon and all images are displayed correctly.

11. Test the page in IE. Then, if necessary make any corrections, and test again in both Firefox and IE. Now, if you've done everything: "Congratulations!"

Want to review our solution files for this web site?

12. If you had any problems along the way and would like to review our solution files, you'll find them in the folder that follows. The only difference is that the home page already has a navigation bar. This is the web site that you'll be using for the exercises in section 2 of this book:

```
c:\html5_css3\exercises\town_hall_2
```

Section 2

More HTML and CSS skills as you need them

In section 1, you learned a professional subset of HTML and CSS skills that you can use for building most web pages. Now, in this section, you can add to those skills by learning new skills whenever you need them. To make that possible, each chapter in this section is an independent training module. As a result, you can read these chapters in whatever sequence you prefer.

Chapter 7 builds on the skills you learned for working with lists and links, and chapter 8 builds on the skills you learned for working with images. Then, the remaining chapters present information on new subjects.

In chapter 9, you'll learn how to code tables that present tabular data. In chapter 10, you'll learn how to code forms using the new HTML5 controls and validation features. In chapter 11, you'll learn how to use the new HTML5 elements for adding audio and video to your web pages. And in chapter 12, you'll learn how to create style sheets for printing web pages.

7

How to work with lists and links

In chapters 3 and 4, you were introduced to the coding for lists and links. Now, in this chapter, you'll review those skills, and you'll learn the other skills that you may need for working with lists and links.

How to code lists

In the topics that follow, you'll learn the HTML skills that you'll need for working with lists. That includes unordered, ordered, and description lists.

How to code unordered lists

Figure 7-1 presents the two elements for coding an *unordered list*. As you learned in section 1, you use the ul element to create a list, and you use the li element to create each item in a list. This is illustrated in the example in this figure.

In addition to containing text, list items can contain inline elements like links and images. They can also contain block elements like headings, paragraphs, and other lists. For example, the first list item in this figure contains text and a link within a paragraph. Then, the second list item contains only text, but it's divided into two paragraphs. As you can see, the second paragraph is aligned with the first paragraph, but it doesn't have a bullet because it's part of the same list item.

Elements that create unordered lists

Element	Description
ul	Creates an unordered list.
li	Creates a list item for the list.

HTML for an unordered list with text, links, and paragraphs

```
<h1>San Joaquin Valley Town Hall Programs</h1>
<ul>
    <li>
        <p>Join us for a complimentary coffee hour at the
        <a href="saroyan.html">William Saroyan Theatre</a>, 9:15 to 10:15
        a.m. on the day of each lecture. The speakers usually attend this
        very special event.</p>
    </li>
    <li>
        <p>Extend the excitement of Town Hall by purchasing tickets to the
        post-lecture luncheons. This unique opportunity allows you to ask
        more questions of the speakers--plus spend extra time meeting new
        Town Hall friends.</p>
        <p>A limited number of tickets are available. Call (559) 555-1212
        for reservations by the Friday preceding the event.</p>
    </li>
</ul>
```

The list in a web browser

San Joaquin Valley Town Hall Programs

- Join us for a complimentary coffee hour at the William Saroyan Theatre, 9:15 to 10:15 a.m. on the day of each lecture. The speakers usually attend this very special event.

- Extend the excitement of Town Hall by purchasing tickets to the post-lecture luncheons. This unique opportunity allows you to ask more questions of the speakers--plus spend extra time meeting new Town Hall friends.

  A limited number of tickets are available. Call (559) 555-1212 for reservations by the Friday preceding the event.

Description

- By default, an *unordered list* is displayed as a bulleted list, but you can change the bullets as shown in figure 7-5.

- An li element typically contains text, but it can also contain other inline elements such as links, as well as block elements such as paragraphs and other lists.

Figure 7-1   How to code unordered lists

How to code ordered lists

If you want to indicate that the items in a list have a sequence like the steps in a procedure, you can use an *ordered list*. To create an ordered list, you use the ol and li elements. These elements are presented in figure 7-2.

The only thing new here is the start attribute of the ol element. You can use this attribute to start a list at a value other than the default. You might want to do that if one list continues from a previous list. For example, this figure shows a procedure that's divided into two parts, and each part is coded as a separate list. Because the first list consists of three items, the start attribute of the second list is set to 4.

Keep in mind if you use the start attribute that it doesn't represent the actual value that's displayed. Instead, it represents the position of the item in the list. When you use decimal values to indicate the sequence of the items in a list as shown here, the position and the value are the same. Later in this chapter, though, you'll learn how to number lists using other values like alphabetic characters. In that case, a start value of 4 would represent the letter "D".

Elements that create ordered lists

Element	Description
ol	Creates an ordered list. You can include the start attribute to specify the starting value for the list. The value represents the position in the list. The default is 1.
li	Creates a list item for the list.

HTML for an ordered list that continues from another ordered list

```
<h1>How to use the WinZip Self Extractor</h1>
<h2>Before you start the WinZip Self Extractor</h2>
<ol>
    <li>Create a text file that contains the message you want to be
        displayed when the executable starts.</li>
    <li>Create a batch file that copies the exercises, and store it
        in the main folder for the files to be zipped.</li>
    <li>Create the zip file.</li>
</ol>
<h2>How to create an executable file</h2>
<ol start="4">
    <li>Run the WinZip Self Extractor program and click through the first
        three dialog boxes.</li>
    <li>Enter the name of the zip file in the fourth dialog box.</li>
    <li>Click the Next button to test the executable.</li>
</ol>
```

The lists in a web browser

How to use the WinZip Self Extractor

Before you start the WinZip Self Extractor

1. Create a text file that contains the message you want to be displayed when the executable starts.
2. Create a batch file that copies the exercises, and store it in the main directory for the files to be zipped.
3. Create the zip file.

How to create an executable file

4. Run the WinZip Self Extractor program and click through the first three dialog boxes.
5. Enter the name of the zip file in the fourth dialog box.
6. Click the Next button to test the executable.

Description

- By default, an *ordered list* is displayed as a numbered list, but you can change that as shown in figure 7-6.
- The start attribute can be used to continue the numbering from one list to another.

Figure 7-2   How to code ordered lists

How to code nested lists

As I mentioned earlier, a list item can contain block elements, including other lists. When you code a list within another list, the lists are referred to as *nested lists*. Figure 7-3 illustrates how nested lists work.

If you look at the HTML in this figure, you'll see that it consists of three lists. The outer list is an unordered list that contains two list items. The first list item defines the first subheading shown in the web browser, along with the three steps that follow it. Then, the second list item defines the second subheading and the remaining steps.

To define the steps, an ordered list is defined within each list item of the unordered list. These lists are coded just like any other ordered list. Because they're nested within other lists, though, they're indented an additional amount.

HTML for ordered lists nested within an unordered list

```
<h1>How to use the WinZip Self Extractor program</h1>
<ul>
    <li>Before you start the WinZip Self Extractor
        <ol>
            <li>Create a text file that contains the message you want
                to be displayed when the executable starts.</li>
            <li>Create a batch file that copies the exercises, and
                store it in the main folder for the files to be zipped.</li>
            <li>Create the zip file.</li>
        </ol>
    </li>
    <li>How to create an executable file
        <ol start="4">
            <li>Run the WinZip Self Extractor program and click through the
                first three dialog boxes.</li>
            <li>Enter the name of the zip file in the fourth dialog
                box.</li>
            <li>Click the Next button to test the executable.</li>
        </ol>
    </li>
</ul>
```

The lists in a web browser

How to use the WinZip Self Extractor

- Before you start the WinZip Self Extractor
    1. Create a text file that contains the message you want to be displayed when the executable starts.
    2. Create a batch file that copies the exercises, and store it in the main directory for the files to be zipped.
    3. Create the zip file.
- How to create an executable file
    4. Run the WinZip Self Extractor program and click through the first three dialog boxes.
    5. Enter the name of the zip file in the fourth dialog box.
    6. Click the Next button to test the executable.

Description

- You can nest lists by coding one list as an item for another list.

- When you nest an unordered list within another list, the default bullet is a circle.

Figure 7-3   How to code nested lists

How to code description lists

In addition to ordered and unordered lists, HTML provides for *description lists*. As the name implies, description lists are typically used to list terms and their descriptions. Figure 7-4 shows how to code description lists.

To code a description list, you use the dl, dt, and dd elements. The dl element creates the description list, the dt element creates the term, and the dd element creates the description for the term. The example in this figure illustrates how this works. Here, the dt and dd elements are coded within the dl element that defines the list. Notice that the dt and dd elements are coded in pairs so there's a description for each term.

When you code a description list, you should know that the dt element can only contain text and inline elements. In contrast, dd elements can also contain block elements. For example, they can contain paragraphs and nested lists.

You should also know that you can code more than one dd element for each dt element. That's useful if you're creating a glossary and a term has more than one meaning. You can also code a single dd element for two or more dt elements. That's useful if you're defining terms that have the same description.

Incidentally, description lists were called *definition lists* in HTML4. The new name implies that a description list can be used for more than just definitions.

Elements that create description lists

Element	Description
dl	Creates a description list that contains pairs of dt and dd elements.
dt	Creates a term in a description list.
dd	Creates a description in a description list.

HTML for a description list

```
<h2>Components of the Internet architecture</h2>
<dl>
    <dt>client</dt>
    <dd>A computer that accesses the web pages of a web application using a
        web browser.</dd>
    <dt>web server</dt>
    <dd>A computer that holds the files for each web application.</dd>
    <dt>local area network (LAN)</dt>
    <dd>A small network of computers that are near each other and can
        communicate with each other over short distances.</dd>
    <dt>wide area network (WAN)</dt>
    <dd>A network that consists of multiple LANs that have been connected
        together over long distances using routers.</dd>
    <dt>Internet exchange point</dt>
    <dd>Large routers that connect WANs together.</dd>
</dl>
```

The list in a web browser

Components of the Internet architecture

client
> A computer that accesses the web pages of a web application using a web
> browser.

web server
> A computer that holds the files for each web application.

local area network (LAN)
> A small network of computers that are near each other and can communicate
> with each other over short distances.

wide area network (WAN)
> A network that consists of multiple LANs that have been connected together
> over long distances using routers.

Internet exchange point
> Large routers that connect WANs together.

Description

- A *description list* consists of terms and descriptions for those terms. In HTML4, this type of list was called a *definition list*.

- The dt element that creates a term in a description list can only contain text. However, dd elements can contain block elements such as headings and paragraphs.

- You can use one or more dd elements to describe a dt element, and you can describe two or more dt elements with a single dd element.

Figure 7-4   How to code description lists

How to format lists

Once you have a list coded the way you want it, you can format it so it looks the way you want. In most cases, that just means changing the spacing above and below the list and its items. But you can also change the bullets that are used for an unordered list. You can change the numbering system that's used for an ordered list. And you can change the vertical alignment of the items in a list. You'll learn these skills in the topics that follow.

How to change the bullets for an unordered list

To change the bullets for an unordered list, you can use the list-style-type and list-style-image properties shown in the first table in figure 7-5. In most cases, you'll use the list-style-type property to specify one of the values listed in the second table.

By default, a list displays a solid round bullet, but you can specify a value of "circle" to display a circle bullet as shown in the first list in this figure. You can also specify a value of "square" to display a square bullet or "none" if you don't want to display any bullets.

If these predefined bullet types aren't adequate, you can display a custom image before each item in an unordered list. To do that, you start by getting or creating the image that you want to use. For instance, you can get many images that are appropriate for lists from the Internet, often for free or for a small charge. The other alternative is to use a graphics program to create your own image. Once you have the image that you want to use, you use the list-style-image property to specify the URL for the image file, as illustrated by the second example in this figure.

In most cases, you'll code the list-style-type and list-style-image properties for the ul element. Then, this property is inherited by all the items in the list. Another way to do that, though, is to code these properties for the li element.

Properties for formatting unordered lists

Property	Description
`list-style-type`	Determines the type of bullet that's used for the items in the list. See the table below for possible values. The default is disc.
`list-style-image`	The URL for an image that's used as the bullet.

Values for the list-style-type property of an unordered list

Value	Description
`disc`	solid circle
`circle`	hollow circle
`square`	solid square
`none`	no bullet

HTML for two unordered lists

```
<h2>Popular web browsers include</h2>
<ul class="circle">
    <li>Internet Explorer</li>
    <li>Firefox</li>
    <li>Chrome</li>
</ul>
<h2>Prime skills for web developers are</h2>
<ul class="star">
    <li>HTML5 and CSS3</li>
    <li>JavaScript</li>
    <li>PHP</li>
</ul>
```

CSS that changes the bullets

```
ul.circle { list-style-type: circle; }
ul.star { list-style-image: url("../images/star.png"); }
```

The lists in a web browser

Description

- You can change the bullet that's displayed for an unordered list by using the list-style-type property. To display an image for the bullet, use the list-style-image property.

Figure 7-5   How to change the bullets for an unordered list

How to change the numbering system
for an ordered list

By default, decimal values are used to number the items in an ordered list. To change that, though, you can use the list-style-type property as shown in figure 7-6. In the example, you can see that "lower-alpha" is used for the value of this property.

Common values for the list-style-type property of an ordered list

Value	Example
decimal	1, 2, 3, 4, 5 ...
decimal-leading-zero	01, 02, 03, 04, 05 ...
lower-alpha	a, b, c, d, e ...
upper-alpha	A, B, C, D, E ...
lower-roman	i, ii, iii, iv, v ...
upper-roman	I, II, III, IV, V ...

HTML for an ordered list

```
<h2>How to create an executable file</h2>
<ol class="lower_alpha">
    <li>Run the WinZip Self Extractor program and click through the first
        three dialog boxes.</li>
    <li>Enter the name of the zip file in the fourth dialog box.</li>
    <li>Click the Next button to test the executable.</li>
</ol>
```

CSS that formats the list

```
ol.lower_alpha { list-style-type: lower-alpha; }
```

The list in a web browser

How to create an executable file

a. Run the WinZip Self Extractor program and click through the first three dialog boxes.
b. Enter the name of the zip file in the fourth dialog box.
c. Click the Next button to test the executable.

Description

- You can change the numbering system that's used for an ordered list using the list-style-type property. The default is decimal.

Figure 7-6   How to change the numbering system for an ordered list

How to change the alignment of list items

Often, the items in a list will be aligned the way you want them. However, you will usually want to adjust the spacing before and after a list, and you will sometimes want to adjust the spacing before or after the list items. Beyond that, you may want to change the indentation of the items in a list or the amount of space between the bullets or numbers in a list.

In figure 7-7, you can see the HTML and the CSS for a formatted list. In this case, the space between the lines has been adjusted. But more important, the list items have been moved left so the bullets are aligned on the left margin instead of being indented. Also, the space between the bullets and the items has been increased. If you compare this list to the one in figure 7-5, you can see the differences.

In the CSS for the list in this figure, you can see that the margins for the unordered list and its list items have been set to 0. Then, the left padding for the ul element has been set to 1 em. This determines the left alignment of the items in the list. Often, though, you have to experiment with this setting to get the alignment the way you want it.

Similarly, the left padding for the li element is set to .25 ems. This determines the distance between the bullet and the text for an item. Here again, you will often have to experiment with this value to get it the way you want it.

For ordered lists, you can use the same techniques to adjust the indentation and to adjust the space between the number and the text in an item. Remember, though, that the numbers in an ordered list are aligned on the right. So if the numbers vary in width, you have to adjust your values accordingly.

HTML for an unordered list

```
<h2>Popular web browsers</h2>
<ul>
    <li>Internet Explorer</li>
    <li>Firefox</li>
    <li>Chrome</li>
    <li>Safari</li>
    <li>Opera</li>
</ul>
```

CSS that aligns the list items

```
h2, ul, li {
    margin: 0;
    padding: 0;
}
h2 {
    padding-bottom: .25em;
}
ul {
    padding-left: 1em;       /* determines left alignment */
}
li {
    padding-left: .25em;   /* space between bullet and text */
    padding-bottom: .25em; /* space after line item */
}
```

The list in a web browser

Popular web browsers
- Internet Explorer
- Firefox
- Chrome
- Safari
- Opera

Description

- You can use margins and padding to control the indentation for the items in an ordered or unordered list, and to control the space between the bullets or numbers and the text that follows.

- You can also use margins and padding to remove the indentation from the items in a list as shown above. However, this doesn't work as well with ordered lists because the numbers or letters are aligned at the right.

- You can remove the indentation from the descriptions in a description list by setting the left margin of the descriptions to zero.

- These techniques work best if you specify the padding and margins using ems.

Figure 7-7   How to change the alignment of list items

How to code links

In section 1, you learn how to code and format simple text links that open another web page in the same window. Now, you'll learn other ways to code and use links.

How to link to another page or start an email message

Figure 7-8 starts by reviewing some of the information that you learned earlier about coding <a> elements that *link* to other pages. Then, it goes on to some new skills.

To start, you code the href attribute so it identifies the page you want the link to display. Then, you code the content that you want to be displayed for the link. The content can be text, an image, or both text and an image.

The first example in this figure illustrates how this works. Here, the first link displays text, and the second link displays an image. Note that this image has a border. Most browsers add this border to identify the image as a link. In that case, the border is the same color as the underline for a text link. However, you can remove the border by using CSS to set the border style to "none".

The third link in the first example shows how the title attribute can be used to improve accessibility. Here, the text for the link is just "TOC", but the title attribute says: "Review the complete table of contents". This title is displayed as a tooltip if the mouse hovers over it, and it can also be read by assistive devices.

The second example in this figure shows how you can use a link to open the user's default email program and start an email message. To do that, you code the href attribute as "mailto:" followed by the email address that the message will be sent to. Although this won't work for users who use email services like gmail or yahoo mail instead of the email programs on their computers, those users can at least get the email address from the text that's displayed for the link.

If you want to populate some of the fields of the email, like the subject, cc, bcc, or body fields, you can add name/value pairs at the end of the email address. To do that, you code a question mark followed by the pairs separated by ampersands (&). In this example, the email will be sent to ed@yahoo.com and the subject line will say "Web mail".

If the user presses the Tab key while a web page is displayed, the focus is moved from one link or form control to another based on the tab sequence. By default, this *tab order* is the sequence in which the links and controls are coded in the HTML. To change that order, though, you can use the tabindex attribute of a link. In the first example in this figure, this is set to zero so that link will be the first one that gets tabbed to.

To set an *access key* for a link, you can code the accesskey attribute. Then, the user can press that key in combination with one or more other keys to activate the link. For example, the accesskey attribute for the first text link in

Four attributes of the <a> element

Attribute	Description
href	A relative or absolute URL that identifies the document a link will display.
title	A description that is displayed as a tooltip. This can clarify where the link is going.
tabindex	Sets the tab order for the links starting with 0. To take a link out of the tab order, code a negative value.
accesskey	Identifies a keyboard key that can be used in combination with other keys to activate the control. The key combination depends on the operating system and browser.

A text link, an image link, and a text link with a title attribute

```
<p>
    <a href="/orders/cart.html" accesskey="c" tabindex="0">Shopping cart</a>
    <a href="/orders/cart.html"><img src="images/cart_animated.gif"
        alt="Shopping cart"></a>
</p>
<p><a href="/books/php_toc.html"
        title="Review the complete table of contents">TOC</a></p>
```

The text and image links in a web browser

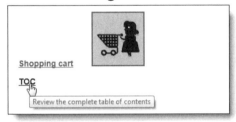

A link that starts an email message

```
<a href="mailto:ed@yahoo.com?subject=Web mail">Email us!</a>
```

Accessibility guidelines

- Always include text that describes where the link is going. If that text has to be short, code the title attribute to clarify where the link is going.

- Don't use image-only links without providing text links that go to the same place.

- If a page contains multiple links, consider improving the tab order by coding tabindex attributes for the links. For instance, you can leave image-only links out of the tab order.

Description

- You use the <a> element to create a *link* that loads another web page. The content of an <a> element can be text, an image, or text and an image.

- You can also use the <a> element to start an email message by coding the href attribute as "mailto:" followed by the email address. To populate the subject, cc, bcc, or body fields in the email, code a question mark after the address followed by one or more name/value pairs separated by ampersands.

- The *tab order* is the sequence that the links will be tabbed to when the user presses the Tab key. For more on this, see chapter 10.

Figure 7-8   How to link to another page or start an email message

this figure is set to the letter "c". Then, the user can activate the link by pressing a control key plus the shortcut key. For instance, Alt+C (the Alt key and the C key) will work in IE, Alt+Shift+C in Firefox, and Ctrl+C in Safari. For more on both access keys and tab order, see chapter 10.

To indicate what the access key for a link or control is, you normally underline the letter in the text for the control. By default, though, the links are underlined so this won't work. But if you remove the underlining, as shown in the next figure, you can use this technique to identify the shortcut keys.

How to format links

Figure 7-9 reviews the formatting skills for links that were introduced in chapter 4. In particular, you can use the pseudo-code selectors to change the default styles for a link.

This figure also shows how to remove the underline for a text link or the border for an image link. To do that, you can set the text-decoration property for a text link or the border property for an image link to "none."

In general, it's good to keep the underlining for text links because that clearly indicates that the text is a link. Similarly, you shouldn't underline text that isn't a link because that can confuse your users. When text links are used in contexts like navigation bars, though, it's okay to remove the underlines. You'll see that illustrated at the end of this chapter.

It's also good to avoid the use of image-only links. The one exception is using the logo in a header to link to the home page of a site because that's become a common practice.

Common CSS pseudo-classes for formatting links

Name	Description
`:link`	A link that hasn't been visited. Blue is the default color.
`:visited`	A link that has been visited. Purple is the default color.
`:hover`	An element with the mouse hovering over it. Hover has no default color.
`:focus`	An element like a link or form control that has the focus.
`:active`	An element that's currently active. Red is the default color.

The properties for removing underlines and borders

Property	Description
`text-decoration`	To remove the underlining from a link, set this to none.
`border`	To remove the border from an image link, set this to none.

The HTML for three links

```
<ul>
    <li><a href="toobin.html">Jeffrey Toobin</a></li>
    <li><a href="sorkin.html">Andrew Ross Sorkin</a></li>
    <li><a href="chua.html">Amy Chua</a></li>
</ul>
```

The CSS for pseudo-class selectors that apply to the links

```
a:link {
    color: green;
}
a:hover, a:focus {
    text-decoration: none;
    font-size: 125%;
}
```

The links in a web browser with the focus on the third link

- Jeffrey Toobin
- Andrew Ross Sorkin
- Amy Chua

Accessibility guideline

- Apply the same formatting for the :hover and :focus selectors. That way, the formatting is the same whether you hover the mouse over a link or use the keyboard to tab to the link.

Figure 7-9   How to format links

How to use a link
to open a new browser window or tab

In most cases, you'll want the page that's loaded by a link to be displayed in the same browser window as the current page. In some cases, though, you may want to open the next page in a new browser window or tab. If, for example, the link loads a page from another web site, you may want to display it in a new window or tab.

To open a new browser window or tab, you set the target attribute of the <a> element to "_blank" as shown in figure 7-10. Here, the link opens a page on another web site in a new tab.

Whether a new window or a new tab is opened depends upon the browser settings. But you can change that. With Firefox, for example, you go to Tools→Options and click on Tabs. With IE, you go to Tools→Internet options and click the Settings button for Tabs.

Incidentally, the target attribute was deprecated in HTML4. However, it is no longer deprecated in HTML5.

HTML for a link that loads the document in a new window or tab

```
<p>Just go to
    <a href="http://www.html5test.com/" target="_blank">
    the HTML5 testing site</a>. It rates your browser as it loads the
    page and also has data on how well other browsers conform to HTML5.
</p>
```

The HTML in one browser tab

The html5test.com home page in another tab

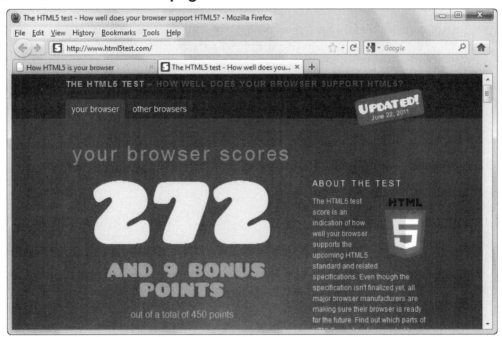

Description

- You can use the target attribute of the <a> tag to specify where the document referred to in a link should be loaded. To load the document in a new browser window or tab, specify "_blank" for this attribute.
- Whether your browser opens a new window or a new tab for the page depends on your browser settings.

Figure 7-10   How to use a link to open a new browser window or tab

How to create and link to placeholders

Besides displaying another page, you can code links that jump to a location on the same page. To do that, you first create a *placeholder* that identifies the location you want the link to jump to. Then, you code a link that points to that placeholder. This is illustrated in figure 7-11.

To create a placeholder, you code the id attribute within an <a> element at the spot where you want the placeholder. In this figure, the first example shows a placeholder with the id "top" that's coded within an h1 element on the page, and the second example shows a placeholder with the id "reason6" that's coded within an h2 element.

Then, the third group of examples shows two links that jump to those placeholders. To do that, the href attributes of these links use the values of the id attributes for the placeholders, preceded by a pound sign (#). When the user clicks on one of these links, the element that contains the placeholder is displayed.

Placeholders can make it easier for users to navigate through a long web page. For pages like these, it's common to include a placeholder at the top of the page along with navigation links for each section of the page. Then, at the end of each section, it's common to include a link to return to the top of the page.

Although placeholders are typically used for navigating within a single page, they can also be used to go to a location on another page. The last example in this figure shows how this works. Here, the name of the page that contains the placeholder is coded before the value of the placeholder's id attribute. Then, when that page is displayed, it will be positioned at the specified placeholder.

Incidentally, placeholders were called *anchors* in HTML4. But since <a> tags are also known as anchor tags, this could be confusing. In HTML5, the term *placeholder* makes this clearer.

A web page that provides links to topics on the same page

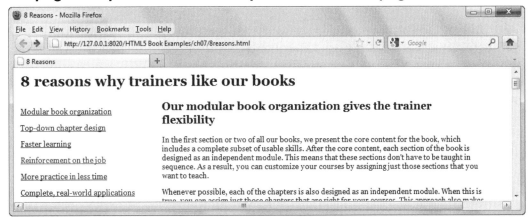

The portion of the page that's displayed when the sixth link is clicked

The HTML for the placeholder at the top of the page

```
<h1><a id="top">8 reasons why trainers like our books</a></h1>
```

The HTML for the placeholder for reason 6

```
<h2><a id="reason6">Our complete, real-world applications ensure
mastery</a></h2>
```

Two links that jump to placeholders on the same page

```
<p><a href="#reason6">Complete,real-world applications</a></p>
<p><a href="#top">Return to top</a></p>
```

A link that jumps to a placeholder on this page from another page

```
<a href="8reasons.html#reason6">Complete, real-world applications</a>
```

Description

- To create a *placeholder*, use the id attribute of the <a> tag.
- To jump to a placeholder, code a link with its href attribute set to the value of the id attribute, preceded by the pound sign.
- To jump to a placeholder on another page, code the URL for the page followed by the id for the placeholder.

Figure 7-11   How to create and link to placeholders

How to link to a media file

If the href attribute of an <a> element addresses a media file, the normal behavior of a browser is to try to display or play it using the right program for that type of file. For instance, the first example in figure 7-12 is a link that opens a PDF file in a new browser window or tab. The second example will play an MP3 audio file. And the third example will play a PowerPoint slide show.

This assumes that the browser has the appropriate program or *media player* for the file. In some cases, this will require that the user install the right player or a *plug-in* for the right player.

To help a browser identify the type of file that the link addresses, you can code the type attribute of an img element. This attribute specifies the *MIME type* for the file. Some of the common MIME types are listed in the first table in this figure, and two of the most popular media players are listed in the second table. To open a PDF for Adobe Reader, for example, you can use the type attribute to specify the MIME type as: application/pdf.

In chapter 11, you'll learn how to add audio and video to your web site. For other types of media, though, the <a> element can do a good job of getting the results that you want.

Popular media formats and MIME types

Format	Description	MIME type
PDF	Portable Document Format file	`application/pdf`
WAV	Waveform audio file	`audio/x-wave`
MP3	MPEG audio file	`audio/mpeg or audio/x-mpeg`
MPG/MPEG	MPEG video file	`video/mpeg`
SWF	ShockWave Flash file	`application/x-shockwave-flash`

Two of the popular media players

Player	Description
Adobe Reader	Used to display PDF files.
Adobe Flash Player	Commonly used to display Flash animation and videos (SWF).

An HTML link that displays a PDF file in a new window

```
<a href="documents/instructors_summary.pdf"
   type="application/pdf"
   target="_blank">Read the Instructor's Summary<a>
```

The PDF file displayed in a browser

An HTML link that plays an MP3 file

```
<a href="music/twist_away.mp3" type="audio/mpeg">MP3 file</a>
```

An HTML link that plays a PowerPoint slide show

```
<a href="media/chapter_01.pps"
   target="_blank">Review the slides for chapter 1</a>
```

Description

- Special *media players* may be required to play a media file in a browser. Often, media players require browser *plug-ins* for playing specific types of files.

- When you use the <a> element to display a media file, the file is typically displayed in its own web page and opened in the default player associated with the file type.

- To help the browser determine which player to use, you can include a type attribute on the <a> element to specify a *MIME type* that identifies the type of content.

Figure 7-12   How to link to a media file

How to create navigation lists and bars

This chapter closes by showing you how to use lists and links in the navigation lists and bars for your web pages. As you will see, the preferred way to do that is to code the <a> elements for the navigation within an unordered list.

How to create a navigation list

Figure 7-13 shows how to create a *navigation list*. This is just a vertical list of links. Here, the <a> elements are coded within an unordered list. This is the preferred way to create a navigation list, because a list is a logical container for the links.

If you look at the CSS for the ul element, you can see that the bullets are removed by the list-style property. If you look at the CSS for the li element, you can see that a border is placed around each item and the width of each item is set to 200 pixels. In addition, the margin property for these elements puts space above and below them.

The most critical CSS, though, is for the <a> elements. First, the display property of these elements is set to "block". This makes the entire block for each link clickable, not just the text. Then, the padding sets the size of each block. Last, the text-decoration property is used to remove the underlining for the text.

Although it's a good practice to keep the underlines for links because that makes it clear that they're links, it's okay to remove the underlines if the formatting makes that clear. In this case, the formatting makes the links within the list items look like buttons. Since buttons are also clickable, the underlines can be removed.

Of course, the simple formatting in this example could be improved by making the list items look even more like buttons. For instance, you could round the corners and add shadows. Or, you could add an icon, like an >> icon, to the right side of the link to indicate that it's a link.

To let the users know which page they're on, it's also a good practice to highlight the link that represents the current page. To do that, the HTML in this example uses the "current" class for the third item, and the CSS changes the background color for that class to silver.

A navigation list

The HTML for the navigation list

```
<h1>Navigation List</h1>
<nav id="nav_list">
    <ul>
        <li><a href="index.html">Home</a></li>
        <li><a href="tickets.html">Get Tickets</a></li>
        <li><a href="members.html" class="current">Become a Member</a></li>
        <li><a href="about_us.html">About Us</a></li>
    </ul>
</nav>
```

The CSS for the navigation list

```
* { margin: 0;
    padding: 0; }
#nav_list ul {
    list-style: none;                  /* removes bullets from list items */
    margin-left: 1.25em;
    margin-bottom: 1.5em; }
#nav_list li {
    width: 200px;
    margin-bottom: .5em;               /* the space after each list item */
    border: 2px solid blue; }          /* adds border around each item */
#nav_list li a {
    display: block;                    /* makes the entire box clickable */
    padding: .5em 0 .5em 1.5em;        /* provides the space around the link */
    text-decoration: none;             /* removes the underlines */
    font-weight: bold;
    color: blue; }
#nav_list a.current {
    backgound-color: silver; }         /* makes current background silver */
```

Description

- The HTML for a *navigation list* is best coded as a series of <a> elements within the li elements of an unordered list.

- To make the entire box for a link clickable, you can set the display property for the <a> elements to block and use padding to provide the space around the links.

- To show the users what page they're on, it's a good practice to highlight the current link. One way to do that is to apply a different color to it.

Figure 7-13   How to create a navigation list

How to create a navigation bar

Figure 7-14 shows how create a *navigation bar*. This is a horizontal list of links that often provide the primary navigation for a site. Here again, the <a> elements are coded within an unordered list because that's the preferred way to do this.

The examples in this figure use the same HTML as the example in the previous figure. Then, in the CSS for the first bar, the bullets are removed from the ul element and the display of the li elements is set to "inline". That displays the links horizontally rather than vertically. In addition, top and bottom borders are added to the ul element and a right border to the li elements. Note here, though, that the user has to click on the underlined text to activate a link. You might also notice that the current link has its underline (text-decoration) removed.

The CSS for the second bar is similar. Here again, the bullets are removed and the li elements are displayed inline. But this time, the background color for the bar is blue, and the text color of the li elements is white. Also, the underlines are removed from links, and the li elements have a right border that is white. Then, because the padding for the <a> elements sets the size of the links within the line items, the entire area for each link is clickable.

Two navigation bars

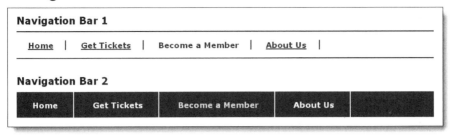

The HTML for the navigation bar

```
<nav id="nav_bar">
    <ul>
        <li><a href="index.html">Home</a></li>
        <li><a href="tickets.html">Get Tickets</a></li>
        <li><a href="members.html" class="current">Become a Member</a></li>
        <li><a href="about_us.html">About Us</a></li>
    </ul>
</nav>
```

The CSS for the first navigation bar

```
#nav_bar ul {
    list-style: none;
    padding: 1em 0;        /* padding above and below li elements */
    border-top: 2px solid black;
    border-bottom: 2px solid black; }
#nav_bar li {
    display: inline;
    padding: 0 1.5em;      /* padding to right and left of items */
    border-right: 2px solid black; }
#nav_bar a {
    font-weight: bold;
    color: blue; }
#nav_bar a.current { color: text-decoration: none; }
```

The CSS for the second navigation bar

```
#nav_bar ul {
    list-style: none;
    padding: 1em 0;        /* padding above and below li elements */
    background-color: blue; }
#nav_bar li { display: inline; }
#nav_bar a {
    padding: 1em 2em;      /* padding around <a> elements */
    text-decoration: none;
    color: white;
    font-weight: bold;
    border-right: 2px solid white; }
#nav_bar a.current { color: yellow; }
```

Description

- The HTML for a *navigation bar* is best coded as a series of <a> elements within the li elements of an unordered list. Then, the CSS gives them the appearance of a bar.

Figure 7-14   How to create a navigation bar

The Town Hall home page with a navigation bar

To put navigation bars in a larger context, figure 7-15 shows the Town Hall home page after a navigation bar has been added to it. The HTML for this bar is the same as in the previous figure, but the first link has "current" as its class attribute because the current page is the home page. You also need to know that this HTML is inserted right after the code for the header and before the code for the section.

The CSS for this bar is somewhat different than in the previous figure because the header for the Town Hall home page already had a bottom border that can be used as the top border for the navigation bar. As a result, the CSS for the bar calls for a bottom border that has the same width and color as the bottom border of the header. The CSS also uses that color for the current link.

The Town Hall home page with a navigation bar

The CSS for the navigation bar

```
#nav_bar {
    clear: left;
    margin: 0;
    padding: 0;
    border-bottom: 2px solid #ef9c00; }
#nav_bar ul {
    margin-left: 0;
    margin-bottom: .5em;
    list-style: none;
    padding: .5em 2em 0 0; }
#nav_bar li {
    display: inline;
    padding: 0 1.5em;
    border-right: 2px solid black; }
#nav_bar a.current { color: #ef9c00; }
```

Description

- The HTML for the bar is almost the same as in the last two figures, but the "current" class is applied to the <a> element for the home link. This HTML is inserted after the header element and before the section element for this page.

- The CSS is similar to the CSS in the last figure, but the bar only requires a bottom border because the header has a bottom border that works as the top border for the bar. The bottom border for the bar is set to the same color as the bottom border for the header. Also, the floating in the header is cleared.

- The link with the class attribute set to "current" is set to the same color as the borders to show the users which link they are currently visiting.

Figure 7-15   The Town Hall home page with a navigation bar

Perspective

Now that you've completed this chapter, you should have a good perspective on what you can do with lists and links. From this point on, you can use this chapter as a reference whenever you need it.

Terms

unordered list	tab order	MIME type
ordered list	access key	navigation list
nested list	placeholder	navigation bar
description list	media player	
link	plug-in	

Summary

- An *unordered list* is displayed as a bulleted list, but you can change the bullets with CSS.

- An *ordered list* is displayed as a numbered list, but you can change the types of numbers that are used with CSS.

- A *description list* consists of terms and descriptions.

- You typically code an <a> element to create a *link* that loads another web page, but you can also use an <a> element to start an email message by coding the href attribute as "mailto:" followed by the email address.

- You can use the tabindex attribute of an <a> element to change the *tab order* of a link, and you can use the accesskey attribute to provide an *access key* for activating the link.

- You can use pseudo-code selectors in CSS to change the default colors for links and to change the styles when the mouse hovers over a link.

- You can use the target attribute to load a linked page in a new browser window or tab. This attribute is no longer deprecated in HTML5.

- A *placeholder* is a location on a page that can be linked to. To create a placeholder, you use the id attribute of an <a> element. To go to the placeholder, you specify that id in the href attribute of another <a> element.

- If an <a> element links to a media file, the browser tries to display or play it by using the right *media player*. To help the browser find the right player, you can use the type attribute to specify a *MIME type*.

- To create a *navigation list* or *navigation bar*, you code a series of <a> elements within the li elements of an unordered list. Then, you can use CSS to remove the bullets and to change the display property so the list is displayed horizontally.

Exercise 7-1   Enhance the Town Hall home page

In this exercise, you'll be working with a second version of the web site that you developed for the chapters in section 1 of this book. This version includes new versions of the HTML and CSS files. In this exercise, you'll enhance the home page so it looks like this:

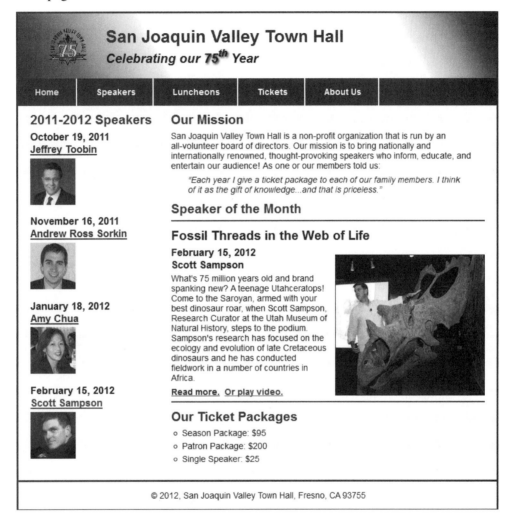

Open the HTML and CSS files for this page

1. Use your text editor to open new versions of the index.html and main.css files for the Town Hall web site:

    ```
    c:\html5_css3\exercises\town_hall_2\index.html
    c:\html5_css3\exercises\town_hall_2\styles\main.css
    ```

2. Test the index file in Firefox and see that a navigation bar has been added to the home page. However, it doesn't look like the one above.

Modify the navigation bar so it looks like the one above

3.   In the HTML file, add the fifth link to the bar.

4.   Using figure 7-14 as a guide, modify the styles for the bar so it looks like the one above. Use #800000 as the background color, #fffded as the color for the text and right borders, and yellow as the text color for the current item. Now, test these changes in Firefox and adjust the CSS until you get it right.

5.   If you've got borders at the top and bottom of the bar, try deleting them so the right borders flow through the bar to the header and section. That's the way it is above. Then, test this change to see whether you like it. If you don't, return it to the way it was.

Play a video

6.   At the bottom of the Speaker of the Month copy, change "Or meet us there!" to a link that plays the sampson.swf file in the media folder in a new window. This link should say: "Or play video." Then, test this change.

Change the bullets in the unordered list

7.   Change the bullets in the unordered list to circles. Then, test this change.

Validate and test in IE

8.   When you've got everything working right, validate the HTML page and test it in IE. If you have any problems, fix them and test again in both Firefox and IE. Remember that in the current version of IE, the gradient in the heading won't be displayed.

Exercise 7-2   Add the bar to the speaker's page

1.   Add the navigation bar of exercise 7-1 to the speaker's page for Scott Sampson. To do that, you need to add the HTML for the bar to the file named sampson.html in the speakers folder, and you need to add the CSS for the bar to the file named speaker.css in the styles folder. You may also need to adjust the CSS.

2.   Test and adjust to get the formatting right.

3.   In the HTML file, make sure the paths in the links for the navigation bar are correct. Because the sampson.html page is in the speakers folder and the index.html and luncheons.html pages are in the root folder, you'll need to use document-relative paths to go to these pages. Also, none of the links in the navigation bar of the sampson.html page should be current.

4.   Test to make sure that the Home and Luncheons links go to the right pages.

8

How to work with images

In chapter 3, you learned the basic skills for including images on a web page. Now, this chapter will expand upon those skills.

Basic skills for working with images

In the topics that follow, you'll learn the basic skills for working with images. This information will review and expand upon the skills you learned in chapter 3.

Types of images for the Web

Figure 8-1 presents the three types of images you can use on a web page. To start, *JPEG files* are commonly used for photographs and scanned images, because these files can represent millions of colors and they use a type of compression that can display complex images with a small file size.

Although JPEG files lose information when they're compressed, they typically contain high quality images to begin with so this loss of information isn't noticeable on a web page. Similarly, although JPEG files don't support transparency, you usually don't need it for any of the colors in a photograph.

In contrast, *GIF files* are typically used for simple illustrations or logos that require a limited number of colors. Two advantages of storing images in this format are (1) they can be compressed without losing any information, and (2) one of the colors in the image can be transparent.

A GIF file can also contain an *animated image*. An animated image consists of a series of images called *frames*. When you display an animated image, each frame is displayed for a preset amount of time, usually fractions of a second. Because of that, the image appears to be moving. For example, the two globes in this figure are actually two of 30 frames that are stored in the same GIF file. When this file is displayed, the globe appears to be rotating.

Unlike the GIF and JPEG formats, which have been used for years in print materials, *PNG files* were developed specifically for the Web. In particular, this format was developed as a replacement for the GIF format. The PNG advantages over the GIF format include better compression, support for millions of colors, and support for variable transparency.

Image types

Type	Description
JPEG	Typically used for photographs and scanned images because it uses a type of compression that can display complex images with a small file size. A JPEG file can represent millions of colors, loses information when compressed, and doesn't support transparency.
GIF	Typically used for logos, small illustrations such as clip art, and animated images. A GIF file can represent up to 256 colors, doesn't lose information when compressed, and supports transparency on a single color.
PNG	Typically used as a replacement for still GIF images. Compressed PNG files are typically smaller than GIF compressed files, although no information is lost. This format can represent millions of colors and supports transparency on multiple colors. Although PNG files are supported by most modern browsers, they have limited support on mobile devices.

Typical JPEG images

Typical GIF images

Description

- *JPEG* (Joint Photographic Experts Group) images are commonly used for the photographs and images of a web page. Although information is lost when you compress a JPEG file, the reduced quality of the image usually isn't noticeable.

- *GIF* (Graphic Interchange Format) images are commonly used for logos and small illustrations. They can also be used for *animated images* that contain *frames*.

- The *PNG* (Portable Network Graphics) format was developed specifically for the web as a replacement for GIF files. Although this format can also be used for photographs, JPEG is the preferred format for photographs because it results in smaller file sizes.

Figure 8-1   Types of images for the Web

How to include an image on a page

To include an image on a web page, you use the img element. Figure 8-2 presents the most common attributes of this element. Because you saw these attributes in chapter 3, you shouldn't have any trouble understanding how they work.

The HTML shown in this figure contains two img elements. Although they both display the same image, the first element includes height and width attributes. These attributes should be used to indicate the actual size of the image in pixels so you shouldn't include any unit of measure when you code them.

When you code them so they represent the actual size of the image, the browser can reserve the correct amount of space for the image as the page is loaded. Then, the browser can reserve the right amount of space for the image and continue rendering the page as it is loaded. This can improve the user experience if a page contains many images.

How to resize an image

If you need to resize an image, figure 8-2 shows how to do that with CSS. Here, the CSS resizes the second image so it's half of its original size. In this example, both the height and width are specified, but if you specify either one, you'll get the same result. That's because the other value will be calculated automatically based on the original proportions of the image.

The trouble with resizing an image is that the image is still downloaded at its full size before it's reduced. The best way to resize an image, then, is to use an image editor to create an image that's the right size. You'll learn more about that later in this chapter.

Attributes of the <img> tag

Attribute	Description
src	The relative or absolute URL of the image to display. It is required.
alt	Alternate text to display in place of the image. It is required.
height	The height of the image in pixels.
width	The width of the image in pixels.

CSS properties for sizing an image

Property	Description
height	A relative or absolute value that specifies the height of the image if the height is different from its original size.
width	A relative or absolute value that specifies the width of the image if the width is different from its original size.

The HTML for two images

```
<p><img src="images/students.jpg" alt="teacher and students"
        height="300" width="400">  
    <img id="small" src="images/students.jpg" alt="teacher and students"></p>
```

CSS for resizing the second image

```
#small {
    height: 150px;
    width: 200px; }
```

The images in a web browser

Accessibility guidelines

- For images with useful content, always code an alt element that describes the content.
- For images that are used for decoration, code the alt attribute as an empty string.

Description

- Use the height and width attributes of the <img> tag only to specify the size of the existing image. Then, the browser can reserve the right amount of space for the image and continue rendering the page while the image is being loaded.
- To display an image at a size other than its full size, you can use the CSS height and width properties. Better, though, is to use an image editor to correctly size the image.

Figure 8-2 How to include and resize an image

How to align an image vertically

When you include an image on a web page, you may want to align it with the in-line elements that surround it. If an image is preceded or followed by text, for example, you may want to align the image with the top, middle, or bottom of the text. To do that, you use the vertical-align property shown in figure 8-3.

To indicate the alignment you want to use, you typically specify one of the keywords listed in this figure. If you specify text-bottom, for example, the image is aligned with the bottom of the adjacent text. In contrast, if you specify bottom, the image is aligned with the bottom of the box that contains the adjacent text.

In most cases, the bottom of the text and the bottom of the box are the same. The exception is if a line height is specified for the box. In that case, the text is centered in the box. Then, if you specify bottom for the image alignment, the image will be aligned at the bottom of the box, which is below the bottom of the text. The top and text-top keywords work the same way.

The middle keyword is useful because it lets you center an image with the surrounding text. This is illustrated in the example in this figure. Here, the HTML includes three paragraphs, each with an image followed by some text. When I didn't specify the vertical alignment for the images, the bottom of each image was aligned with the bottom of the text. When I specified middle for the vertical alignment, the center of each image was aligned with the center of the text.

Note that I specified a right margin for the images for both the aligned and unaligned examples to create space between the images and the text. You can also use padding and borders with images. This works just like it does for block elements.

The property for aligning images vertically

Property	Description
vertical-align	A relative or absolute value or a keyword that determines the vertical alignment of an image. See the table below for common keywords.

Common keywords for the vertical-align property

Keyword	Description
bottom	Aligns the bottom of the image box with the bottom of the box that contains the adjacent in-line elements.
middle	Aligns the midpoint of the image box with the midpoint of the containing block.
top	Aligns the top of the image box with the top of the box that contains the adjacent in-line elements.
text-bottom	Aligns the bottom of the image box with the bottom of the text in the containing block.
text-top	Aligns the top of the image box with the top of the text in the containing block.

The HTML for a web page with three images

```
<h2>To order now:</h2>
<p><img src="images/computer.gif" alt="web address">
   <b>Web:</b> www.murach.com</p>
<p><img src="images/telephone.gif" alt="phone">
   <b>Phone:</b> 1-800-221-5528</p>
<p><img src="images/fax.gif" alt="fax">
   <b>Fax:</b> 1-559-440-0963</p>
```

CSS that aligns the images in the middle of the text

```
img {
    vertical-align: middle;
    margin-right: 10px; }
```

The images in a web browser before and after they're aligned

Description

- If you use pixels, points, or ems to specify the value for the vertical-align property, the image is raised if the value is positive and lowered if it's negative. If you specify a percent, the image is raised or lowered based on the percentage of the line height.

- You can use margins, padding, and borders with images just like block elements.

Figure 8-3   How to align an image vertically

How to float an image

In section 1, you learned how to float a logo in a heading and how to float block elements for page layout. Now, figure 8-4 reinforces what you've learned.

At the top of this figure, you can see the two properties for floating images: float and clear. These properties work just like they do for block elements. You use the float property to determine whether the image should be floated to the right or to the left. And you use the clear property to stop an element from floating to the right or left of a floated image.

In the HTML in this figure, you can see that the first element defines an image. This image is followed by an unordered list and a paragraph. In the CSS that follows, you can see that the image is floated to the left. In addition, top and bottom margins are specified for the image to create space between the image and the text that precedes and follows it. In this case, you don't need to specify a right margin for the image because the items in the list are indented by default. Also note that you don't have to specify a width when you float an image. That's because the width can be determined from the actual width of the image.

Finally, notice that the clear property with a value of "left" is specified for the paragraph that follows the list. Because of that, this paragraph won't flow into the space to the right of the image. Instead, the text starts below the image.

The properties for floating images

Property	Description
float	A keyword that determines how an image is floated. Possible values are left, right, and none. None is the default.
clear	A keyword that determines if an element that follows a floated element flows into the space left by the floated element. Possible values are left, right, both, and none. None is the default.

Some of the HTML for a web page

```
<img src="images/students.jpg" alt="teacher and students">
<ul>
    <li>in college and university MIS programs that focus on providing
        students with practical, real-world experience</li>
    <li>by technical institutes and community colleges that focus on the
        skills that employers are looking for</li>
    <li>in Continuing Ed and Extension programs where the students are
        professionals who are expanding their skills</li>
</ul>
<p id="last">So if your program fits one of those profiles, please take
a look at our books. I&rsquo;m confident you&rsquo;ll discover a new level
of structure, clarity, and relevance that will benefit both you and your
students.</p>
```

CSS that floats the image and clears the last paragraph

```
img {
    float: left;
    margin-top: 15px;
    margin-bottom: 10px; }
#last { clear: left; }
```

The HTML in a web browser

Teach your students using the books the professionals use

Although our books are written for professional programmers who need to master new job skills, there have always been instructors teaching job-oriented curricula who've adopted our books. For example, our books are used:

- in college and university MIS programs that focus on providing students with practical, real-world experience
- by technical institutes and community colleges that focus on the skills that employers are looking for
- in Continuing Ed and Extension programs where the students are professionals who are expanding their skills

So if your program fits one of those profiles, please take a look at our books. I'm confident you'll discover a new level of structure, clarity, and relevance that will benefit both you and your students.

Description

- You can use the same techniques to float an image that you use to float a block element.

Figure 8-4   How to float an image

Advanced skills for working with images

The topics that follow present some advanced skills for working with images. One or more of these may come in handy as you develop web pages that use images.

How to use the HTML5 figure and figcaption elements

The HTML5 figure and figcaption elements can be used with anything that is used as a figure, like an image or table. Because an image is often used as a figure, though, we're presenting these elements in this chapter.

Figure 8-5 shows how to use these elements for an image that's used as a figure. Here, the figure contains one img element plus one figcaption element that provides a caption below the image. Then, the figure is floated within an article, and the image and caption float along with it.

By default, a figcaption element is an inline element, not a block element. As a result, you will usually want to use the CSS display property to change it to a block element. That makes it easier to format the caption. In this example, the figcaption element comes after the image in the HTML so the caption is displayed below the image. But you can change that by coding the figcaption element before the image in the HTML.

Although you can get the same results without using these HTML5 elements, it's better to use these semantic elements. That way, it's easy to tell that the image is used as a figure, and it's easy to tell that the caption applies to the image.

A web page that uses figure and figcaption elements

The HTML for the figure and figcaption elements

```
<article>
    <h1>Fossil Threads in the Web of Life</h1>
    <figure>
        <img src="images/sampson_dinosaur.jpg" alt="Scott Sampson">
        <figcaption>Scott Sampson and friend</figcaption>
    </figure>
    <p>What's 75 million years old and brand spanking new? A teenage
    ...
    </p>
</article>
```

The CSS for the figure and figcaption elements

```
figure {
    float: left;
    margin-right: 1.5em; }
figcaption {
    display: block;
    font-weight: bold;
    padding-top: .25em;
    margin-bottom: 1em;
    border-bottom: 1px solid black; }
```

Description

- The figure element can be used as a container for anything that is used as a figure, like an image or a table.

- The figcaption element can be used within a figure to provide a caption that describes the figure, but it is optional. When coded, it can be anywhere within the figure.

- By default, the figcaption element is an inline element so you usually need to change that.

Figure 8-5   How to use the HTML5 figure and figcaption elements

How to work with thumbnails

For some pages, you will want to display images at a small size because you can fit more on the page. However, you will also want to provide a way for the user to display the images at a larger size. For example, many e-commerce pages display small images of their products. Then, the user can click on one of the images to see a larger version of the same image.

When a group of small images is displayed, the images are typically referred to as *thumbnails*. Although this name implies that an image is about the size of a thumbnail, it can be used to refer to any small image.

Figure 8-6 presents an example that uses thumbnails. At the top of this figure, you can see part of a web page with six thumbnails. If you look at the HTML for this page, you can see that the thumbnail images are coded within <a> elements. That way, when the user clicks on an image, the page specified on the href attribute of the <a> element will be displayed. In this case, the page displays a description of the photo along with a larger image.

In this example, the thumbnails are displayed on one web page and the full photos are displayed on separate pages. In other words, a new web page is displayed with a full photo each time a thumbnail is clicked. By using JavaScript, though, you can display the full photos on the same page as the thumbnails by replacing the current photo with a new one each time a thumbnail is clicked. That way, you can greatly reduce the number of web pages that are needed to display a series of photos. In chapter 13, you'll learn more about this JavaScript capability.

For accessibility, you should normally avoid the use of images as links. But this type of page is a common exception. At the least, though, you can provide alt attributes that give the visually-impaired a sense of what's going on. These attributes should be better, of course, than the ones in this example.

Thumbnails in a web page

The photo that's displayed when the fifth thumbnail is clicked

The HTML for the page that contains the thumbnails

```
<h3>Ram Tap Combined Test</h3>
<p>
    <a href="p1.html"><img src="thumbnails/t1.jpg" alt="Photo 1"></a>
    <a href="p2.html"><img src="thumbnails/t2.jpg" alt="Photo 2"></a>
    <a href="p3.html"><img src="thumbnails/t3.jpg" alt="Photo 3"></a>
    <a href="p4.html"><img src="thumbnails/t4.jpg" alt="Photo 4"></a>
    <a href="p5.html"><img src="thumbnails/t5.jpg" alt="Photo 5"></a>
    <a href="p6.html"><img src="thumbnails/t6.jpg" alt="Photo 6"></a>
</p>
```

Description

- A *thumbnail* is a small version of an image that can be used to make downloading the image faster and to save space on a web page that contains multiple images.

- To create a thumbnail, you can use an image editor for sizing an image.

- A thumbnail can be used as the image for a link that displays a page with a larger version of the image.

- A larger version of a thumbnail can be displayed on the same page by using JavaScript for an image swap. See chapter 13 for more information.

Figure 8-6   How to work with thumbnails

How to do image rollovers

You may remember from chapter 1 that an image rollover occurs when the mouse hovers over an image and the image is replaced by another image. Although JavaScript is often used for image rollovers, you can do them without JavaScript as shown in figure 8-7.

The HTML in this figure consists of just an h1 and a <p> element within the body element. Also, the <p> element is given an id so CSS can be applied to it. But note that the <p> element is empty. So where is the image for this page?

In the CSS for the <p> element, the first rule set specifies a background image. That displays the image within the element. Then, the second rule set specifies a different background image when the mouse is hovering over the <p> element. That accomplishes the image rollover.

This is a relatively simple technique that you can use for a limited number of image rollovers. But if coding these rule sets gets cumbersome, you can use JavaScript to simplify the process.

The image has been rolled over because the mouse is hovering over it

The HTML for the page

```
<body>
    <h1>Ram Tap Combined Test</h1>
    <p id="image1"></p>
</body>
```

The CSS for the image rollover

```
#image1 {
    background-image: url("h1.jpg");
    width: 434px;
    height: 312px;
}
#image1:hover {
    background-image: url("h2.jpg");
}
```

Description

- An *image rollover* is an image the gets changed when the mouse hovers over it.
- One way to do image rollovers is to use background images and the :hover selector.
- When you use this method, the first background image is applied to a block element like a <p> element. Then, the second background image is displayed when the mouse hovers over it.

Figure 8-7   How to do image rollovers

How to create image maps

You've probably seen web pages that display an image and go to other pages depending on where you click in the image. For example, you might be able to click on a state within a United States map to go to a page with information about that state.

To make this work, you use an *image map* as shown in figure 8-8. Here, the image in the browser consists of pictures of two books. Then, when the PHP book is clicked, one page is displayed. When the JavaScript book is clicked, another page is displayed. Within the image map, each clickable area is called a *hotspot*.

To define an image map, you use the img, map, and area elements. In the usemap attribute of the img element, you code the name of the map element that will be used. In the map element, you code the name that the img element refers to. Then, within the map element, you code one or more area elements that define the hotspots of the map.

The key to defining an area map is coding the area elements. Here, you code the href attribute to specify what page you want to display when the area is clicked. Then, you code the shape attribute to identify the type of shape you want to use for the region. In this example, I used two polygons.

To identify the actual shape and location of an area, you code the coords attribute. The values for this attribute depend on the shape of the area. For rectangular areas, which assumes that the rectangle is vertical, not at an angle, four values are specified. The first two identify the x, y coordinates in pixels of the upper left corner of the area relative to the upper left corner of the image. The second two identify the x, y coordinates in pixels of the lower right corner of the area.

If you want to define a more complex shape than a rectangle or circle, you can specify "poly" for the value of the shape attribute. Then, the coords attribute will consist of a series of x, y coordinates that start in the upper-left corner and travel clockwise around the shape. To identify the shape for the PHP book, for example, I included five sets of x, y coordinates because part of the book is hidden. To identify the shape for the JavaScript book, I only used four sets of coordinates.

To get the coordinates that you need for an image map, you can use an image editor. Then, you just point to the locations in the image and record the coordinates that are shown.

The attribute of the img element that identifies the related map element

Attribute	Description
usemap	Identifies the related map element. The value of this attribute is the value of the name attribute of the map element, preceded by a pound sign (#).

The attribute of the map element that gives it a name

Attribute	Description
name	Provides a name for the map.

The attributes of the area elements that create the image maps

Attribute	Description
href	Specifies a relative or absolute URL that identifies the page that will be displayed when the area is clicked.
shape	A keyword that indicates the type of shape the area represents. Possible keywords are rect, circle, poly, and default, which is the same as rect.
coords	Values that indicate the shape and location of the area. Two sets of x, y coordinates are required for a rectangle to identify the upper left and lower right corners. Three values are required for a circle to identify the x, y coordinates of the center and the radius. Polygonal shapes require a series of x, y coordinates.
alt	Text that's displayed in place of the area if the image can't be displayed.

An image in a web browser with hotspots created by an image map

The HTML for the image and image map

```
<img src="images/web.jpg" alt="PHP and JavaScript books" usemap="#books">
<map name="books">
    <area href="php.html" alt="PHP book" title="PHP"
        shape="poly" coords="0,44, 170,1, 202,13, 170,230, 57,258">
    <area href="javascript.html" alt="JavaScript book" title="JavaScript"
        shape="poly" coords="223,40, 393,88, 336,302, 166,252">
</map>
```

Description

- You can use the map and area elements to define an *image map* that provides clickable areas for the image called *hotspots*.

- The coordinates for an area are relative to the upper left corner of the image and are measured in pixels.

Figure 8-8   How to create image maps

Related skills for working with images

At this point, you've learned the HTML and CSS skills that you need for working with images. If someone else is responsible for getting and sizing the images that you use, that may be all you need to know. But if you need to get and size your own images, here are some other skills that you'll need.

When to use an image editor

When you use images on a web page, you want them to be the right size and format. If they aren't that way, you can use an image editor like the one in figure 8-9 to make the adjustments. Today, one of the most popular and expensive editors is Adobe Photoshop, but Adobe also offers a moderately-priced consumer product called Photoshop Elements. Beyond that, there are many other image editors that range from free to hundreds of dollars. One of the most popular free editors is GIMP, which can be downloaded from the GIMP web site.

Because using an image editor goes beyond HTML5 and CSS3, this book doesn't show you how to use one. However, this figure does summarize some of the common uses of an image editor.

The primary use of an image editor is to size the images and save them in the right format so they will load as quickly as possible. In this figure, you can see some of the controls for doing that. Usually, you save an image for the web with a resolution of 72 dpi (dots per inch) because most monitors support that resolution, and lower resolution means faster loading.

By default, an image is displayed on a page only after the entire file has been loaded. In many cases, that's okay. But if a page contains many images, waiting for the page to load can be an unpleasant user experience. One way to improve that is to use an image editor to create *progressive JPEGs*, *interlaced GIFs*, or *interlaced PNGs*. Then, the images will slowly come into view as the page is loaded.

You can also use an image editor to work with an *animated image* like a GIF file that contains *frames*. For instance, you can specify whether the frames are shown only once or repeated. You can also set the timing between the frames.

If an image has a transparent color, you can save it as a GIF or PNG file with *transparency*. To understand how this works, you need to know that an image is always rectangular. This is illustrated by the first starburst example in this figure. Here, the area that's outside the starburst is white, and it isn't transparent. As a result, you can see the white when the image is displayed over a colored background. In contrast, the area outside the second starburst image is also white, but it is transparent. Because of that, you can see the background color behind it.

The second image in this example also uses a *matte*. A matte is useful when a GIF or PNG image with a transparent color is displayed against a colored background. Without a matte, the edges of the image can appear jagged. But if you add a matte that's the same color as the background, it will help the image blend into the background and minimize the jagged edges.

An image editor as it is used to change the size of an image

Typical editing operations

- Change the size, image type, or quality of an image.
- Control the animation of an animated GIF file.
- Save an image with transparency or a matte.
- Get the coordinates for an image map.

Three popular image editors

- Adobe Photoshop (the industry standard for graphic artists)
- Adobe Photoshop Elements (an inexpensive editor)
- GIMP (a free editor)

An image without transparency and with transparency and a matte

Description

- If an image with *transparency* is displayed over a colored background, the background color will show through the transparent portion of the image.
- If an image with a transparent color is displayed over a colored background, a *matte* of the same color will help the image blend into the background.

Figure 8-9   When to use an image editor

You can also use a matte with a JPEG image. Then, all of the transparent area in the original image is filled with the color you choose. Later, when the image is displayed against a background that's the same color as the matte, the matte area appears to be transparent.

How to get images and icons

For most web sites, you'll use your own photos and create most of the graphic images that you use. But sometimes, you may need to get images or icons from another source. The easiest way to do that is to copy or download them from another web site.

Figure 8-10 lists several of the most popular web sites you can use to get and search for images and icons. For example, www.freefoto.com, openphoto.com, and www.sxc.hu are three of the most popular web sites for getting images.

Although you can find many images and icons that are available for free on the Web, most require a Creative Commons license. The types of licenses that are available and the conditions required by these licenses are summarized in this figure. As you can see, all of the licenses require attribution, which means that you must give credit to the author of the image or the web site that provided the image. The other license conditions determine how an image can be shared, whether it can be used for commercial purposes, and whether you can derive new images from the existing image.

Stock photos are special images that are typically produced in a studio. For example, the JPEG file in figure 8-4 is a stock photo. You must pay for these types of images, and they can be expensive.

Incidentally, you can also get an image or the link to an image from another site by right-clicking on the image and selecting the appropriate command from the shortcut menu. Then, if you save the link to the image in the href attribute of an <img> tag, your web page will display the image that's actually stored on the other site. This is known as "hot linking" and it is highly discouraged unless you have an agreement with the other site. If, for example, you agree to provide a link to another site and that site agrees to provide a link to your site, this is a quick way to get the images and URLs that you will need.

Creative Commons license conditions for images and icons

Conditions	Description
Attribution	You can use the image and images derived from it as long as you give credit as requested by the author or web site providing the image.
Share Alike	You can distribute the image based on the license that governs the original work.
Non-Commercial	You can use the image and images derived from it for non-commercial purposes only.
No Derivative Works	You can use only the original image and not images derived from it.

Creative Commons licenses

- Attribution
- Attribution No Derivatives
- Attribution Non-Commercial Share Alike
- Attribution Share Alike
- Attribution Non-Commercial
- Attribution Non-Commercial No Derivatives

Popular web sites for images

- www.sxc.hu
- www.freefoto.com
- www.openphoto.net
- www.google.com/imghp

Popular web sites for stock photos

- www.istockphoto.com
- www.gettyimages.com

A popular search engine for stock photos

- www.everystockphoto.com

Description

- Many of the images and icons that are available from the Web are licensed under a Creative Commons license. The license can restrict the use of an image to one or more of the conditions listed above. The most common condition is attribution.
- Stock photos are typically produced in studios and can be purchased for a one-time fee of one dollar to several hundred dollars.
- You can also search for specific images and icons from a generic search engine such as Google.

Figure 8-10   How to get images and icons

How to create favicons

In chapter 3, you learned how to add a *favicon* to a web page. Now, figure 8-11 shows you how to create a favicon. As a refresher, this figure also includes the link element for a favicon. As you can see in the browser display, this favicon is displayed in the address bar and in the tab for the page. It may also be displayed as part of the bookmark for the page.

To start, you should know that a favicon is just a special-purpose icon. Like other icons, a favicon should always be stored in a file with the ico extension. That's because this is the only extension Internet Explorer supports for favicons.

To create a favicon, you can use a program or tool like the ones described in this figure. If you want to create your own icons from scratch, you can purchase a program like Axialis Icon Workshop. Otherwise, you can get one of the free products listed here.

If you're using Photoshop, for example, you can get the free plug-in that's available for that program. You can also download a free image converter such as IrfanView from the Internet. Or, you can use an online image converter such as FavIcon from Pics.

Although they can be larger, most favicons are 16 pixels wide and tall. In fact, some image converters will automatically convert the image you specify to 16x16 pixels. That's the case with FavIcon from Pics.

Other image converters will maintain the original size of the image when they create the favicon. When the favicon is displayed on the web page, however, it will be cropped so it's square. That's the case with IrfanView. To make sure a favicon is displayed the way you want, you should make sure the original image is square before you convert it to a favicon.

A web page with favicons (circled)

The link element in the head section that links to the favicon

```
<link rel="shortcut icon" href="images/favicon.ico">
```

Popular programs and tools for creating favicons

Program/tool	Description
Axialis Icon Workshop	A software product that lets you create, edit, and convert icons. For more information, go to www.axialis.com/iconworkshop/.
Photoshop plug-in	Free software that you can use with Photoshop. To download, go to www.telegraphics.com.au/sw/.
IrfanView	A free image converter that you can download from www.irfanview.com.
FavIcon from Pics	A free image converter that you can run online at: www.html-kit.com/favicon/.

Description

- A *favicon* is a small image that appears to the left of the URL in the browser's address bar. It may also appear to the left of the title in a browser tab, and it may be used by the browser for a favorite or bookmark.

- A favicon is typically 16 pixels wide and tall and typically has the extension ico since that's the only extension currently supported by Internet Explorer for icons.

- You can create an ico file by using an icon editor, a program that converts an image to an ico file, or a web-based converter.

Figure 8-11   How to create favicons

Perspective

Now that you've finished this chapter, you should have all the HTML and CSS skills that you need for developing web pages with images. But if you're going to need to do your own image editing, you'll also need to get an image editor and learn how to use it. At the least, the image editor that you choose should provide for sizing images and changing the image type and quality.

Terms

JPEG file	thumbnail	interlaced GIF
GIF file	image rollover	interlaced PNG
animated image	image map	transparency
frame	hotspot	matte
PNG file	progressive JPEG	favicon

Summary

- The three common formats for images are *JPEG* (for photographs and scanned images), *GIF* (for small illustrations, logos, and animated images), and *PNG* (typically used as a replacement for still GIF images).

- You should use the height and width attributes of an <img> tag only to specify the size of the image, not to resize it. Then, the browser can reserve the right amount of space for the image and continue rendering the page, even if the image is still being loaded.

- You can use CSS to vertically align an image within the block element that contains it. You can also use CSS to float an image.

- The HTML5 figure element can be used to treat an image as a figure that's referred to outside of the figure. The HTML5 figcaption element can be used within a figure element to provide a caption for the figure.

- A *thumbnail* is a small version of an image that is often used as a link to a page that displays a larger version of the image.

- An *image rollover* occurs when the mouse hovers over an image and the image is replaced by another image.

- An *image map* defines the clickable *hotspots* for an image. To define these hotspots, you code map and name elements in the HTML for the image.

- To resize an image so it's the right size for a web page, you can use an image editor like Photoshop or Photoshop Elements.

- To reduce the loading time for an image, you can use an image editor to change the image type or quality. To improve the user experience as images load, you can create *progressive JPEGs*, *interlaced GIFs*, and *interlaced PNGs*.

- A GIF file with two or more *frames* is an *animated image*. Then, you can use an image editor to control how that animation works.

- GIF and PNG files support *transparency*. Then, the background color that's behind the image shows through the transparent parts of the image.

- If you use an image editor to specify a *matte* for an image and then set the matte color to the same one that's used for the background color, the image will blend in better with the background.

- The Internet has many sites that offer images, stock photos, and icons that you may want to use for your site.

- A *favicon* is a small image that appears to the left of the URL in the browser's address bar. It is typically 16 pixels wide and has ico as its extension.

Exercise 8-1   Use a figure on the speaker's page

In this exercise, you'll enhance the speaker page by adding figure and figcaption elements so the page looks like the one that follows. If you didn't do exercise 7-2, your page won't have the navigation bar.

1. Use your text editor to open the HTML and CSS files for this speaker's page, which will be in the exercises/town_hall_2/speakers folder.

2. In the HTML file, enclose the img element at the top of the article in a figure element. Then, add a figcaption element below the img element.

3. In the CSS file, add the rule sets for formatting the figure and figcaption.

4. Test this enhancement in both Firefox and IE.

9

How to work with tables

If you look at the HTML for some of the web sites that are in use today, you'll see that many of them still use tables to control the page layout. As you saw in chapter 6, however, the right way to do that is to use CSS. As a result, you should only use tables to display tabular data. In this chapter, you'll learn how to do that.

Basic skills for using tables

In the topics that follow, you'll learn the basic skills for coding and formatting tables. But first, I want to introduce you to the structure of a table in HTML.

An introduction to tables

Figure 9-1 presents a simple table and points out its various components. To start, a table consists of one or more *rows* and *columns*. As you'll see in the next figure, you define a table by defining its rows. Then, within each row, you define a *cell* for each column.

Within each row, a table can contain two different kinds of cells. *Header cells* identify what's in the columns and rows of a table, and *data cells* contain the actual data of the table. For example, the three cells in the first row of the table in this figure are header cells that identify the contents of the columns. In contrast, the cells in the next four rows are data cells. The last row starts with a header cell that identifies the contents of the cells in that row.

In broad terms, a table starts with a *header* that can consist of one or more rows. Then, the *body* of the table presents the data for the table. Last, the *footer* provides summary data that can consist of one or more rows. For accessibility, a table should also have a caption above or below it that summarizes what's in the table.

A simple table with basic formatting

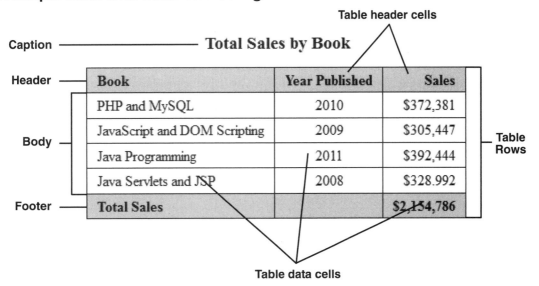

Description

- A *table* consists of *rows* and *columns* that intersect at *cells*.
- Cells that contain the data of the table are called *data cells*.
- Cells that identify the data in a column or row are called *header cells*.
- The *header* for a table can consist of more than one row, and the *footer* for a table can consist of more than one row.
- The *body* of a table, which contains the data, usually consists of two or more rows.
- Now that CSS can be used for page layout, you should only use tables for tabular data.

Figure 9-1   An introduction to tables

How to create a table

Figure 9-2 presents the four most common elements for coding tables. The table element defines the table itself. Then, you code the other elements within this element.

To define each row in a table, you use the tr (table row) element. Within each row, you code one th (table header) or td (table data) element for each cell in the row. You can see how this works in the table in this figure. This is the same table that's in figure 9-1, but without the formatting. In the last row, note that the first cell is coded as a th element. That's because it identifies the data in the last row.

By default, the content of a header cell is boldfaced and centered in the cell, and the content of a data cell is left-aligned. Also, the width of the cells is determined by the data they contain, with each cell in a column being as wide as the widest cell. You can see how this works in the browser display in this figure. In the next figure, though, you'll learn how to use CSS to format a table.

Common elements for coding tables

Element	Description
table	Defines a table. The other elements for the table are coded within this element.
tr	Defines a row.
th	Defines a header cell within a row.
td	Defines a data cell within a row.

The HTML for the table in figure 9-1 before it's formatted

```
<table>
    <tr>
        <th class="left">Book</th>
        <th>Year Published</th>
        <th>Sales</th>
    </tr>
    <tr>
        <td class="left">PHP and MySQL</td>
        <td>2010</td>
        <td>$372,381</td>
    </tr>
    <tr>

        .
        .
        .
    </tr>
    <tr id="total">
        <th class="left">Total Sales</th>
        <td></td>
        <td>$2,154,786</td>
    </tr>
</table>
```

The table in a web browser with no CSS formatting

Book	Year Published	Sales
PHP and MySQL	2010	$372,381
JavaScript and DOM Scripting	2009	$305,447
Java Programming	2011	$392,444
Java Servlets and JSP	2008	$328.992
Total Sales		$2,154,786

Description

- By default, the width of each column in a table is determined automatically based on its contents.
- By default, the content of a th element is boldfaced and centered, and the content of a td element is left-aligned.

Figure 9-2   How to create a table

How to use CSS to format a table

Figure 9-3 presents some of the common CSS properties for formatting tables. However, you can also use many of the other CSS properties that you've already learned to format a table.

As you saw in the last figure, a table doesn't include borders by default (the border around that table was added by the program that we use for capturing screens). In many cases, though, you'll want to add a border around a table to make it stand out on the page. You may also want to add borders around the cells or rows in a table to help identify the columns and rows.

To do that, you can use any of the border properties you learned about in chapter 5. In the CSS in this figure, for example, the shorthand border property adds a solid black border around the table and around each cell in the table.

By default, a small amount of space is included between the cells of a table. To remove that space, you can set the border-collapse property to a value of "collapse". Then, the borders between adjacent cells will be collapsed to a single border as shown in the first table in this figure. But note that if two adjacent cells have different borders, the most dominant border will be displayed. If one border is wider than the other, for example, the wider border will be displayed.

When you use the padding property with tables, it works similarly to the way it works with the box model. That is, it specifies the amount of space between the contents of a cell and the outer edge of the cell. In this figure, for example, you can see that .2 em of space has been added above and below the contents of each cell, and .7 em of space to the left and right of the contents.

To complete the formatting, the CSS left aligns those elements that are in the "left" class. It also bolds the type for the element with "total" as its id. If you look at the HTML in the last figure, you can see how this works. In figure 9-5, though, you'll learn how you can use CSS3 to do this without using ids and classes.

Common properties for formatting table, tr, th, and td elements

Property	Description
border-collapse	A keyword that determines whether space exists between the borders of adjacent cells or the borders are collapsed to a single border between cells. Possible values are collapse and separate. The default is separate.
border-spacing	A relative or absolute value that specifies the space between cells when the borders aren't collapsed. Not supported by IE7 and earlier.
padding	The space between the cell contents and the outer edge of the cell.
text-align	The horizontal alignment of text.
vertical-align	The vertical alignment of text.

The CSS for the table in figure 9-2

```
table {
    border: 1px solid black;
    border-collapse: collapse; }
th, td {
    border: 1px solid black;
    padding: .2em .7em;
    text-align: right; }
th.left, td.left { text-align: left; }
#total { font-weight: bold; }
```

The table in a web browser

Book	Year Published	Sales
PHP and MySQL	2010	$372,381
JavaScript and DOM Scripting	2009	$305,447
Java Programming	2011	$392,444
Java Servlets and JSP	2008	$328.992
Total Sales		$2,154,786

The table without collapsed borders

Book	Year Published	Sales
PHP and MySQL	2010	$372,381
JavaScript and DOM Scripting	2009	$305,447
Java Programming	2011	$392,444
Java Servlets and JSP	2008	$328.992
Total Sales		$2,154,786

Description

- In HTML5, the attributes that were commonly used for formatting tables have been deprecated. As a result, you should use CSS for all table formatting.

Figure 9-3   How to use CSS to format a table

How to add a header and footer

Figure 9-4 presents the elements for grouping rows into headers and footers. It also presents the element for grouping rows in the table body, which you'll typically do when you use a header and footer.

To code a header, you simply code the rows that make up the header between the opening and closing tags of the thead element. Similarly, you code a footer by coding rows within a tfoot element. And you code a body by coding rows within a tbody element.

The example in this figure illustrates how this works. Here, the first row of the table is coded within a thead element, the last row of the table is coded within a tfoot element, and the remaining rows are coded within a tbody element. Then, the CSS for this page applies a background color to the header and footer using a selector that includes the thead and tfoot elements. It also changes the font weight for the footer to bold. You can see the results in the browser.

The elements for coding the header, body, and footer

Element	Description
thead	Groups one or more rows into a table header.
tbody	Groups the rows between the header and footer into a table body.
tfoot	Groups one or more rows into a table footer.

The HTML for a table with a header, body, and footer

```
<table>
    <thead>
        <tr>
            <th class="left">Book</th>
            <th>Year published</th>
            <th>Total sales</th>
        </tr>
    </thead>
    <tbody>
        <tr>
            <td class="left">PHP and MySQL</td>
            <td>2010</td>
            <td>$372,381</td>
        </tr>
        .
        .
    </tbody>
    <tfoot>
        <tr>
            <th class="left">Total Sales</th>
            <td></td>
            <td>$2,154,786</td>
        </tr>
    </tfoot>
</table>
```

The CSS for the header and footer

```
thead, tfoot { background-color: aqua; }
tfoot { font-weight: bold; }
```

The table in a web browser

Book	Year Published	Sales
PHP and MySQL	2010	$372,381
JavaScript and DOM Scripting	2009	$305,447
Java Programming	2011	$392,444
Java Servlets and JSP	2008	$328,992
Total Sales		**$2,154,786**

Description

- The thead, tbody, and tfoot elements make it easier to style a table with CSS.

Figure 9-4   How to add a header and footer

How to use the CSS3 structural pseudo-classes for formatting tables

In chapter 4, you were introduced to a few of the CSS3 pseudo-classes. Now, figure 9-5 presents some of the ones that are especially useful for formatting tables. These classes can be referred to as the structural pseudo-classes, because they let you select elements by their structural location. By using these pseudo-classes in your selectors, you can avoid the use of id and class selectors, which simplifies your HTML.

To illustrate, the first example in this figure uses the first-child pseudo-class to select the first th and the first td element in each row. This is a structural pseudo-class that you were introduced in chapter 4. Then, the rule set left aligns the data in these cells. This means that you don't need to use the "left" class that was used in figure 9-3 for formatting.

The second example uses the nth-child selector to select the second th and td element in each row. Then, the rule set centers the heading and data in those cells. The result is that the contents of the cells in the second column of the table are centered.

The last example also uses the nth-child selector to select all even rows in the body of the table. Then, it applies silver as the background color for these rows. If you look at the table of n values in this figure, you can see that the n value could also be coded as 2n to select all even rows or 2n+1 to select all odd rows. If you want to apply a different color to every third row, you can use other combinations of n values to get that result.

The syntax for the CSS3 structural pseudo-class selectors

Syntax	Description
`:nth-child(n)`	nth child of parent
`:nth-last-child(n)`	nth child of parent counting backwards
`:nth-of-type(n)`	nth element of its type within the parent
`:nth-last-of-type(n)`	nth element of its type counting backwards

Typical n values

Value	Meaning
`odd`	Every odd child or element
`even`	Every even child or element
`n`	The nth child or element
`2n`	Same as even
`3n`	Every third child or element (3, 6, 9, ...)
`2n+1`	Same as odd
`3n+1`	Every third child or element starting with 1 (1, 4, 7, ...)

The CSS3 code for formatting a table without using classes

```
th:first-child, td:first-child {
    text-align: left; }
th:nth-child(2), td:nth-child(2) {
    text-align: center; }
tbody tr:nth-child(even) {
    background-color: silver; }
```

The table in a browser

Book	Year Published	Sales
PHP and MySQL	2010	$372,381
JavaScript and DOM Scripting	2009	$305,447
Java Programming	2011	$392,444
Java Servlets and JSP	2008	$328,992
ASP.NET with Visual Basic	2011	$351,200
ASP.NET with C#	2011	$404,332
Total Sales		$2,154,786

Description

- The CSS3 structural pseudo-classes let you format a table without using classes or ids.

Figure 9-5   How to use the CSS3 structural pseudo-classes for formatting tables

How to use the HTML5 figure and figcaption elements with tables

If you read chapter 8, you already know how to treat an image as a figure by using the HTML5 figure and figcaption elements. Now, figure 9-6 shows how to use these elements for a table that's used as a figure. Here, the figure element contains a figcaption element followed by a table element.

By default, a figcaption element is an inline element, not a block element. As a result, you will usually want to use the CSS display property to change it to a block element. That makes it easier to format the caption. In this example, the figcaption element comes before the table in the HTML so the caption is displayed above the table. But you can change that by coding the figcaption element after the table in the HTML.

In the CSS for the table element, you can see that the top and bottom margins are set to 10 pixels, and the right and left margins are set to "auto". As a result, the table is centered within the figure element.

In figure 9-8, you'll see that you can also use the caption element within a table element to provide a caption for a table. In general, though, it's better to use the fig and figcaption elements to present a table. That way, it's easier for a screen reader to tell that the table is used as a figure and that the caption applies to the table.

A table within a figure

Total Sales by Book		
Book	**Year Published**	**Sales**
PHP and MySQL	2010	$372,381
JavaScript and DOM Scripting	2009	$305,447
Java Programming	2011	$392,444
Java Servlets and JSP	2008	$328.992
ASP.NET with Visual Basic	2011	$351,200
ASP.NET with C#	2011	$404.332
Total Sales		**$2,154,786**

The HTML for the figure and figcaption elements

```
<figure>
    <figcaption>Total Sales by Book</figcaption>
    <table>
            .
            .
    </table>
</figure>
```

The CSS for the figure and figcaption elements

```
figure, figcaption {
    margin: 0;
    padding: 0; }
figure {
    border: 1px solid black;
    width: 450px;
    padding: 15px; }
figcaption {
    display: block;
    font-weight: bold;
    text-align: center;
    font-size: 120%;
    padding-bottom: .25em; }
table {
    border-collapse: collapse;
    border: 1px solid black;
    margin: 10px auto; }
```

Description

- The figure element can be used as a container for anything that is used as a figure. The figcaption element can be used within a figure to provide a caption that describes the figure, but it is optional. When coded, it can be anywhere within the figure.

- By default, the figcaption element is an inline element.

- Although you can use the HTML caption element to provide a caption for a table, it's better semantically to use the fig and figcaption elements.

Figure 9-6   How to use the HTML5 figure and figcaption elements with tables

How to merge cells in a column or row

For complicated tables, it often makes sense to *merge* some of the cells. This is illustrated in figure 9-7. Here, four cells are merged in the first row so "Sales" spans the last four columns of the table. Also, two cells are merged in the first column, so "Book" is in its own cell.

To merge cells, you use the two attributes of the th and td elements that are summarized in this figure. To merge cells so a cell in a row spans two or more columns, you use the colspan attribute. To merge cells so a cell in a column spans two or more rows, you use the rowspan attribute. The value you use for these attributes indicates the number of cells that will be merged.

The example in this figure illustrates how these attributes work. Here, you can see a table header that consists of two rows and five columns. However, the first header cell spans two rows. As a result, the second row doesn't include a th element for the first column.

Now, take a look at the second header cell in the first row of the header. This cell spans the remaining four columns of the row. As a result, this row includes only two th elements: the one that defines the cell that contains the "Book" heading, and the one that defines the cell that contains the "Sales" heading.

In the CSS for the merged cells, you can see how the CSS3 structural pseudo-classes are used in the selectors. First, the first-child class is used to bottom align "Book" in the merged cell that spans two rows. Second, the nth-child class is used to center "Sales" in the merged cell that spans four columns. Third, the nth-child class is used to right align the th cells within the second row of the table.

Attributes of the <th> and <td> tags for merging cells

Attribute	Description
colspan	Identifies the number of columns that a cell will span. The default is 1.
rowspan	Identifies the number of rows that a cell will span. The default is 1.

A table with merged cells

Book	Sales			
	North	South	West	Total
PHP and MySQL	$55,174	$73,566	$177,784	$306,524
JavaScript and DOM Scripting	$28,775	$24,349	$168,228	$221,352
Java Programming	$27,688	$39,995	$239,968	$307,651
Java Servlets and JSP	$23,082	$24,858	$129,619	$177,559
Sales Totals	$140,775	$165,550	$762,794	$1,069,119

The HTML for the table

```
<table>
    <thead>
        <tr>
            <th rowspan="2">Book</th>
            <th colspan="4">Sales</th>
        </tr>
        <tr>
            <th>North</th>
            <th>South</th>
            <th>West</th>
            <th>Total</th>
        </tr>
    </thead>
    <tbody>
        .
        .
    </tbody>
    <tfoot>
        <tr>
            <th>Sales Totals</th>
            <td>$140,775</td>
            <td>$165,550</td>
            <td>$762,794</td>
            <td>$1,069,119</td>
        </tr>
    </tfoot>
</table>
```

The CSS for the merged cells

```
th:first-child { vertical-align: bottom; } /* bottom aligns "Book" */
th:nth-child(2) { text-align: center; }    /* centers "Sales" */
tr:nth-child(2) th { text-align: right; }  /* right aligns 2nd row hdgs */
```

Figure 9-7   How to merge cells in a column or row

How to provide for accessibility

Because tables are difficult for visually-impaired users to decipher, HTML provides a few attributes that can improve accessibility. These attributes are summarized in figure 9-8, and they can be read by screen readers.

First, it's important to provide a caption for each table that summarizes what the table contains. To do that, you can use the caption element as shown in this figure or the fig and figcaption elements as shown in figure 9-6.

Second, you can code the headers attribute on a td or th element to identify one or more header cells that the cell is associated with. To identify a header cell, you code the value of the cell's id attribute. In the example in this figure, you can see that an id attribute is coded for each of the three th elements in the table header as well as the th element in the table footer. Then, each of the td elements includes a headers attribute that names the associated th element or elements.

For instance, the headers attribute for the first td element in each row of the body names the header cell that contains the header "Book" because the content of these cells are book names. Similarly, the td element in the footer includes a headers attribute that names two th elements. The first one is for the header cell in the third column of the first row (the one with the heading "Sales"), and the second one is for the header cell in the first column of the last row (the one with the heading "Total Sales").

The last attribute for accessibility is scope. Although you can code this attribute on either a td or th element, it's used most often with the th element. The scope attribute indicates whether a cell is associated with a column, a row, or a group of merged cells in a column. In this figure, for example, this attribute indicates that each of the three th elements in the header row is associated with a column.

Even if you use these attributes, a table can be difficult for a visually-impaired person to interpret. So besides coding these attributes, try to keep your tables simple. That is not only good for the visually-impaired, but also for all the users of your web site.

Attributes that can be used for accessibility

Attribute	Description
caption	Describes the contents of the table. The other alternative is to treat the table as a figure and use the figcaption element to describe the table.
headers	Identifies one or more header cells that describe the content of the cell.
scope	A keyword that tells if a cell is associated with a column or row. Common keywords are col and row. You can also use the keyword rowgroup to refer to merged cells.

The HTML for a table that provides for accessibility

```
<table>
<caption>Total sales for books published from 2008 to 2011</caption>
<thead>
    <tr>
        <th id="hdr_book" scope="col">Book</th>
        <th id="hdr_year" scope="col">Year Published</th>
        <th id="hdr_sales" scope="col">Sales</th>
    </tr>
</thead>
<tbody>
    <tr>
        <td headers="hdr_book">PHP and MySQL</td>
        <td headers="hdr_year">2010</td>
        <td headers="hdr_sales">$372,381</td>
    </tr>
    <tr>
        <td headers="hdr_book">JavaScript and DOM Scripting</td>
        <td headers="hdr_year">2009</td>
        <td headers="hdr_sales">$305,447</td>
    </tr>
</tbody>
<tfoot>
    <tr>
        <th id="hdr_total" scope="row">Total Sales</th>
        <td></td>
        <td headers="hdr_sales hdr_total">$2,154,786</td>
    </tr>
</tfoot>
</table>
```

Accessibility guideline

- Use the attributes listed above to make a table more accessible to visually-impaired users who use screen readers.

Figure 9-8   How to provide for accessibility

Other skills for working with tables

For most tables, the skills you've just learned will be all you need. But here are two other skills that you should at least be aware of.

How to nest tables

In the past, when tables were used for laying out pages, it was common to nest one table within another table. Today, that type of page layout should be replaced by the techniques that you learned in chapter 6.

Occasionally, though, *nested tables* can be useful for presenting tabular data. That's why figure 9-9 shows how nested tables work. Here, the example is a simple table that lists the year-to-date sales by region. For the West and East regions, a single sales amount is displayed. But for the Central region, two sales amounts for two different areas within the region are displayed. To accomplish that, the cell for this region contains another table.

To code a table within another table, you simply code a table element within a td element. Then, you code the other elements of the table within the table element just like you would any other table. In this case, the table consists of two rows, each with two cells, but there's no limit to the size of a nested table or the number of levels of nesting.

In general, though, you shouldn't need to nest tables for two reasons. First, you can get the same result in other ways. Second, it's better to keep your tables simple so it's easier for your users to understand them, especially your visually-impaired users.

A table with another table nested within one of its cells

Region	YTD sales		
West	$68,684.34		
Central		North	$21,223.08
		South	$41,274.06
East	$72,741.06		

The HTML for the table

```
<table id="outer">
    <caption>YTD Sales by Region</caption>
    <tr>
        <th>Region</th>
        <th>YTD sales</th>
    </tr>
    <tr>
        <th>West</th>
        <td>$68,684.34</td>
    </tr>
    <tr>
        <th>Central</th>
        <td>
            <table id="inner">
                <tr>
                    <th>North</th>
                    <td>$21,223.08</td>
                </tr>
                <tr>
                    <th>South</th>
                    <td>$41,274.06</td>
                </tr>
            </table>
        </td>
    </tr>
    <tr>
        <th>East</th>
        <td>$72,741.06</td>
    </tr>
</table>
```

Description

- You can *nest* one table within another table by coding a table element within a td element.

- Nested tables were used frequently when tables were used for page layout. Now that tables should only be used for tabular data, you should rarely need nesting.

Figure 9-9   How to nest tables

How to control wrapping

By default, the content of the cells in a table will *wrap* to two or more lines if you size the browser window so the content can't be displayed on a single line. This is illustrated by the table in the browser at the top of figure 9-10. Here, you can see that the heading in the second column and some of the data in the first column have been wrapped onto two lines.

In some cases, though, you won't want the headings and data to wrap. Then, you can use the white-space property to prevent that from happening. In the CSS in this figure, for example, I coded this property with a value of "nowrap" for the table element. Then, the table appears as in the second browser in this figure. Here, the table is too wide for the window. As a result, the browser displays a horizontal scroll bar so the user can scroll to the rest of the table.

A table with wrapping

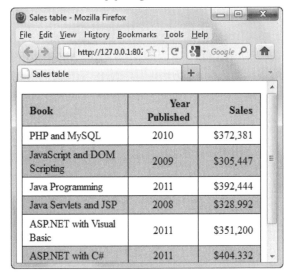

A table without wrapping

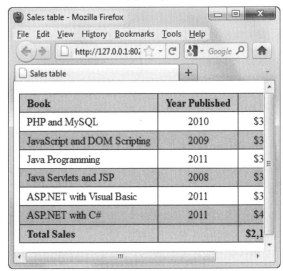

The property that stops wrapping

```
table { white-space: nowrap; }
```

Description

- You can use the white-space property to keep table data from wrapping if the table doesn't fit in the browser window. To do that, code the value "nowrap" for this property.

- You can code the white-space property for an entire table or individual cells.

Figure 9-10   How to control wrapping

Perspective

As you've seen in this chapter, it's relatively easy to create and format simple tables. Remember, though, that you should only use tables when you're presenting tabular data. You should be using CSS, not tables, for page layout.

Terms

table	header
row	footer
column	body
cell	merged cells
data cell	nested tables
header cell	wrapped rows

Summary

- A *table* consists of *rows* and *columns* that intersect at *cells*. *Data cells* contain the data of a table. *Header cells* identify the data in a column or row.

- The rows in a table can be grouped into a *header*, a *body*, and a *footer*.

- To define a table in HTML, you use the table, tr, th, and td elements. Then, you can use CSS to apply borders, spacing, fonts, and background colors to these elements.

- If you use the thead, tfoot, and tbody elements to group the rows in a table, it's easier to style the table with CSS.

- You can use the CSS3 structural pseudo-classes to format the rows or columns of a table without using id or class selectors.

- The HTML5 figure element can be used to treat a table as a figure. The HTML5 figcaption element can be used within a figure element to provide a caption for the figure.

- To make tables more accessible to visually-impaired users, you can use the HTML attributes that can be read by screen readers.

- You will often want to *merge* two or more cells in a column or row, and you may occasionally want to *nest* one table within another.

- If a table doesn't fit in the browser window, the browser will *wrap* the data so it does fit. If you don't want that, you can use CSS to turn the wrapping off.

Exercise 9-1   Add a table to the luncheons page

In this exercise, you'll enhance the luncheons page by adding a table to it so it looks like the one that follows. If you didn't do exercise 7-1, the navigation bar will be formatted differently.

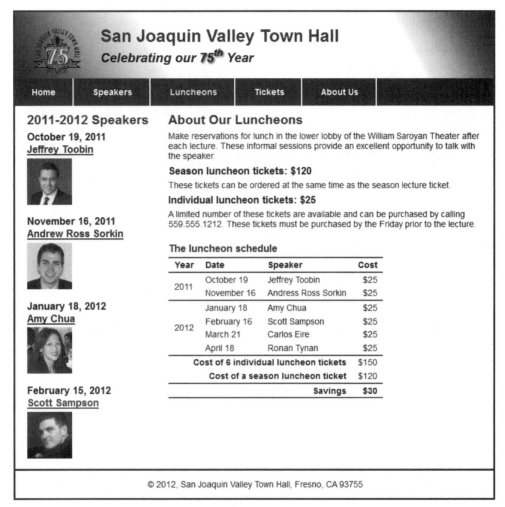

Enter the table into the luncheons.html file

1. Use your text editor to open the luncheon.html page in the town_hall_2 folder. Then, run the page to see that everything but the table is already in the file.

2. Add the table shown above to the page. To start the table, you may want to copy the HTML for one of the tables in the book examples into the file. Then, you can modify that code and add the data for the new table. To quickly add new rows to the table, you can copy and paste earlier rows.

3. Test the page to make sure the contents are all there, even though the table won't be formatted right.

Add the CSS for the table to the main.css file

4. Use your text editor to open the main.css file in the styles folder. To start that code, copy the CSS for one of the tables in the book applications into the file. Then, test to see how the table looks.

5. Modify the CSS so the table looks like the one above. Here, all of the borders and the text in the heading above the table should have #800000 as their color. To do some of the alignment and to add borders to some of the rows, you should use classes.

6. Test and adjust until the table looks the way you want it to.

Treat the table as a figure, provide for accessibility, and experiment

7. Enclose the table within a figure element, and code a figcaption element above the table, but within the figure element. Then, copy the h2 element that says: "The luncheon schedule" into the figcaption element.

8. Test this change. The page should look the same as it did in step 6. If necessary, adjust the HTML or the CSS.

9. Using figure 9-8 as a guide, add the attributes for user accessibility.

10. Experiment with the CSS3 structural pseudo-classes to see whether you can replace some of your use of class selectors with pseudo-class selectors.

10

How to work with forms

To create dynamic web pages, you use HTML to create forms that let the user enter data. Then, the user can click on a button to submit the data to a web server for processing.

In this chapter, you'll learn how to code forms and the controls they contain. You'll also learn how to use the new HTML5 features for data validation and how to use the new HTML5 controls.

How to use forms and controls

A *form* contains one or more *controls* such as text boxes and buttons. In the topics that follow, you'll learn how to create a form and how to add the controls that are currently supported by all browsers to a form. If you already know how to create forms with HTML4, you can skim the topics that follow until you come to the new material on HTML5 validation and controls.

How to create a form

Figure 10-1 shows how to code a form that contains two controls: a text box and a button. To start, you code the form element. On the opening tag for this element, you code the action and method attributes. The action attribute specifies the file on the web server that should be used to process the data when the form is submitted. The method attribute specifies the HTTP method that should be used for sending the form to the web server.

In the example in this figure, the form will be submitted to the server using the HTTP "post" method when the user clicks the Subscribe button. Then, the data in the form will be processed by the code that's stored in the file named subscribe.php.

When you use the post method, the form data is packaged as part of an HTTP request and isn't visible in the browser. Because of that, the submission is more secure than it is when you use the "get" method, but the resulting page can't be bookmarked.

When you use the get method, the form data is sent as part of the URL for the HTTP request. That means that the data is visible and the page can be bookmarked. This is illustrated by the URL in this figure. Here, the URL is followed by a question mark and name/value pairs separated by ampersands. In this case, two values are submitted: the email address that has been entered, and the value of the Submit button. Because browsers and servers limit the amount of data that can be in a URL, you often are forced to use the post method.

Within the opening and closing tags of the form element, you code the controls for the form. In this example, the first input element is for the text box that will receive the user's email address. The second input element displays a button. You'll learn how to code these controls in the next two figures.

But first, this figure summarizes the four attributes that are common to most controls. Here, the type attribute specifies the type of control you want to use, like the button and text types used in this example. In contrast, the name attribute is only required for radio buttons and check boxes (see figure 10-4). Although the name attribute can also be referred to by JavaScript or server-side code, the id attribute is more commonly used for that today. Nevertheless, most of the examples in this chapter include the name attribute.

In contrast, the disabled and readonly attributes are Boolean attributes that you'll use infrequently. The disabled attribute disables a control so the data in the control isn't submitted with the form. And the readonly attribute provides a value that can't be changed but is submitted with the form.

Attributes of the form element

Attribute	Description
name	A name that can be referred to by client-side or server-side code.
action	The URL of the file that will process the data in the form.
method	The HTTP method for submitting the form data. It can be set to either "get" or "post". The default value is "get".
target	Where to open the page that's specified in the action attribute. If you specify, _blank, the page is opened in a new window or tab.

Attributes common to most input elements

Attribute	Description
type	The type of control like "button", "text", or "checkbox".
name	A name that can be referred to by client-side or server-side code.
disabled	A Boolean attribute that disables and grays out the control. Then, the control can't receive the focus, the user can't tab to it, and the value isn't submitted with the form.
readonly	A Boolean attribute that means a user can't change the control's value. But the control can receive the focus, the user can tab to it, and the value is submitted with the form.

The HTML for a form

```
<form name="email_form" action="subscribe.php" method="post">
    <p>Please enter your e-mail address to subscribe to our newsletter.</p>
    <p>E-Mail: <input type="text" name="email"></p>
    <p><input type="submit" name="submit" value="Subscribe"></p>
</form>
```

The form in a web browser

The URL that's used when the form is submitted with the get method

```
subscribe.php?email=zak%40modulemedia.com&submit=Subscribe
```

Description

- A *form* contains one or more *controls* like text boxes, radio buttons, lists, or check boxes that can receive data.
- You should code the name attribute to uniquely identify each form and control. You only need to code the id attribute if you want to use it as a CSS selector.
- When a form is submitted to the server for processing, the data in the controls is sent along with the HTTP request.
- For the get method, the URL is followed by a question mark and name/value pairs that are separated by ampersands. For the post method, the data is hidden.

Figure 10-1   How to create a form

How to use buttons

Figure 10-2 shows five different types of *buttons*. To code the first four, you use the input element as shown in the HTML in this figure.

In the examples, the first button is a generic button, defined by the type attribute as "button". When the user clicks this type of button, client-side code is usually run. For instance, JavaScript can be used to validate the data on the form. Then, if the data is valid, the script can submit the form to the server.

The second button is a *submit button*. When it is clicked, the form and its data is submitted to the server for processing. Unlike a generic button, a submit button sends the data to the server automatically without using client-side code.

The third button is a *reset button*. When it is clicked, the values in all of the controls on the form are reset to their default values.

The fourth button is an *image button*. It works like a submit button. The difference is that an image button displays an image rather than text. To specify the URL for the image, you use the src attribute. To specify text if the image can't be displayed, you use the alt attribute. And if you want to size the image, you can set the width and height attributes.

If you don't specify a value attribute for the first three types of buttons, the web browser supplies a default value depending on the button type. For example, the default text for a submit button is usually "Submit", the default text for a reset button is usually "Reset", and the default text for a generic button is usually "Button."

To code the fifth type of button, you use the button element instead of the input element. When you use the button element, you can format the text that's displayed on the button, and you can include elements other than text. In the example in this figure, the img element has been used to add a shopping cart image in front of the "Add to Cart" text for the button. When you use the button element, you still need to set the type attribute so the browser knows how to treat the button when it is clicked by the user.

Attributes of the input element for buttons and for the button element

Attribute	Description
type	The type of button. Valid values include "submit", "reset", "button", or "image". The "submit" and "image" types submit the form to the server, the "reset" type resets all fields to their default values, and the "button" type is typically used to run a client-side script.
value	The text that's displayed on the button and submitted to the server when the button is clicked.
src	For an image button, the relative or absolute URL of the image to display.
alt	For an image button, alternate text to display in place of the image.
height	For an image button, the height of the button in either pixels or percent.
width	For an image button, the width of the button in either pixels or percent.

Four buttons that are created by the input element

```
<input type="button" name="message" value="Alert Me">
<input type="submit" name="checkout" value="Checkout">
<input type="reset" name="resetform" value="Reset">
<input type="image" src="images/submit.jpg" alt="Submit button"
       width="114" height="42">
```

A button that is created by the button element

```
<button type="submit">
    <img src="images/addtocart.png" width="30" height="23"
        alt="Add to Cart">Add to Cart</button>
```

The buttons in a web browser

Description

- You can use the input element to create four different types of *buttons*.

- You can also use the button element to create a button. The main difference between the input and button elements is that the input element only allows a button to contain plain text or an image, but the button element allows a button to contain formatted text as well as other HTML elements such as images.

- When you click on a *submit button* for a form (type is "submit"), the form data is sent to the server as part of an HTTP request. When you click on a *reset button* (type is "reset"), the data in all of the fields is reset to the default values.

- You can use the "button" type to perform processing on the client before the form is submitted to the server. For instance, when the user clicks on the button, a client-side script can be run to validate the form data. Then, if the data is valid, the script can submit the form to the server.

Figure 10-2   How to use buttons

How to use text fields

Figure 10-3 shows how to use the input element to create three types of *text fields*, also referred to as *text boxes*. In the example in this figure, the first and second input elements display text fields that accept input from a user. To do that, the type attribute for both elements is set to "text". In addition, the name attribute is set to "quantity" for the first text box and "username" for the second text box.

If you want to put a starting value into a text field, you use the value attribute. For instance, the value attribute for the first text field is set to 1. As a result, this field will contain a value of 1 when the browser displays this page for the first time. Then, the user has the option of changing that value. If the value attribute is omitted, as in the second example, no value is displayed when the text box is displayed for the first time.

The first input element in this figure illustrates the use of the readonly attribute. This Boolean attribute doesn't let the user enter data into the field. However, the field can receive the focus, and the data in the field is submitted with the form. In contrast, the disabled attribute grays out a field, the field can't receive the focus, and the data in the field isn't submitted with the form.

The second input element illustrates the use of the new HTML5 autofocus attribute. This instructs the browser to put the focus in the text box when the page is loaded.

The third input element in this figure creates a *password field* that works much like the first two text fields. However, the value in the field is displayed as bullets or asterisks. This improves the security of an application by preventing others from reading a password when a user enters it.

This password field also shows how to use the maxlength attribute. Here, this attribute is set to 6. As a result, the user can enter a maximum of six characters into this field. This is useful if you're working with a database that limits the number of characters that can be stored in a field.

The password field also demonstrates how to use the new HTML5 placeholder attribute. Like the value attribute, the placeholder attribute displays text within the control. The difference is that the placeholder text disappears when the focus is moved to the field.

The fourth input element in this figure creates a *hidden field* that works much like the other three text fields. However, this field isn't displayed by the browser. Nevertheless, you can use client-side or server-side code to work with the value that's stored in this field. Because the user can't enter text into a hidden field, you usually code a value attribute for a hidden field.

In these examples, the username and password fields are displayed at their default width. One way to change that is to include the size attribute as shown in the quantity field. A better way, though, is to use CSS, which you can also use to align the controls. You'll learn how to format and align controls later in this chapter.

Attributes of the input element for text fields

Attribute	Description
type	The type of text field. Valid values include "text", "password", and "hidden".
value	The default value for the field, but the user can change this value. If a reset button is clicked, the field will revert to this value.
maxlength	The maximum number of characters that the user can enter in the field.
size	The width of the field in characters based on the average character width of the font. However, it's better to use CSS to set the size of a field.
autofocus	New to HTML5, a Boolean attribute that tells the browser to set the focus on the field when the page is loaded.
placeholder	New to HTML5, this attribute puts a default value or hint in the field. Unlike the value attribute, though, this value is removed when the user's cursor enters the control.

The HTML for text fields

```
Quantity:<input type="text" name="quantity" value="1" size="5"
          readonly><br><br>
Username:<input type="text" name="username" autofocus><br><br>
Password:<input type="password" name="password" maxlength="6">
          placeholder="Enter your password"><br><br>
Hidden:<input type="hidden" name="productid" value="widget">
```

The text fields in a web browser

Quantity: 1

Username: |

Password: Enter your password

Hidden:

Description

- There are several types of *text fields*. The three most common are text, password, and hidden.

- A normal text field accepts input data from the user. Then, when the form is submitted, the name and value attributes are passed to the server.

- A *password field* also accepts input data that is submitted to the server, but the entry is obscured by bullets or asterisks.

- A *hidden field* has name and value attributes that are sent to the server when the form is submitted, but the field isn't displayed in the browser. However, if you view the source code for the web page, you can see the data for the hidden field.

Figure 10-3   How to use text fields

How to use radio buttons and check boxes

Figure 10-4 shows how to use the input element to code *checkbox fields* and *radio fields*, commonly referred to as *check boxes* and *radio buttons*. Although check boxes work independently of each other, radio buttons are typically set up so the user can select only one radio button from a group of buttons. In the example in this figure, for instance, you can select only one of the three radio buttons. However, you can select or deselect any combination of check boxes.

To create a radio button, you set the type attribute of the input element to "radio". Then, to create a group, you set the name attribute for all of the radio buttons in the group to the same value. In this figure, all three radio buttons have "crust" as their name attribute. That way, the user will only be able to select one of these radio buttons at a time. Note, however, that each of these buttons has a different value attribute. That way, your client-side or server-side code can get the value of the selected button.

To create a check box, you set the type attribute of the input element to "checkbox". Then, you set the name attribute so you can access the control from your client-side and server-side code. When you submit the form to the server, a name/value pair for the check box is submitted only if it's selected.

If you want a check box or radio button to be selected by default, you can code the checked attribute. In this figure, for example, the second radio button has been selected by default.

Attributes of the input element for radio buttons and check boxes

Attribute	Description
type	The type of control, either "radio" or "checkbox".
value	The value to submit to the server when the control is checked and the form is submitted.
checked	A Boolean attribute that causes the control to be checked when the page is loaded. If a reset button is clicked, the control reverts to the checked state.

The HTML for radio buttons and check boxes

```
Crust:<br>
<input type="radio" name="crust" value="thin">Thin Crust<br>
<input type="radio" name="crust" value="deep" checked>Deep Dish<br>
<input type="radio" name="crust" value="hand">Hand Tossed<br><br>
Toppings:<br>
<input type="checkbox" name="topping1" value="pepperoni">Pepperoni<br>
<input type="checkbox" name="topping2" value="mushrooms">Mushrooms<br>
<input type="checkbox" name="topping3" value="olives">Olives
```

The radio buttons and check boxes in a web browser

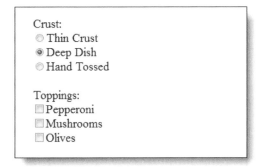

Description

- Only one *radio button* in a group can be selected at one time. The radio buttons in a group must have the same name attribute, but different values.

- *Check boxes* are unrelated, so more than one check box can be checked at the same time.

Figure 10-4   How to use radio buttons and check boxes

How to use drop-down lists

Figure 10-5 shows how to code a *drop-down list*. With a drop-down list, the user can select one option from a list of options. To display the list of options, the user must click the arrow at the right side of the control. In this figure, for example, you can see a drop-down list of sizes after the list is displayed.

To code a drop-down list, you use a select element. For this element, you code the name attribute. Then, between the opening and closing tags, you code two or more option elements that supply the options that are available for the list. For each option element, you code a value attribute. In addition, you supply the text that's displayed in the list for the content of the element. This text is often the same as or similar to the value for the option.

If you want to group the options in a drop-down list, you can code one or more optgroup elements. In this figure, for example, two optgroup elements are used to divide the options that are available into two groups: The New Yorker and The Chicago. To do that, the label attribute specifies the label for each group. Note, however, that the user can't select a group, only the options it contains.

When a drop-down list is first displayed, the first option in the list is selected by default. If that's not what you want, you can code the selected attribute for the option you want to be selected.

Attributes of the optgroup and option elements

Element	Attribute	Description
optgroup	label	The text that's used to identify a group of options.
option	value	The value of the selected option that will be sent to the server for processing.
option	selected	A Boolean attribute that causes the option to be selected when the page is loaded.

The HTML for a drop-down list

```
Style:<br>
<select name="style_and_size">
    <optgroup label="The New Yorker">
        <option value="ny10">10"</option>
        <option value="ny12">12"</option>
        <option value="ny16">16"</option>
    </optgroup>
    <optgroup label="The Chicago">
        <option value="chi10">10"</option>
        <option value="chi12">12"</option>
        <option value="chi16">16"</option>
    </optgroup>
</select>
```

The drop-down list in a web browser when the user clicks on the arrow

Description

- To create a *drop-down list*, you code a select element that contains option elements.
- To group the options in a list, you can code the options within an optgroup element. However, that isn't required.
- To use a drop-down list, the user clicks the arrow at the right side of the field to display the list, and then clicks on an option to select it. Or, the user can press the Tab key until the focus is on the list, and then press the down arrow to cycle through the options.
- By default, the first option in the list is selected when the page is loaded. To change the default option, code the selected attribute for the option you want to be selected.

Figure 10-5   How to use drop-down lists

How to use list boxes

In addition to drop-down lists, you can code another type of list called a *list box*. A list box differs from a drop-down list in that two or more of its options are always displayed. You can also define a list box so two or more options can be selected at the same time.

Figure 10-6 shows how to code list boxes. To start, you code a select element with a name attribute. You also code the size attribute to indicate the number of options that are displayed at a time. In the example in this figure, the size attribute is set to 4. However, because the list contains seven options, the browser adds a scroll bar to the list.

By default, the user can select only one option from a list box. In some cases, though, it makes sense to let the user select two or more options. To do that, you code the multiple attribute. Then, the user can select multiple options by holding down the Ctrl key in Windows or the Command key in Mac OS and clicking on the options.

Attributes of the select element for list boxes

Attribute	Description
size	The number of items to display in the control. If the value is 1, the control will be a drop-down list. The default value is 1.
multiple	A Boolean attribute that determines whether multiple items can be selected. It is only valid if size is greater than 1.

The HTML for a list box

```
<select name="toppings" size="4" multiple>
    <option value="pepperoni">Pepperoni</option>
    <option value="sausage" selected>Sausage</option>
    <option value="mushrooms">Mushrooms</option>
    <option value="olives">Black olives</option>
    <option value="onions">Onions</option>
    <option value="bacon">Canadian bacon</option>
    <option value="pineapple">Pineapple</option>
</select>
```

The list box in a web browser with a scroll bar

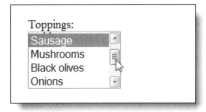

Description

- A *list box* displays the number of options you specify on the size attribute. If the list contains more options than can be displayed at once, a scroll bar is added to the list box.

- By default, only one option can be selected from a list box. To allow two or more selections, include the multiple attribute.

- You use the option element to define the options in a list box, and you can use the optgroup element to define option groups, just as you can with drop-down lists.

Figure 10-6   How to use list boxes

How to use text areas

Figure 10-7 shows how to code a *textarea field*, or just *text area*. Although a text area is similar to a text field, a text area can display multiple lines of text. As the user enters text into a text area, the text is automatically wrapped to the next line when necessary. Or, the user can start a new line by pressing the Enter key. If the user enters more lines than can be displayed at one time, the browser adds a scroll bar to the text area.

To code a text area, you use a textarea element with a name attribute just as you do for other controls. You can also code the initial text for an area by using the value attribute. Or, you can use the placeholder attribute to display text that disappears when the text area receives the focus, as illustrated by the example in this figure.

You can also code the rows attribute to specify the approximate number of visible rows the text area will contain, and you can code the cols attribute to specify the approximate number of columns. Although these attributes were required with HTML4, they are no longer required with HTML5. As a result, it's better to size the area by using CSS.

Attributes of the textarea element

Attribute	Description
rows	The approximate number of rows in the text area. Not required in HTML5.
cols	The approximate number of columns in the text area. Not required in HTML5.
wrap	Specifies how the text should wrap. Possible values include soft and hard, and soft is the default.

The HTML for a text area with default text

```
Comments:<br>
<textarea name="comments"
    placeholder="If you have any comments, please enter them here.">
</textarea>
```

The CSS for the text area

```
textarea {
    height: 5em;
    width: 25em;
    font-family: Arial, Helvetica, sans-serif; }
```

The text area in a web browser

The text area after text has been entered into it

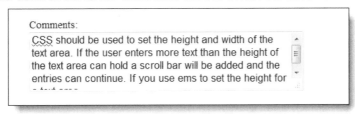

Description

- A *textarea field* (or just *text area*) can be used to get multi-line text entries.
- Any whitespace in the HTML for the content of a text area is shown in the value that's displayed in the browser.
- To set the height and width for a text area, you should use the CSS height and width properties. If you use ems to specify the height, the text area will hold approximately as many lines as ems.
- If you use ems to specify the width, each line in the text area will provide for more characters than ems except for a mono-spaced font. That's because an em is approximately the width of a capital M and most characters are narrower than that.

Figure 10-7   How to use text areas

How to use labels

The first label element in the example in figure 10-8 shows how to use a *label* to display text that identifies the contents of a related text field. To do that, the for attribute of the label element is used to specify the id of the related text field. Thus, the label is associated with the text field. This is a simple but common use of labels that makes it easier to align the controls of a form with CSS. You'll see how this works in figure 10-11.

The other label elements in this example show how labels can be used with radio buttons and check boxes to improve the accessibility of these items. Here again, the for attribute of the label is used to specify the id of a related radio button or check box. If you compare this coding to the coding in figure 10-4, you'll see that the label elements, not the input elements, now provide the text that is displayed after the buttons and check boxes.

When you code radio buttons and check boxes in this way, the user can click on the label text to turn a button or check box on or off. For instance, the mouse pointer in the browser display has clicked on the text for the third radio button to turn it on. This makes the buttons and check boxes more accessible to users who lack the motor control to click on the smaller button or box.

Coding buttons and check boxes this way also makes it easier for assistive devices such as screen readers to read the text associated with a control and tell it to the user. If you don't use labels in this way, the assistive devices have to scan the text around a control and guess which snippet of text is associated with the control.

Attribute of the label element

Attribute	Description
for	Should be set to the id of the related control. Although the id attribute is optional in forms that don't rely on client-side scripting, it is required when using labels and the for attribute.

The HTML for a form with label elements

```
<label for="quantity">Quantity:</label>
<input type="text" name="quantity" id="quantity" value="1" size="5"><br><br>

Crust:<br>
<input type="radio" name="crust" id="crust1" value="thin">
<label for="crust1">Thin Crust</label><br>
<input type="radio" name="crust" id="crust2" value="deep">
<label for="crust2">Deep Dish</label><br>
<input type="radio" name="crust" id="crust3" value="hand">
<label for="crust3">Hand Tossed</label><br><br>

Toppings:<br>
<input type="checkbox" name="topping1" id="topping1" value="pepperoni">
<label for="topping1">Pepperoni</label><br>
<input type="checkbox" name="topping2" id="topping2" value="mushrooms">
<label for="topping2">Mushrooms</label><br>
<input type="checkbox" name="topping3" id="topping3" value="olives">
<label for="topping3">Black Olives</label><br><br>
```

The HTML in a browser as the user clicks on a label to check its box

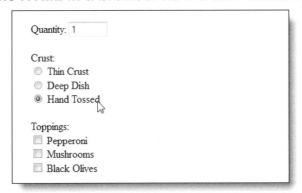

Accessibility guideline

- Use labels with radio buttons and check boxes so the user can click on the label text to select the control that the label is associated with. This also helps assistive devices.

Description

- A *label* is commonly used to identify a related field. However, labels should also be used to improve the accessibility of radio buttons and check boxes.
- Labels also make it easier to align the controls on a web page (see figure 10-11)

Figure 10-8   How to use labels

How to group controls with fieldset and legend elements

In many cases, you'll want to group related controls on a form to make it easy for users to see that they're related. To group controls, you use the fieldset and legend elements as shown in figure 10-9.

To start, you code the fieldset element. Then, you code the legend element right after the opening tag of the fieldset element. The content of this legend element determines the text that's displayed for the group. Then, the controls in the group follow the legend element.

The example in this figure illustrates how this works. Here, two groups are defined: one that contains radio buttons and one that contains check boxes. By default, this code places a thin gray border around the groups, as shown in this figure. To change the appearance of this border, though, you can use CSS.

HTML that uses fieldset and legend elements

```
<form name="order" action="order.php" method="post">
<fieldset>
    <legend>Crust</legend>
    <input type="radio" name="crust" id="crust1" value="thin">
    <label for="crust1">Thin Crust</label><br>
    <input type="radio" name="crust" id="crust2" value="deep">
    <label for="crust2">Deep Dish</label><br>
    <input type="radio" name="crust" id="crust3" value="hand">
    <label for="crust3">Hand Tossed</label>
</fieldset>
<br>
<fieldset>
    <legend>Toppings</legend>
    <input type="checkbox" name="topping1" id="topping1" value="pepperoni">
    <label for="topping1">Pepperoni</label><br>
    <input type="checkbox" name="topping2" id="topping2" value="mushrooms">
    <label for="topping2">Mushrooms</label><br>
    <input type="checkbox" name="topping3" id="topping3" value="olives">
    <label for="topping3">Black Olives</label>
</fieldset>
</form>
```

The elements in a web browser

Description

- The fieldset element is used to group controls.
- The legend element can be coded within a fieldset element. It is used to label the group of controls.
- If you want to disable all of the controls within a fieldset element, you can code the disabled attribute for the fieldset element.

Figure 10-9   How to group controls with fieldset and legend elements

How to use a file upload control

Figure 10-10 shows how to use the *file upload control*. This control lets users upload one or more files to your web server. Typically you'll use this control with a server-side programming language such as PHP, which transfers the file or files from the user's computer to the web server. When you code a file upload control, you set the type attribute to "file" and set the name attribute as you would for any other control.

You can also code the accept attribute for a file upload control. This attribute lets you specify the types of files that will be accepted by this control. In the example in this figure, the JPEG and GIF types are specified so the control will only display those types of files when the Browse button is clicked and the files are displayed. If you omit this attribute, all types of files will be displayed.

When using the file upload control, the method attribute of the form should be set to "post". In addition, the enctype attribute of the form should be set to multipart/form-data. This is typically the only time this attribute will be modified within the form element.

Attributes of the input element for a file upload control

Attribute	Description
accept	The types of files that are accepted for upload. When the operating system's open dialog box opens, only files of those types will be shown.
multiple	A Boolean attribute that lets the user upload more than one file.

The HTML for a file upload element that accepts JPEG images

```
<form name="upload_form" action="sendemail.php" method="post"
    enctype="multipart/form-data">
  Attach an image:<br>
  <input type="file" name="fileupload" accept="image/jpeg, image/gif">
</form>
```

The file upload control in the Firefox browser

This Windows dialog box that's displayed when Browse is clicked

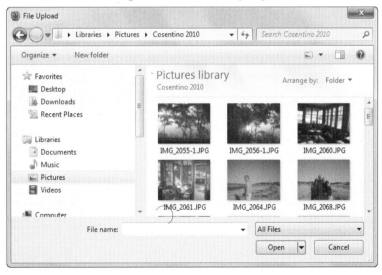

Description

- To create a *file upload control*, code the input element with "file" as the type attribute. This control lets your users select the files they want to upload to your web server.

- In the form element that contains the file upload control, the method attribute must be "post", and you must code the enctype attribute as shown above.

- How the file upload control is implemented varies by browser. For example, the Chrome browser displays a Choose File button instead of a Browse button.

Figure 10-10   How to use a file upload control

Other skills for working with forms

Now that you know how to code forms using common controls, you're ready to learn some other skills for working with forms and controls. In particular, you should know how to use CSS to align and format the controls. You should also know how to set the tab order of the controls on a form and how to assign access keys to the controls. Here again, if you already have these skills, you can skip ahead to the HTML5 features for data validation.

How to align controls

The best way to align controls is to use the technique shown in figure 10-11. Here, the rule set for the labels starts by floating the labels to the left. That causes the labels to be treated like block elements. Then, the rule set sets the width property so all the labels are the same width, and it sets the text-align property so the labels are aligned at the right. This makes the form more readable.

After the rule set for labels, a rule set is coded for the input controls. Here, the margin-left property increases the space between the labels and text boxes to 1 em. Then, the margin-bottom property sets the space after the text boxes to .5 ems.

The last rule set aligns the buttons on the form by adjusting the left margin of just the Register button to 7 ems. To do that, it uses the Register button's id as the selector. This aligns that button with the text boxes above it. Then, the Reset button is 1 em to the right of the Register button because the left margin for all input controls is set to 1 em.

Label, text box, and button controls aligned on a form

First name: |

Last name:

Address:

City:

State:

Zip code:

[Register] [Reset]

The HTML for the form

```
<label for="firstname">First name:</label>
<input type="text" name="firstname" id="firstname" autofocus><br>
<label for="lastname">Last name:</label>
<input type="text" name="lastname" id="lastname"><br>
<label for="address">Address:</label>
<input type="text" name="address" id="address"><br>
<label for="city">City:</label>
<input type="text" name="city" id="city"><br>
<label for="state">State:</label>
<input type="text" name="state" id="state"><br>
<label for="zip">Zip code:</label>
<input type="text" name="zip" id="zip"><br>
<input type="submit" name="register" id="button" value="Register">
<input type="reset" name="reset" id="reset">
```

The CSS for the controls

```
label {
    float: left;
    width: 5em;
    text-align: right;}
input {
    margin-left: 1em;
    margin-bottom: .5em;}
#button {
    margin-left: 7em;}
```

Description

- If a form includes a series of controls and labels that identify them, you can align the labels by floating them to the left of the controls and setting a width that provides enough space for all the labels. Then, you can set a left margin for the controls to add space between the labels and the controls.

- A series of labels is typically more readable if the labels are aligned at the right.

Figure 10-11   How to align controls

How to format controls

In the last topic, you learned how to use a few of the CSS properties to align the controls on a form. But you can also use CSS properties to format controls. Figure 10-12 shows how this works. The form shown here has the same HTML that's in the previous figure, but with some additional formatting.

First, the font property is used to change the font family and font size for the entire page. This not only affects the label elements but also the text that the user enters into the control and the font on the buttons.

Second, the color for the labels has been set to navy, and the font weight for the labels has been set to bold. This is done by using a selector for all labels.

Third, the :focus pseudo-class is used to change the appearance of the text box that has the focus. In this case, a 2px solid navy border is added to the text box. You can see that in the first text box in the browser.

Last, both of the buttons have been formatted with a box shadow and a silver background color. To select these buttons, I used a combination of two id selectors: #button and #reset.

The form in figure 10-11 with some additional formatting

First name:	[ ]
Last name:	[ ]
Address:	[ ]
City:	[ ]
State:	[ ]
Zip code:	[ ]
	[Register] [Reset]

The CSS for the form

```
body {
    font: 90% Arial, Helvetica, sans-serif;
    margin: 20px; }
label {
    color: navy;
    float: left;
    width: 8em;
    font-weight: bold;
    text-align: right;}
input {
    width: 15em;
    margin-left: 1em;
    margin-bottom: .5em;}
input:focus {
    border: 2px solid navy; }
#button, #reset {
    width: 7em;
    box-shadow: 2px 2px 0 navy;
    background-color: silver; }
#button { margin-left: 9.5em; }
```

Description

- You can use many of the properties you learned about in chapters 4 and 5 to format controls.

- You can use the :focus pseudo-class to change the appearance of a control when it has the focus.

Figure 10-12   How to format controls

How to set the tab order and assign access keys

Figure 10-13 shows how to set the tab order of the controls and how to assign access keys to controls. By default, when the user presses the Tab key on a web page, the focus moves from one control to another in the sequence that the controls appear in the HTML, not including labels. This sequence is referred to as the *tab order* of the controls, and it includes the links created by <a> elements.

To change this default tab order, you can code tabindex attributes. To remove a control from the tab order, for example, you assign a negative number to its tabindex attribute. To include a control in the order, you start the tabindex attribute at zero or any positive number and then increment the index by any amount as you add more controls. You can also code the same tabindex value for more than one control. Then, within those controls, the tab order will be the sequence that the controls appear in the HTML.

Controls that aren't assigned a tabindex value will also receive the focus in the sequence that the controls appear in the HTML. These controls will receive the focus after all the controls that are assigned tabindex values. As a result, you usually assign tabindex values to all of the controls on a form if you assign values to any of the controls.

With HTML5, though, you can use the autofocus attribute to put the focus in the control that you want the user to start with. This is often all you need to do to get the tab order the way you want it.

When you work with the tab order, you should be aware of browser variations. That is, when you press the Tab key right after a page is loaded, the focus may move to a browser control like the address bar instead of the first control on the page. In fact, you may have to press the Tab key several times before the focus is moved to the first control. Here again, you can use the autofocus attribute to get around this problem.

When you provide an *access key* for a control, the user can press that key in combination with one or more other keys to move the focus to a control. If the page is displayed in Internet Explorer, for example, the user can move the focus to a control by pressing the Alt key and the access key.

To define an access key for a control, you code the accesskey attribute as shown in this figure. The value of this attribute is the keyboard key you want to use to move the focus to the control. In the first example in this figure, you can see that the accesskey attribute is coded for the three text boxes on the form. The access key for the First name text box is "F", the access key for the Last name text box is "L", and the access key for the Email text box is "E". Here, the letters that are used for the access keys are underlined in the labels that are associated with the controls. This is a common way to identify the access key for a control.

The second example in this figure shows another way to code access keys for controls that have labels associated with them. Here, the accesskey attribute is coded for each of the labels instead of for the text boxes. Then, when the user activates one of these access keys, the focus is moved to the associated text box (the one specified by the for attribute) because labels can't receive the focus.

The attributes for setting the tab order and access keys

Attribute	Description
tabindex	To set the tab order for a control, use a value of 0 or more. To take a control out of the tab order, use a negative value like -1.
accesskey	A keyboard key that can be pressed in combination with a control key to move the focus to the control.

Three labels with access keys

The HTML for the controls

```
<label for="firstname"><u>F</u>irst name:</label>
<input type="text" name="firstname" id="firstname" accesskey="F"><br>
<label for="lastname"><u>L</u>ast name:</label>
<input type="text" name="lastname" id="lastname" accesskey="L"><br>
<label for="email"><u>E</u>mail:</label>
<input type="text" name="email" id="email" accesskey="E">
```

Another way to define the access keys

```
<label for="firstname" accesskey="F"><u>F</u>irst name:</label>
<input type="text" name="firstname" id="firstname"><br>
<label for="lastname" accesskey="L"><u>L</u>ast name:</label>
<input type="text" name="lastname" id="lastname"><br>
<label for="email" accesskey="E"><u>E</u>mail:</label>
<input type="text" name="email" id="email">
```

Accessibility guideline

- Setting a proper tab order and providing access keys improves the accessibility for users who can't use a mouse.

Description

- The *tab order* for a form is the sequence in which the controls receive the focus when the Tab key is pressed. By default, the tab order is the order of the controls in the HTML, not including labels, and most browsers include links in the default tab order.

- *Access keys* are shortcut keys that the user can press to move the focus to specific controls on a form. If you assign an access key to a label, the focus is moved to the control that's associated with the label since labels can't receive the focus.

- To use an access key, you press a control key plus the access key. For IE, Chrome, and Safari, use the Alt key. For Firefox, use Alt+Shift. And for Opera, use Alt+Esc to get a list of available access keys.

Figure 10-13   How to set the tab order and assign access keys

How to use the HTML5 features for data validation

Now, it's on to the new HTML5 features for *data validation*. These features let you validate some of the data that the user enters into a form without using client-side or server-side scripting languages!

The HTML5 attributes and CSS3 selectors for data validation

As figure 10-14 shows, HTML5 provides three new attributes for data validation. The autocomplete attribute is on by default in all modern browsers, which means that a browser will use its *auto-completion feature* to display a list of entry options when the user starts the entry for a field. These options will be based on the entries the user has previously made for fields with similar names. If you're using a modern browser, you've probably noticed that your browser does this.

If you don't want the browser to use this feature, you can use the autocomplete attribute to turn it off for an entire form or for one or more fields. For instance, you may want to turn this off for fields that accept credit card numbers. In the example in this figure, this attribute is turned off for the phone field.

In contrast, the required attribute causes the browser to check whether a field is empty before it submits the form for processing. If the field is empty, it displays a message like the one in this figure. The browser also highlights all of the other required fields that are empty when the submit button is clicked. However, the message, how it's displayed, and how the other empty fields are highlighted vary from one browser to another.

If you would like to stop one or more controls from being validated, you can code the novalidate attribute for the form or for the controls. This is illustrated by the address field in the example.

To format required, valid, and invalid fields, you can use the new CSS3 pseudo-classes that are listed in this figure. For instance, you can use the :required pseudo-class to format all required fields. If your browser doesn't support these pseudo-classes, you can still format the required fields by using the attribute selector shown in this figure. You'll see these pseudo-classes in action in the web page at the end of this chapter.

The HTML5 attributes for data validation

Attribute	Description
`autocomplete`	Set this attribute to off to tell the browser to disable auto-completion. This can be coded for a form or a control.
`required`	This Boolean attribute indicates that a value is required for a field. If the form is submitted and the field is empty, the browser displays its default error message.
`novalidate`	This Boolean attribute tells the browser that it shouldn't validate the form or control that it is coded for.

HTML that uses the validation attributes

```
Name:     <input type="text" name="name" required><br>
Address: <input type="text" name="address" novalidate><br>
Zip:      <input type="text" name="zip" required><br>
Phone:    <input type="text" name="phone" required autocomplete="off"><br>
<input type="submit" name="submit" value="Submit Survey">
```

The error message and highlighting used by Firefox

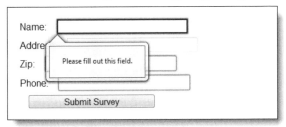

The CSS3 pseudo-classes for required, valid, and invalid fields

```
:required
:valid
:invalid
```

A CSS attribute selector for all controls with the required attribute

```
input[required]
```

Description

- By default, the *auto-completion feature* is on in all modern browsers. That means that the browser will display entry options when the user starts an entry. These options will be based on previous entries for fields with similar names.

- If the required attribute is coded for a field, the browser checks to see whether the field is empty when the form is submitted. If it is, the browser displays its default error message for the field. But what this message says and how it's displayed are browser-dependent.

- At this writing, Chrome, Firefox, and Opera support these HTML5 attributes, as well as the three CSS3 pseudo-classes shown above.

- To select all the input elements with the required attribute, you can also use the attribute selector shown above.

Figure 10-14   The HTML5 attributes and CSS3 selectors for data validation

How to use regular expressions for data validation

A *regular expression* is a standard language that provides a way to match a user entry against a *pattern* of characters. As a result, regular expressions can be used for validating user entries that have a standard pattern, such as credit card numbers, zip codes, dates, phone numbers, URLs, and more. Regular expressions are supported by many programming languages including JavaScript and PHP, and now regular expressions are supported by HTML5.

As figure 10-15 shows, HTML5 provides a pattern attribute that is used for the regular expression that will be used to validate the entry for the field. In the example, regular expressions are used for the zip code and phone fields. As a result, the user must enter a zip code that has either 5 digits or 5 digits, a hyphen, and 4 more digits. And the phone number must be 3 digits, a hyphen, 3 more digits, another hyphen, and 4 more digits. If these fields don't match those patterns when the user clicks the submit button, an error message is displayed by the browser and the form isn't submitted.

If you code a title attribute for a field that is validated by a regular expression, the value of that attribute is displayed when the mouse hovers over the field. It is also displayed at the end of the browser's standard error message for a field that doesn't match the regular expression. In the example, the browser's standard message is: "Please match the requested format:", which is followed by the value of the title attribute. But here again, the message that's displayed and how it's displayed are browser-dependent.

The trick of course is coding the regular expressions that you need, and that can be difficult. For more information or to find the expressions that you need, you can search the web. Or, you can refer to our JavaScript or PHP book, which gives detailed instructions on how to create regular expressions.

Attributes for using regular expressions

Attribute	Description
pattern	Specifies the regular expression that is used to validate the entry.
title	Text that is displayed in the tooltip when the mouse hovers over a field. This text is also displayed after the browser's error message.

Patterns for common entries

Used for	Pattern
Password (6+ alphanumeric)	`[a-zA-Z0-9]{6,}`
Zip code (99999 or 99999-9999)	`\d{5}([\-]\d{4})?`
Phone number (999-999-9999)	`\d{3}[\-]\d{3}[\-]\d{4}`
Date (MM/DD/YYYY)	`[01]?\d\/[0-3]\d\/\d{4}`
URL (starting with http:// or https://)	`https?://.+`
Credit card (9999-9999-9999-9999)	`^\d{4}-\d{4}-\d{4}-\d{4}$`

HTML that uses regular expressions

```
Name: <input type="text" name="name" required autofocus><br>
Zip: <input type="text" name="zip" required
    pattern="\d{5}([\-]\d{4})?"
    title="Must be 99999 or 99999-9999"><br>
Phone: <input type="text" name="phone" required
    pattern="\d{3}[\-]\d{3}[\-]\d{4}"
    title="Must be 999-999-9999"><br>
<input type="submit" name="submit" value="Submit Survey">
```

The form in Firefox

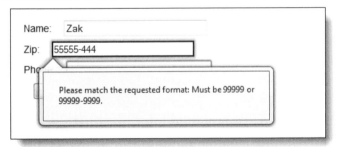

Description

- To use *regular expressions* to validate entries in text fields, you code the expression in the pattern attribute of the control. Then, the user's entry must have the *pattern* that's defined by the regular expression.

- At this writing, Chrome, Firefox, and Opera support this feature.

- To learn how to code regular expressions, you can search the web or use our JavaScript or PHP book.

Figure 10-15   How to use regular expressions for data validation

How to use a datalist to present entry options

Figure 10-16 shows how you can use the new HTML5 datalist element to provide a *datalist* of entry options for a field. Then, when the cursor is placed in the field, the list of options appears below the text box. At that point, the user can either use the mouse to select an option or use the down-arrow key to highlight an option and the Enter key to select it. This can assure that the user's entry is valid.

To provide a datalist, you code a datalist element that contains the option elements that define the options in the datalist. For each option element, you code value and label attributes. The value is what is shown on the left side of the list and in the text box if the user selects that option. The label is what is shown on the right side of the list, and it should be a friendly text-based description of the value on the left.

To associate a datalist with a text field, you add a list attribute to the field that specifies the id of the datalist element. In the example in this figure, the text field has a list attribute with a value of "links" that is the same as the id attribute of the datalist element.

Attributes for the option elements within a datalist element

Attribute	Description
value	The value of an option in the datalist. It is left-aligned.
label	The description of the item in the datalist. It is right-aligned.

HTML that uses a datalist element

```
<p>Our company is conducting a survey. Please answer the question below.</p>
<label for="link">What is your preferred search engine:</label>
<input type="url" name="link" id="link" list="links">
<datalist id="links">
    <option value="http://www.google.com/" label="Google">
    <option value="http://www.yahoo.com/" label="Yahoo">
    <option value="http://www.bing.com/" label="Bing">
    <option value="http://www.dogpile.com/" label="Dogpile">
</datalist>
<br><br>
<input type="submit" name="submit" value="Submit Survey">
```

The form in Opera after the user moves the focus to the field

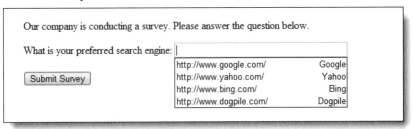

Description

- You can use the new datalist element to define a *datalist* that appears under a text field when a user begins typing in the field. This is similar to the "auto suggest" feature that's used by search engines.

- To associate a control with a datalist, you set the list attribute of the control to the id of the datalist element.

- To define the items in the datalist, you use option elements.

- At this writing, the datalist element is only supported by Firefox and Opera, and the operation of this feature is browser-dependent.

Figure 10-16   How to use a datalist to provide entry options

How to use the HTML5 controls

Besides the validation features that you've just learned, HTML5 provides several new controls. Some of these do some validation. Some provide better ways to enter data. And all of them are good semantically.

How to use the email, url, and tel controls

Figure 10-17 presents the new email, url, and tel controls. To use one, you code an input element with the type attribute set to "email", "url", or "tel". That is good semantically, because the type clearly indicates what type of data the control is for: an email address, a URL, or a telephone number.

Beyond that, a browser that supports the email and url controls will validate the data in the controls when the form is submitted. For instance, the Opera browser in this figure is displaying its error message for an invalid email address. This works the same for a url control.

At this writing, though, validation isn't done for tel fields. That's because the format of telephone numbers can vary so much from one country to another. However, this may change as browsers evolve.

If you experiment with the validation that's done by the browsers that currently support these elements, you'll see that it isn't foolproof for email and url fields. In fact, you can do a better job of validation by using regular expressions. But this too may change as browsers evolve.

If a browser doesn't support these controls, they are treated as text boxes. Since this doesn't cause any problems, you can start using these controls right away. That way, you still get the semantic benefits.

The email, url, and tel controls

Control	Description
email	A control for receiving an email address. This implies that the entry will be validated by the browser when the form is submitted.
url	A control for receiving a URL. This implies that the entry will be validated by the browser when the form is submitted.
tel	A control for receiving a telephone number, but currently this doesn't imply validation because the formats vary from one country to another.

HTML code that uses the email, url, and tel elements

```
<form name="email_form" action="survey.php" method="post">
    <h3>Your information:</h3>
    <label for="email">Your email address:</label>
    <input type="email" name="email" id="email" required><br>
    <label for="link">Your web site:</label>
    <input type="url" name="link" id="link"><br>
    <label for="phone">Your phone number:</label>
    <input type="tel" name="phone" id="phone" required><br><br>
    <input type="submit" name="submit" value="Submit Survey">
</form>
```

The form in Opera

Description

- The HTML5 email, url, and tel controls are designed for email address, URL, and telephone number entries. The first two imply that validation will be done by the browser when the form is submitted, but phone numbers aren't validated.

- It's good to use these controls for semantic reasons because they indicate what type of data each control is for.

- At this writing, the email control is supported by Firefox, Chrome, and Opera, and the iPhone and iPad support this control by displaying a keyboard that is optimized for email addresses when this control receives the focus.

- At this writing, the url control is supported by all browsers except IE, and the tel control is essentially supported by all browsers since data validation isn't required.

- Here again, the wording of the error messages and the way they're displayed depends upon the browser.

Figure 10-17   How to use the email, url, and tel controls

How to use the number and range controls

Figure 10-18 shows how to use the new number and range controls. In browsers that support these controls, the number control is presented as a text box with up and down arrows that can increase or decrease the value in the box. And the range control is presented as a slider that the user can use to increase or decrease the initial value.

When you code these controls, you usually include the min, max, and step attributes. Those attributes set the minimum and maximum values that the control will accept, as well as the amount to increase or decrease the value when a number arrow is clicked or the slider is moved.

The examples in this figure show how this works. Here, the number control has 100 as its minimum value, 1000 as its maximum value, and 100 as the step value when an arrow is clicked. In contrast, the range control has 1 as its minimum value, 5 as its maximum value, and 1 as the step value.

If you code a value attribute for a number control, it will appear in the text box as the starting value. Otherwise, no value is displayed. This is illustrated by the example in this figure. If you code a value attribute for a range control, the slider will be set to that value. Otherwise, it will be set to the middle of the slider.

Here again, if a browser doesn't support these controls, they are treated as text boxes. Since this doesn't cause any problems, you can start using these controls right away. That way, you still get the semantic benefits.

Attributes for the number and range controls

Attribute	Description
`min`	The minimum value that may be entered.
`max`	The maximum value that may be entered.
`step`	The value that the entry is increased or decreased by when the user clicks on the up or down arrow for a number field or moves the slider for a range field.

HTML that uses number and range controls

```
<h3>Your information:</h3>
<form name="test_form" action="test.php" method="get">
    <label for="investment">Monthly investment: </label>
    <input type="number" name="investment" id="investment"
           min="100" max="1000" step="100" value="300"><br><br>
    <label for="book">Rate the book from 1 to 5: </label>
    <input type="range" name="book" id="book"
           min="1" max="5" step="1"><br><br>
    <input type="submit" name="submit" value="Submit Survey">
</form>
```

The form in Opera

Description

- The HTML5 number and range controls are designed for numeric entries.
- It's good to use these controls for semantic reasons because they indicate what type of data each control is for.
- In Chrome, Opera, and Safari, a text box with up and down arrows is rendered for the number control and a slider is rendered for the range control.
- If these controls aren't supported by a browser, a text box is displayed.

Figure 10-18   How to use the number and range controls

How to use the date and time controls

Figure 10-19 shows how to use the new date and time controls for user entries. When the user clicks on the down arrow for any one of the date types, the calendar is displayed, as shown by the last control in this figure. Then, the user can select the date, month, or week. When the user clicks on the up or down arrow for a time, the time is increased or decreased.

If you study the examples, you can see how to code the input elements for these controls. The only difference between the datetime and the datetime-local types is that datetime is formatted in Coordinated Universal Time, or UTC. This is the time by which the world sets its clocks. In contrast, datetime-local is based on the date and time used by your system's clock.

At this writing, Firefox, Internet Explorer, and Safari treat these controls as text boxes. Chrome supports these controls but not the popup calendar, and Opera has the best support for these controls. Nevertheless, it's good to use these controls for semantic reasons. And there's no harm done if they're rendered as text boxes.

Attributes for the date and time controls

Attribute	Description
max	The maximum value that may be entered within a date or time field.
min	The minimum value that may be entered within a date or time field.

HTML that uses the date and time controls

```
Date and time:  
    <input type="datetime" name="datetime"><br><br>
Local date and time:  
    <input type="datetime-local" name="datetimelocal"><br><br>
Month:  
    <input type="month" name="month"><br><br>
Week:  
    <input type="week" name="week"><br><br>
Time:  
    <input type="time" name="time"><br><br>
Date:  
    <input type="date" name="date">
```

The controls in Opera

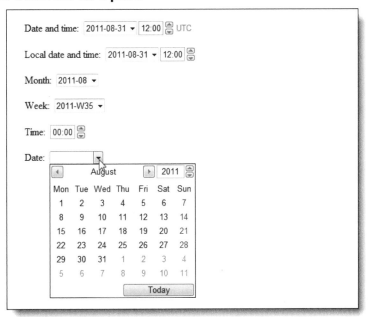

Description

- The HTML5 date, datetime, datetime-local, month, week, and time controls are designed for date and time entries. Here again, it's good to use these controls for semantic reasons.

- At this writing, Safari, Firefox, and Internet Explorer ignore the date and time elements and render text fields instead. In contrast, Chrome has some support for these elements, and Opera fully supports them by showing calendar widgets.

Figure 10-19   How to use the date and time controls

How to use the search control for a search function

Figure 10-20 shows how you can add a search function to a web site. To do that, you use the new search control along with several hidden fields to create a form that submits the search data to a search engine.

At the top of this figure, you can see the two controls that are needed for a search function: a search element for the search entry and a Search button that submits the search entry to the search engine. This is the standard way to set up the controls for a search function, and this mimics the way Google uses these controls. If you want to vary from this at all, you can use a Go button instead of a Search button, but users expect all search functions to look this way. You should also make the text box large enough for a typical entry.

If you look at the HTML code for the search form, you will see that the form is submitted to www.google.com/search, which is the Google search engine. That's why the results of the search are displayed on the standard Google results page.

In the code for this search form, the first input element is for the search control. Although a text field would also work, the new search control is rendered differently in the browser. For instance, as the Safari browser at the top of this figure shows, the search box is highlighted and has an "x" at the right of the box. This is meant to mimic the look of other Apple products such as the iPad, iPhone, iPod, the Apple website, and more.

To limit the search to www.murach.com, this HTML uses two hidden fields that pass the required data to the Google search engine. To use this HTML for a Google search of your site, you just need to change the value attribute in the two hidden fields to the URL for your web site.

The trouble with the standard Google search engine is that sponsored links will be displayed on the results page. That's why it's better to use a search engine that can be customized so it returns results that are appropriate for users of your site. To find a search engine like this, you can search the web for "add search function to web site." Some of these search engines are free, and some like Google Site Search charge a nominal fee like $100 a year for a small site.

A search function that uses a search control in the Safari browser

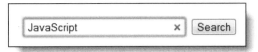

The results of a search when the Google search engine is used

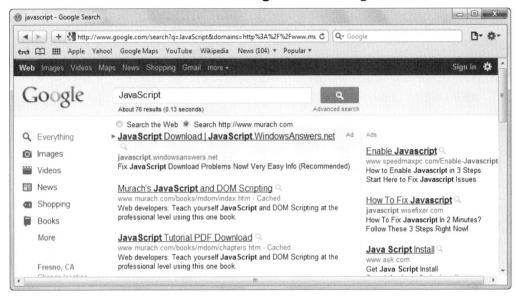

The HTML for using the Google search engine

```
<form method="get" action="http://www.google.com/search">
    <input type="search" name="q" size="30" maxlength="255">
    <input type="hidden" name="domains" value="http://www.murach.com">
    <input type="hidden" name="sitesearch" value="http://www.murach.com">
    <input type="submit" name="search" value="Search">
</form>
```

Description

- To implement a search function, you use an HTML form to submit the search text and other required data to the search engine.

- Within the form for the search function, you can use an input element of the "search" type for the text that's entered. This is good for semantic reasons.

- This control should be followed by a submit button that says Search or Go. The form must also include one hidden field to specify the domain for the search and another one to specify that only that domain should be searched.

- If you use a search engine like Google, you have no control over the search results. If you want to customize the results, you can use a search engine like Google Site Search.

- At this writing, Safari and Chrome are the only browsers that stylize the search control when the user enters data into it. Other browsers treat this control as a text box.

Figure 10-20   How to use the search control for a search function

How to use the color control

Figure 10-21 demonstrates the use of the new color control. In browsers that support this control, a color palette is displayed when the user clicks on the down arrow. Then, if the user clicks on Other button, the color palette for the user's operating system is displayed. Later, when the color selection is submitted to the browser, it is sent as a hexadecimal code.

At present, only Opera supports this control, and the other browsers treat it as a text box. But here again, it's good to use this control for semantic reasons, and there's no harm done if the control is treated as a text box.

The HTML for a color control

```
<label for="firstcolor">Choose your first background color:</label>
<input type="color" name="firstcolor" id="firstcolor">
```

The color control in Opera

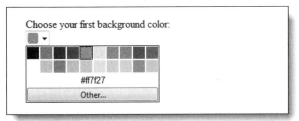

The Windows color palette

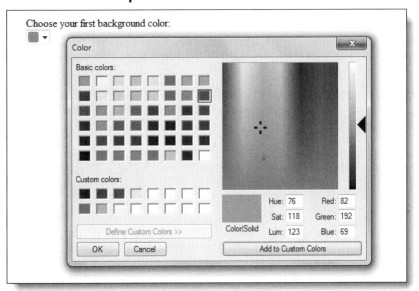

Description

- Use the input element with "color" as its type to let the users select a color from the color palette. When the user selects a color, the hexadecimal value for that color is displayed above the Other button.

- If the user clicks on the Other button, the color palette for the user's operating system is opened. Then, the user can use the controls of this palette to create custom colors.

- When the form is submitted, the hexadecimal value is used as the data for the control.

- At this writing, only Opera supports this control. Other browsers treat this control as a text box. But here again, using this control is good for semantic reasons.

Figure 10-21   How to use the color control

How to use the output element to display output data

Figure 10-22 shows how to use the new output element. Unlike the other controls that you've seen in this chapter, the output element is used to display output data, not to accept input data. To create the output, though, you need to use client-side code like JavaScript or server-side code like PHP.

In the example in this figure, JavaScript is used to add the values in the number controls and display the output in the output element. In this case, I used CSS to add a border to the output element so it's easy to spot. Otherwise, this element wouldn't have a border.

To show which fields the output element is associated with, you can code the for attribute. In this example, this attribute is used to show that the result is derived from the input fields that are named x and y.

Although you could use a label or text box to display the output, using the output element is good for semantic reasons. Also, browsers that don't support it render the output control as a text box. As a result, you can start using this control right now.

If you don't know how to use JavaScript or PHP, you won't be able to provide the code that calculates the result. But as a web designer, you may be asked to provide controls that the programmers for your site can use for their results. In that case, the output element is a good option.

An attribute for the output element

Attribute	Description
for	Can be used to associate an output element with one or more form controls.

The HTML for a form that uses an output element

```
<p>Enter numbers in both fields and click the Calculate button.</p>
<form onsubmit="return false">
    <input name="x" type="number" min="100" step="5" value="100"> +
    <input name="y" type="number" min="100" step="5" value="100"><br><br>
    <input type="button" value="Calculate"
        onClick="result.value = parseInt(x.value) + parseInt(y.value)">
    <br><br>
    Total: <output name="result" for="x y"></output>
</form>
```

The form in Safari with a border around the output element

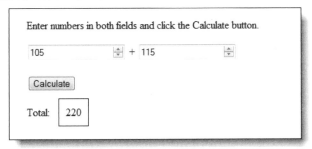

Description

- This control is designed to display data that is calculated by a client-side or server-side scripting language.

- Although you could use a textbox or label to display the output data, using the output element is better for semantic reasons.

- In this example, JavaScript is used for the onClick event of the Calculate button. This code just adds the values in the number controls that are named x and y. For more on JavaScript, see chapter 13.

- At this writing, IE is the only browser that doesn't support this element.

Figure 10-22   How to use the output element to display output data

How to use the progress and meter elements to display output data

Like the output element, the progress and meter elements are designed for output data that's developed by JavaScript. However, both of these controls present the data in a graphical form as shown in figure 10-23. By default, the color used in these controls is green.

To use these elements, you code an id attribute that can be referred to by the JavaScript code. Then, you can code some of the attributes supported by these elements including the high, low, min, max, optimum, and value attributes.

The high and low attributes can be used to define the points at which the progress or meter element's value is considered a high or low point. When the low and high attributes are set for the meter element, the meter color changes from green to yellow when the indicator is either below the low or above the high value.

The min and max attributes can be used to define the lower and upper limits of the progress or meter elements. Typically, you use 0 to represent 0% for the min attribute of a progress element and 100 to represent 100% for the max attribute because most progress indicators work within that range. In contrast, a meter might work differently. If, for example, a meter element is used to represent a car's speed, 0 will still be the min value, but 140 might be the max value, which represents that maximum speed that the car will go.

You can use the optimum attribute to define the point at which the progress or meter element's value is considered the optimum value. Again, if we use the speedometer in a car as an example, the optimum value might be 65 to represent 65 miles per hour.

The value attribute works the same as it does for most other form controls in that it allows you to define a default value that you want the progress or meter element to start at. However, JavaScript can be used to change this value.

One reason for using these elements is semantics because they clearly indicate the type of data that will be presented. The other reason is that these elements make it easier to display progress and meter data in a graphical form. The problem is that only Opera fully supports these elements right now.

Here again, if you don't know how to use JavaScript, you won't be able to provide the code that changes the values in these controls. But as a web designer, you should know how to code these elements so they can be used by the programmers for your site.

Attributes for the progress and meter elements

Attribute	Description
high	The point at which the element's value is considered a high point.
low	The point at which the element's value is considered a low point.
min	The lower limit of the element. Typically, this will be 0 to represent 0%.
max	The upper limit of the element.
optimum	The point at which the element's value is considered optimum.
value	The current value of the element.

The HTML for progress and meter elements

```
<body onLoad="setProgressAndMeter()">
    <h3>Progress Element</h3>
    Progress set by JavaScript on page load:
    <progress id="progressBar" max="100" value="0"></progress>
    <h3>Meter Element</h3>
    Meter set by JavaScript on page load:
    <meter id="meterBar" max="100" value="0" optimum="50" high="60"></meter>
</body>
```

The progress and meter elements in Opera

Progress Element

Progress set by JavaScript on page load:

Meter Element

Meter set by JavaScript on page load:

The JavaScript that manipulates the progress and meter elements

```
<script>
    function setProgressAndMeter() {
        var progress = document.getElementById("progressBar");
        setInterval(setProgressAndMeter, 500);
        progress.value += 10;
        var meter = document.getElementById("meterBar");
        setInterval(setProgressAndMeter, 500);
        meter.value += 10;
    };
</script>
```

Description

- These controls are designed to display data in progress bar or meter form. This is good semantically, and these controls also make it easier to display the data graphically.

- In this example, JavaScript is used to update these controls as the page is loaded. For more on JavaScript, see chapter 13.

- At this writing, Opera is the only browser that fully supports these elements, although Chrome provides minimal support.

Figure 10-23   How to use the progress and meter elements to display output data

A web page
that uses HTML5 data validation

To show how the new HTML5 features for forms can be used in a web page, this chapter ends by presenting a complete example.

The page layout

Figure 10-24 presents a web page that contains a form that uses some of the new HTML5 controls. This includes an email control for the email address entry, a date control for the starting date entry, and a number control for the number of tickets entry.

Because this page is displayed in Opera, which supports these controls, you can click on the down arrow for the date control to display a calendar like the one in figure 10-19. You can also click on the up or down arrow for the number control to change the number of guest tickets.

The CSS for this form, puts a 3-pixel, red border around the required fields and a 1-pixel, black border around the fields that have valid entries. In this example the first two fields, the address field, and the guest tickets field are considered valid.

Because the autofocus attribute is used for the email field, you don't need to change the tab order for this form. But otherwise, the tab order would start with the four links in the navigation bar and continue with the six links in the navigation list in the right sidebar before the focus got to the first field in the form.

A web page in Opera with a form that uses HTML5 validation

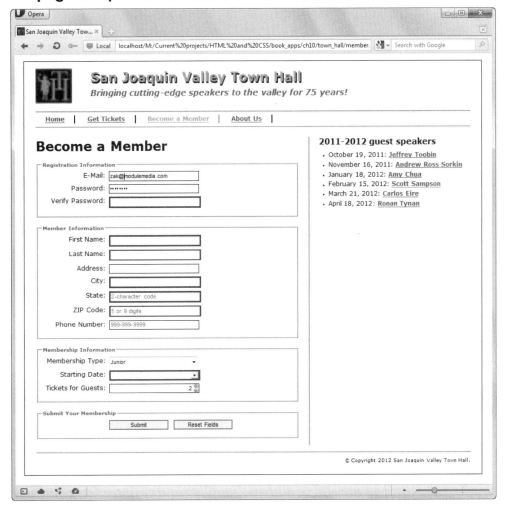

Description

- The form in this web page uses many of the HTML5 controls that were presented in this chapter. Its controls are formatted and aligned with CSS, and the CSS3 pseudo-classes are used to format the required, valid, and invalid fields.

- Form validation is done by using required attributes, regular expressions, and the email, date, and number controls.

- The autofocus attribute is used for the first control in the form so the tab order doesn't need to be changed. Otherwise, the navigation links and sidebar links would come before the form controls in the tab order.

- The placeholder attribute is used in some fields to indicate how the user should enter the data. When the focus moves to the field, the placeholder text is removed.

Figure 10-24   A web page with a form that uses HTML5 validation

The HTML

Figure 10-25 presents most of the HTML for the form within this web page. The rest of the code for this page is like the code that you've seen for this web site in earlier chapters.

To help you focus on the HTML5 elements for a form, most of them are highlighted in this figure. For instance, the type attributes for the email, tel, date, and number controls are highlighted. Also, the new autofocus and required attributes are highlighted. Last, the pattern and title attributes are highlighted for those fields that use regular expressions for data validation.

If you study this code, you'll see that it doesn't do a complete job of data validation. For instance, there's no way to verify that the second entry of the password is the same as the first entry when you use HTML5.

Similarly, the state field uses the maxlength attribute to limit the entry to two characters, but those characters won't necessarily be a valid state code. In fact, they may not even be letters. You could fix this by using a regular expression that requires two letters, but even then the code may not be valid.

This illustrates some of the limitations of HTML5 data validation. That's why JavaScript is commonly used to do client-side data validation. For instance, JavaScript could check to make sure that the second password entry is the same as the first entry. And JavaScript could look up the state entry in a table that contains the 50 state codes that are valid. Then, any entry that isn't in the table would be considered invalid.

Keep in mind, though, that the entries for a form should always be validated by the server-side code too. Like JavaScript, that code can validate data more thoroughly than the HTML5 features. As a result, the data validation on the client doesn't have to be thorough. In fact, the main point of client-side validation is to save some of the round trips that would be required if the validation was only done by the server. And if you use the HTML5 features for data validation, you will certainly save many round trips.

In that context, it's okay to start using the HTML5 features for data validation right now. Then, if a browser doesn't support them, you can rely on the server-side programming for data validation.

The HTML for the form

```html
<form action="register_account.html" method="get"
    name="registration_form" id="registration_form">
<fieldset>
    <legend>Registration Information</legend>
    <label for="email">E-Mail:</label>
    <input type="email" name="email" id="email" autofocus required><br>
    <label for="password">Password:</label>
    <input type="password" name="password" id="password" required
        pattern="[a-zA-Z0-9]{6,}"
        placeholder="At least 6 letters or numbers"><br>
    <label for="verify">Verify Password:</label>
    <input type="password" name="verify" id="verify" required><br>
</fieldset>
<fieldset>
    <legend>Member Information</legend>
    <label for="first_name">First Name:</label>
    <input type="text" name="first_name" id="first_name" required><br>
    ...
    ...
    ...
    <label for="state">State:</label>
    <input type="text" name="state" id="state" required maxlength="2"
        placeholder="2-character code"><br>
    <label for="zip">ZIP Code:</label>
    <input type="text" name="zip" id="zip" required
        placeholder="5 or 9 digits"
        pattern="^\d{5}(-\d{4})?$" title="Either 5 or 9 digits"><br>
    <label for="phone">Phone Number:</label>
    <input type="tel" name="phone" id="phone" placeholder="999-999-9999"
        pattern="\d{3}[\-]\d{3}[\-]\d{4}"
        title="Must be 999-999-999 format"><br>
</fieldset>
<fieldset>
    <legend>Membership Information</legend>
    <label for="membership_type">Membership Type:</label>
    <select name="membership_type" id="membership_type">
        <option value="j">Junior</option>
        <option value="r">Regular</option>
        <option value="c">Charter</option>
    </select><br>
    <label for="starting_date">Starting Date:</label>
    <input type="date" name="starting_date" id="starting_date" required><br>
    <label for="tickets">Tickets for Guests:</label>
    <input type="number" name="tickets" id="tickets"
        value="2" min="1" max="4" placeholder="from 1 to 4"><br>
</fieldset>
<fieldset id="buttons">
    <legend>Submit Your Membership</legend>
    <label> </label>
    <input type="submit" id="submit" value="Submit">
    <input type="reset" id="reset" value="Reset Fields"><br>
</fieldset>
</form>
```

Figure 10-25   The HTML for the form

The CSS

Figure 10-26 presents the CSS for the form that's used in the web page. Of most interest is the use of the CSS3 selectors. For instance, the input:required selector is used to put a 3-pixel, red border around required fields in browsers that support the :required pseudo-class. But note that this attribute selector

```
input[required]
```

is also used to apply the red border in browsers that don't support that pseudo-class, but do support the required attribute.

You can also see how the :valid and :invalid pseudo-classes are used to format the invalid fields. First, a black border is applied to valid fields, as shown in figure 10-24. Then, the box shadow is removed from invalid fields. This is done specifically for the Firefox browser because it's the only one that applies a box shadow to those fields.

The CSS for the form

```
fieldset {
    margin-top: 1em;
    margin-bottom: 1em;
    padding-top: .5em;
}

legend {
    color: green;
    font-weight: bold;
    font-size: 85%;
}

label {
    float: left;
    width: 10em;
    text-align: right;
}

input, select {
    width: 15em;
    margin-left: 0.5em;
    margin-bottom: 0.5em;
}

input:required, input[required] {
    border: 3px solid red;
}

input:valid {
    border: 1px solid black;
}

input:invalid {
    box-shadow: none;
}

br {
    clear: both;
}

#buttons input {
    width: 10em;
}
```

Figure 10-26   The CSS for the form

Perspective

Now that you've completed this chapter, you should have all the skills you need for creating forms, including forms that use HTML5 controls. You should also be able to use the HTML5 features for data validation.

Remember, though, that you can do a better job of data validation by using JavaScript. You'll see this illustrated at the end of chapter 13 by the same web page that's presented at the end of this chapter. On the other hand, data validation should always be done on the server too, so the client-side data validation doesn't have to be foolproof.

At present, the main problem with the HTML5 features for data validation is that they aren't supported consistently by all browsers. Until that changes, it's okay to use the new controls because they are treated as text boxes if they aren't supported. But for client-side data validation, JavaScript is still the best solution.

Terms

form	drop-down list
control	list box
button	text area
submit button	label
reset button	file upload control
image button	tab order
text field	access key
text box	data validation
password field	auto-completion feature
hidden field	regular expression
check box	pattern
radio button	datalist

Summary

- A *form* contains one or more *controls* like text boxes, radio buttons, or check boxes that can receive data. When a form is submitted to the server for processing, the data in the controls is sent along with the HTTP request.

- When the get method is used to submit a form, the data is sent as part of the URL for the next web page. When the post method is used, the data is hidden.

- A *submit button* submits the form data to the server when the button is clicked. A *reset button* resets all the data in the form when it is clicked. Buttons can also be used to start client-side scripts when they are clicked.

- The controls that are commonly used within a form are *labels*, *text fields*, *radio buttons*, *check boxes*, *drop-down lists*, *list boxes*, and *text areas*.

- A *text field* is used to get data from a user. A *password field* also gets data from the user, but its data is obscured by bullets or asterisks. A *hidden field* contains data that is sent to the server, but the field isn't displayed on the form.

- A *label* is commonly used to identify a related control. To associate a label with a control, you use the for attribute of the label to specify the id value of the control.

- You can use a *file upload control* to upload a file from the user's system. Then, server-side code is used to store the file on the web server.

- You can use CSS to align controls by floating the labels to the left of the controls. You can also use CSS to format the controls.

- The *tab order* of a form is the order in which the controls receive the focus when the Tab key is pressed. By default, this is the sequence in which the controls are coded in the HTML. To change that, you can use tabindex attributes.

- *Access keys* are shortcut keys that the user can press to move the focus to specific controls on a form. To assign an access key to a control, you use its accesskey attribute. To let the user know that an access key is available, you can underline the access key in the label for the control.

- HTML5 introduces some attributes for *data validation*, and CSS3 introduces some pseudo-classes for formatting required, valid, and invalid fields. The HTML5 attributes for data validation include the required attribute and the pattern attribute that provides for *regular expressions*.

- HTML5 also introduces some input controls including the email, url, tel, number, range, date, time, search, and color controls. These are good semantically because they indicate what types of data the controls are for.

- HTML5 also introduces some output controls that can receive the results of client-side or server-side programming. These include the output, progress, and meter controls.

Exercise 10-1   Create a form for getting tickets

In this exercises, you'll create a form like the one that follows. To do that, you'll start from the HTML and CSS code that is used for the form in the chapter application.

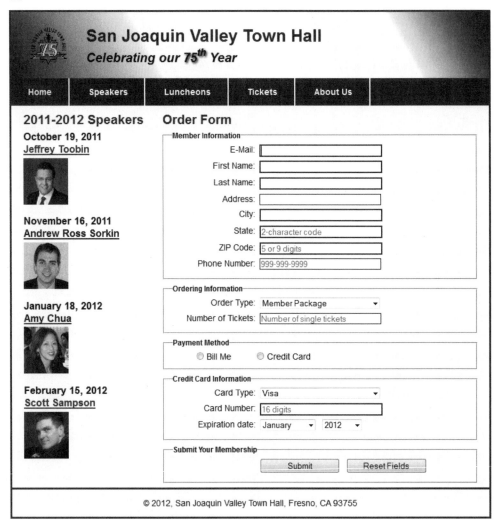

Open the HTML and CSS files

1. Use your text editor to open the HTML and CSS files for the Tickets page:

   ```
   c:\html5_css3\exercises\town_hall_2\tickets.html
   c:\html5_css3\exercises\town_hall_2\styles\tickets.css
   ```

2. Run the HTML file in Firefox to see that this page contains the form and the formatting that is used in the application at the end of the chapter. Your job is to modify the form and its CSS so the page looks like the one above.

Fix the formatting of the form and test after each change

3. Change the fieldset margins and padding so there is no top margin, the bottom margin is .5em, the top and bottom padding is .5em, and the right and left padding is 1em.

4. Change the legend formatting so the color is black.

5. Change the formatting so the required and the invalid fields have a 2px border with #800000 as the font color, and the valid fields have a 1px black border.

Fix the HTML one fieldset at a time and test after each change

6. In the HTML, change the heading before the form to "Order Form". Then, combine the first two fieldsets, change the legend to "Member Information", and delete the password fields so the first fieldset looks like the one above.

7. In the Membership Information fieldset, change the legend to "Ordering Information" and modify the HTML for the fields. Here, the Order Type list should have these choices: Member Package, Donor Package, and Single Tickets. Also, the Number of Tickets field should be a text field with the placeholder shown above.

8. Add the Payment Method fieldset with two radio buttons, and use the coding method in figure 10-8 so the user can activate the buttons by clicking on the labels. Then, adjust the CSS so the buttons are side by side as shown above.

    One way to do that is to code an id for the fieldset, and then use an id selector to turn off the float for the labels, to set the width of the buttons to "auto", and to set the left margin for the buttons to 3em.

9. Add the Credit Card Information fieldset. Here, the Card Type list should have these choices: Visa, MasterCard, and Discovery. The Card Number field should have the placeholder shown. The month list should have values from January through December. And the year list should have values from 2012 through 2016.

    To format these lists, you can use id selectors and set the width of the month to 7em and the width of the year to 5em. To check the validity of the card number, you can use this pattern: \d{16}.

10. For the Submit Your Order fieldset, you just need to change the legend.

Test, validate, and test in other browsers

11. Test the validation that's done by the form by entering combinations of invalid data. Then, enter valid data for all the fields and click the Submit button. This should display a page (register_account.html) that shows the data that has been submitted.

12. Validate the HTML file, and test the form in IE. Then, if you have the time, test the form in Chrome, Opera, and Safari too.

11

How to add audio and video to your web site

In this chapter, you'll learn how to add audio and video to your web site. As you will see, HTML5 provides new audio and video elements that make this easier than before. To make sure that your audio and video will work on older browsers, though, you'll also learn how to use the old elements for delivering audio and video.

An introduction to media on the web

Before I show you how to include media files in a web page, you need to be familiar with the various media types and codes that are used for video and audio. You also need to know what media types and encoders work with the browsers that are used today.

Common media types for video and audio

When most of us think about *media types*, a short list comes to mind: MPEG, AVI, MP3, and maybe even AAC. The reality, though, is that there are dozens of media types for both video and audio. Some of them are summarized in figure 11-1.

These media types are nothing more than containers of information that are used by *media players* to play the content that the types contain. For example, an MPEG file contains a video track, which is what the users see, and one or more audio tracks, which is what the users hear. To keep the video coordinated with the audio, a media type can also contain markers that help the audio sync up with the video. In addition, a media type can contain metadata, such as the title of the video, any still imagery related to the video (cover art), the length of the video, and digital rights management information.

For some media types, a browser will require a *plug-in* that plays that type. These plug-ins are generally released by the player manufacturers. For instance, Apple provides a QuickTime plug-in, Windows provides a Windows Media Player plug-in, and Adobe provides a Flash Player plug-in. If a browser supports a media type without requiring a plug-in, you can say that the browser "natively" supports that media type.

Common media types for video

Type	Description
MPEG-4	Commonly found with either an .mp4 or .m4v extension. The MPEG-4 media type is loosely based on Apple's QuickTime (.mov) media type. Although movie trailers on Apple's website are still delivered in the older QuickTime .mov media type, iTunes uses the newer MPEG-4 media type for delivering video.
Flash Video	Commonly found with either the .flv or .f4v extension. Flash Video, developed by Adobe, is currently the most common media type for delivering video on the web. At this writing, YouTube delivers its video using this format.
Ogg	Usually found with the .ogg extension. Ogg is an open-source, open-standard media type currently supported natively by Firefox 3.5 and above, Chrome 4 and above, and Opera 10.5 and above. The video stream of an ogg media type is technically referred to as Theora.
WebM	A relatively new file format which is usually found with the .webm extension. WebM is currently supported natively by Chrome, Firefox, and Opera, and Adobe has recently announced that future releases of Flash will also support WebM video.
ASF	The Advanced Systems Format is commonly found with the .asf extension. ASF is a Microsoft proprietary media type and is specifically meant for streaming media. The video stream of an ASF media type is typically Windows Media Video (WMV).
AVI	Audio Video Interleave is commonly found with the .avi extension and is another Microsoft proprietary media type. It is one of the oldest media types and was introduced in 1992 when computer-based video was largely a hope for the future.

Common media types for audio

Type	Description
MP3	MPEG-1 Audio Layer 3, which is commonly known as MP3, is one of the most widely-used media types for audio.
AAC	Advanced Audio Coding or AAC is the format that Apple uses to deliver audio for its iTunes store. AAC was originally designed to deliver better quality audio than MP3.
Ogg	Usually found with the .ogg extension. Ogg is an open-source, open-standard media type currently supported natively by Firefox 3.5+, Chrome 4+, and Opera 10.5+. The audio stream of an ogg media type is technically referred to as Vorbis.
WMA	Windows Media Audio or WMA are usually found with the .wma extension. The audio stream of an ASF media type is typically Windows Media Audio.

Description

- A *media type* is a container for several components, including an encoded video track, one or more encoded audio tracks, and metadata.

- To play a media type, a browser requires a *media player* for that type.

- For specific media players, browsers often require special *plug-ins*. These plug-ins are generally released by the player manufacturers, and include QuickTime, Windows Media Player, and Adobe Flash Player.

- To say that a browser "natively" supports a media type means that the browser doesn't require a plug-in for it.

Figure 11-1   Common media types for video and audio

Video codecs

Within a media type, a video is encoded with a specific type of code. Although there are dozens of different codes used for video, figure 11-2 summarizes the three that are most noteworthy. H.264 is usually mentioned in the same breath as MPEG since it was developed by MPEG in 1993. Theora is the video stream portion of the Ogg media type. And VP8 was originally developed by On2 Technologies and more recently acquired by Google.

When a media player plays a media type, it has to do the five tasks that are summarized in this figure. Of these tasks, it's the decoding of the video and audio tracks that is the most difficult.

To decode, media players use software components called *codecs*. This name is derived from COmpressor/DECompressor, because video and audio are compressed when they're encoded and decompressed when they're decoded. You can also think of codec as COder/DECoder. Once the codecs have been used to "crack the codes," the media players display a series of images (otherwise known as frames) on the screen.

Video codecs

Codec	Description
H.264	Developed by the MPEG group in 1993. The goal of the Movie Picture Experts Group (MPEG) was to provide a single "all inclusive" codec that would support low bandwidth, low-CPU devices (think mobile phones); and high bandwidth, high-CPU devices (think your computer); and everything in between.
Theora	Theora is a royalty free codec which can produce video streams that can be embedded in virtually any format. Theora is typically mentioned in the same breath as Ogg.
VP8	Originally developed by On2 Technologies (recently acquired by Google), VP8 is an open-source, royalty-free encoder.

What a media player does when it plays a video

- Determines the media type that the user is attempting to play.
- Determines whether it has the capability of decoding its video and audio streams.
- Decodes the video and displays it on the screen.
- Decodes the audio and sends it to the speakers.
- Interprets any metadata and makes it available.

Description

- A *codec* (derived from COmpressor/DECompressor or COder/DECoder) is a software component that is used to code and decode the algorithms that are used for a media type.
- A codec also compresses the code so it will load faster in a browser and decompresses the code before it is played.
- Although there are dozens of codecs for video, the three most common are H.264, Theora, and VP8.

Figure 11-2   Video codecs

Audio codecs

Like video, dozens of audio codecs are available. In fact, it's safe to say that there are many more audio codecs than there are video codecs. That's because there's a multi-billion dollar industry that revolves around the delivery of audio streams via MP3 players as well as iPods and iPhones.

An audio codec is used to decode the audio portion of an audio or video file, convert it to audible waveforms, and send it to the speakers of a system, which convert those waveforms into sound. The biggest difference between video and audio is that audio can store channels that let the sound be delivered to different speakers at the same time.

Most audio files contain two channels, which represent the left and right speakers, but it's common for video media types to have several channels of audio that represent left, right, and center speakers plus speakers in the rear. This is commonly referred to as "surround sound."

Unlike video, where the codecs have different names than their media types, audio codecs often have names that are the same as or similar to their media types. MP3 is one example, which can be played on a dedicated MP3 player or as part of a video track. Another example is AAC, which was adopted by Apple and is currently supported by all of Apple's products, including iTunes, iPod, and iPad. Similarly, Vorbis is commonly used for the Ogg media types (both audio and video), and Windows Media Audio (WMA) is commonly used for Microsoft's WMA and ASF media types.

Audio codecs

Codec	Description
AAC	AAC is one of the most common media types and is also the encoding standard for the media type. It is currently used on all Apple products, as well as Nintendo's DSi and Wii, Sony's Playstation 3 and Portable, as well as several mobile devices including phones powered by Sony Ericsson, Nokia, Android, and WebOS.
FLAC	Free Lossless Audio Codec (FLAC) is a free, open-source codec that has seen its popularity increase over the years due in large part to its high compression ratio. Audio files that uses FLAC can have their file sizes reduced by up to 60%.
MP3	MPEG-1 Audio Layer 3, commonly known as MP3, is one of the most widely-used media types for audio.
Vorbis	Typically packaged within the .ogg extension and commonly referred to as Ogg Vorbis. Vorbis is a free, open source format that is supported natively by most popular Linux installations as well as the newer editions of Chrome, Firefox, and Opera browsers.
WMA	Windows Media Audio (WMA) is usually found with the .wma extension. The audio stream of an ASF media type is typically Windows Media Audio.

Description

- Although there are more than a dozen codecs for audio, the five most common are those in the table above.

- When you watch a video or listen to audio in your browser, your media player is responsible for interpreting the media type. It is also responsible for decoding the audio so it can direct the sound to the speakers on your device.

- Unlike video codecs, audio codecs often have the same name as their media type or a similar name.

Figure 11-3   Audio codecs

Audio and video support in current browsers

One of the problems when adding audio or video to a web site is that there isn't a single combination of codecs that will work on all browsers. This is shown by the tables in figure 11-4.

One solution to this problem is to encode your media in the Flash file format (SWF) and rely on the browser's Flash Player plug-in to play your media. Although this has worked well for many years, it presents three problems. First, you're forcing your users to rely on a plug-in to view your media. Although it's true that 97% of the users have the Flash plug-in installed, this plug-in consumes resources and that still leaves 3% who won't be able to play your media. Second, what about the ever-expanding use of mobile devices such as iPhones that don't support Flash? That segment, which currently represents about 10% of Internet traffic, is also left out. Third, the Flash player is unstable in some browsers so it sometimes crashes, which is one of the biggest reasons why the iPhone doesn't support Flash.

This is where HTML5 and its new video and audio elements come in. To use them, though, you need to encode your media into multiple formats so they can be run on all browsers. You will also need to specify the MIME types that are used for these formats, as summarized in this figure. A *MIME type* describes the contents of a file and helps a browser determine what player to use to open the file. To refer to an MP3 file, for example, you will code "audio/mp3". Or, to refer to a Flash file, you will code "application/x-shockwave-flash".

Audio codec support in current browsers

Browser	Ogg Vorbis	MP3	AAC
IE	-	9.0+	9.0+ (with VP8 codec)
Firefox	3.6+	-	-
Safari	with QuickTime installed	3.0+	5.0+
Chrome	5.0+	10.0+	6.0+
Opera	10.5+	-	-

Video codec support in current browsers

Browser	Ogg Theora	H.264	WebM
IE	-	9.0+	9.0+ (with VP8 codec)
Firefox	3.5+	-	4.0+
Safari	-	3.0+	-
Chrome	5.0+	10.0+	6.0+
Opera	10.5+	-	10.6+

The MIME types you will need for identifying audio and video files

Media type	MIME type	Codec
MP3	`audio/mp3`	
Ogg Vorbis	`audio/ogg`	
WebM	`video/webm`	`theora, vorbis`
Ogg Theora	`video/ogg`	`theora, vorbis`
Flash	`application/x-shockwave-flash`	

Description

- The most common audio codecs are Ogg Vorbis, MP3, and AAC. Chrome has the best audio codec support of the five browsers above.

- The most common video codecs are Ogg Theora, H.264, and WebM. Again, Chrome has the best support of the five browsers above.

- Mobile devices such as Apple's iPhone and Google's Android support H.264 video and AAC audio within the MPEG media type.

- One of the problems when adding audio or video to a web site is that there isn't a single combination of codecs that will work on all browsers. To support all browsers, then, you need to encode your media into more than one media type.

- A *MIME type* describes the contents of a file and can assist browsers in determining what player to use to open the file. The table above summarizes the MIME types and codecs that you will need to specify for audio and video that will work on all browsers.

Figure 11-4   Audio and video support in current browsers

How to encode media

Figure 11-5 shows how easy it is to use software products that can convert a media file from one type to another, like MPEG/AAC to Ogg Theora/Vorbis. A product like this can also convert a raw, uncompressed video or audio file that you've recently captured on a digital video camera into a compressed format that targets one of the codecs.

Although many free and commercial software packages are available for encoding media types, one free product that I like is Miro Converter (www.mirovideoconverter.com). It lets you convert a file from just about any media type into the types needed for web applications. Miro Converter also supports audio-only formats including MP3 and Ogg as well as formats for mobile devices such as iPhone, Android, and PSP.

To use Miro Converter, you just drag the media type that you'd like to convert into the file pane, select the media type/codec that you'd like to target from the drop-down menu, and click Convert. Depending on the size of your file, the conversion process will take anywhere from seconds to minutes to hours. When the conversion process is finished, your new media file will be in the same folder as the file that you converted from.

Other converters that warrant mention are: Apple's iTunes (for audio) and QuickTime Pro (for just about anything); Microsoft's Windows Media Encoder; Adobe's Media Encoder (great for Flash); Firefogg, which is a handy add-in to Firefox and specifically supports the Ogg file format; FFmpeg, which is great for batch encoding; and Handbrake, which is ideally suited for mobile device output and comes as a graphical user interface or command line install.

Miro Converter as it's about to convert a .wmv file to MP4 Video

Description

- To encode audio and video files in the formats that you need, you can use one of the many encoders that are currently available, including Miro Converter, iTunes, QuickTime, Windows Media Encoder, Adobe Media Encoder, Firefogg, FFmpeg, and Handbrake.

- One encoder that I recommend is Miro Converter. It is a free program that lets you convert audio and video from one format to another as well as encode video for the popular media types including Ogg, WebM, and MPEG-4.

- Miro Converter also supports mobile devices including iPhone, Android, and PSP.

Figure 11-5   How to encode media

How to add audio and video to a web page

With that as background, you're ready to learn how to add audio and video to your web pages. As you'll see, there are several ways to do that. To start, you'll learn how to use the older HTML elements that are still required by some of the older browsers. Then, you'll learn how to use the new HTML5 elements for audio and video. Last, you'll learn how to use a combination of these elements with a twist of Flash to provide the best solution for cross-browser compatibility.

How to use the object and param elements

Figure 11-6 shows how you can use the object element to embed a media type in a web page. For years, this element was the standard element for doing that. When you use the object element, you can include one or more param elements to provide values to the media player that's being used. This has always been one of the advantages of using an object element since this lets you vary the way the media player works.

When you code the object element, you usually code the four attributes listed in this figure. The type attribute specifies the MIME type. The data attribute specifies the URL of the file you want to play. And the width and height attributes specify the width and height of either the media type or the player.

For a Flash file, these attributes apply to the file. For other types of media, they apply to the media player. Also, if a file doesn't have a visual element, you can omit the width and height attributes or set their values to 0. You can use this technique, for example, to play an audio file in the background.

This figure also presents the two attributes of the param element that you're most likely to use. For the name attribute, you specify the name of a parameter for a specific media player. Then, you specify the parameter's value on the value attribute. In the example in this figure, you can see how this works for the autoplay parameter. Here, the autoplay parameter tells the player to start playing the file as soon as the page is loaded.

The parameters that you can use depend on the media player that you're targeting. For a complete list of parameters, you need to review the Internet documentation for the targeted media player.

Of note in this example is that the object element doesn't specify what media player to use. Instead, the player depends on what media player the user has installed and, worse, whether or not that player is capable of playing the media type that's offered by the object element. For this reason, the use of the object element is on the decline and for the most part has been relegated to serving as a "fallback" mechanism that serves up a "safe" media type such as Flash for browsers that don't support the HTML5 video and audio elements.

The object and param elements

Element	Description
object	Embeds a media file into a web page.
param	Provides parameters to the media player that's used to open a file.

Attributes of the object element

Attribute	Description
type	The MIME type of the file.
data	The URL of the file.
width	The width of the file or the media player that's used.
height	The height of the file or the media player that's used.

Attributes of the param element

Attribute	Description
name	The name of the parameter. Each media player has its own parameters.
value	The value of the parameter.

An object element for playing a Flash file

```
<object type="application/x-shockwave-flash"
        data="media/sjv_anniversary.swf" width="400" height="150">
    <param name="autoplay" value="true">
</object>
```

Description

- When you use the object element, you can control the appearance and operation of the media player by coding parameter elements. These elements are standard HTML.

- If you don't specify the MIME type for a file, the file will be opened in the browser's default media player for the media type.

- Because different players accept different parameters, you typically specify the parameters for all the players you want to provide for. Then, if a player doesn't support a parameter, it will ignore it.

- If you don't want to display the interface for a media player, you can omit the width and height attributes or set them to 0.

- Some browsers require a param element that specifies the URL of the file even if the file is identified in the object element.

- The object element is still used today, but its use is slowly declining thanks in large part to the video and audio elements in HTML5 and the growing support for these elements in today's modern browsers.

Figure 11-6   How to use the object and param elements

How to use the embed element

Another element that is commonly used in existing sites for embedding media files is the embed element. Although this element wasn't supported by previous HTML standards, it was supported by all of the major browsers, and it is now supported by the HTML5 standard. As a result, you should feel free to use it, especially if you're having trouble getting the object and param elements to work right.

Figure 11-7 presents some of the most useful attributes of the embed element. As you can see, all of these are the same or similar to the attributes you code on the object element.

In addition to the basic attributes, you can code the parameters for media players as attributes, rather than as separate param elements. For instance, the first example in this figure uses the autoplay attribute to pass a parameter to the default player for an MP3 file that tells the player to start playing the file as soon as the page is loaded.

Here again, these attributes vary depending on the target media player and you should consult the documentation for the players to find out which media player supports which attributes. In this figure, you can see the URLs for the documentation of some of the common media players.

Like the object element, you'll notice that the embed element doesn't explicitly specify what player to use. For this reason, the use of the embed element is also on the decline and for the most part has been relegated to the role of serving as a "fallback" mechanism for browsers that don't support the HTML5 video or audio elements.

Attributes of the embed element

Attribute	Description
type	The MIME type of the file to be played.
src	The URL of the file to be played.
width	The width of the file or the media player that's used.
height	The height of the file or the media player that's used.

An embed element for playing an MP3 file

```
<embed type="audio/mpeg"
       src="media/sjv_welcome.mp3"
       width="300" height="25"
       autoplay="true">
```

An embed element that plays a YouTube video

```
<embed type="application/x-shockwave-flash"
       src="http://www.youtube.com/v/LgDqE2Tlz_U"
       width="560" height="349">
```

Web sites for information about other attributes

QuickTime attributes
```
http://support.apple.com/kb/TA26485
```

Flash attributes
```
http://kb2.adobe.com/cps/127/tn_12701.html
```

Windows Media Player attributes
```
http://www.microsoft.com/windows/windowsmedia/howto/articles/adsolutions2.aspx
```

Description

- When you use the embed element, you code all parameters as attributes, not as param elements.

- Although the embed element wasn't part of the HTML4 specification, this element was supported by all major browsers, and now it is included in the HTML5 specification.

- Often, an embed element is easier to code and works better than a comparable object element. That's why the embed element is currently in use on many web sites.

- If you don't specify the MIME type for a file, the file will be opened in the browser's default media player for the media format.

- Using the embed element is a good way to display YouTube videos within your web pages.

- The HTML specification lists four standard attributes, but other attributes are supported for specific media players.

Figure 11-7   How to use the embed element

How to use the HTML5 video and audio elements

Figure 11-8 shows how to use the new HTML5 video and audio elements to add video and audio to your web pages. In their simplest form, you just add the video and audio elements to a page and code the src attributes that point to the media files to be played. This is illustrated by the first example in this figure.

If you want to set some of the options that these elements support, you can code the other attributes that are summarized in this figure. This is illustrated by the second and third examples. Here, the width and height attributes are used to set the dimensions of the media player in the browser. The controls attribute instructs the browser to display a toolbar that displays play, pause, volume, and progress controls. And the autoplay attribute tells the browser to begin playing the media as soon as the page is loaded.

Within the video and audio elements in these examples, you can see the source elements that refer to the different media types that are needed for browser compatibility. For the video files, the codecs attribute is also coded. The end result is that the source elements provide for all of the media types in figure 11-4. As a result, these examples will run on any modern browser.

Please note, however, that the MPEG video is listed as the first source element for the video element. That's important because a bug in iPads that are running iOS 3.x prevents the browser from ignoring media types that it doesn't understand so the browser won't move down to the first one that it does understand. By putting its source element first, you avoid that problem because other browsers will skip to the first source element that they understand.

Note too the way the type attribute is coded in the video source elements. Here, the attribute value is enclosed within single quotation marks. Then, within the type attribute, the value of the codecs attribute is enclosed within double quotation marks.

These examples show how the HTML5 audio and video elements can be used to simplify the way that audio and video are added to a web page. To start, this coding will work for all modern browsers. But even better, these elements provide video and audio that is native to all current editions of the major browsers.

That means that you no longer have to worry about whether or not your users have the right player or plug-in installed on their browsers. That also means you don't have to worry about whether or not their browsers will crash because of the instabilities of the Flash player. The only problem is that the older browsers don't support these elements, but the next topic will show you how to fix that.

Last, if you're using Aptana to run pages that use video elements, they may not work. If that happens, you need to run the pages from the browser instead. To do that, you can use the browser's File→Open or Open File command, or you can type the complete path and filename into the address bar and press Enter. This applies to any page that uses the video element including those in the next two figures.

Common attributes for the audio and video elements

Attribute	Description
src	The URL of the file to be played.
poster	Supported only by the video element, this attribute provides the path to a static image to be displayed in place of the video file before it is played.
preload	One of three possible values that tell the browser whether to preload any data: none (the default), metadata (only preload metadata like dimensions and track list), or auto (preload the entire media file).
autoplay	Starts playing the media as soon as the web page is loaded in the browser.
loop	Causes the media to repeat playing when it reaches the end.
muted	Supported only by the video element, this attribute causes the video to begin playing (if autoplay is also coded) with the volume muted.
controls	Displays the default control toolbar underneath the audio or video being played.
width	Specifies the width of the media file to be played within the browser.
height	Specifies the height of the media file to be played within the browser.

The attributes for the source element

Attribute	Description
src	The URL of the file to be played.
type	The MIME type of the file to be played, including the codec for video files, but the codec isn't needed for MPEG (MP4).

The easiest way to add a video or audio element to your web page

```
<video src="media/sjv_speakers_sampson.mp4"></video>
<audio src="media/sjv_welcome.mp3"></audio>
```

A video element for playing MPEG-4, Ogg (Theora), and WebM media types

```
<video id="videoplayer" width="480" height="270" controls autoplay>
    <source src="media/sjv_speakers_sampson.mp4">
    <source src="media/sjv_speakers_sampson.webm"
        type='video/webm; codecs="vp8, vorbis"'>
    <source src="media/sjv_speakers_sampson.ogv"
        type='video/ogg; codecs="theora, vorbis"'>
</video>
```

An audio element for playing MP3 and Ogg (Vorbis) media types

```
<audio id="audioplayer" controls autoplay>
    <source src="media/sjv_welcome.ogg" type="audio/ogg">
    <source src="media/sjv_welcome.mp3" type="audio/mp3">
</audio>
```

Description

- The video and audio elements play the various media types natively within a browser.
- To make your media work on all browsers, you need to add one source element for each of the required media types in figure 11-4, plus the codec for all video files except MP4.

Aptana warning

- Don't use Aptana to run pages that use the video element. They won't work correctly.

Figure 11-8   How to use the HTML5 video and audio elements

How to fall back to Flash
for backward compatibility

Figure 11-9 shows how to use the HTML5 audio and video elements and still provide backward compatibility with older browsers. The key point here is that you also provide the audio or video as a Flash media type and fall back to that file in browsers that don't support the HTML5 elements. Since a majority of the browsers today support the audio and video elements and since 97% of Internet users have the Flash plug-in installed on their browsers, this means that just about everyone will be able to play your media.

As you can see in the first example in figure 11-9, the code for doing this is relatively straightforward. To start, a video element that contains three source elements provides the video for all modern browsers. This is the same as in the previous figure.

Then, to provide for backward compatibility, the code nests an object element that refers to a Flash video within the video element. This will work in older IE browsers because they will ignore elements that they don't understand (the video element) and pick up on the nested object element.

After that, a second object element is nested within the first object element. This is like the first object element, but it uses the data attribute instead of the param element to refer to the media type. This will work in older browsers other than IE.

As the second example shows, you use this same approach for audio-only media types. For audio, though, only two source elements are required within the audio element. But a Flash file is still used as the fallback mechanism for older browsers.

HTML for playing a video that falls back to Flash

```
<video id="videoplayer" width="480" height="270" controls autoplay>
    <source src="media/sjv_speakers_sampson.mp4">
    <source src="media/sjv_speakers_sampson.webm" type='video/webm;
            codecs="vp8, vorbis"'>
    <source src="media/sjv_speakers_sampson.ogv" type='video/ogg;
            codecs="theora, vorbis"'>

    <object type="application/x-shockwave-flash" width="480" height="270">
        <param name="movie" value="media/sjv_speakers_sampson.swf">
        <param name="wmode" value="transparent">
        <param name="quality" value="high">
        <!--[if !IE]>-->
            <object type="application/x-shockwave-flash"
                    data="media/sjv_speakers_sampson.swf"
                    width="480" height="270">
                <param name="wmode" value="transparent">
                <param name="quality" value="high">
            </object>
        <!--<![endif]-->
    </object>
</video>
```

HTML for playing an audio that falls back to Flash

```
<audio id="audioplayer" controls>
    <source src="media/sjv_welcome.ogg" type="audio/ogg">
    <source src="media/sjv_welcome.mp3" type="audio/mp3">

    <object type="application/x-shockwave-flash" width="50" height="50">
        <param name="movie" value="media/sjv_welcome.swf">
        <param name="wmode" value="transparent">
        <param name="quality" value="high">
        <!--[if !IE]>-->
            <object type="application/x-shockwave-flash"
                    data="media/sjv_welcome.swf" width="50" height="50">
                <param name="wmode" value="transparent">
                <param name="quality" value="high">
            </object>
        <!--<![endif]-->
    </object>
</audio>
```

Description

- For browsers that don't support the video and audio elements, you can nest an object element within the video or audio element to play a Flash file.
- This also works for browsers that don't support any of the media types listed within the source elements of the video or audio element.
- If you prefer, you can use an embed element instead of an object element to fall back to Flash.

Aptana warning

- If you use Aptana to run a page that uses the video element, it won't work correctly. Instead, use the browser's File→Open command or comparable method to run the page.

Figure 11-9   How to fall back to Flash for backward compatibility

A web page that offers both audio and video

Now that you've seen how the object, param, video, and audio elements work, it's time to put it all together into a simple web page that uses these elements.

The page layout

The web page in figure 11-10 starts with a short audio message that welcomes the visitor to the site. Then, it offers a video of one of the speakers who's scheduled to speak. In the embedded video, you can see an image of the speaker that will disappear when the video is played.

A web page that offers both audio and video

Description

- This web page offers both audio and video to the user. The audio is a brief introduction to the speakers. The video is a video of the selected speaker.

- The poster attribute of the video element is used to display a static image in place of the media type when the page is displayed. The poster file will be replaced with the actual video when the user clicks on the play button.

- The controls toolbar automatically appears when the page loads and while your cursor is over the video. As you move your cursor off the video, the control toolbar automatically drops off and becomes hidden. Moving your cursor back onto the video causes the control toolbar to reappear.

Aptana warning

- If you use Aptana to run a page that uses the video element, it won't work correctly. Instead, use the browser's File→Open command or comparable method to run the page.

Figure 11-10   A web page that offers both audio and video

The HTML

Figure 11-11 presents the HTML file for the web page. Here, both the audio and video fall back to Flash in browsers that don't support the audio and video elements. You shouldn't have any trouble following this code because it is so similar to what you saw in figure 11-9.

In the code for the audio element, you might notice the absence of the autoplay attribute. This prevents the browser from automatically playing the sound when the page loads.

In the code for the video element, you might notice the addition of the poster attribute. This displays a static image in place of the video that would otherwise begin playing automatically.

The HTML for a page that uses both audio and video elements

```
<body>
<h1>Welcome to the San Joaquin Valley Town Hall</h1>
<audio id="audioplayer" controls>
    <source src="media/sjv_welcome.ogg" type="audio/ogg">
    <source src="media/sjv_welcome.mp3" type="audio/mp3">

    <object type="application/x-shockwave-flash" width="50" height="50">
        <param name="movie" value="media/sjv_welcome.swf">
        <param name="wmode" value="transparent">
        <param name="quality" value="high">
        <!--[if !IE]>-->
            <object type="application/x-shockwave-flash"
                    data="media/sjv_welcome.swf" width="50" height="50">
                <param name="wmode" value="transparent">
                <param name="quality" value="high">
            </object>
        <!--<![endif]-->
    </object>
</audio>

<h2>San Joaquin Valley Town Hall welcomes Dr. Scott Sampson</h2>
<p>On February 15, 2012, Dr. Scott Sampson will present a lecture titled
&lsquo;Fossil Threads in the Web of Life&rsquo;<br>In the meantime, you can
see a video of Dr. Sampson below.</p>

<video id="videoplayer" controls width="480" height="270"
    poster="images/poster.png">
    <source src="media/sjv_speakers_sampson.mp4">
    <source src="media/sjv_speakers_sampson.webm" type='video/webm;
            codecs="vp8, vorbis"'>
    <source src="media/sjv_speakers_sampson.ogv" type='video/ogg;
            codecs="theora, vorbis"'>

    <object type="application/x-shockwave-flash" width="480" height="270">
        <param name="movie" value="media/sjv_speakers_sampson.swf">
        <param name="wmode" value="transparent">
        <param name="quality" value="high">
        <!--[if !IE]>-->
            <object type="application/x-shockwave-flash"
                    data="media/sjv_speakers_sampson.swf"
                    width="480" height="270">
                <param name="wmode" value="transparent">
                <param name="quality" value="high">
            </object>
        <!--<![endif]-->
    </object>
</video>
</body>
```

Figure 11-11   The HTML for the web page

Perspective

Now that you know how to embed media files within your web pages, here's a caution about overusing them. First, remember that media files are often large so web pages that embed media files are likely to load slowly, particularly on systems that have slow Internet connections. Second, remember that users who can't see or hear won't benefit from video or audio. As a result, if the audio and video are essential to the site, you should also provide text versions of the audio and video. So, before you decided to use media files, please be sure that they support the goals of your web site and enhance the user experience.

Terms

media type
media player
plug-in
codec
MIME type

Summary

- A browser uses a *media player* to play an audio or video *media type* when media are embedded in a web page.

- Some browsers require *plug-ins* for the media players that play specific media types.

- Audio and video files come in a variety of media types. MPEG, Ogg, and WebM are common types for video, and AAC and MP3 are common types for audio.

- *Codecs* are software components that are used by browsers to decipher the algorithms in a media type.

- A *MIME type* describes the contents of a file and can help a browser determine what media player to use for the file.

- To embed media types in the web page for older browsers, you can either use the object and param elements or the embed element.

- The HTML5 video and audio elements are supported by modern browsers and will play media without the need for special plug-ins.

- You can nest object or embed elements within video and audio elements to fall back to the Flash media type. This allows you to target older browsers that don't support the HTML5 video and audio elements.

Exercise 11-1   Add video to a speaker's page

In this exercise, you'll add video to a copy of the speaker's page for Scott Sampson. This will show you how easy it is to add video to a page. When you're through, the page should look like the one that follows. But if you haven't done exercise 7-2, your page won't have a navigation bar.

Open the page, copy it, and copy in the HTML for running a video

1. Use your text editor to open this page:

   ```
   c:\html5_css3\exercises\town_hall_2\speakers\sampson.html
   ```

2. Make a copy of this page in the same folder, and name it sampson_video.html. If you're using Aptana, you can use the File→Save As command to do that.

3. Open the book application for this chapter, and copy the code for running the video to the clipboard. Then, paste in into the sampson_video.html file so it replaces either the figure element (if your file has one) or the img element.

4. Test the page to see what the result is. But don't run it from Aptana because the video won't work right. Instead, run the page using one of the other methods.

Modify the HTML to get this working right

5. Modify the references to the media files so they point to the right files. To do that, you need to use a document-relative path that goes up one level, and you need to use the right filenames. For instance, the reference in the first source element should be:

    ```
    src="../media/sampson.mp4"
    ```

    To find out what the right filenames are, you can look in the media folder.

6. You also need to modify the reference to the poster file that's in the images folder with a similar document-relative path.

7. Test this page again and it should work. This shows how easy it is to add a video to a page because you'll use the same code each time. Only the references will change.

12

How to format web pages for printing

To this point, you've learned how to create and format web pages that will be displayed on a computer screen. From a browser, the users can print those web pages, but the browser determines how they're printed. Now, in this chapter, you'll learn how to control the printing of a web page.

The skills for formatting printed web pages

To format the printing of a web page, you need to know how to define the styles for printing and you need to know how to use the special properties for printing. So those skills are presented first in this chapter.

How to define the style sheets and rule sets for printed pages

To define the rule sets for the printing of a web page, you can use the link element to include another style sheet for the page that's just for printing. This is illustrated by the first example in figure 12-1. To do that, you code the media attribute with "print" as the value. Then, assuming that the link element for the *print style sheet* is coded last, the rule sets in the print style sheet override the styles for the same elements in the *screen style sheet*.

If you only need a few extra styles for printing, you can define them in the screen style sheet by using @media print to identify the rule sets for printing. This is illustrated by the second example in this figure. If you need more than a few extra styles for printing, though, this can get complicated.

A third way to provide styles for printing is to use the styles element in the head section of the HTML. This is illustrated by the third example in this figure. But if you want to use these styles for other web pages, you have to copy these styles to the HTML of the other pages.

Link elements that include style sheets for screen and print media

```
<link rel="stylesheet" href="styles/main.css">
<link rel="stylesheet" href="styles/print.css" media="print">
```

A rule set for printing that's embedded within a screen style sheet

```
@media print {
    body {
        font-family: "Times New Roman", Times, serif;
        background-color: white;
    }
}
```

A style element for printing in the head section of the HTML

```
<style media="print">
    font-family: "Times New Roman", Times, serif;
    background-color: white;
</style>
```

Description

- The default media type for a link element is "screen" so you don't have to specify that for a web page that's going to be displayed by a browser.

- The media type for a link element that specifies a style sheet for printing a web page is "print".

- Within a style sheet, you can specify a rule set or a group of rule sets for the printed page by coding @media print.

- You can also embed a style element within the head section of the HTML that provides rule sets for printing.

- When you provide a link element for both screen and print, you usually code the link element for the print style sheet last. That way, the print style sheet just needs to override the screen rules that need to be changed.

Figure 12-1   How to define the style sheets and rule sets for printed pages

Recommendations for print formatting

Figure 12-2 starts by presenting some basic recommendations for formatting printed pages. As you can see, the first three recommendations have to do with changing the fonts so they're more readable. In particular, a serif font should be used for text because that makes the printed text easier to read (although sans-serif text is more readable on the screen).

The fourth recommendation is to remove site navigation. That makes sense because navigation can't be used when the page is printed. You may, however, want to print links that link to other topics to show the reader what is available.

The last recommendation is to remove any images that aren't needed to understand the content of the page. That will make the page print more quickly.

CSS properties for printed pages

Figure 12-2 also shows the CSS properties that you can use to control printing. The one you'll probably use the most is display. Although you can use it to display an inline element as a block element and vice versa, you're most likely to use it to exclude an element such as an image from a page when it's printed. To do that, you set this property to "none".

You can also use the visibility property to hide an element when a page is printed. When you use this property, though, the space occupied by the element is still included on the page. If that's not what you want, you should use the display property.

The remaining properties let you control page breaks. A *page break* is the point at which the printing skips from the bottom of one page to the top of the next page.

The page-break-before and page-break-after properties let you specify whether a page break always occurs before or after an element, may occur before or after an element, or shouldn't occur before or after an element. The page-break-inside property is similar, but it specifies whether a page break can occur within an element. For headings, you will usually want to set the page-break-after property to "avoid" so a heading isn't printed on one page and the text that follows on another page.

When a page break occurs within an element, the orphans and widows properties specify the minimum number of lines that can be printed at the bottom of the current page and the top of the next page. In printing terminology, *orphan* refers to the first line of a paragraph by itself at the bottom of a page, and *widow* refers to the last line of a paragraph by itself at the top of a page. To avoid orphans and widows, which you usually want to do, you can set these properties to 2 or more.

Although some browsers don't support the orphan, widow, and some of the page break properties, that's usually okay. If these properties are ignored, the page breaks will occur where you don't want them, but the users will still be able to read them.

Recommendations for formatting printed pages

- Change the text color to black and the background color to white.
- Change text other than headings to a serif font to make the text easier to read when printed.
- Use a base font size that's easy to read when printed.
- Remove site navigation since it can't be used from a printed page.
- Remove as many images as possible, particularly Flash and animated images.

CSS properties for printing

Property	Description
display	A keyword that determines how an element is displayed. Common keywords are block, inline, and none.
visibility	A keyword that determines if an element is visible. Common keywords are visible and hidden.
page-break-before	A keyword that determines when a page break is allowed before an element's box. Common keywords are always, auto, and avoid.
page-break-after	A keyword that determines when a page break is allowed after an element's box. Common keywords are always, auto, and avoid.
page-break-inside	A keyword that determines when a page break is allowed within an element's box. Possible keywords are auto and avoid.
orphans	An integer that determines the minimum number of lines within an element that can be printed at the bottom of a page when a page break occurs within the element.
widows	An integer that determines the minimum number of lines within an element that can be printed on the next page when a page break occurs within the element.

CSS that uses two of the properties for printing

```
img { display: none; }
h1, h2, h3 { page-break-after: avoid; }
```

Description

- If you don't want an element to be included when a page is printed, you can set its display property to none. Then, no space is allocated for the element's box.
- If you don't want an element to be included when a page is printed but you want to allocate space for the element's box, you can set the visibility property to hidden.
- The auto keyword for the page-break properties indicates that a break may occur, but doesn't have to occur, like it does when you use the always keyword.
- The avoid keyword for the page-break properties tells the browser to avoid a page break if it can.
- Although the widows, orphans, and some of the page break properties aren't supported by all browsers, it's usually okay if they're ignored.

Figure 12-2   Formatting recommendations and CSS properties for printed pages

A two-column web page
with special formatting for printing

To illustrate the use of a style sheet for a printed page, the next three figures present a two-column web page, the HTML that includes the screen and print style sheets, the printed version of the page, and the CSS for the print style sheet.

The web page

Figure 12-3 presents the two-column web page that you studied in chapter 6. However, this web page has been enhanced by a navigation bar and by fig and figcaption elements.

To understand the style sheet for printing that you're going to see in a moment, you shouldn't need to review the HTML for this page. Just keep in mind that the major structural elements in sequence are header, nav, aside, article, and footer.

The links to the style sheets

Figure 12-3 also presents the links for the screen and print style sheets. Note here that the print style sheet comes after the screen style sheet so the print rules override the screen rules for the same elements. If, for example, the print rules for the headings in the header set the font color to black, the printed headings will be in black. However, the other screen rules for headings, like the text shadow and italics will be retained.

A web page with two columns

The link elements in the head section

```
<link rel="stylesheet" href="styles/speaker.css">
<link rel="stylesheet" href="styles/speaker_print.css" media="print">
```

Description

- This is the same page that is presented in chapter 6, plus the navigation bar that was added in chapter 7 and the fig and figcaption elements that were added in chapter 8.

- The main structural elements in sequence are header, nav, aside, article, and footer.

- In the CSS for the article, the CSS3 column-count property is used so the first column contains two text columns.

- Since IE9 doesn't support the column-count property, you won't see two columns of text in that browser.

Figure 12-3   The screen layout for a two-column web page

The printed page

Figure 12-4 shows the print layout for the web page. If you compare this layout with the screen layout, you'll notice a number of differences. For instance, the navigation bar and aside are removed. All of these differences are summarized in this figure.

This figure also shows how to print a page. For instance, this printed page is displayed in Print Preview mode. Then, to print the page, you can just click on the Print button. You can also print a page by using the Print command in the File menu of the browser or by clicking on the Print button in the browser's tool bar.

As a developer, you can make it easy for the user to print a page by including a Print button on the web page that uses JavaScript to print the page when the button is clicked. This is illustrated in chapter 13. No matter how the page is printed, though, the style sheet for print media is used if one is available.

Incidentally, Print Preview mode is helpful when you're designing a print style sheet because it lets you see the layout without having to print the page. Then, when you have the layout the way you want it, you can print it as a final check that everything is working right.

The layout for the web page in Print Preview mode

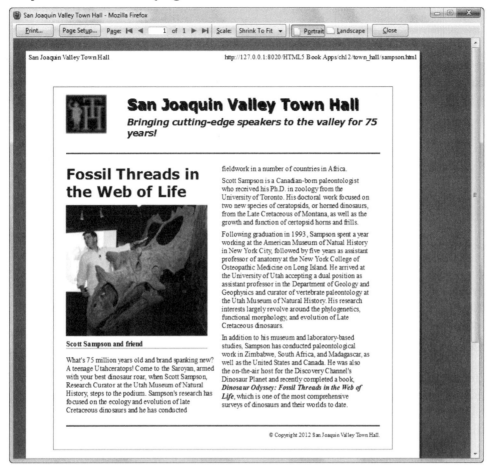

Changes to the printed page

- The navigation bar and aside aren't printed.
- The headings, text, and borders are set to black.
- The width of the article is wider and the right border is removed.
- The font for the text has been changed to a serif font so it's easier to read.

How to preview and print a web page

- To display a page in Print Preview mode, choose the File→Print Preview command from the browser's menu.
- To print a page, you can click the Print button in the browser's toolbar, choose the File→Print command from the menu, or click the Print button in Print Preview mode.
- Another option is to include a Print button on a page and use JavaScript to print the page when the button is clicked.

Figure 12-4   The print layout for the web page

The CSS for the print style sheet

Figure 12-5 presents the CSS for the printed web page. Remember that the print style sheet only needs to include rule sets for screen rules that must be overridden. For instance, since the screen rule for the body sets the width to 962 pixels, the print rule for the body needs to override that by setting the width to auto. That way, the body will fill the printed page. Similarly, the width for the article is set to auto and its border is set to none so the right border in the article in the web page won't be printed.

Because this page is simple, you should be able to understand the rules sets in the print style sheet without much trouble. But take a moment to consider what you would need to do if you wanted to print the aside before the article. Since the aside comes before the article in the HTML, you would just need to override the float property of the aside by setting it to none.

Now consider what you would have to do to print the aside after the article. First, you would have to code the article before the aside in the HTML and float the article to the left in the CSS for the web page. Then, you would need to remove the float in the print style sheet. This illustrates that when you code the HTML for a web page that you know will be printed, you need to keep in mind the sequence in which the content will be printed as well as how the content will be displayed.

Incidentally, when you use the margin or padding property to set margins or padding for boxes that will be printed, you may want to use inches (in) as the unit of measure. For instance, you could set the margin of the body to .25in. Note, however, that this value doesn't replace the default margin provided by a browser for printed output. Instead, this value is added to the default margin.

Unfortunately, different browsers can have different default margins. Because of that, it's often best to specify no margin at all, which is the way this is handled in the CSS in this figure.

The CSS for the printed web page

```
body {
    font-family: "Times New Roman", Times, serif;
    width: auto;
}
h1, h2 {
    font-family: Verdana, Arial, Helvetica, sans-serif;
}
/* the styles for the navigation bar */
#nav_bar {
    display: none;
}
/* the styles for the sidebar */
aside {
    display: none;
}
/* the styles for the article */
article {
    border: none;
    width: auto;
}
/* the styles for the header */
header {
    border-bottom: 2px solid black;
}
header h1, header h2 {
    color: black;
}
/* the styles for the footer */
footer {
    border-top: 2px solid black;
}
```

Description

- All of the rules in the print style sheet override the settings in the style sheet for the screen.

- The width of the body and article are set to auto so they will be as wide as the printed page permits.

- The font-family for the body is set to a serif font, and the font-family for the headings is set to a sans-serif font.

- The display properties for the navigation bar and aside are set to none so they aren't included in the printed page.

- The border for the article is set to none, and the borders for the header and footer are set to black.

- The color of the h1 and h2 elements in the header is set to black.

- To set margins and padding, you can use *in* (inches) as the unit of measure, which makes sense when you're printing on pages that are 8½ by 11 inches.

Figure 12-5   The CSS for the print style sheet

Perspective

You probably know from experience how frustrating it can be to print a web page and have part of the content cut off or have it print so small that you can barely read it. So if the information on a page is important enough to print, be sure to provide a style sheet that will make it easy to read when printed.

Terms

print style sheet
screen style sheet
page break
widow
orphan

Summary

- If you want to format the way a web page is printed, you can use a link element to include a separate style sheet for printing. This link element should come after any *screen style sheets* so the styles in the *print style sheet* will override the screen styles.

- CSS provides several properties for printing, including the display property for omitting an element from a web page, several page-break properties for controlling where *page breaks* occur, and orphans and widows properties for avoiding *orphans* and *widows*.

- When you code the CSS for a page that's going to be printed, you should remove site navigation and unnecessary images, use dark print on a white background, and use a serif font for the text on a page in a size that's easy to read.

Exercise 12-1   Format the printing for a page

In this exercise, you'll style the printing for the speaker's page for Scott Sampson so it prints like this:

San Joaquin Valley Town Hall   file:///M:/Current projects/HTML and CSS/exercise_solutions/town_h...

San Joaquin Valley Town Hall
Celebrating our 75th Year

October 19, 2011
Jeffrey Toobin

November 16, 2011
Andrew Ross Sorkin

January 18, 2012
Amy Chua

February 15, 2012
Scott Sampson

Fossil Threads in the Web of Life
February 15, 2012
Scott Sampson

Scott Sampson and Friend

What's 75 million years old and brand spanking new? A teenage Utahceratops! Come to the Saroyan, armed with your best dinosaur roar, when Scott Sampson, Research Curator at the Utah Museum of Natural History, steps to the podium. Sampson's research has focused on the ecology and evolution of late Cretaceous dinosaurs and he has conducted fieldwork in a number of countries in Africa.

Scott Sampson is a Canadian-born paleontologist who received his Ph.D. in zoology from the University of Toronto. His doctoral work focused on two new species of ceratopsids, or horned dinosaurs, from the Late Cretaceous of Montana, as well as the growth and function of certopsid horns and frills.

Following graduation in 1993, Sampson spent a year working at the American Museum of Natural History in New York City, followed by five years as assistant professor of anatomy at the New York College of Osteopathic Medicine on Long Island. He arrived at the University of Utah accepting a dual position as assistant professor in the Department of Geology and Geophysics and curator of vertebrate paleontology at the Utah Museum of Natural History. His research interests largely revolve around the phylogenetics, functional morphology, and evolution of Late Cretaceous dinosaurs.

In addition to his museum and laboratory-based studies, Sampson has conducted paleontological work in Zimbabwe, South Africa, and Madagascar, as well as the United States and Canada. He was also the on-the-air host for the Discovery Channel's Dinosaur Planet and recently completed a book, *Dinosaur Odyssey: Fossil Threads in the Web of Life*, which is one of the most comprehensive surveys of dinosaurs and their worlds to date.

© 2012, San Joaquin Valley Town Hall, Fresno, CA 93755

Open the HTML and CSS files for this page

1. Use your text editor to open these pages:

   ```
   c:\html5_css3\exercises\town_hall_2\speakers\sampson.html
   c:\html5_css3\exercises\town_hall_2\styles\speaker.css
   ```

2. Run this page in Firefox, and use the File→Print Preview command to see what it will look like when printed.

Add the styles for printing the page to the style sheet

3. In the style sheet for this page, add a @media print selector to the end of the file, as shown in figure 12-1. Then, add rules sets that do the following:

    Change the font family for the body to Times New Roman, Times, or the default serif font.

    Change the width of the body to "auto", the background color to white, and the border to none.

    Turn off the display for the navigation bar (if your page has one), the first heading in the aside, and the return link in the aside. To do that for the link, you can use an id selector.

    Set the padding for the section and the aside to zero.

    Set the width of the section to 5 inches and the width of the aside to 2 inches.

    Now, test these changes to see how things are going.

4. Add the other rule sets that are needed to get the print preview to look like the one above, such as:

    Change the font family for the h1 and h2 elements to Arial, Helvetica, and the default sans-serif font.

    If it isn't already there, add a 3px bottom border to the header with #800000 as its color.

    Reduce the font-size for the h2 elements in the aside to 100%.

    Remove the underlines from the <a> elements in the aside and set their color to black.

    Now, test these changes. The page should be looking pretty good.

5. Make whatever final adjustments are needed, and test one last time.

Section 3

JavaScript and jQuery skills

Sections 1 and 2 of this book present the HTML and CSS skills that you use as you build web sites. But a modern web site requires more than that. That's why this section presents some of the JavaScript and jQuery skills that you'll need as you develop a web site. Although these chapters won't teach you how to write your own JavaScript code, they will teach you how to use code that was written by others to get the results that you want.

In chapter 13, for example, you'll learn how to enhance your web pages by using JavaScript to add features like image rollovers, image swaps, slide shows, tabs, and data validation. In chapter 14, you'll learn how to use jQuery, which consists of JavaScript libraries, to add features like accordions, carousels, slide shows, and sortable lists. In chapter 15, you'll learn how to use jQuery Mobile to develop web sites for mobile devices. And in chapter 16, you'll learn how to use the HTML5 features that require the use of JavaScript or jQuery.

13

How to use JavaScript to enhance your web pages

In this chapter, you'll learn how you can use JavaScript to enhance your web pages. Although you won't learn how to code in JavaScript, you will learn the concepts and terms that you need for understanding how JavaScript works. Then, you'll learn how you can use tested JavaScript code to get the results you want.

Introduction to JavaScript and DOM scripting

In this introduction, you'll learn how JavaScript and DOM scripting work together. You'll also learn how to include JavaScript in your HTML documents.

How JavaScript works

Figure 13-1 presents a diagram that shows how JavaScript fits into the client/server architecture. Here, you can see that the *JavaScript* code is executed in the web browser by the browser's *JavaScript engine*. This is referred to as *client-side processing,* in contrast to the *server-side processing* that's done on the web server. This takes some of the processing burden off the server and makes the application run faster. Today, almost all web browsers have JavaScript enabled so JavaScript applications will run on them.

To illustrate the use of JavaScript code, the example in this figure gets the current date and the current year and inserts both into an HTML document. To do that, the JavaScript code is embedded within script elements in the body of the document. This code is executed when the page is loaded.

You can see the results in the web browser in this figure. In this case, the JavaScript code in the first script element writes the first line into the web page, which includes the current date. And the JavaScript code in the second script element writes the copyright line into the web page, which includes the current year.

How JavaScript fits into the client/server architecture

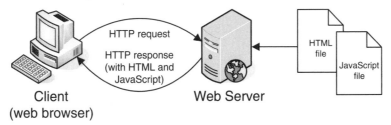

JavaScript in an HTML document that gets the current date and year

```
<p>
    <script>
        var today = new Date();
        document.write("Current date: ");
        document.write(today.toDateString());
    </script>
</p>
<p>
    <script>
        var today = new Date();
        document.write("&copy; ");
        document.write(today.getFullYear());
        document.write(", San Joaquin Valley Town Hall")
    </script>
</p>
```

The JavaScript in a web browser

Current date: Thu Sep 15 2011

© 2011, San Joaquin Valley Town Hall

Description

- *JavaScript* is a scripting language that is run by the *JavaScript engine* of a browser. As a result, the work is done on the client, not the server.

- JavaScript can modify the contents of a web page when the page is loaded or in response to a user action. In this example, JavaScript inserts the current date and the current year into the web page when the page is loaded.

Figure 13-1   How JavaScript works

How the DOM (Document Object Model) works

The *DOM (Document Object Model)* is an internal representation of the HTML elements in a web page. As an HTML page is loaded by the web browser, the DOM for that page is created in the browser's memory. In figure 13-2, you can see a simple HTML document and the structure of the DOM for that document.

Each element of the web page is represented by a *node* in the DOM. The nodes in the DOM have a hierarchical structure based on how the HTML elements are nested inside each other. The DOM starts with the html element and follows the nesting of the elements down to the text that is in each element.

Within the DOM, several types of nodes are used to represent the contents of the web page. HTML elements are stored in *element nodes*, and text is stored in *text nodes*. In this figure, element nodes are shown as ovals, and text nodes are shown as rectangles. Other common node types are *attribute nodes* and *comment nodes*.

The nodes that make up the DOM can be modified by JavaScript. This allows the web page to be modified after it is displayed by the web browser. Whenever a change is made to the DOM, the web browser displays the updated page in the browser window.

The code for a web page

```
<!DOCTYPE HTML>
<html lang="en">
<head>
    <meta charset="utf-8">
    <title>San Joaquin Valley Town Hall</title>
</head>
<body>
    <h1>San Joaquin Valley Town Hall</h1>
    <p>Welcome to Town Hall. We have some fascinating speakers this season.
    </p>
    <h2>Our 2011-2012 Lineup of Speakers</h2>
    <ul>
        <li>Jeffrey Toobin</li>
        <li>Andrew Ross Sorkin</li>
        <li>Amy Chua</li>
    </ul>
    <p>Contact us by phone at 559-555-1212 to get tickets.</p>
</body>
</html>
```

The DOM for the web page

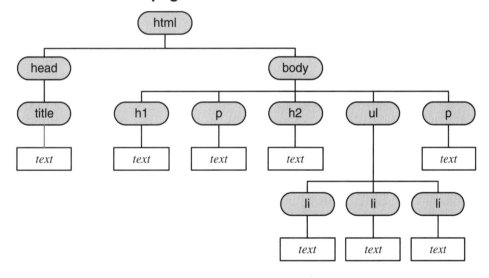

Description

- The *DOM* (*Document Object Model*) is a hierarchical collection of *nodes* in the web browser's memory that represents the current web page.
- The DOM for a web page is built as the page is loaded by the web browser.
- JavaScript can modify the web page in the browser by modifying the DOM. Whenever the DOM is changed, the web browser displays the results of the change.
- Many JavaScript applications manipulate the DOM based on user actions.

Figure 13-2   How the DOM (Document Object Model) works

How DOM scripting works

DOM scripting lets you use JavaScript to update a web page in response to user actions that are called *events*. An event is typically an action the user performs with the mouse or keyboard. The JavaScript code that is executed in response to an event is called an *event handler*.

The diagram in figure 13-3 describes the event cycle that drives DOM scripting. First, the page is loaded and the event handlers are attached to the events that will be processed. Next, when an event occurs, the appropriate event handler is executed. Then, if this event handler modifies the DOM, the page is immediately updated.

The example in this figure illustrates the event cycle. It shows how DOM scripting can be used to print a web page when the Print button is clicked. In contrast to the JavaScript code in figure 13-1, the majority of code in this example is embedded in the head section of the HTML document. That's because this code doesn't generate any output.

In this application, the JavaScript event handler is embedded in the head section of the HTML document. This code consists of a function named printTOC() that will print the page. However, you don't need to know how this function works in order to use it. You just embed it in your HTML document.

Then, in the body of the HTML document, the button for printing the document is coded. This button is coded the way chapter 10 shows how to code buttons, but it also includes an onclick attribute with a value of "printTOC()". This means that the printTOC() function should be executed when the button is clicked.

So, when the page is loaded and the user clicks the button, the click event occurs. This calls the event handler named printTOC() that's in the head section. Then, that function starts the printing process, which displays the system's dialog box for the printing.

Although this example illustrates event handling, it doesn't change the DOM. As a result, this isn't an example of DOM scripting. However, you'll soon see examples that do change the DOM.

A web page that uses a JavaScript button for printing

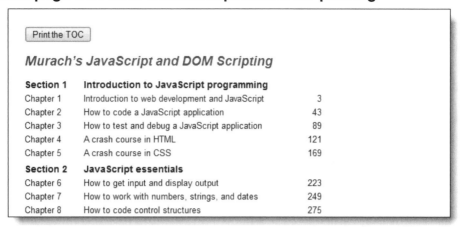

The DOM event cycle

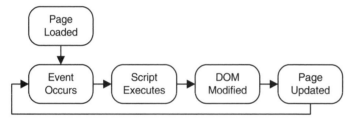

The JavaScript in the head section

```
<script>
    function printTOC() {
        window.print();
    }
</script>
```

The HTML code for the button in the body section

```
<input type="button" id="print" value="Print the TOC" onClick="printTOC()">
```

Description

- *DOM scripting* is the process of manipulating the DOM by using JavaScript.
- An *event* is an action the user performs like clicking a mouse button. When the event occurs, JavaScript is used to process it. This code is called an *event handler*.
- As an event handler executes, it has full access to the DOM so it can read the elements on the page, and it can change their attributes and contents. When the DOM is modified, the web browser detects the changes and updates the web page that's in the browser.
- When the event handler is finished, the web browser waits for another event to occur and the cycle starts over again until another page is loaded.

Figure 13-3   How DOM scripting works

How to include JavaScript in an HTML document

Figure 13-4 shows how to include JavaScript in an HTML document. To start, this figure describes two attributes that can be used with the script element. The src attribute specifies the location of the external JavaScript file that should be included in the document. The type attribute specifies that JavaScript is the client-side scripting language.

In HTML5, though, the type attribute can be omitted since JavaScript is assumed to be the scripting language. That's why the type attribute is omitted in the examples that follow. These examples illustrate the three ways that you can include JavaScript in an HTML document.

In the first example, the script element is coded in the head section of an HTML document, and the src attribute identifies an external JavaScript file named image_swap.js. This assumes that the external file is in the same folder as the HTML page. If it isn't, you can code the path to the file along with the filename.

In the second example, the script element is coded in the head section of an HTML document. Since the JavaScript is coded within this element, the JavaScript is embedded in the head of the document. As you saw in figure 13-3, JavaScript code in the head section is typically used to define event handlers.

In the third example, a script element that contains JavaScript is embedded in the body of an HTML document. As you saw in figure 13-1, a script element like this is replaced by the output of the JavaScript code when the application is loaded.

In the last example in this figure, you can see how the noscript element can be used. It is usually coded after a script element in the body of a document. Then, if JavaScript is disabled in a user's browser, the content of the noscript tag is displayed. But if JavaScript is enabled, the script element is replaced by the output of the JavaScript code and the noscript tag is ignored. This way some output will be displayed whether or not JavaScript is enabled.

Two attributes of the script element

Attribute	Description
src	Specifies the location and name of an external JavaScript file.
type	With HTML5, this attribute can be omitted. If you code it, use "text/javascript" for JavaScript code.

A script element in the head section that loads an external JavaScript file

```
<script src="image_swap.js"></script>
```

A script element that embeds JavaScript in the head section

```
<head>
    ...
    <script>
        function printTOC() {
            window.print();
        }
    </script>
</head>
```

A script element that embeds JavaScript in the body

```
<p>&copy;
    <script>
        var today = new Date();
        document.writeln(today.getFullYear());
    </script>
</p>
```

How to use the noscript tag in the body of an HTML document

```
<script>
    var today = new Date();
    document.writeln(today.getFullYear());
</script>
<noscript>2011</noscript>
```

Description

- You can have more than one script element in a web page. These elements are executed in the order that they appear in the document.

- If a script element in the head section includes an external JavaScript file, the JavaScript in the file runs as if it were coded in the script element.

- If a script element is coded in the body of a document, it is replaced by the output of the JavaScript code.

- The noscript element can be used to display content when JavaScript is disabled in a user's browser.

- The HTML document must be valid before and after all scripts have been executed.

Figure 13-4   How to include JavaScript in an HTML document

How to use JavaScript to enhance your web pages

This topic shows you how to use tested JavaScript code in your own web pages, even though you didn't write the code and may not understand how it works. This is the way many web developers work in the real world today.

If these applications are hard to follow as you read about them, you will get a chance to experiment with some of them in the exercises for this chapter. That should resolve any questions that you have.

JavaScript for opening a popup window

Figure 13-5 presents an application that opens a new browser window when the book image is clicked. This is sometimes called a *popup window*, but the window that is opened is actually a second web page. In this example, the new window is named newwindow.html.

To use this function, you first copy the script element into the head section of your HTML document. Within the JavaScript for that element, you can see that the function name is enlargeImage().

Then, in the body of the document, you code an <a> element for the image or text that you want to start the event. In this example, an img element is coded within the <a> element, and the image is the JavaScript book that you can see in the browser window. In the HTML for the <a> element, you also code an onclick attribute so the enlargeImage() function will be run when the user clicks on the book image.

Finally, you need to create the web page named newwindow.html that is opened in the new window. In this example, this consists of an img element that specifies a larger version of the JavaScript book.

If you look at the JavaScript code in the script element, you can see this line of code:

```
window.open('newwindow.html','newwin','width=425,height=525');
```

This is the code within the function that actually opens the new window. Within the parentheses, you can see three parameters that are separated by commas. The first parameter is the name of the HTML file that will be opened in the new window. The second parameter is a name for the window. And the third parameter specifies the width and height of the window in pixels.

If necessary, you can change one or more of these parameters. If, for example, you want to change the size of the window, you can change the width and height parameters. Or, if you want a different file opened in the new window, you can change the first parameter. However, if the size of the window is okay and the file you want opened is named newwindow.html, you won't need to change these parameters.

A web page that opens a new browser window when the book is clicked

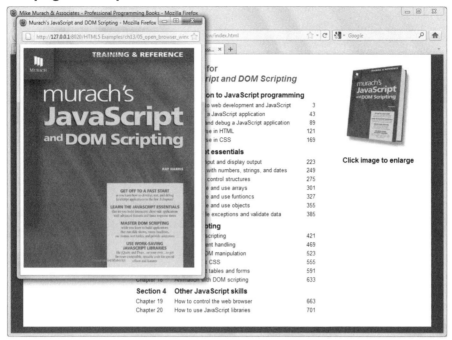

The JavaScript event handler in the head section

```
<script>
    function enlargeImage() {
        window.open('newwindow.html','newwin','width=425,height=525');
    }
</script>
```

The HTML for the link that starts the event

```
<a href="#" onClick="enlargeImage()">
    <img src="images/javascriptbook.jpg" alt="JavaScript book">
</a>
```

The body of the page named newwindow.html

```
<body>
    <img src="images/javascriptbook_500.jpg" width="400" height="500"
        alt="JavaScript and DOM Scripting">
</body>
```

How to use this JavaScript

- Copy the JavaScript event handler into the head section of the HTML. If you want to adjust the width and height of the new window, you can change the width and height parameters in this event handler.

- Code an <a> element for the image or text that you want to start the event. Then, code an onClick attribute for this element with the name of the event handler as the value.

- Create a new web page named newwindow.html that contains an enlarged version of the image that starts the event.

Figure 13-5   JavaScript for opening a popup window

JavaScript for image rollovers

Figure 13-6 presents an application that does image rollovers. An *image rollover* occurs when the user moves the mouse pointer over one image and that image is temporarily replaced by another image. Then, when the user moves the mouse pointer off the image, the rollover ends. When you use rollovers, you often replace the current image with a close-up of it or with the same image shot from another angle.

In this example, three images of C# books are set up for image rollovers. Then, when the mouse hovers over one of the books, the VB version of the book replaces the C# version. This is illustrated by the first book on the page, which has been rolled over to the VB version.

To use the JavaScript code for this application for image rollovers, you need to code the two script elements in the head section of your HTML. You also need to copy the file named rollover_library.js into the folder for your application.

Then, in the body of the document, you need to code one img element for each image that is going to be rolled over. If you're going to use two images, the ids for these elements should be "image1" and "image2" so they match the ids that are used in the JavaScript code. If you're going to use more images, you continue this id pattern.

Now, back to the JavaScript code that's embedded in the document. For each image rollover, you need to code one JavaScript statement like this:

```
rollover1 = new Rollover("image1", "images/vb10.jpg");
```

Here, "rollover1" is a name used by the JavaScript in the rollover library; "image1" is the id of the image; and "images/vb10.jpg" is the path and filename for the rollover image, which is the VB version of the book.

If you're going to use just one image rollover on a page, you can delete the statement that starts with rollover2. If you're going to use more than two rollovers, you can continue with rollover3 and image3. In this application, you're actually changing the embedded JavaScript code, but as you will see, you don't always need to do that.

By the way, this is an example of DOM scripting. When the mouse pointer hovers over an image, that event triggers a JavaScript event handler that changes the DOM so the src attribute in the img element points to the rollover image.

A web page with the first image rolled over

The script elements in the head section

```
<script src="rollover_library.js"></script>
<script>
    var $ = function (id) { return document.getElementById(id); }
    var rollover;
        window.onload = function () {
        // You need to provide one statement for each rollover here
        rollover1 = new Rollover("image1", "images/vb10.jpg");
        rollover2 = new Rollover("image2", "images/asp_vb.jpg");
        rollover3 = new Rollover("image3", "images/ado_vb.jpg");
        }
</script>
```

The HTML for the img elements that get rolled over

```
<p><img src="images/cs10.jpg" alt="" id="image1"></p>
<p><img src="images/asp_cs.jpg" alt="" id="image2"></p>
<p><img src="images/ado_cs.jpg" alt="" id="image3"></p>
```

How to use this JavaScript

- Copy the two script elements into the head section of the HTML and make sure that the external JavaScript file has been copied into the current folder.

- In the body of the HTML document, code one img element for each image that you want rolled over. The ids for these elements should be image1, image2, and so on.

- In the embedded JavaScript, provide one statement for each rollover. For these statements, you can use rollover1, rollover2, and so on as the names before the equal signs. Then, within the parentheses for each statement, you code (1) the id of the image to be rolled over, and (2) the location of the rollover image.

Figure 13-6   JavaScript for image rollovers

JavaScript for image swaps

Figure 13-7 presents an application that does image swaps. An *image swap* occurs when an event handler uses DOM scripting to replace one image with another. In this application, an image swap occurs each time the user clicks on one of the thumbnail images at the top of the web page. Here, the user has clicked on the fourth thumbnail so the caption and image in the body of the document have been replaced with the caption and image that correspond to that thumbnail image.

The benefit of image swapping is that you use one web page to present more than one image. In this case, you use one page to present five different images. If you didn't use image swapping, that would require six different web pages.

To use the JavaScript for this application for your own image swaps, you start by copying the two JavaScript files into the folder for your application. Then, you code two script elements in the head section of the HTML document that include those two files. For this application, you don't have to modify any of the JavaScript code.

What's most important, though, is that you code the HTML for the thumbnails, caption, and image exactly as shown in this figure. For the caption, you must code a span element within any block element like the h2 element in this example, and the id attribute for the span element must be "caption". For the image, you must code an img element with "image" as its id, and its src attribute must locate the first image that will be used for the page.

For the thumbnails, you code an unordered list with "image_list" as its id. Then, you code one li element for each item swap. Within each li element, you code an <a> element that uses the href attribute to identify the image to be swapped and the title attribute to identify the caption. Last, you code an img element for the thumbnail as the content for the <a> element within each li element.

When the page is loaded, the JavaScript code uses the attributes in the unordered list to build a list of the captions and images that are going to be swapped when the thumbnails are clicked. Then, the caption and image are swapped each time a thumbnail is clicked.

This is another example that illustrates the power of DOM scripting. Each time the click event occurs, the related event handler changes the DOM so the contents of the span element and the src attribute in the img element display the swapped caption and image.

Incidentally, to get the thumbnails displayed in a row the way they are in this example, you need a CSS file that does that formatting. If you're interested, you can review the file in the downloaded application.

A web page after the second thumbnail has been clicked

The script elements for the JavaScript files

```
<script src="image_swap_library.js"></script>
<script src="image_swap.js"></script>
```

The HTML for the images, captions, and thumbnails

```
<ul id="image_list">
    <li><a href="images/ss08.jpg" title="SQL Server 2008 for developers">
        <img src="thumbnails/ss08.jpg" alt=""></a></li>
    <li><a href="images/php.jpg" title="PHP and MySQL">
        <img src="thumbnails/php.jpg" alt=""></a></li>
    <li><a href="images/vb10.jpg" title="Visual Basic 2010">
        <img src="thumbnails/vb10.jpg" alt=""></a></li>
    <li><a href="images/ado_vb.jpg"
            title="ADO.NET 4 database programming with VB 2010">
        <img src="thumbnails/ado_vb.jpg" alt=""></a></li>
    <li><a href="images/asp_vb.jpg"
            title="ASP.NET 4 web programming with VB 2010">
        <img src="thumbnails/asp_vb.jpg" alt=""></a></li>
</ul>
```

The HTML for the caption and image that get swapped

```
<h2><span id="caption">SQL Server 2008 for developers</span></h2>
<p><img id="image" src="images/ss08.jpg" alt=""></p>
```

How to use this JavaScript

- Code an unordered list with "image_list" as its id. Then, within each list item, code an <a> element. In each <a> element, the href attribute should locate the image to be swapped, and the title attribute should provide the caption for the swapped image.

- As the contents for the <a> elements in the image list, code the img elements for the thumbnails.

- For the caption of the main image, code a span element within any block element with "caption" as its id. For the main image, code an img element with "image" as its id.

Figure 13-7   JavaScript for image swaps

JavaScript for slide shows

Figure 13-8 presents an application that does a slide show. In this case, the caption and image change every few seconds. The user can also use the controls above the image to change the time between image changes or to stop the slide show and manually move forward or backward through the images.

To use the JavaScript code for this application for your own slide show, you set up the slide show in a way that's similar to using the JavaScript for image swaps. First, you code two script elements in the head section that include the required JavaScript files. Second, you code an unordered list that contains <a> elements that identify the images and captions for the slide show. Third, you include the HTML for the controls. Last, you code a span element for the slide caption and an img element for the slide.

To make this work, you must also copy the JavaScript files and control images into the folder for your application. In addition, you must use a CSS file that provides the right formatting for the controls. Here again, if you're interested in the CSS, you can review the file in the downloaded application.

A web page with a slide show that's on the second slide

The script elements for the JavaScript files

```
<script src="slide_show_library.js"></script>
<script src="slide_show.js"></script>
```

The HTML for the slides and captions

```
<ul id="image_list">
    <li><a href="images/js.jpg" title="JavaScript and DOM Scripting<a></li>
    <li><a href="images/php.jpg" title="PHP and MySQL"></a></li>
    <li><a href="images/vb10.jpg" title="Visual Basic 2010"></a></li>
    <li><a href="images/cs10.jpg" title="C# 2010"></a></li>
    <li><a href="images/asp_vb.jpg" title="ASP.NET 4 with VB 2010"></a></li>
    <li><a href="images/asp_vb.jpg" title="ASP.NET 4 with C# 2010"></a></li>
</ul>
```

The HTML for the controls

```
<p id="controls">
    <button id="btn_previous" disabled>
        <img src="images/prev.gif" alt="Previous Image">
    </button>
    <button id="btn_play">
        <img src="images/pause.gif" alt="Play or Pause" id="img_play_pause">
    </button>
    <input type="button" id="btn_speed" value="Slow">
    <button id="btn_next" disabled>
        <img src="images/next.gif" alt="Next Image">
    </button>
</p>
```

The HTML for the caption and image area

```
<h2><span id="caption">JavaScript and DOM Scripting</span></h2>
<p><img src="images/book1.jpg" alt="" id="image"></p>
```

How to use this JavaScript

- The HTML is similar to the HTML for image swaps, but you don't code img elements within <a> elements, and you do need to add the HTML for the controls.

Figure 13-8   JavaScript for slide shows

JavaScript for tabbed data

Figure 13-9 shows how *tabs*, or *tabbed data*, can be used in a web application. When the user clicks on a tab, the display is changed so it looks like the tab is active and the data for that tab is displayed.

This is an interface that users are familiar with so it's easy for them to use. Please note, however, that the current "best practices" for the use of tabbed data include these guidelines:

- Tabs should be used for secondary data, not the primary data on a page.
- The graphics should clearly indicate which tab is active, usually by showing a border below the inactive tabs and no border below the active tab.
- The text on each tab should be short and clearly indicate what type of data the tab holds.
- The data for each tab should be independent of the other tabs so the users aren't forced to switch back and forth between tabs to see related data
- The data for each tab should be part of a single HTML page so clicking on a tab doesn't load a new page.

To implement that last guideline, of course, you need to use a client-side scripting language like JavaScript.

To use the JavaScript for the tabs in this figure, you code the HTML the way it's illustrated. First, you code the two script elements for the JavaScript files. Second, you code an unordered list that will be converted into the tabs. Third, you code a div element that contains one div element for the contents of each tab.

The keys here are that the ul element must have "tab_list" as its id, and the div element for the tab contents must have "tab_contents" as its id. Also, the <a> element for the active tab when the page is loaded should have "active" as its class attribute, and the div elements for the tab contents that aren't active when the page is loaded should have "hide" as their class attributes. Note here that you don't need to code id attributes for the content divisions, but you do need to code them in the same sequence as the related list items.

When the user clicks on a tab after the page is loaded, the JavaScript applies the "active" class to the corresponding <a> element, and it sets the class attribute for the other <a> elements to an empty string. Then, the JavaScript sets the class attribute for the contents div that corresponds to the active tab to an empty string, and it sets the class attribute for the other div elements to "hide".

The key to this application, then, is the CSS that creates the tabs, shows which one is active, and shows the contents for that tab. That CSS is on the next page.

Tabbed data with the first tab active

The script elements for the JavaScript files

```
<script src="tabs_library.js"></script>
<script src="tabs.js"></script>
```

The HTML for the tabs and tab contents

```
<ul id="tab_list">
    <li><a href="" id="tab1" class="active">Contents</a></li>
    <li><a href="" id="tab2" class="">Author</a></li>
    <li><a href="" id="tab3" class="">Downloads</a></li>
</ul>
<div id="tab_contents">
    <div class="">
        <h2>The table of contents</h2>
        <p>The descriptive text for this tab.</p>
    </div>
    <div class="hide">
        <h2>About the author</h2>
    </div>
    <div class="hide">
        <h2>About the downloads</h2>
    </div>
</div>
```

How to code the HTML that is processed by the JavaScript

- For the tabs, code an unordered list with "tab_list" as its id. Then, within each list item, code an <a> element with an empty href attribute.

- For the tab that you want to be active when the page is loaded, code a class attribute for the <a> element with "active" as its value.

- For the tab contents, code a div element with "tab_contents" as its id. Within this div element, code one div element for each tab. These div elements don't need id attributes, but they should be in the same sequence as the related list items.

- For each div element that isn't going to be active when the page is loaded, code a class attribute with "hide" as its value.

- Within the div element for a tab, code whatever content you want.

Figure 13-9   JavaScript for tabbed data

The CSS for the tabbed data in figure 13-10 is interesting because it shows how easy it is to create simple, but effective tabs. In fact, another guideline for using tabs is to keep the graphics simple.

To some extent, you need to experiment with this CSS to see how easily you can change the size of the tabs, the spacing between the tabs, the background colors of the tabs and contents, and so on. But here are some of the key points that you should be aware of.

First, the rule set for the unordered list (#tab_list) sets the border below the tabs. Second, the rule set for the li elements in the tab list removes the bullets and displays the list items in-line. Third, the rule set for the <a> elements in the tab list sets the background color for the inactive tabs to a light blue. More important, this rule set puts a black border around each <a> element, including a black bottom border.

How then does that bottom border get removed for the active tab? The rule set for the active class of an <a> element sets the bottom border to white. Then, this border overlays the black border for that portion of the tab list, so it looks like the tab is active.

Last, the rule set for the hide class turns the display of the related element off. That's what hides the contents for the tabs that aren't active. Because the CSS works this way, all the JavaScript has to do is turn on the "active" class for the active tab and the "hide" class for the content elements that aren't active.

The CSS for the tabbed data

```css
#tab_list {
    margin:0;
    padding: 3px 6px;
    border-bottom: 1px solid black;
}
#tab_list li {
    list-style: none;
    display: inline;
}
#tab_list li a {
    padding: 3px 1em;
    margin-left: 3px;
    text-decoration: none;
    font-weight: bold;
    background: #ccffff;
    border: 1px solid black;
}
#tab_list li a:hover {
    background: silver;
    border-color: black;
}
#tab_list li a.active {
    background-color: white;
    border-bottom: 1px solid white;
}
#tab_contents div {
    padding: 5px 10px 10px;
    border: 1px solid black;
    border-top: 0;
    height: 100px;
    overflow: auto;
}
.hide {
    display: none;
}
```

Description

- The rule set for the ul element (#tab_list) puts a black border at the bottom of all the tabs.

- The rule set for the li elements displays them inline with no bullets.

- The rule set for the <a> elements within the li elements displays them with a black border on all four sides, including the bottom.

- The rule set for the <a> element with the "active" class applies a white bottom border, which overlays the black border. That shows which tab is selected.

- The "hide" class doesn't display any element that it is coded for.

- When the user clicks on a tab, the JavaScript applies the "active" class to the underlying <a> element and removes it from the other <a> elements. It also removes the "hide" class from the related contents division and applies the "hide" class to the other contents divisions.

Figure 13-10   The CSS for the tabbed data

What to do if the JavaScript doesn't work

Whenever you use JavaScript, errors can occur. When you're using tested JavaScript code, however, the errors aren't likely to be in the JavaScript code. More likely, they'll be in the HTML code that is used by the JavaScript code.

For instance, figure 13-11 shows the slide show application in Firefox. However, the slide show didn't start after the page was loaded into the browser. So what's the problem?

To help figure that out, you can display the Firefox Error Console by using the command in this figure. In this example, the message in this console says: "SlideShow isn't defined". Then, you can click on the message to display the statement in the JavaScript code that initiated the error. Here again, you can see a reference to SlideShow.

Even if you don't know JavaScript, this should tell you that the JavaScript file that contains SlideShow hasn't been loaded into storage. Then, you can check the script elements that load the files to make sure the paths and filenames are correct.

If Firefox has detected JavaScript errors in previous web pages when you first display the Error Console, the dialog box may contain messages for those pages. To clear those messages, you can click the Clear button at the top of the dialog box. Then, when you reload the page and display the Error Console, it will display only the current error.

When you use tested JavaScript code, one common error is not providing the script elements that include the required JavaScript files. In this case, though, a JavaScript error won't occur unless other JavaScript code refers to code in the missing JavaScript file.

Another common error is coding the wrong ids for elements that are used by the JavaScript code. Then, the JavaScript code won't be able to find the nodes in the DOM that it's looking for.

Perhaps the best debugging advice when you're using JavaScript code that you don't understand is to be especially careful when you code the HTML that the JavaScript code is going to use. If you code all of the attributes right in the first place, that's easier than looking for problems later on.

A web page in Firefox with the Error Console displayed

The code that's displayed when the link in the Error Console is clicked

How to display the Firefox Error Console

- Use the Tools→Web Developer→Error Console command or press Ctrl+Shift+J.

How to tell when a JavaScript error has occurred

- The JavaScript for the web page doesn't do anything
- An error message is displayed

Common HTML errors when using tested JavaScript code

- Omitting the script elements that load the JavaScript files or misspelling the filenames.
- Coding the wrong ids for the HTML elements that are used in the DOM scripting.

Description

- Some browsers will display an error message when a JavaScript error occurs, but some won't. To some extent, that depends on how the browser is set up.
- One way to tell if a JavaScript error has occurred is to load the page in Firefox and display the Error Console. That may also give you a clue to what you've done wrong.

Figure 13-11   What to do if the JavaScript doesn't work

Web sites for JavaScript code

You can, of course, use any of the JavaScript code in the applications that you've just reviewed because the code is available in the downloadable applications for this book. But you should also know that many web sites provide JavaScript code that you can use in your programs, and much of it is free.

In figure 13-12, for example, you can see a web page that offers free JavaScript code for doing Image Slideshows. This web page is on the Dynamic Drive web site, and it's one of my favorite sites for getting JavaScript code. The other is The JavaScript Source.

To find sites like this, you can search for "free javascript code" or "javascript code examples". Often, these sites provide JavaScript for games and special effects that you can easily add to your site. Remember, though, that you don't want to distract the users of your site from doing what you see as the primary goals of your site.

One of the problems with the code that you get from web sites like this is that it can be difficult to figure out how to use, especially if you don't understand JavaScript. Another problem is that web sites like this often provide code that you embed in your HTML, instead of code that's in separate JavaScript files. But that often makes your code more difficult to create, test, and maintain.

With these problems in mind, it still makes sense to search for free JavaScript code, especially if you're looking for code that does a specific function. Eventually, though, you should learn how to do your own JavaScript programming. That will not only make it easier for you to use the code that you get from JavaScript web sites, but it will also let you write your own code if you can't find what you want.

A web site that offers free JavaScript code

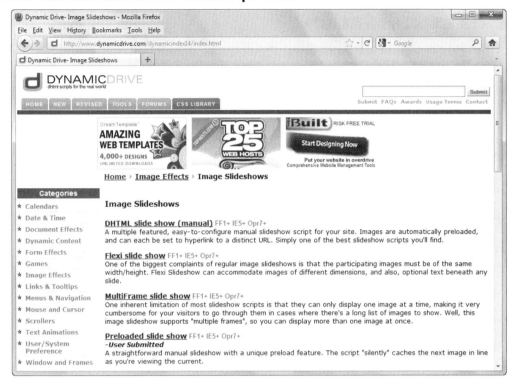

Zak's recommendations for JavaScript web sites

- Dynamic Drive (http://www.dynamicdrive.com)
- The JavaScript Source (http://javascript.internet.com)

Description

- Many web sites provide JavaScript code that you can download or cut-and-paste into your web pages. Most of these sites also provide instructions for using that code.

- To find sites that provide JavaScript code, you can search for terms like "free javascript code" or "javascript code examples".

- These sites often provide JavaScript code that provides special effects or games that you can add to your site. Remember, though, to keep your focus on the goals of your web site.

- One of the problems with the code that you get from these sites is that it is often hard to figure out how to use it. Another problem is that these sites often provide code that you embed in your HTML, but that can make your code more difficult to create and maintain.

Figure 13-12   Web sites for JavaScript code

Another example: JavaScript for data validation

In chapter 10, you learned how you could use the new HTML features and controls for client-side data validation. Now, you'll see how JavaScript can be used for validating the data in the same application.

The page layout

Figure 13-13 presents a web page that provides *data validation* before the form data is sent to the server for processing. In this example, the user entered some valid data and some invalid data and clicked on the Register button. Then, the JavaScript code for this application displayed an error message in a dialog box along with error messages to the right of the invalid fields.

When the user corrects all the errors so all the data is valid and then clicks on the Register button, the form and all of its data will be submitted to the web server for processing. To reset all of the fields in the form to what they were when the web page was loaded, the user can click on the Reset button.

As you will see, the HTML for the form in this web page uses some of the HTML5 features for data validation. That's why the invalid fields have a red border around them. But note that the Verify Password text box doesn't have a red border, even though its entry doesn't match the entry in the Password dialog box. That's because there's no way of comparing the two password entries with HTML5. But the JavaScript for data validation has caught this error and displayed an error message to the right of the Verify Password text box.

Similarly, the ZIP code text box doesn't have a red border to indicate that its entry is invalid. Here again, that's because HTML5 has no way of knowing that CC is an invalid state code. But here again, the JavaScript data validation caught the error by looking for the code in a table of the 50 valid codes and not finding it.

You might also be interested in the way that Safari renders the date control near the bottom of the form. Although Safari doesn't offer a drop-down calendar, it will display a valid date for tomorrow if the user clicks on the up button or a valid date for yesterday if the user clicks on the down button.

A web page in Safari with a form that uses JavaScript validation

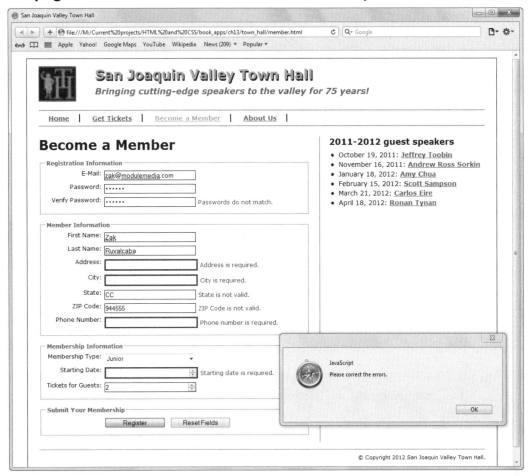

The script elements for the JavaScript files

```
<script src="register_library.js"></script>
<script src="register.js"></script>
```

How to use the JavaScript for this application in your own application

- In the HTML for your application, use the same ids for the fields that this application uses. Note, however, that your fields don't have to be in the same sequence.

- If you don't include all of the fields shown above, you must modify the first page of the register_library.js file. To do that, delete all lines of code that refer to the fields that you haven't included in your HTML.

- Code the form element and the Register and Reset buttons the same way they're coded for this application. However, you can change the value properties of the buttons.

Figure 13-13   The user interface for the data validation application

The HTML

Figure 13-14 presents the HTML for this application. Not shown are the two script elements for the JavaScript files that are required for this application. These elements are presented in the previous figure.

For this HTML to work right with the JavaScript code, the form element and the elements for the Register and Reset buttons must be coded just as they are. However, you can change the value attributes for the buttons if you want different text displayed on them.

Similarly, the ids for the fields must be just as they are in this HTML because those are the field names that the JavaScript is programmed for. For instance, "email", "password", and "verify" must be used for the first three fields on the form. Last, the ids for the span elements for the error messages after the fields must be the same as in this HTML. For instance, "email_error", "password_error", and "verify_error" must be used for the span elements that follow the first three fields on this form.

If you study this HTML, you can see that it uses several of the HTML5 features and controls for data validation. For instance, both the autofocus and required attributes are coded for the email control, and the email type is used for this input element. Similarly, the date type with the required attribute is used for the data control. This shows that the new features can be used along with the JavaScript code for data validation. Then, if a browser doesn't support the new features, you can rely on the JavaScript for data validation.

If you want to use the JavaScript files in a similar application, you just need to adhere to the naming conventions that I just described. You don't need to present the controls in the same sequence. However, if you don't want to use all of the controls in your form, you will need to modify the JavaScript code as described in the next figure.

Some of the HTML for the form

```
<form action="register_account.html" method="get"
      name="registration_form" id="registration_form">
<fieldset>
    <legend>Registration Information</legend>
    <label for="email">E-Mail:</label>
    <input type="email" name="email" id="email" autofocus required>
        <span id="email_error">Must be a valid  email address.</span><br>
    <label for="password">Password:</label>
    <input type="password" name="password" id="password" required>
        <span id="password_error">Must be at least 6 characters.</span><br>
    <label for="verify">Verify Password:</label>
    <input type="password" name="verify" id="verify" required>
        <span id="verify_error"> </span><br>
</fieldset>
<fieldset>
    <legend>Member Information</legend>
    <label for="first_name">First Name:</label>
    <input type="text" name="first_name" id="first_name" required>
        <span id="first_name_error"> </span><br>
    ...
    ...
    ...
    <label for="state">State:</label>
    <input type="text" name="state" id="state" maxlength="2" required>
        <span id="state_error">Use 2 character abbreviation.</span><br>
    <label for="zip">ZIP Code:</label>
    <input type="text" name="zip" id="zip" required>
        <span id="zip_error">Use 5 or 9 digit ZIP code.</span><br>
    <label for="phone">Phone Number:</label>
    <input type="tel" name="phone" id="phone" required>
        <span id="phone_error">Use 999-999-9999 format.</span><br>
</fieldset>
<fieldset>
    <legend>Membership Information</legend>
    <label for="membership_type">Membership Type:</label>
    <select name="membership_type" id="membership_type">
        <option value="j">Junior</option>
        <option value="r">Regular</option>
        <option value="c">Charter</option>
    </select><br>
    <label for="starting_date">Starting Date:</label>
    <input type="date" name="date" id="date" required>
        <span id="date_error"> </span><br>
    <label for="tickets">Tickets for Guests:</label>
    <input type="number" name="tickets" id="tickets" value="2" min="1"
           max="4" placeholder="from 1 to 4"><br>
</fieldset>
<fieldset id="buttons">
    <legend>Submit Your Membership</legend>
    <label> </label>
    <input type="button" id="register" value="Register">
    <input type="button" id="reset_form" value="Reset Fields"><br>
</fieldset>
</form>
```

Figure 13-14   The HTML for the data validation application

The JavaScript code

Figure 13-15 presents the first page of the register_library.js file for this application. This code sets up the fields that are going to be validated. If you're going to use this code for a form that uses all of the fields, you don't need to do anything to this code.

However, if you don't want to use all of the fields, you must modify the code on the first page of this file. Specifically, you must either delete or comment out any of the lines of code that refer to a field that you're not using. If, for example, you aren't going to use the phone field, you must delete or comment out the second to last line of code in the array of fields, the last line of code in the default field messages, and the second and third to last lines of code in the field error messages.

What if you want to add fields that aren't included in this application? What if you want to change the rules for what a valid field is? That would require changes to the JavaScript code, and that would mean that you would have to know how to modify the code. That's why every serious web developer should eventually learn how to develop JavaScript and DOM scripting applications.

The first page of the register_library.js file

```
var $ = function (id) { return document.getElementById(id); }

var RegisterForm = function () {
    // Array of fields
    this.fields = [];
    this.fields["email"] = {};
    this.fields["password"] = {};
    this.fields["verify"] = {};
    this.fields["first_name"] = {};
    this.fields["last_name"] = {};
    this.fields["address"] = {};
    this.fields["city"] = {};
    this.fields["state"] = {};
    this.fields["zip"] = {};
    this.fields["phone"] = {};
    this.fields["date"] = {};

    // Default field messages
    this.fields["email"].message = "Must be a valid email address.";
    this.fields["password"].message = "Must be at least 6 characters.";
    this.fields["state"].message = "Use 2 letter abbreviation.";
    this.fields["zip"].message = "Use 5 or 9 digit ZIP code.";
    this.fields["phone"].message = "Use 999-999-9999 format.";

    // Field error messages
    this.fields["email"].required = "Email is required.";
    this.fields["email"].isEmail = "Email is invalid.";
    this.fields["password"].required = "Password is required.";
    this.fields["password"].tooShort = ["Password is too short.", 6];
    this.fields["verify"].required = "Confirm password.";
    this.fields["verify"].noMatch = ["Passwords do not match.", "password"];
    this.fields["first_name"].required = "First name is required.";
    this.fields["last_name"].required = "Last name is required.";
    this.fields["address"].required = "Address is required.";
    this.fields["city"].required = "City is required.";
    this.fields["state"].required = "State is required.";
    this.fields["state"].isState = "State is invalid.";
    this.fields["zip"].required = "ZIP is required.";
    this.fields["zip"].isZip = "ZIP is invalid.";
    this.fields["phone"].required = "Phone is required.";
    this.fields["phone"].isPhone = "Phone is invalid.";
    this.fields["date"].required = "Starting date is required.";
}
```

Figure 13-15   The JavaScript for the first page of the register_library.js file

Perspective

Now that you've completed this chapter, you should be able to use tested JavaScript code to enhance your web pages. Eventually, though, you should take the time to learn how to do your own JavaScript programming. For that, we recommend *Murach's JavaScript and DOM Scripting*. By learning JavaScript, you will not only be able to make better use of existing JavaScript code, but you will also be able to write your own JavaScript code so it works just the way you want it to.

Terms

JavaScript	element node	popup window
JavaScript engine	text node	image rollover
client-side processing	attribute node	image swap
server-side processing	comment node	tabs
DOM (Document	DOM scripting	tabbed data
Object Model)	event	data validation
node	event handler	

Summary

- *JavaScript* is a scripting language that is run by the *JavaScript engine* of a browser. As a result, the work is done on the client, not the server, and that takes some of the processing burden off the server.

- The *DOM (Document Object Model)* is a hierarchical collection of *nodes* in the web browser's memory that represents the current web page. The DOM for each page is built as the page is loaded.

- *DOM scripting* is the process of changing the DOM by using JavaScript. When the DOM changes, the browser immediately displays the results of the change.

- An *event* is an action the user performs, like clicking on a button or image. When an event occurs, it can be handled by JavaScript code known as an *event handler*.

- To run an event handler for the click event of an HTML element, you can code the onClick attribute with the name of the event handler as its value.

- To embed JavaScript code or to include JavaScript files in an HTML document, you code a script element.

- If a script element is coded in the body of a document, it is replaced by the output of the JavaScript code. This element can be followed by a noscript element that displays content if JavaScript isn't enabled in the user's browser.

- Common uses for JavaScript are *popup windows*, *image rollovers*, *image swaps*, slide shows, *tabs*, and *data validation*.

Exercise 13-1   Enhance a page with JavaScript

In this exercises for this section, you'll be working with a third version of the Town Hall web site. In this exercise, you'll make two minor JavaScript enhancements to the speaker's page for Scott Sampson:

Open the HTML and CSS files for this page

1. Use your text editor to open the HTML and CSS files for this page:

    ```
    c:\html5_css3\exercises\town_hall_3\speakers\sampson.html

    c:\html5_css3\exercises\town_hall_3\styles\speaker.css
    ```

2. Test the file in Firefox and see that it looks like the one above, but without the Print Page button.

Add the Print Page button

3. Add the JavaScript for printing a page to the head section as shown in figure 13-3. Then, add the Print Page button to the page at the top of the aside.

4. Test this code. It should work, although the formatting for the button won't be right. If it doesn't work, make sure that you have entered everything exactly as it is in figure 13-3.

5. Modify the JavaScript so the function name is printPage() instead of printTOC(). Then, modify the value for the button so it is "Print Page" instead of "Print TOC", and modify the value for the onClick attribute so it is "printPage()".

6. Test again, and it still should work. However, the formatting of the button still won't be right. Also, when you print the page, the button will be printed on the page, which isn't what you want. To fix these problems, adjust the CSS file for the page, and test again.

Automatically update the year in the footer

7. Using figure 13-1 as a guide, use JavaScript to get the current year and put it into the copyright line in the footer. Then, test this change.

Exercise 13-2 Use JavaScript for image swaps

In this exercise, you'll enhance a page so it uses JavaScript to do image swaps. That page will look like the one below. Then, when the user clicks on a small image, a larger image of that speaker is displayed below the small images.

This is the page that is displayed when you click on the Speakers link in the navigation bar on any of the other pages. On the left side of this page, you can see the links that will be used to go to other pages that will be used for the applications in this section.

Open the HTML and CSS files for this page

1. Use your text editor to open the HTML and CSS files for this page:

   ```
   c:\html5_css3\exercises\town_hall_3\speakers\image_swaps.html
   c:\html5_css3\exercises\town_hall_3\styles\speakers_pages.css
   ```

2. Look in the head section of the HTML file to see that it contains two script elements that load the two JavaScript files for this application. Then, test the file in Firefox to see that it looks okay, but it doesn't work.

Modify the HTML so the image swaps work

3. Using figure 13-7 as a guide, modify the HTML so it should work. Then, test and adjust until it does.

4. Click on the Home link in the navigation bar to go to that page; click on the Speakers link to return to the Image Swaps page; and click on the links in the sidebar to see that these links go to the starting pages for other exercises.

14

How to use jQuery
to enhance your web pages

In the last chapter, you learned how to use JavaScript to enhance your web pages. Now, you'll learn how to use jQuery to enhance your web pages. As you will see, jQuery consists of JavaScript libraries that make it easier for you to enhance your web pages, whether or not you know how to program in JavaScript.

Introduction to jQuery

In this introduction, you'll learn what jQuery is and how to use it. Specifically, you'll learn how to code the script elements that load jQuery into your web pages and how to use the jQuery methods.

What jQuery is and where to get it

As figure 14-1 summarizes, *jQuery* is a free, open-source, JavaScript library that provides dozens of functions for common web features. This means that you don't have to write your own JavaScript code for these functions. You just need to know how to use the jQuery functions. Beyond that, the jQuery functions are coded and tested for cross-browser compatibility, so they will work in all browsers.

That's why jQuery is used by almost half of the 10,000 most-visited web sites today. And that's why jQuery is commonly used by professional web developers. In fact, you can think of jQuery as one of the four technologies that every web developer should know how to use: HTML, CSS, JavaScript, and jQuery. But don't forget that jQuery is actually JavaScript.

Besides the core jQuery library, jQuery provides the *jQuery UI* (User Interface) library. The functions in this library use the components of the core library to build advanced features that can be created with just a few lines of code.

For instance, an accordion is a jQuery UI widget that uses the selectable interaction and the slide effect of jQuery. Similarly, a sortable list is a jQuery UI widget that uses the draggable, selectable, and sortable interactions and the fade effect of jQuery. jQuery UI also provides themes that are used to format the widgets, and this overrides the themes component of jQuery.

As you will see in the next figure, you don't have to download the jQuery files if you use a Content Delivery Network. If you decide to download them, though, you can download the jQuery file from the jQuery web site that's shown in this figure. This web site also provides documentation, sample applications, and links to other web sites that provide jQuery information and enhancements. Then, to get the jQuery UI files, go to the jQuery UI web site. One quick way to do that is to click on the *UI* link in the top navigation bar on the jQuery site.

The jQuery web site at www.jQuery.com

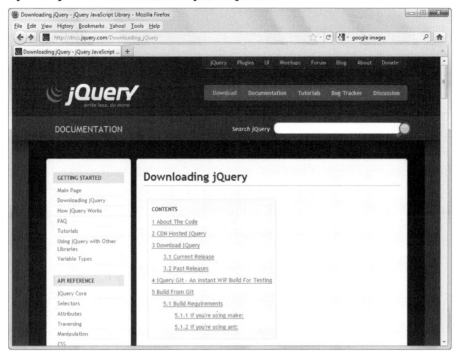

The two jQuery libraries

- jQuery (the core library)
- jQuery UI (User Interface)

What jQuery offers

- Dozens of functions that make it easier to add JavaScript features to your web pages.
- Functions that are tested for cross-browser compatibility.

Description

- Today, jQuery is used by almost 50% of the 10,000 most-visited web sites, and its popularity is growing rapidly.
- *jQuery* is a free, open-source, JavaScript library that makes JavaScript programming easier. It provides widgets, interactions, effects, and themes that can be used to build features like carousels and slide shows.
- *jQuery UI* is a free, open-source, JavaScript library that provides higher-level functions like advanced widgets that can be easily customized by using *themes* that override the themes component of jQuery.
- As you will see in the next figure, you don't have to download the jQuery libraries if you use a Content Delivery Network. If you decide to download them, though, you can download jQuery from the jQuery web site. Then, you can download jQuery UI from its site (www.jqueryui.com). To get to that site, you can click *UI* in jQuery's navigation bar.

Figure 14-1   What jQuery is and where to get it

How to include jQuery and jQuery UI in your web pages

To use jQuery and jQuery UI, you need to include the three files listed at the top of figure 14-2 in your web pages. As this figure shows, there are two ways to do that.

The first way to include the three files in your web pages is illustrated by the first set of examples. Here, the script elements get the files from a *Content Delivery Network* (*CDN*). A CDN is a web server that hosts open-source software, and Google, Microsoft, and jQuery are good CDNs for getting the jQuery libraries. In the example in this figure, the Google CDN is used.

The benefit to using a CDN is that you don't have to download the jQuery and jQuery UI files, and you don't have to manage the versions as new ones become available. Instead, you just have to change the version numbers in the script elements for these libraries. This is the method that's used in all of the examples in this chapter.

The second way to include the jQuery files in your web pages is to download the three files from the jQuery web site and deploy them on your system or web server. To do that, you download the compressed zip files that contain the files, extract the files from the zip files, and copy the files to your web server.

Then, for each web page that uses jQuery, you code one link element that includes the CSS file for jQuery UI and two script elements that include the jQuery and jQuery UI files. This is illustrated by the second set of examples in this figure. Here, the names for the current versions of the files are retained. Although you can change those names once they're on your server, keeping the downloaded names makes it easy to tell which versions of the files you're using.

No matter which method you use for including the jQuery files, be sure that the script element for jQuery UI comes after the one for jQuery. That's because the jQuery UI functions often refer to functions in the jQuery file.

The three files that you need to include for jQuery applications

- The jQuery JavaScript file
- The jQuery UI JavaScript file
- The jQuery UI stylesheet

Two ways to include the jQuery files

- Include the files from a Content Delivery Network (CDN) like Google, Microsoft, or jQuery.
- Download and deploy the files on your web server. Then, include them from the server.

How to include the jQuery files from a Content Delivery Network (CDN)

```
<!-- include the jQuery UI stylesheet -->
<link rel="stylesheet"
    <!-- the attribute that follows should be on a single line -->
    href="https://ajax.googleapis.com/ajax/libs/jqueryui/1.8.16/
        themes/base/jquery.ui.all.css">

<!-- include the jQuery and jQuery UI JavaScript files -->
<script
    src="https://ajax.googleapis.com/ajax/libs/jquery/1.6.2/jquery.min.js">
</script>
<script
    src="https://ajax.googleapis.com/ajax/libs/jqueryui/1.8.16/jquery-ui.js">
</script>
```

How to include the jQuery files when they're on your web site

```
<!-- include the jQuery UI stylesheet -->
<link rel="stylesheet" href="jquery.ui.all.css">

<!-- include the jQuery and jQuery UI JavaScript files -->
<script src="jquery-1.6.2.min.js"></script>
<script src="jquery-ui.js"></script>
```

Description

- To use jQuery, you need to include the three files shown above. The first two are the JavaScript files for jQuery and jQuery UI. The third is the CSS file for styling the widgets that you build with jQuery UI.
- The jQuery and jQuery UI filenames always include the version numbers.
- If you include the files from a *Content Delivery Network* (*CDN*), you don't have to download the files. You just have to update the version numbers in the filenames when new versions become available.
- If you download and deploy the jQuery files to your system, you can change the filenames so they're simpler. But that way, you can lose track of what versions you're using and when you need to upgrade to newer versions.
- jQuery and jQuery UI are continually being refined and improved, so check the web sites often for the latest versions.

Figure 14-2   How to include jQuery and jQuery UI in your web pages

How to use jQuery

In this chapter, you're not going to learn how to write the JavaScript code that uses jQuery, but you should be aware of what's going on. To that end, figure 14-3 provides the coding techniques that you should know.

To start, you should know that the $ sign always refers to the jQuery libraries. Then, in the parentheses after the dollar sign, you code a selector that identifies the HTML element or elements that jQuery will be applied to.

This is illustrated by the first set of examples in this figure. Here, the first selector is a type selector that applies to all h1 elements. The second selector is an id selector that applies to the HTML element with "accordion" as its id. And the third selector is a class selector that applies to all of the elements with "fadein" as their class name. This shows how closely the jQuery selectors relate to the CSS selectors.

After the selector, you can use this syntax to run a jQuery *method* on the *object* that's referred to by the selector:

```
object.method
```

This is illustrated by the second set of examples in this figure. Here, the first statement runs the hide method on all h1 elements. The second statement runs the accordion method on the HTML element with "accordion" as its id. In the first statement, the value in the parentheses for the hide method is a parameter that tells the method to hide the elements at a slow speed.

The third group of examples shows two ways to code a JavaScript function that uses the jQuery ready method. The ready method tests to see whether the DOM has been created while a web page is being loaded. When the ready method detects that the DOM has been created, it passes control to the method or methods that follow it. In both of these examples, the alert method of the window object is executed when the ready method finishes. This is a JavaScript method that displays a message box.

The ready method is important because the jQuery methods in this chapter can't be run until the DOM has been created. As a result, the JavaScript code that calls these methods must be run after the ready method has finished. If the code were run before the DOM was built, it wouldn't work correctly because the methods use the DOM. Because of that, every one of the features that follows is coded within a function that starts with the short version of the ready method.

Incidentally, the code in these examples is actually JavaScript code that accesses jQuery methods. For short, the JavaScript code is commonly referred to as a *script*, and the script is coded within a script element in the head section of the HTML. You'll see this illustrated in all of the examples that follow.

How to code jQuery selectors

A type selector that selects all h1 elements
```
$("h1")
```

An id selector that selects the element with "accordion" as its id
```
$("#accordion")
```

A class selector that selects all elements in the "fadein" class
```
$(".fadein")
```

How to use the dot syntax to call jQuery methods

A call to the hide method of an h1 object
```
$("h1").hide("slow")
```

A call to the accordion method of the element with "accordion" as its id
```
$(#accordion).accordion()
```

Two ways to code a function that uses the jQuery ready method

The long way
```
$(document).ready(function(){
    window.alert("The DOM is ready.");
});
```

The short way
```
$(function(){
    window.alert("The DOM is ready.");
});
```

The message box that's displayed when the DOM is ready

Description

- When you use jQuery, the dollar sign ($) is used to refer to the jQuery library. Then, you can code selectors by using the CSS syntax within quotation marks within parentheses.

- To call a jQuery *method*, you code a selector that refers to an *object*, followed by the dot operator (.), followed by the method name. Then, that method is applied to the object.

- A function for the ready method will run any methods that it contains as soon as the DOM is ready. In the example above, the JavaScript alert method displays a dialog box as soon as the DOM is ready for the page that's being loaded.

Figure 14-3   How to use jQuery

How to use two of the jQuery features

Now that you've been introduced to jQuery, you'll learn how to use two common web features that require the use of the jQuery core library. As you will see, using these jQuery features requires more code than using jQuery UI features.

jQuery for carousels

Figure 14-4 shows how to use jQuery to build a *carousel*. What makes this carousel unique is that you can add as many images as you like to the list of images, but only three will appear. Then, the user can click on the arrows at the sides of the carousel to display more images. With each click, the images slide sideways so one image disappears and a new one appears.

In the HTML for a carousel, you code the div, ul, li, and img elements shown in the example in this figure. You also code the id and class attributes for these elements as shown in this example. Within the div elements for the two buttons, the img elements must refer to the left.jpg and right.jpg files. These are the images for the buttons that move the carousel to the left and right.

If you want the images in the carousel to be clickable, you can code them within <a> elements. Then, the user can click an image to go to a web page that describes the object in detail.

To use the script for a carousel, you just copy the script element in this figure into the head section of your HTML. But note that this element must come after the script element for the jQuery library because it refers to functions and methods in that library. Note too that the jQuery UI files aren't required for a carousel because it only uses functions from the jQuery library. Because this script doesn't use any of the higher-level functions of jQuery UI, it is more extensive than the scripts for the jQuery UI features.

In this example and all the ones that follow, the JavaScript for the feature is coded within a function for the ready method of the document. This means that the code won't be run until the DOM is ready. Then, the code prepares the carousel so it's ready for use.

To make this script easier to use, you can copy it into a new JavaScript file (but just the script, not the script tags). Then, you can use the script element to include the file after the script element for loading the jQuery library. If, for example, you name the file carousel.js, the script element just needs to include that file. When that file is loaded with the web page, the function is run just as it is if the script is embedded in the head section.

A carousel

The script element for the carousel

```
<script>
$(function() {
    var $slider = $('.panel-inner');
    var liW = 101;
    var liFW = parseInt(liW * ($slider.find('li').length + 1));
    $slider.css('width', liFW + 'px');
    $('.button').click(function() {
        var leftX = (this.id == 'right') ?
            parseInt($slider.css('left').toString().replace('-', '')) :
            parseInt($slider.css('left'));
        var leftY = (this.id == 'right') ? ((leftX + 404) == liFW) ? 0: -
            (leftX + liW) : (leftX < 0) ? -
            (parseInt(leftX.toString().replace('-', '')) - liW) : 0;
        rotate(leftY);
    });
    var rotate = function(leftY) {$slider.animate({left: leftY},500);}
});
</script>
```

The HTML for the carousel

```
<div id="carousel">
    <div class="button" id="left"><img src="images/left.jpg"></div>
    <div class="panel">
        <ul class="panel-inner">
            <li><img src="images/book1.jpg" alt="SQL Server 2008"></li>
            <li><img src="images/book2.jpg" alt="PHP and MySQL"></li>
            <!-- add as many images as you want -->
        </ul>
    </div>
    <div class="button" id="right"><img src="images/right.jpg"></div>
</div>
```

How to code the HTML and the script for a carousel

- Code a div element with "carousel" as its id. Within this element, code one div element for the left button, one div element that contains one ul element, and one div element for the right button. For each element, use the id and class attributes that are shown above.

- Within the ul elements, code as many li elements that contain img elements as you want. Within the button div elements, code img elements for the left.jpg and right.jpg files.

- Copy the script element into the head section after the element for the jQuery file.

Figure 14-4   jQuery for carousels (part 1 of 2)

Part 2 of this figure presents the CSS for the carousel in part 1. Here, the width, height, and margin properties are highlighted because they are the ones you might want to change. If, for example, you want the carousel to show four images instead of three, you can change the width property of the panel. Similarly, if you want to increase the size of the images or the space between them, you can adjust the properties for the inner panel including the li and img elements within the inner panel.

Here again, because this application doesn't use jQuery UI, the CSS is more extensive than it would be if it did. This is illustrated by the jQuery UI examples that follow.

The CSS for the carousel in part 1 of this figure

```css
/* the styles for the carousel */
#carousel {
    margin: 10px 0 0 0;
    padding: 0;
    width: 400px;
    height: 125px;
}
.button {
    margin: 45px 10px 0 10px;
    float: left;
    height: 25px;
    width: 25px;
}
.panel {
    margin: 0;
    overflow: hidden;
    position: relative;
    float: left;
    width: 300px;
    height: 125px;
}
.panel-inner {
    position: absolute;
    left: 0;
    height: 125px;
    list-style: none;
    margin: 0;
    padding: 0;
}
.panel-inner li {
    text-align: center;
    padding: 0;
    margin: 1px 1px 0 0;
    float: left;
    width: 100px;
    height: 125px;
    background: #FFF;
}
.panel-inner li img {
    width: 100px;
    height: 125px;
    margin: 1px 0 0 1px;
}
```

How to code the CSS for a carousel

- Copy the CSS above into the CSS file for the web page. Or, save the above CSS in a new CSS file and add a link that includes that file for the web page.

- To change the size of the images, the space between them, and the number of images that are shown at one time, you can adjust the height, width, and margin properties for the elements of the carousel.

Figure 14-4 jQuery for carousels (part 2 of 2)

jQuery for slide shows

Figure 14-5 shows how to use jQuery to create a *slide show*. When the page loads, the first image is displayed. Then, every five seconds, the image fades out and the next image fades into its place.

To code the HTML for a slide show, you code one div element that contains as many img elements as you want. This is illustrated by the HTML in this example. As you can see, the class attribute for the div element must be set to "fadein".

To use the script for a slide show, just copy the script element in this figure into the head section of the HTML. Here again, this script element must come after the script element that includes the jQuery library, and the jQuery UI library isn't required. And here again, you could copy the script into a new file and include that file instead of embedding the script in the head section.

If you want to change the speed at which the slides are displayed, you can change the 5000 milliseconds (5 seconds) to a smaller or larger number. Similarly, if you want to change the speed at which the slides fade out and in, you can change the 1000 millisecond values to smaller or larger numbers.

Like the carousel application, this application requires some CSS. This time, the width and height properties are used to set the size of the division that's used for the slide show. And the position properties are used to place each image within the division starting in the upper-left corner.

Unlike the carousel application, you can't make the images in the slide show clickable by coding them within <a> elements. If you do that, the slide show won't work correctly.

A slide show that fades one image out and the next image in

The script element for the slide show

```
<script>
    $(function(){
        $('.fadein img:gt(0)').hide();
        setInterval(function(){
            $('.fadein :first-child').fadeOut(1000)
                .next('img').fadeIn(1000)
                .end().appendTo('.fadein');}, 5000);
    });
</script>
```

The HTML for the slide show

```
<div class="fadein">
    <img src="images/book1.jpg" alt="SQL Server 2008 for Developers">
    <img src="images/book2.jpg" alt="PHP and MySQL">
    <img src="images/book3.jpg" alt="Visual Basic 2010">
</div>
```

The CSS for the slide show

```
.fadein {
    position: relative;
    width: 200px;
    height: 250px; }
.fadein img { position: absolute; }
```

How to code the HTML for a slide show

- Code a div element with "fadein" as its class name. Within this element, code as many img elements as you need for the slide show.

How to code the script for a slide show

- Copy the script element shown above into the head section after the script elements that include the jQuery files.

- To adjust the speed of the slideshow, change the 5000 milliseconds (5 seconds) to a smaller or larger value. To change the fade-out and fade-in time, change the 1000 milliseconds to smaller or larger values.

Figure 14-5   jQuery for slide shows

How to use four of the jQuery UI features

Next, you're going to learn how to use four of the jQuery UI features. As you will see, using these features requires smaller scripts and less CSS than using jQuery features.

jQuery UI for accordions

Figure 14-6 shows how to build an *accordion* using jQuery and jQuery UI. An accordion consists of two or more panels that you can open by clicking on the heading for a panel. These panels open by sliding up or down, depending on the location of the panel.

The HTML for an accordion consists of one div element with "accordion" as its id that contains one h3 element followed by a div element for each panel in the accordion. In this example, the accordion consists of three panels so there are three h3 elements and each is followed by a div element.

Within each h3 element, you code an <a> element with its href attribute set to a hash value (#). Then, for the contents of the <a> element, you code the heading that you want for the panel.

Within each div element for a panel, you can code whatever HTML elements you want. For instance, you could code a heading, an image, one or more paragraphs, and an <a> element. You'll see that illustrated in the web page at the end of this chapter.

To use the script for an accordion, you just copy the script element in this figure at the end of the head section, after the script elements for the jQuery and jQuery UI files. This shows the power of jQuery UI. With one line of code within a ready function, the accordion is implemented. And this application doesn't require any CSS code either, although you'll typically use CSS to format the elements that you code for the contents of the panels.

An accordion within a web page

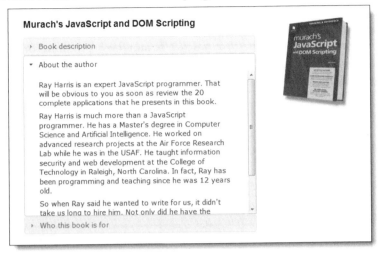

The script element for the accordion

```
<script>
    $(function() {
        $("#accordion").accordion();
    });
</script>
```

The HTML for the accordion

```
<div id="accordion">
    <h3><a href="#">Book description</a></h3>
    <div> <!-- panel contents --> </div>
    <h3><a href="#">About the author</a></h3>
    <div> <!-- panel contents --> </div>
    <h3><a href="#">Who this book is for</a></h3>
    <div> <!-- panel contents --> </div>
</div>
```

How to code the HTML for an accordion

- Code a div element with "accordion" as its id.
- For the title of each panel in the accordion, code an <a> element within an h3 element. In each <a> element, the href attribute should contain a # symbol, and the content should be the title of the panel.
- For the contents of each panel, code a div element that contains whatever HTML elements the content requires.

Description

- The jQuery accordion method creates the accordion from the HTML.
- The basic formatting of the accordion is done by jQuery UI, but you can use CSS to format the contents within the panels.
- The script in the head section must come after the scripts that include the jQuery files.

Figure 14-6   jQuery UI for accordions

jQuery UI for auto-completion

Figure 14-7 shows how to implement the *auto-completion* feature with jQuery UI. When this feature is implemented for a text box and the user starts an entry, a list of possible entries drops down from the box. Then, the user can select one of the entries by clicking on it or by pressing the down-arrow key to cycle through the words and the Enter key to select a word.

To code the HTML for a text box that uses this feature, you code a label and text box within a div element. For the div element, you use "ui-widget" as the value for the class attribute. For the text box, you use an id attribute that can be referred to by the script. But note that the input element for the text box doesn't include a type attribute that specifies what kind of input should be rendered by the browser. Instead, jQuery UI will see to it that the input element is rendered as a text or search box.

To code the script for this feature, you can start by copying the script element in this figure into the head section of the HTML, after the script elements for the jQuery and jQuery UI files. Then, within this script, you need to change the variable name that's used (murachBooks) and the list of words for the completion list. You also need to change the selector for the autocomplete method to the id you used for the input element in the HTML. Last, you need to change the source name to the variable name that you used for the list of words.

You can of course use this feature for more than one text box on a web page. For each text box, you just need a unique id in the HTML and a unique variable name in the script.

A text box that that displays an auto-completion list

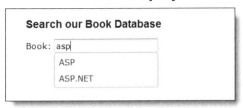

The script element for auto-completion

```
<script>
    $(function() {
        var murachBooks =
            ["ASP", "ASP.NET", "C#", "C++", "CICS", "CSS", "COBOL",
            "DB2", "HTML", "IMS", "Java", "JavaScript", "LINQ", "OS/390",
            "PHP", "VB", "VB.NET", "Visual Basic", "Web Development",
            "Web Programming", "XHTML", "z/OS JCL"];
        $("#books").autocomplete({
            source: murachBooks
        });
    });
</script>
```

The HTML for the text box

```
<h1>Search our Book Database</h1><br>
<div class="ui-widget">
    <label for="books">Book: </label>
    <input id="books">
</div>
```

How to code the HTML for the text box

- Code a div element with "ui-widget" as its class. This is a jQuery UI class name that is used to style the text box and the auto-completion list.
- Within the div element, code a label element and an input element, and code the for attribute of the label so it points to the id of the input element.

How to code the script for auto-completion

- Copy the script element shown above into the head section after the script elements that include the jQuery files.
- Replace the variable (var) name "murachBooks" with a name of your choosing, and code a list of the words for the auto-completion list between the brackets.
- Replace the selector "#books" with the id of the input element in the HTML code. Replace the source name with the name you used for the variable.

Figure 14-7   jQuery UI for auto-completion

jQuery UI for popup dialog boxes

Figure 14-8 shows a *popup dialog box* that pops open when the user clicks on the smaller book image on the right. Once the dialog box appears, the user can move it by dragging its heading bar, close it by clicking on the x in its heading bar, or resize it by dragging the resize handle in the lower-right corner. The jQuery dialog box is a good alternative to opening a browser window with JavaScript, as shown in figure 13-5, since most browsers block that type of popup window.

To code the HTML for a dialog box, you code a div element with its id attribute set to "dialog" and its title attribute set to the title that you want in the heading bar. You also need to code a style attribute that sets the display property to "none" so the dialog box isn't displayed when the page is loaded.

Then, within this div element, you can code whatever you want to include in the dialog box. In this example, the dialog box contains just one image, but it could include a heading, image, text, and more. You'll see that illustrated in the web page at the end of this chapter.

Besides the HTML for the dialog box, you need to set up an image or some other clickable object that can be used to pop open the dialog box. In this example, the clickable object is an image with its id set to "book", but you can change the id so it's appropriate for the object that you're using.

To code the script that makes the dialog box work, you can start by copying the script element in this figure into the head section of the HTML, after the script elements for the jQuery and jQuery UI files. Then, you need to change the id selectors so they refer to the ids that you used in the HTML. If you want to change the width of the dialog box, you can also change the 300 value that's highlighted to a larger or smaller value. By default, this value is 300 pixels, and you can't change it by using CSS to set the width of the div element.

In case you're interested, the code in this script sets up an event handler for the click event of the object with "book" as its id, but only after the ready method has been executed and the DOM has been built. This event handler runs the dialog method of the div element with "dialog" as its id. This means that the dialog box is opened when the book image is clicked.

A dialog box that opens when the image on the right is clicked

The script element for the dialog box

```
<script>
    $(function() {
        $("#book").click(function(event){
            $("#dialog").dialog({width:300});
        });
    });
</script>
```

The HTML for the dialog box

```
<h1>Featured Book</h1>
<img src="images/javascriptbook.jpg" id="book" width="159" height="192">
<div id="dialog" title="JavaScript and DOM Scripting"
    style="display:none;">
    <img src="images/javascriptbook_300.jpg" width="250" height="313">
</div>
```

How to code the HTML for the dialog box

- Code an element that can be used to start a click event that can be used to open the dialog box, and give it an id attribute that can be used by the script.
- Code a div element that will serve as the dialog box that will pop open. Use "dialog" as its id, code a title attribute that will be displayed in the header of the dialog box, and code a style attribute of "display:none" to prevent the dialog box from appearing when the page is loaded.
- In the div element, code whatever elements you want for the contents of the dialog box.

How to code the script for a dialog box

- Copy the script element shown above into the head section after the script elements for the jQuery files. Then, replace the ids in the code with the ids in the HTML.
- If necessary, you can also change the width of the dialog box by modifying the width parameter, which by default is 300 pixels.

Figure 14-8   jQuery UI for popup dialog boxes

jQuery UI for sortable lists

Figure 14-9 shows how to use jQuery UI to create a *sortable list*. When you use this feature, a list is displayed when the web page is loaded. Then, the user can drag the items in the list to new locations.

To code the HTML for a sortable list, you code a ul element with "sortable" as its id that contains one li element for each item in the list. For each li item, you use the same class name that's shown in the example in this figure. Then, for the content of each li item, you code an empty span tag with the class name shown in this example. This is used by jQuery UI to set the double-arrow icon that's shown to the left of each item. After the span tag, you code the text that you want to use for the item.

To code the script that makes the sortable list work, you can copy the script element in this figure into the head section of your HTML, but after the script elements for the jQuery and jQuery UI files. Unless you change the name that you use for the ul element for the list, you won't have to change any of this code. In case you're interested, the last line in this script calls the disableSelection method. This method prevents the text within the li element from being accidentally selected while the user is dragging an item.

A sortable list as one of the items is dragged upward

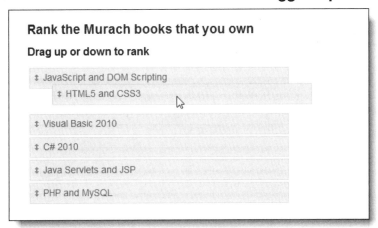

The script element for the sortable list

```
<script>
    $(function() {
        $("#sortable").sortable();
        $("#sortable").disableSelection();
    });
</script>
```

The HTML for the sortable list

```
<ul id="sortable">
    <li class="ui-state-default">
        <span class="ui-icon ui-icon-arrowthick-2-n-s"></span>
        JavaScript and DOM Scripting</li>
    <li class="ui-state-default">
        <span class="ui-icon ui-icon-arrowthick-2-n-s"></span>
        Visual Basic 2010</li>
    <!-- Add as many list items as you want -->
</ul>
```

How to code the HTML for a sortable list

- Code a ul element with "sortable" as its id. Within this element, code the li elements for the items in your list and use the class name shown above for each element. This class is used by jQuery UI to style the items.
- After the opening tag for each li element, code an empty span element with the class attribute shown above. This class name represents the small double-arrowhead icon that appears to the left of each item in the list.
- After the span element, code the text for the sortable item. This is what the user will see in the list.

How to code the script for a sortable list

- Copy the script element shown above into the head section after the script elements for the jQuery files.

Figure 14-9   jQuery UI for sortable lists (part 1 of 2)

When you use a sortable list, you will need to provide some CSS for it. This is illustrated by the CSS in part 2 of this figure. In particular, you need to provide CSS for the span elements in the list. Here, each span element is positioned absolutely starting in the upper-left corner of the li element. Then, the margin-left property is set to -1.3 ems so the double-arrow icons are to the left of the text for the item.

You might also want to change the height, width, or margins of some of the elements in the list. If you experiment with these settings, you'll see how easy it is to get your sortable list looking the way you want it.

The CSS for the sortable list in part 1 of this figure

```
/* the styles for the sortable list */
#sortable {
    list-style-type: none;
    margin: 0;
    padding: 0;
    width: 80%;
}
#sortable li {
    margin: 0 3px 3px 3px;
    padding: 0.4em;
    padding-left: 1.5em;
    height: 18px;
}
#sortable li span {
    position: absolute;
    margin-left: -1.3em;
}
```

How to code the CSS for a sortable list

- Copy the CSS above into the CSS file for the web page. Or, save the above CSS in a new CSS file and add a link that includes that file for the web page.

- To adjust the height, width, and margins of the items in the sortable list, you can change the properties highlighted above.

- To adjust the location of the icon to the left of each item, you can change the margin-left property of the span element.

Figure 14-9   jQuery UI for sortable lists (part 2 of 2)

A web page that uses jQuery

Now that you've seen how you can use jQuery and jQuery UI to add special features to your web pages, it's time to put it all together into a more realistic web page that uses two of these features.

The page layout

Figure 14-10 shows another version of the Town Hall home page. This time it uses an accordion to list the six speakers for the year. Then, if the user clicks on one of the headings in the accordion, the content for that speaker is displayed. In this example, the user has clicked on the fourth heading so that panel is displayed. It contains a heading, an image that has been floated left, a paragraph of text, and a link that the user can click on to go to the page for that speaker.

This web page also uses a popup dialog box that is displayed when the user clicks on the small image of this month's speaker. The content of this dialog box contains a heading, an image, and a paragraph.

The Town Hall home page with an accordion and a popup dialog box

Description

- This web page contains an accordion and a dialog box that pops up when the user clicks on the speaker of the month.

- As you can see in the accordion for the fourth speaker, the contents include a heading, an image, a paragraph, and a link.

- As you can see in the dialog box, the contents include a heading, an image, and a paragraph.

Figure 14-10   The Town Hall home page with an accordion and a popup dialog box

The HTML for the accordion and the popup dialog box

Figure 14-11 shows the HTML for the accordion and dialog box. In the head section, you can see the script element that contains the script that implements these features. Here, the script sets up the accordion and dialog box, but only after the DOM has been built.

The first statement in this script sets up the event handler for the click event of the image that has "speaker" as its id. Later, when the user clicks on the image, this event handler is executed. Then, it calls the dialog method, which pops open the dialog box for the div element that has "dialog" as its id. Since the width parameter for this method is set to 400 pixels, that's what the width of the dialog box will be.

The next statement runs the accordion method of the div element that has "accordion" as its id. But note that both the dialog box and the accordion are set up within one ready function. That makes sense because the statements for both of these features need to be run after the DOM is ready. If you were to add other jQuery features to this application, you could also code them within this one ready function.

In the HTML for the dialog box that's coded in the aside element, you can see the contents for that box. It contains an h2 element, an img element, and a <p> element. This shows that you can include whatever content you want in a dialog box.

In the HTML for the accordion that's coded in the section element, you can see the contents for the fourth speaker. It consists of an h2 element, an img element within an <a> element, a <p> element, and another <a> element within a <p> element. This means that the user can click on the image or the link at the end of the contents to go to the web page for the speaker.

The HTML for the accordion and dialog box

```html
<head>
    <!-- the normal elements for the head section -->
    <!-- the link and script elements for the jQuery files -->
    <script>
        $(function() {
            $("#speaker").click(function(event){
                $("#dialog").dialog({width:400});
            });
            $("#accordion").accordion();
        });
    </script>
</head>

<body>
<aside>
    <h1>This month's speaker</h1>
    <img src="images/sampson75.jpg" id="speaker" alt="Scott Sampson">
    <div id="dialog" title="February 15, 2012: Scott Sampson"
        style="display:none">
        <h2>Fossil Threads in the Web of Life</h2>
        <img src="images/sampson_dinosaur.jpg"
            alt="Scott Sampson" width="260">
        <p>What's 75 million years old and brand spanking new? Find out
            this month by attending Scott Sampson's fascinating
            presentation.
        </p>
    </div>
    <!-- the rest of the aside -->
</aside>
<section>
    <h1>2011-2012 guest speakers</h1>
    <div id="accordion">
        <!-- the h3 and div elements for the first 3 speakers -->
        <h3><a href="#">February 15, 2012: Scott Sampson</a></h3>
        <div>
            <h2>Fossil Threads in the Web of Life</h2>
            <a href="sampson.html">
                <img src="images/sampson75.jpg" alt="Scott Sampson">
            </a>
            <p>What's 75 million years old and brand spanking new? A teenage
                Utahceratops! Come to the Saroyan, armed with your best
                ...
                ...
                of countries in Africa.</p>
            <p><a href="sampson.html">For more, click here</a></p>
        </div>
        <!-- the h3 and div elements for the last 2 speakers -->
    </div>
    <br>
    <h2>Looking for a unique gift?</h2>
    <!-- the rest of the section -->
</section>
```

Figure 14-11   The HTML for the accordion and the popup dialog box

The CSS for the accordion
and the popup dialog box

Figure 14-12 presents the CSS for just the accordion and the popup dialog box. This shows how you can use CSS to format the contents of each panel in an accordion and the contents of a dialog box. For example, the height of the accordion is set to 220 pixels, and that becomes the height of each panel. Also, the images within the accordion panels have been floated left and the padding has been set so there is adequate space between the image and the text that flows around it.

Similarly, the margins and padding have been set for the contents of the popup dialog box. But remember that the height and width properties can't be used to set the size of the dialog box. To do that, you need to change the width parameter in the script for the dialog box, which for this dialog box has been set to 400 pixels.

The CSS for the accordion and dialog box

```css
#accordion div {
    height: 220px;
}
#accordion img {
    padding: .5em 1em .5em 0;
    border: none;
    float: left;
}
#dialog h2 {
    color: blue;
    margin: 0;
    padding: .5em 0;
}
#dialog p {
    margin: 0;
    padding: .5em 0;
}
```

Description

* This shows how you can use CSS to format the HTML in an accordion or dialog box.

Figure 14-12   The CSS for the accordion and the popup dialog box

Perspective

Now that you've completed this chapter, you should be able to use jQuery and jQuery UI to add features to your web pages. Besides the ones presented in this chapter, you may be able to find others that you can implement by searching the web. You may also be able to find jQuery plug-ins that implement the features that you're looking for. Although it would be even better to learn how to write your own jQuery code, this is a quick way to implement the features that you want without learning JavaScript and jQuery.

Terms

jQuery
jQuery UI
CDN (Content Delivery Network)
object
method
script
carousel
slide show
accordion
auto-completion
popup dialog box
sortable list

Summary

- *jQuery* is a JavaScript library that makes it easier to use JavaScript features that have been tested for cross-browser compatibility.

- *jQuery UI* is a related JavaScript library that uses the jQuery library to build higher-level features.

- To use the jQuery and jQuery UI libraries, you code script elements in the head section that load these files with the web page. Because jQuery UI uses jQuery, the script element for jQuery UI must be coded after the one for jQuery.

- When you code statements that use jQuery, you use selectors that are much like those for CSS. You also use a dot syntax that consists of the selector for one or more elements (or *objects*), the dot, and the name of the *method* that should be executed.

- Six common uses of jQuery and jQuery UI that can be copied into your own pages are *carousels*, *slide shows*, *accordions*, *auto-completion*, *popup dialog boxes*, and *sortable lists*.

Exercise 14-1   Use jQuery for a carousel

In this exercise, you'll enhance a page so it uses jQuery for a carousel.

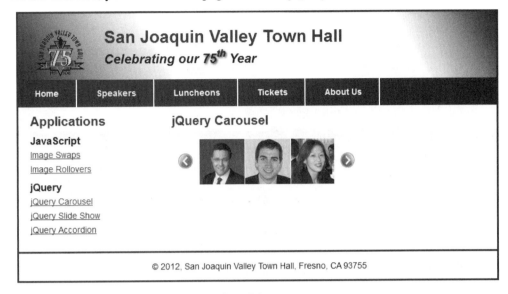

Open the HTML and CSS files for this page

1. Use your text editor to open the HTML and CSS files for this page:

    `c:\html5_css3\exercises\town_hall_3\speakers\carousel.html`

    `c:\html5_css3\exercises\town_hall_3\styles\speakers_pages.css`

2. Test the file in Firefox and see that it shows six images in a row. These are the images that you will use in the carousel.

3. Review the code in the head section and note that it contains all of the JavaScript code that you need for the carousel.

Enhance the HTML and CSS for this page

4. Using figure 14-4 as a guide, enhance the HTML code so it will work properly with the JavaScript and jQuery code. Then, test this page to see that CSS is desperately needed.

5. Copy the CSS that's shown in figure 14-4 from the chapter application to the CSS file for this page. Then, test this page again. The carousel should work, but its formatting won't be like the one above.

6. Modify the CSS for the carousel until the carousel looks and works the way you want it to.

Exercise 14-2   Use jQuery for a slide show

In this exercise, you'll enhance a page so it uses JavaScript and jQuery to run a slide show. This exercise is like the earlier ones in this section, but this time you will copy the JavaScript and CSS code into the HTML and CSS files for this application. That's a common way to develop an application like this.

Copy the required HTML and CSS into the exercise files

1. Open the HTML and CSS files for this page:

    ```
    c:\html5_css3\exercises\town_hall_3\speakers\slideshow.html
    c:\html5_css3\exercises\town_hall_3\styles\speakers_pages.css
    ```

2. Open the HTML and CSS files for the slide show example:

    ```
    c:\murach\html5_css3\book_examples\ch14\05_slide_show\index.html
    c:\murach\html5_css3\book_examples\ch14\05_slide_show\styles\main.css
    ```

3. Copy the script elements for the slide show from the HTML file for the example to the head section of the HTML file for the exercise.

4. Copy the CSS rule sets for the slide show from the CSS file for the example to the CSS file for the exercise.

Modify the HTML, test it, and experiment

5. Using figure 14-5 as a guide, modify the HTML for the exercise so it will work for the slide show. Then, test the slide show. It should work, although the formatting may not be exactly the way you want it.

6. If you have the time, adjust the formatting and experiment with the fadeIn and fadeOut values in the script element of the head section.

15

How to use jQuery Mobile to build mobile web sites

In sections 1 and 2, you learned how to create and format web pages that will be displayed on a computer screen. Now, you'll learn how to create web pages that are displayed on mobile devices like cell phones, tablets, and PDAs. To do that, you'll use an exciting new jQuery library called jQuery Mobile.

How to work with mobile devices

Many different types of mobile devices are in use today, and these devices are frequently used to access web sites. Because the screens on these devices are much smaller than standard computer screens, a web site that's designed to be used on the desktop can be difficult to work with on a mobile device. To accommodate mobile users, then, web developers typically provide pages that are designed specifically for mobile devices.

How to provide pages for mobile devices

Figure 15-1 presents five ways to provide web pages for mobile devices. To start, you can use a style sheet for the "handheld" media type. Unfortunately, that media type is considered antiquated and not all mobile browsers recognize it. That includes the Safari browser used by Apple's iPhone, current versions of the Opera Mobile and Opera Mini browsers, and others. These browsers support the standard screen media type instead of the handheld type.

On the other hand, iPhone's Safari and other mobile browsers including Opera's Mobile and Mini browsers do support a new feature of CSS3 called *media queries*. These queries let you use a conditional expression for a media type. If, for example, the maximum screen width for a mobile device is 480 pixels, you can code a link element like this if you want to use a different style sheet for those devices:

```
<link rel="stylesheet" href="styles/mobile.css"
      media="only screen and (max-device-width: 480px)">
```

Then, you can code another link element for screen media with a minimum screen width of 481 pixels. The style sheet for this element would then be used for standard computer screens.

The next technique requires that you develop a separate web site for mobile devices. When you use this technique, you include a link on the home page that lets the user switch to the mobile version of the site. The trouble with this is that users don't always enter a site at the home page, so you may need to provide links to the mobile site on other pages.

When you use the last three techniques in this figure, the web site detects when a mobile device is being used and then redirects the user to the mobile version of the site automatically. This is what is done on most commercial web sites that service many mobile device users. For these sites, one common convention for the mobile site name is to precede the domain name for the main site with m and a period as in m.yahoo.com.

To detect a mobile device, a web site can use JavaScript on the client, a scripting language on the server, or *WURFL* on the server. Because this book isn't about JavaScript or server-side programming, though, these techniques aren't presented in this book. Instead, this chapter shows you how to develop the web pages for a mobile web site, which you need to learn how to do no matter how the user gets to that site.

Define a style sheet for mobile devices

- One way to define a style sheet for mobile devices is to set the media attribute in the link element to "handheld". However, many mobile browsers don't recognize this media type.

- CSS3 provides a new feature called *media queries* that gives you more control over the style sheet for a web page. The downside is that older browsers don't support this feature so this technique isn't backward compatible. For more information, see http://www.w3.org/TR/css3-mediaqueries/.

Include a link to a mobile version of the web site

- When you use this technique, you display the desktop version of the web site no matter what device accesses it. Then, you include a link to a mobile version of the site near the top of the home page.

Use JavaScript to detect mobile devices and redirect

- When you use this technique, you use JavaScript to detect mobile devices. Then, if a mobile device is detected, the user is redirected to the mobile version of the web site.

- The problem with this is that there are so many different mobile devices that it's difficult to detect them all. Also, some mobile devices don't support JavaScript.

Use a server-side scripting language to detect and redirect

- With this technique, you use a server-side scripting language such as PHP to detect mobile devices. To do that, the script looks at the web browser that made the request to see if a mobile device is being used. If so, the user is redirected to the mobile version of the web site.

- The problem with this is that there are so many mobile browsers that it's difficult to detect them all.

Use the WURFL to detect mobile devices

- The *WURFL* (*Wireless Universal Resource File*) is an XML configuration file that contains information about a variety of mobile devices, including the features and capabilities they support. This file is updated frequently with new devices.

- To use the WURFL, you implement the API (Application Programming Interface) using languages such as Java, PHP, C++, or C#.NET. This API lets you determine the browser that's being used and then retrieve information about that browser from the XML file. When you use this technique, you have to download the XML configuration file periodically so it's up-to-date.

Description

- At present, the best way to provide for mobile devices is to redirect the user to a mobile version of the main web site. That can be done by providing a link to the mobile version or by automatically detecting mobile devices and redirecting them to that version.

- To detect mobile devices, you can use the last three techniques above. However, these techniques aren't illustrated in this chapter. Instead, this chapter assumes that you'll provide a link to a mobile version of your web site.

Figure 15-1   How to provide pages for mobile devices

How to set the viewport properties

When you develop a web site for mobile devices, you can use a special meta element that lets you configure a device's *viewport*. This meta element is presented in figure 15-2.

To start, you should know that the viewport on a mobile device works differently from the viewport on a computer screen. On a computer screen, the viewport is the visible area of the web page. However, the user can change the size of the viewport by changing the size of the browser window.

In contrast, the viewport on a mobile device can be larger or smaller than the visible area and determines how the page content appears in that area. In this figure, for example, you can see that the first web page is displayed so almost all of the width of the page is visible. In contrast, the second web page extends beyond the visible area of the screen. Because this display is larger, however, it's easier to work with.

To configure the viewport, you use a meta element with the name attribute set to "viewport". Then, for the content attribute, you can specify any of the properties listed in this figure to set the dimensions and scaling of the web page within the mobile device.

The two coding examples in this figure illustrate how this meta element works. The first example sets the width of the viewport to the width of the mobile device. You can use this setting if a page is wider than the device width but narrower than the default viewport width. Then, the page will be enlarged so it fills the visible area. Because this example also sets the user-scalable property to "no", the user can't zoom in or out of the page.

The second example shows the code that is used for the pages in the rest of this chapter. Here again, this example sets the width of the viewport to the width of the mobile device, but it also sets the zoom factor, or *scale*, for the viewport. In this case, this scale is set to 1, which represents the default width for the viewport. For the iPhone, that means the viewport width is set to 320 pixels.

If you want the viewport to appear to be larger or smaller, you can change the initial scale to a value that is higher or lower than 1. This is illustrated by the two screens in this figure. Since the HTML for the first screen doesn't include a viewport meta element, its initial scale is 1 and the content for this full screen is small. For the second screen, though, a meta element sets the initial scale to .5. As a result, a smaller portion of the page is shown on a mobile device, but what's shown is easier to read because it's larger.

A web page on an iPhone before and after scaling

No viewport meta element

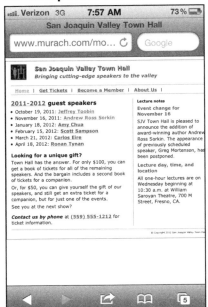

width=device-width, initial-scale=.5

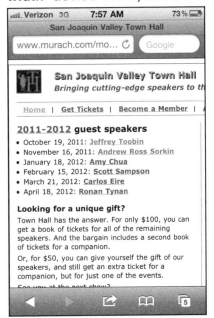

Content properties for viewport metadata

Property	Description
width	The width of the viewport in pixels. You can also use the device-width keyword to indicate that the viewport should be as wide as the screen.
height	The height of the viewport specified in pixels. You can also use the device-height keyword to indicate that the viewport should be as tall as the screen.
initial-scale	A number that indicates the initial zoom factor that's used to display the page.
minimum-scale	A number that indicates the minimum zoom factor for the page.
maximum-scale	A number that indicates the maximum zoom factor for the page.
user-scalable	Indicates whether the user can zoom in and out of the viewport. Possible values are yes and no.

Meta elements that set viewport properties

```
<meta name="viewport" content="width=device-width, user-scalable=no">
<meta name="viewport" content="width=device-width, initial-scale=1">
```

Description

- The *viewport* on a mobile device determines the content that's displayed on the page. It can be larger or smaller than the actual visible area of the screen.

Figure 15-2   How to set the viewport properties

Guidelines for designing mobile web pages

If you create web pages specifically for mobile devices, you should follow some general guidelines so it's easy for users to work with those pages. Figure 15-3 presents these guidelines.

In general, you want to simplify the layout and content of your pages. This is illustrated by the two pages in this figure. The first shows the home page for the mobile version of a large web site. Here, the page consists primarily of links to the major types of products that the site offers. The second page shows how the page for one product has been simplified. If you review the full version of this site, you'll get a better idea of just how much the full version has been simplified.

Guidelines for testing mobile web pages

Because there are so many different mobile devices, it's important to test a mobile web page on as many devices and in as many browsers as possible. Although the best way to test a mobile web page is to deploy the page on a web server and then display it on a variety of devices, that isn't always possible. In that case, you may want to use the device emulators and browser simulators that are available for many of the mobile devices and browsers.

In most cases, you need to download the required emulator or simulator from the manufacturer's web site so you can run it on your desktop. In a few cases, though, you can run the emulator or simulator online. To do that, though, you sometimes need to deploy the web page so it can be accessed online. Also, when you use an emulator or a simulator, it may not always provide accurate results, although it should approximate what a page will look like.

To capture the screens for this chapter, I used my iPhone. To do that, I first deployed the pages to my web server. Then, I used the Safari browser on my iPhone to display the pages. To capture each page image, I held down the Home button and pressed the Power button. After I captured all of the page images, I copied the images from my iPhone to my computer.

If you don't have a web server that you can deploy the mobile pages on, one easy option is to size your browser window so it's about the size of a mobile device. That will give you a good idea of what the pages will look like on a mobile device. Another option is to use the iPhone simulator that's available at

`www.testiphone.com`

With this simulator, you can paste the location of a page on your computer into the address bar and click the Refresh button to display the page.

Two pages from the mobile web site for www.orvis.com

The Home page

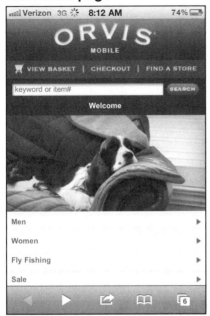

A product page

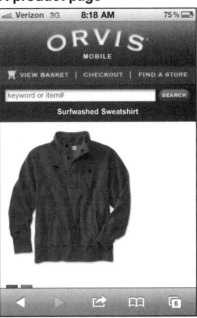

Guidelines for designing mobile web pages

- Keep your layout simple so the focus is on the content. One-column layouts typically work best.
- Include only essential content.
- Keep images small and to a minimum.
- Avoid using Flash. Most mobile devices, including the iPhone don't support it.
- Include only the essential navigation in the header of the page. The other navigation should be part of the content for the page.
- Make links and other elements large enough that the user can easily manipulate them.
- Use relative measurements so the page looks good regardless of the scale.

Guidelines for testing mobile web pages

- Test all pages on as many different mobile devices and in as many different mobile browsers as possible.
- The best way to test mobile web pages is to deploy them to your Internet server and test them on the devices themselves.
- When you can't test your pages on the devices themselves, you can use device emulators and browser simulators.

Figure 15-3   Guidelines for designing and testing mobile web pages

An introduction to jQuery Mobile

In chapter 14, you learned how to use jQuery to enhance your web pages. Now, in this chapter, you'll learn how to use the new jQuery Mobile library to develop mobile web sites. Although there are other ways to develop mobile web sites, we think jQuery Mobile sets a standard that other development methods are going to have a hard time beating.

What jQuery Mobile is and where to get it

As figure 15-4 summarizes, *jQuery Mobile* is a free, open-source, cross-platform, JavaScript library that you can use for developing mobile web sites. This library lets you create pages that look and feel like the pages of a native mobile application.

Although jQuery Mobile is currently available as a beta test version, this version already provides all of the features that you need for developing an excellent mobile web site. As a result, you can start using it right away. You can also expect this version to be continually enhanced, so jQuery Mobile will only get better.

To include jQuery Mobile in your pages, you can use a Content Delivery Network as shown in the next figure. Otherwise, you will need to download the files that it requires. To download the jQuery library that jQuery Mobile requires, go to the jQuery web site that you learned about in the last chapter. To get the jQuery Mobile files, go to the jQuery Mobile web site.

The jQuery Mobile web site (www.jquerymobile.com)

The two jQuery libraries that you need

- jQuery (the core library)
- jQuery Mobile

Description

- jQuery Mobile is a free, open-source, JavaScript library that makes it much easier to develop web sites for mobile devices. It is used in combination with the core jQuery library.

- jQuery Mobile lets you store multiple pages in a single HTML file, create dialog boxes, buttons, and navigation bars; format your pages without coding your own CSS; lay out pages with two columns, collapsible content blocks, and accordions; and much more.

- jQuery Mobile is supported by most devices including iPhone iOS, Android, BlackBerry, Windows Phone, Palm WebOS, and Symbian.

- The jQuery Mobile web site features all of the documentation, sample code, and downloads that you need for beginning your work with mobile devices.

- To download jQuery Mobile, go to its web site (www.jquerymobile.com). However, you won't need to do that if you include it from a Content Deliver Network (see figure 15-5).

Figure 15-4   What jQuery Mobile is and where to get it

How to include jQuery Mobile in your web pages

To use jQuery Mobile, you need to include the three files listed at the top of figure 15-5 in your web pages: the jQuery file, the jQuery Mobile file, and the jQuery Mobile CSS style sheet. As this figure shows, there are two ways to do that.

The first way to include the three files is illustrated by the first set of examples in this figure. Here, the link element for the CSS file and the script elements for the jQuery and jQuery Mobile files use a *Content Delivery Network (CDN)*. A CDN is a web server that hosts open-source software, and Microsoft and jQuery are the only CDNs at this writing that you can use for getting the jQuery Mobile library. In this example, the jQuery CDN is used.

The benefit to using a CDN is that you don't have to manage the jQuery and jQuery Mobile versions on your server as new ones become available. Instead, you just have to change the version numbers in the link and script elements for these files.

The second way is to download the three files and deploy them on your system or web server. To do that, you download the compressed zip files, extract the files from the zip files, and copy the files to your web server.

Then, for each web page that uses jQuery Mobile, you code one link element that includes the CSS file and two script elements that include the jQuery and jQuery Mobile files. This is illustrated by the second set of examples in this figure. Here, the names for the current versions of the files are retained. Although you can change those names once they're on your server, keeping the downloaded names makes it easy to tell which versions of the files you're using.

No matter which method you use, you must code the script element for jQuery Mobile after the one for jQuery. That's because jQuery Mobile uses functions that are in the jQuery file.

The three files that you need to include for jQuery applications

- The jQuery JavaScript file
- The jQuery Mobile JavaScript file
- The jQuery Mobile CSS style sheet

Two ways to include the jQuery files

- Include the files from a Content Delivery Network (CDN) like Microsoft or jQuery.
- Download and deploy the files on your web server. Then, include them from the server.

How to include the jQuery Mobile files from a Content Delivery Network

```
<!-- include the jQuery Mobile stylesheet -->
<link rel="stylesheet"
    href="http://code.jquery.com/mobile/1.0b3/jquery.mobile-1.0b3.min.css">

<!-- include the jQuery and jQuery Mobile JavaScript files -->
<script src="http://code.jquery.com/jquery-1.6.3.min.js"></script>
<script
    src="http://code.jquery.com/mobile/1.0b3/jquery.mobile-1.0b3.min.js">
</script>
```

How to include the jQuery Mobile files when they're on your web server

```
<!-- include the jQuery Mobile stylesheet -->
<link rel="stylesheet" href="jquery.mobile-1.0b3.min.css">

<!-- include the jQuery and jQuery Mobile JavaScript files -->
<script src="jquery-1.6.3.min.js"></script>
<script src="jquery.mobile-1.0b3.min.js"></script>
```

Description

- To use jQuery, you need to include the three files shown above. The first two are the JavaScript files for jQuery and jQuery Mobile. The third is the CSS file for the jQuery Mobile style sheet.
- jQuery Mobile is currently in a beta release, but it is continually being improved and enhanced, so check the web site often for the latest version.
- At this writing, only Microsoft and jQuery provide *Content Delivery Networks (CDNs)* that can be used to access the jQuery Mobile files.
- The jQuery and jQuery Mobile filenames always include the version number. At this writing, the latest version of jQuery Mobile is 1.0b3, where b3 means "beta 3."
- If you download and deploy the jQuery files to your system, you can change the filenames so they're simpler. But that way, you can lose track of what versions you're using and when you need to upgrade to newer versions.

Figure 15-5   How to include jQuery Mobile in your web pages

How to create one web page with jQuery Mobile

To give you an idea of how jQuery Mobile works, figure 15-6 shows how to create one web page with it. In the HTML for a page, you use data-role attributes to identify the components of the page: page, header, content, and footer. You also use an h1 element for the content of the header, and an h4 element for the content of the footer.

In the page that's displayed, you can see how jQuery Mobile automatically formats these components. Here the text for both the header and footer is centered in white type against a black background, while the text for the content is black against a gray background. This is the default styling that's done by jQuery Mobile, and it's similar to the styling for a native iPhone application.

Within the header, footer, and content components, you can code the HTML for whatever content you need. You'll see this illustrated in the examples that follow. However, this simple example should give you some idea of how easy it is to code and format a single web page.

A web page that uses jQuery Mobile

The HTML for the mobile web page

```
<div data-role="page">
    <header data-role="header">
        <h1>Header</h1>
    </header>

    <section data-role="content">
        <p>The page content</p>
    </section>

    <footer data-role="footer">
        <h4>Footer</h4>
    </footer>
</div>
```

Description

- The HTML for a typical web page that uses jQuery Mobile will contain div, header, section, and footer elements.

- The data-role attribute is used to identify the different parts of a mobile web page. To identify the four major parts of a mobile web page, set the values of this attribute to "page", "header", "content", and "footer".

- In the header, the content should be coded within an h1 element. In the footer, the content should be coded within an h4 element.

- In the section with "content" as its data-role attribute, you can code whatever elements you need.

- The style sheet for jQuery Mobile formats the web page based on the values in the data-role attributes.

Figure 15-6   How to create one web page with jQuery Mobile

How to use jQuery Mobile to create a mobile web site

In the four topics that follow, you'll learn the basic techniques for creating the pages of a mobile web site. That will include the use of dialog boxes, buttons, and navigation bars.

How to code multiple pages in a single HTML file

In contrast to the way you develop the web pages for a screen web site, jQuery Mobile lets you create multiple pages in a single HTML file. This is illustrated by figure 15-7. Here, you can see two pages of a site along with the HTML for these pages. What's surprising is that both pages are coded within a single HTML file.

For each page, you code one div element with "page" as its id. Then, within each of those div elements, you code the div elements for the header, content, and footer of each page. Later, when the HTML file is loaded, the first page in the body of the file is displayed.

To link between the pages in the HTML file, you use placeholders as shown in figure 7-11 of chapter 7. For instance, the <a> element in the first page in this example goes to "#toobin" when the user taps on the h2 or img element that is coded as the content for this link. This refers to the div element with "toobin" as its id attribute, which means that tapping the link takes the reader to the second page in the file.

Although this example shows only two pages, you can code many pages within a single HTML file. Remember, though, that all of the pages along with their images, JavaScript, and CSS files are loaded with the single HTML file. As a result, the load time will become excessive if you store too many pages in a single file. When that happens, you can divide your pages into more than one HTML file.

Two web pages that use jQuery Mobile

The HTML for the two pages in the body of one HTML file

```
<div data-role="page">
    <header data-role="header"><h1>SJV Town Hall</h1></header>
    <section data-role="content">
        <h3>The 2011-2012 Speakers</h3>
        <a href="#toobin">
            <h4>Jeffrey Toobin<br>October 19, 2011</h4>
            <img src="images/toobin75.jpg" alt="Jeffrey Toobin"></a>
        <!-- THE ELEMENTS FOR THE REST OF THE SPEAKERS -->
    </section>
    <footer data-role="footer"><h4>&copy; 2011</h4></footer>
</div>
<div data-role="page" id="toobin">
    <header data-role="header"><h1>SJV Town Hall</h1></header>
    <section data-role="content">
        <h3>The Supreme Nine:<br>Black Robed Secrets</h3>
        <img src="images/toobin_court.cnn.jpg" alt="Jeffrey Toobin">
        <p>Author of the critically acclaimed best seller, <i>The Nine:
        <!-- THE COPY CONTINUES -->
    </section>
    <footer data-role="footer"><h4>&copy; 2011</h4></footer>
</div>
```

Description

- When you use jQuery Mobile, you don't have to develop a separate HTML file for each page. Instead, within the body element of a single HTML file, you code one div element for each page with its data-role attribute set to "page".

- For each div element, you set the id attribute to a placeholder value that can be accessed by the href attributes in the <a> elements of other pages.

Figure 15-7   How to code multiple pages in a single HTML file

How to use dialog boxes and transitions

Figure 15-8 shows how to create a *dialog box* that opens when a link is tapped. To do that, you code the dialog box just as you would any page. But in the <a> element that goes to that page, you code a data-rel attribute with "dialog" as its value.

As the examples in this figure show, the jQuery Mobile CSS file formats a dialog box differently than a normal web page. By default, a dialog box will have a dark background with white foreground text, and the header and footer won't span the width of the page. A dialog box will also have an "X" in the header that the user must tap to return to the previous page.

When you code an <a> element that goes to another page or dialog box, you can also use the data-transition attribute to specify one of the six *transitions* that are summarized in the table in this figure. Each of these transitions is meant to mimic an effect that a mobile device like an iPhone uses.

A page and a dialog box that have the same HTML

The web page

The dialog box

The transitions that can be used

Transition	Description
slide	The next page slides in from right to left.
slideup	The next page slides in from bottom to top.
slidedown	The next page slides in from top to bottom.
pop	The next page fades in from the middle of the screen.
fade	The next page fades into view.
flip	The next page flips from back to front similar to a playing card being flipped over. This transition isn't supported on some devices.

HTML that opens the page as a dialog box with the "pop" transition

```
<a href="#toobin" data-rel="dialog" data-transition="pop">
```

HTML that opens the page with the "fade" transition

```
<a href="#toobin" data-transition="fade">
```

Description

- The HTML for a *dialog box* is coded the way any page is coded. However, the <a> element that links to the page includes the data-rel attribute with "dialog" as its value. To close the dialog box, the user taps the X in the header of the box.

- To specify the way a page or a dialog box is opened, you can use the data-transition attribute with one of the values in the table above. If a device doesn't support the transition that you specify, the attribute is ignored.

- The styling for a dialog box is done by the jQuery Mobile CSS file.

Figure 15-8   How to use dialog boxes and transitions

How to create buttons

Figure 15-9 shows how to use buttons to navigate from one page to another. To do that, you just set the data-role attribute for an <a> element to "button", and jQuery Mobile does the rest.

However, you can also set some other attributes for buttons. If, for example, you want two or more buttons to appear side by side, like the first two buttons in this figure, you can set the data-inline attribute to "true".

If you want to add one of the 18 icons that are provided by jQuery Mobile to a button, you also code the data-icon attribute. For instance, the third button in this example uses the "delete" icon, and the fourth button uses the "home" icon. All of these icons look like the icons that you might see within a native mobile application. Incidentally, these icons are not separate files that the page must access. Instead, they are provided by the jQuery Mobile library.

If you want to group two or more buttons horizontally, like the Yes, No, and Maybe buttons in this figure, you can code the <a> elements for the buttons within a div element that has "controlgroup" as its data-role attribute and "horizontal" as its data-type attribute. Or, to group the buttons vertically, you can change the data-type attribute to "vertical".

If you set the data-rel attribute for a button to "back" and the href attribute to the pound symbol (#), the button will return to the page that called it. In other words, the button works like a Back button. This is illustrated by the last button in the content for the page.

The last two buttons show how buttons appear in the footer for a page. Here, the icons and text are white against a black background. In this case, the class attribute for the footer is set to "ui-bar", which tells jQuery Mobile that it should put a little more space around the contents of the footer. You'll learn more about that in figure 15-12.

A mobile web page that displays buttons

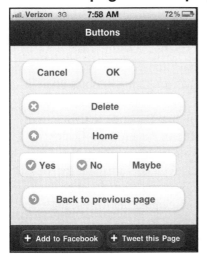

The icons that are provided by jQuery Mobile

delete	arrow-l	arrow-r	arrow-u	arrow-d	search
plus	minus	check	gear	refresh	forward
back	grid	star	alert	info	home

The HTML for the buttons in the section

```
<!-- For inline buttons, set the data-line attribute to true -->
<a href="#" data-role="button" data-inline="true">Cancel</a>
<a href="#" data-role="button" data-inline="true">OK</a>
<!-- To add an icon to a button, use the data-icon attribute -->
<a href="#" data-role="button" data-icon="delete">Delete</a>
<a href="#" data-role="button" data-icon="home">Home</a>
<!-- To group buttons, use a div element with the attributes that follow -->
<div data-role="controlgroup" data-type="horizontal">
    <a href="#" data-role="button" data-icon="check">Yes</a>
    <a href="#" data-role="button" data-icon="arrow-d">No</a>
    <a href="#" data-role="button">Maybe</a>
</div>
<!-- To code a Back button, set the data-rel attribute to back -->
<a href="#" data-role="button" dat-rel="back" data-icon="back">
    Back to previous page</a>
```

The HTML for the buttons in the footer

```
<footer data-role="footer" class="ui-bar">
    <a href="http://www.facebook.com" data-role="button"
        data-icon="plus">Add to Facebook</a>
    <a href="http://www.twitter.com" data-role="button"
        data-icon="plus">Tweet this Page</a>
</footer>
```

Description

- To add a button to a web page, you code an <a> element with its data-role attribute
  set to "button".

Figure 15-9   How to create buttons

How to create a navigation bar

Figure 15-10 shows how you can add a navigation bar to a web page. To do that, you code a div element with its data-role set to "navbar". Within this element, you code a ul element that contains li elements that contain the <a> elements for the items in the navigation bar. Note, however, that you don't code the data-role attribute for the <a> elements.

To change the color for the items in the navigation bar, the code in this example includes the data-theme-b attribute for each item. As a result, jQuery Mobile changes the background color of each item from black, which is the default, to an attractive blue. In addition, this code sets the class attribute for the active button to "ui-btn-active" so jQuery Mobile changes the color for the active button to a lighter blue. This shows how you can change the formatting that's used by jQuery Mobile, and you'll learn more about that next.

A mobile web page with a navigation bar

The HTML for the navigation bar

```html
<header data-role="header">
    <h1>SJV Town Hall</h1>
    <div data-role="navbar">
        <ul>
            <li><a href="#home" class="ui-btn-active"
                    data-icon="home" data-theme="b">Home</a></li>
            <li><a href="#speakers"
                    data-icon="star" data-theme="b">Speakers</a></li>
            <li><a href="#contactus"
                    data-icon="grid" data-theme="b">Contact Us</a></li>
        </ul>
    </div>
</header>
```

How to code the HTML for a navigation bar

- Code a div element within the header element. Then, set the data-role attribute for the div element to "navbar".

- Within the div element, code a ul element that contains one li element for each link.

- Within each li element, code an <a> element with an href attribute that uses a placeholder for the page that the link should go to. Then, set the data-icon attribute to the icon of your choosing.

- For the active item in the navigation bar, set the class attribute to "ui-btn-active". Then, the color of this item will be lighter than the other items in the navigation bar.

- You should also use the data-theme attribute to apply a jQuery Mobile theme to each item in the navigation bar. Otherwise, the buttons in the bar will be the same color as the rest of the header. To learn more about applying themes, see figure 15-12.

Figure 15-10   How to create a navigation bar

How to format content with jQuery Mobile

As you've already seen, jQuery Mobile automatically formats the components of a web page based on its own style sheet. Now, you'll learn more about that, as well as how to adjust the default styling that jQuery Mobile uses.

The default styles that jQuery Mobile uses

Figure 15-13 shows the default styles that jQuery Mobile uses for common HTML elements. For all of its styles, jQuery Mobile relies on the browser's rendering engine so its own styling is minimal. This keeps load times fast and minimizes the overhead that excessive CSS would impose on a page.

As you can see, jQuery Mobile's styling is so effective that you shouldn't need to modify its styling by providing your own CSS style sheet. For instance, the spacing between the items in the unordered list and the formatting of the table are both acceptable the way they are. Also, the black type on the gray background is consistent with the formatting for native mobile applications.

The default styles for common HTML elements

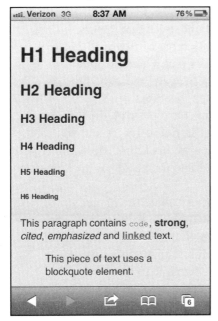
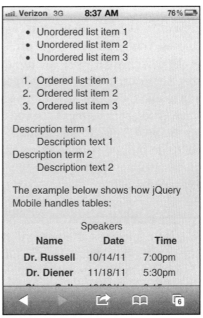

Description

- By default, jQuery Mobile automatically applies styles to the HTML elements for a page. These styles are not only attractive, but also mimic a browser's native styles.

- By default, jQuery Mobile applies a small amount of padding to the left, right, top, and bottom of each mobile page.

- By default, links are slightly larger than normal text. This makes it easier for the user to tap the links.

- By default, links are underlined with blue as the font color.

Figure 15-11   The default styles that jQuery Mobile uses

How to apply themes to HTML elements

In some cases, you will want to change the default styles that jQuery Mobile uses. You've already seen that in the navigation bar of figure 15-10. To change the default styles, you can use the five *themes* that jQuery Mobile provides. These are summarized in figure 15-12. Here again, these themes are meant to mimic the appearance of a native mobile application.

One way to apply themes is to code a data-theme attribute with the theme letter as its value. You saw this in the navigation bar in figure 15-10, and you can see this in the code for the second navigation bar in this figure. Here, the data-theme attribute applies theme "e" to the header and theme "d" to the items in the navigation bar.

The other way to apply themes is to set the class attribute for an element to a class name that indicates a theme. This is illustrated by the first example after the table. Here, the class attribute is used to apply both the "ui-bar" and "ui-bar-b" classes to the div element. As a result, jQuery Mobile first applies its default styling for a bar to the element and then applies the b theme to that styling. In the pages that follow, you'll see other examples of this type of styling.

Please note that the table in this figure says to use theme e sparingly. That's because it uses an orange color that works okay for accenting an item, but isn't attractive in large doses. This is illustrated by the second header and navigation bar in this figure, which tends to be jarring when you see it in color.

In general, it's best to stay with the default styles and the first three themes, which usually work well together. Then, you can experiment with themes d and e when you think you need something more.

Two headers and navigation bars that illustrate the use of themes

Header "a", bar "b"

Header "e", bar "d"

The HTML for the second header and navigation bar

```
<header data-role="header" data-theme="e">
    <h1>SJV Town Hall</h1>
    <div data-role="navbar">
        <ul>
            <li><a href="#home" data-icon="home"
                data-theme="d">Home</a></li>
            <li><a href="#speakers" data-icon="star"
                data-theme="d" class="ui-btn-active">Speakers</a></li>
            <li><a href="#news" id="news" data-icon="grid"
                data-theme="d">News</a></li>
        </ul>
    </div>
</header>
```

The five jQuery Mobile themes

Theme	Description
a	Black background with white foreground. This is the default.
b	Blue background with white foreground.
c	Light gray background with a black foreground. Text will appear in bold.
d	Dark gray background with black foreground. Text will not appear in bold.
e	Orange background with black foreground. Use for accents, and use sparingly.

Two ways to apply a theme

By using a data-theme attribute

```
<li><a href="#home" class="ui-btn-active"
    data-icon="home" data-theme="b">Home</a></li>
```

By using a class attribute that indicates the theme

```
<div class="ui-bar ui-bar-b">Bar</div>
```

Description

- By using the five themes that are included with jQuery Mobile, you can make appropriate adjustments to the default styles for the HTML elements.
- Although you can use your own CSS style sheet with a jQuery Mobile application, you should avoid doing that whenever possible.

Figure 15-12   How to apply themes to HTML elements

How to use jQuery Mobile for page layout

The last four topics in this chapter show how to use jQuery Mobile for special page layouts.

How to lay out your content in two columns

Figure 15-13 shows how you can lay out the content for a page in two columns. This can be useful for a photo gallery or product list because it can reduce the amount of scrolling that's needed to see all of the items.

In the HTML for a two-column layout, you start with a section (or div) element that has its class set to "ui-grid-a". Then, within this section, code one div element for each column with the class for the first element set to "ui-block-a" and the class for the second element set to "ui-class-b". Within these two div elements, you code the content for each column.

In this example, the content for each speaker consists of a paragraph, an image, and another paragraph. Also, all of the speakers for the first column are coded in the first block, and all of the speakers for the second column are coded in the second block. However, you could also code this as a series of grids with just two blocks (or speakers) in each grid: one for the left column, and one for the right column.

In the code for this example, you may note the heading for each speaker is coded as a strong element within a paragraph. Although it would be better semantically to code this as a heading element, you sometimes need to make an accommodation like this to get the content to fit in the mobile web page. Also, you can see that speaker name and date are coded as the content for <a> elements within paragraphs. As a result, these items are formatted in blue and underlined.

A mobile web page that has two columns

The HTML for the two columns

```
<section data-role="content">
    <section class="ui-grid-a">
        <div class="ui-block-a">
            <p><strong>Black Robed Secrets</strong></p>
            <img src="images/toobin75.jpg" alt="Jeffrey Toobin"><br>
            <p><a href="#toobin"><strong>Jeffrey Toobin</strong></a>
                <br>October 19, 2011</p>
            <p><strong>Babylon<br>to Beijing</strong></p>
            <!-- the rest of the code for this speaker -->
        </div>
        <div class="ui-block-b">
            <p><br><strong>Too Big to Fail</strong></p>
            <img src="images/sorkin75.jpg" alt="Andrew Ross Sorkin">
            <p><a href="#sorkin"><strong>Andrew Sorkin</strong></a>
                <br>November 16, 2011</p>
            <!-- the code for next speaker in the second column -->
        </div>
    </section>
</section>
```

How to code the HTML for two columns

- Code a section (or div) element for the two-column area, and set its class to "ui-grid-a". Within this section, code one div element for each column, and set their classes to "ui-block-a" and "ui-block-b". In the div elements for the columns, code the content for the columns.

Description

- The ui-block-a and ui-block-b classes are formatted by jQuery Mobile so they float left. As a result, the div elements are displayed in two columns.

Figure 15-13   How to lay out your content in two columns

How to create collapsible content blocks

Figure 15-14 shows how you can display content in *collapsible content blocks*. Then, the user can tap on an item to display (or expand) the content within the block. By default, jQuery Mobile formats these blocks and adds plus and minus signs to them as shown in this figure.

In the code for this feature, you can see that there's one div element for all of the blocks with its data-role attribute set to "content". You can also see that there's one div element for each content block with its data-role attribute set to "collapsible". By default, the content blocks are collapsed when the page is loaded, but you can change that by setting the data-collapsed attribute for one or more blocks to "false".

A mobile web page with collapsible content blocks

With all blocks collapsed

With the second block expanded

The HTML for the collapsible content blocks

```
<section data-role="content">
    <div data-role="collapsible">
        <h3>Jeffrey Toobin<br>October 19, 2011</h3>
        <h3>Black Robed Secrets</h3>
        <img src="images/toobin75.jpg" alt="Jeffrey Toobin">
        <p>Author of the critically acclaimed best seller...</p>
    </div>
    <div data-role="collapsible" data-collapsed="false">
        <h3>Andrew RossSorkin<br>November 16, 2011</h3>
        <h3>Too Big to Fail</h3>
        <img src="images/sorkin75.jpg" alt="Andrew Ross Sorkin">
        <p>A leading voice on Wall Street and corporate America...</p>
    </div>
    <!-- THE DIV ELEMENTS FOR THE OTHER CONTENT BLOCKS -->
</section>
```

How to code the HTML for collapsible content blocks

- Code a div element for each content block with the data-role attribute set to "collapsible".
- By default, each content block will be collapsed when the page is displayed. To expand a content block, add the data-collapsed attribute with its value set to "false".
- Within each div element, you can code the HTML for whatever content you want.

Description

- More than one content block can be expanded at the same time.
- jQuery Mobile automatically adds the plus and minus icons for the content blocks.

Figure 15-14   How to create collapsible content blocks

How to create an accordion

When you create an *accordion*, you code the content blocks the same way you code the collapsible content blocks of the previous figure. This is illustrated by figure 15-15. However, you code these content blocks within a section or div element that has its data-role attribute set to "collapsible-set".

One difference between an accordion and collapsible content blocks is that jQuery Mobile formats the blocks in the accordion as a unit. You can see this if you compare the example in this page with the one in the previous page. The other difference is that the user can only expand one block at a time in an accordion. So, when one block is expanded, the other block is collapsed.

A mobile web page with an accordion

With all blocks collapsed

With the first block expanded

The HTML for the accordion

```
<section data-role="content">
    <section data-role="collapsible-set">
        <div data-role="collapsible" data-collapsed="false">
            <h3>Jeffrey Toobin<br>October 19, 2011</h3>
            <h3>Black Robed Secrets</h3>
            <img src="images/toobin75.jpg" alt="Jeffrey Toobin">
            <p>Author of the critically acclaimed best seller,
                <i>The Nine: Inside the Secret World of the Supreme
                Court</i>, Jeffrey Toobin brings us the inside story
                of one of America's most mysterious and powerful
                institutions.</p>
        </div>
        <!-- THE DIV ELEMENTS FOR THE OTHER CONTENT BLOCKS -->
    </section>
</section>
```

How to code the HTML for an accordion

- Code a section (or div) element for the accordion within the section for the page and set its data-role attribute to "collapsible-set".
- Code the content blocks the same way you code collapsible content blocks (figure 15-14).

Description

- In contrast to collapsible content blocks, only one block in an accordion can be expanded at the same time.
- jQuery Mobile automatically adds the plus and minus icons for the content blocks.

Figure 15-15   How to create an accordion

How to create a contents list

Figure 15-16 shows how to create a list that can be used to link to other pages. In the first example, the user can tap on the image, the text, or the right-arrow icon to go to a page that gives more information about the speaker. In the second example, the user can tap on the image or the text to go to the speaker's page, or the user can tap on the gear icon to go to a Buy Tickets dialog box.

To create a list like this, you start with a ul element that has "listview" as its data-role attribute. Then, you code the HTML for each block in an li element. Within each li element, you code an <a> element that contains the image and text that you want in the first two columns. After that, you can code another <a> element that provides the icon in the third column.

In the HTML for the first example, both <a> elements in each block link to the page for the speaker. As a result, the user can tap anywhere in the block to go to the speaker's page. In this case, the default icon is used for the second link, and that icon is the right arrow.

In the HTML for the second example, the first <a> element in each block is coded the same way it is in the first example. However, the second <a> element links to a page with "buytix" as its id, and it treats this page as a dialog box. The HTML for the second example also uses the data-split-attribute to set the icon that's used to a gear, and it uses the data-inset attribute to inset the list as shown in this example.

When you code the HTML for a list, especially an inset list, it's often difficult to get all the information to display fully. For instance, none of the items in the second example display the date fully. That's why you may be forced to limit the information that each block provides.

A mobile web page that displays a contents list
Using the defaults   With data-inset="true"

The HTML for the first list (tapping the arrow goes to the speaker's page)

```
<section data-role="content">
    <ul data-role="listview">
        <li>
            <a href="#toobin">
                <img src="images/toobin75.jpg">
                    <p><strong><br>Jeffrey Toobin<br>
                        October 19, 2011</strong></p></a>
            <a href="#toobin">Jeffrey Toobin</a>
        </li>
        <!-- THE LI ELEMENTS FOR THE OTHER CONTENT BLOCKS -->
    </ul>
</section>
```

The HTML for the second list (tapping the gear goes to a Buy Tickets page)

```
<section data-role="content">
    <ul data-role="listview" data-split-icon="gear" data-inset="true">
        <li><!-- SAME AS ABOVE -->
            <a href="#buytix" data-rel="dialog">Buy Tickets</a>
        </li>
        <!-- THE LI ELEMENTS FOR THE OTHER CONTENT BLOCKS -->
```

How to code the HTML for a list

- Code a ul element with its data-role attribute set to "listview". If you set the data-inset attribute for this element to "true", the list will be inset as in the second example above.

- Within the ul element, code one li element for each item in your list. Within each li element, code an <a> element that links to a page that contains more information about the item. The link can contain can contain text and images.

- To add a column that contains an icon, code another <a> element.

Figure 15-16   How to create a contents list

A mobile web site that uses jQuery Mobile

To show how the features you've just learned work together in a complete web site, this chapter ends by presenting several pages of a mobile web site that uses jQuery Mobile. This should give you a better idea of how you can use jQuery Mobile to build your own sites.

The layout for the mobile web site

Figure 15-17 presents four pages of the mobile version of the Town Hall web site. That includes the Home, Speakers, and Contact Us pages, as well as one of the speaker's pages. On all of these pages, you can see the navigation bar that lets the user go from one page to another.

On the Home page, you can see the speaker of the month, and the link that will take the user to that speaker's page. This is followed by copy that tells what the web site does.

On the Speakers page, the user can tap on any item in the first column of the contents list to go to the page for that speaker. Or, the user can tap on the gear icon to open a dialog box that shows how to buy tickets. Unlike the contents list in the previous figure, this one doesn't include images so the text is more prominent.

On the Contact Us page, you can see a phone number, an email address, and a Buy Tickets button that includes a gear icon. If the user taps on the phone number, the user's device will try to call that number. If the user taps on the email address, the user's system will try to start an email to that address. And if the user taps on the Buy Tickets button, the Buy Tickets page will be opened as a dialog box. This is the same page that's opened when the user taps on the gear icon on the Speakers page.

The page layouts for a mobile web site that uses jQuery Mobile

The Home page

The Speakers page

The Scott Sampson page

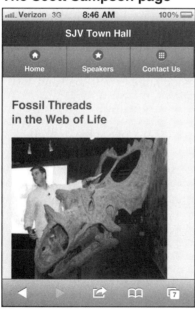

The Contact Us page

Description

- When the user taps a speaker on the Speakers page, a page for that speaker is opened. When the user taps a gear, a Buy Tickets dialog box is opened.
- When the user taps the phone number on the Contact Us page, the device's phone feature will try to call the number.

Figure 15-17   A mobile web site for Town Hall

The HTML for the mobile web site

Figure 15-18 presents the primary HTML for this web site in three parts. Since this HTML uses the features that you've learned about in this chapter, you should be able to understand it on your own. In case you're interested, though, here are a few highlights.

In the head section in part 1, the viewport metadata specifies a width equal to the devices width and an initial scale of 1. This should work for all mobile devices, include iPhones and Android devices.

In the body section in part 1, you can see the HTML for the Home page of the site. Since this page is first in the file, it is the one that will be displayed when the HTML file is loaded. Other than the data-role attributes, this page uses normal HTML code with none of the features that jQuery Mobile provides.

In part 2 of this figure, you can see the code for the Speakers page. This uses a list like the one in figure 15-16, but without the images. That provides more room for the text so none of the text is missing, even though heading elements are used for the text and the list is inset. This list also includes the gear icon that opens the Buy Tickets page as a dialog box when it is tapped.

In part 3 of this figure, you can see the code for Scott Sampson's page. This page can be reached from the Home page as well as the Speakers page. Then, to return to the previous page, the button at the bottom of this page is coded as a Back button. In other words, it will return to either the Home or the Speakers page based upon which page linked to it.

In part 3, you can also see the code for the Contact Us page. Here, <a> elements are used for the phone number and email address. That's why the device will try to call the phone number when the phone number is tapped and why the device will try to start an email message when the email address is tapped.

This Contact Us page uses a third <a> element for the button on the page. It specifies the gear icon in its data-icon attribute, so the gear appears on the button. It also specifies "b" as its data-theme attribute so the button is blue. Note, however, that it doesn't have a data-role attribute that is set to "button". Instead, this <a> element is coded within a div element that has its class set to "ui-bar", and that's what makes the link look like a button.

The HTML for the head section and the Home page

```
<!DOCTYPE HTML>
<html lang="en">
<head>
    <meta charset="utf-8">
    <meta name="viewport" content="width=device-width, initial-scale=1">
    <title>San Joaquin Valley Town Hall</title>
    <link rel="stylesheet"
        href="http://code.jquery.com/mobile/1.0b3/jquery.mobile-1.0b3.min.css">
    <script src="http://code.jquery.com/jquery-1.6.3.min.js"></script>
    <script
        src="http://code.jquery.com/mobile/1.0b3/jquery.mobile-1.0b3.min.js">
    </script>
</head>

<body>
<div data-role="page" id="home">
    <header data-role="header">
        <h1>SJV Town Hall</h1>
        <div data-role="navbar">
            <ul>
                <li><a href="#home" data-icon="home" data-theme="b"
                        class="ui-btn-active">Home</a></li>
                <li><a href="#speakers" data-icon="star"
                        data-theme="b">Speakers</a></li>
                <li><a href="#contact" data-icon="grid"
                        data-theme="b">Contact Us</a></li>
            </ul>
        </div>
    </header>
    <section data-role="content">
        <h3>Speaker of the month<br>February 15, 2012</h3>
        <a href="#sampson">
            <img src="images/sampson75.jpg" alt="Scott Sampson">
            <h4>Fossil Threads in the Web of Life<br>Scott Sampson</h4>
        </a>
        <h3>Cutting-edge speakers <br>for 75 years</h3>
        <p>Since 1936, San Joaqin Valley Town Hall has showcased nationally
            and internationally renowned, thought-provoking, speakers who
            inform, educate, and entertain our audience.</p>
        <h3>Our History</h3>
        <p>1937: In the town of Hanford, California, Clio Lee Aydelott—a woman
        ...
        ...
    </section>

    <footer data-role="footer">
        <h4>&copy; 2011</h4>
    </footer>
</div>
```

Figure 15-18   The HTML for the mobile web site (part 1 of 3)

The HTML for the Speakers page

```
<div data-role="page" id="speakers">
<header data-role="header">
    <!-- same header and navigation bar that's in the other pages
         but the Speakers button is the active button -->
</header>

<section data-role="content">
    <h3>The 2011-2012 Speakers</h3>
    <ul data-role="listview" data-split-icon="gear" data-inset="true">
        <li>
            <a href="#toobin">
                <h4>Jeffrey Toobin<br>Black Robed Secrets</h4>
                <h4>October 19, 2011</h4>
            </a>
            <a href="#buytix" data-rel="dialog" data-transition="pop">
                Buy Tickets</a>
        </li>
        <li>
            <a href="#sorkin">
                <h4>Andrew Ross Sorkin<br>Too Big to Fail</h4>
                <h4>November 16, 2011</h4>
            </a>
            <a href="#buytix" data-rel="dialog" data-transition="pop">
                Buy Tickets</a>
        </li>
        <li>
            <a href="#chua">
                <h4>Amy Chua<br>Babylon to Beijing</h4>
                <h4>January 18, 2012</h4>
            </a>
            <a href="#buytix" data-rel="dialog" data-transition="pop">
                Buy Tickets</a>
        </li>
        <li>
            <a href="#sampson">
                <h4>Scott Sampson<br>Fossil Threads <br>
                    in the Web of Life</h4>
                <h4>February 15, 2012</h4>
            </a>
            <a href="#buytix" data-rel="dialog" data-transition="pop">
                Buy Tickets</a>
        </li>
        <li>
            ...
            ...
        </li>
    </ul>
</section>

<footer data-role="footer">
    <h4>&copy; 2011</h4>
</footer>
</div>
```

Figure 15-18   The HTML for the mobile web site (part 2 of 3)

The HTML for Scott Sampson's page

```
<div data-role="page" id="sampson">
    <header data-role="header">
        <!-- same header and navigation bar that's in the other pages
             but there is no active button -->
    </header>

    <section data-role="content">
        <h3>Fossil Threads<br>in the Web of Life</h3>
        <img src="images/sampson_dinosaur.jpg" alt="Scott Sampson">
        <p>What's 75 million years old and brand spanking new? A teenage
            <!—the rest of the copy for this speaker -->
        </p>
        <p><a href="#" data-role="button" data-rel="back" data-theme="b">
            Back to previous page</a></p>
    </section>

    <footer data-role="footer">
        <h4>&copy; 2011</h4>
    </footer>
</div>
```

The HTML for the Contact Us page

```
<div data-role="page" id="contact">
    <header data-role="header">
        <!-- same header and navigation bar that's in the other pages
             but the Contact Us button is the active button -->
    </header>

    <section data-role="content" style="text-align:center;">
        <strong>Phone</strong><br>
        <a href="tel:15594442180">559.444.2180</a><br><br>
        <strong>Mail</strong><br>
            San Joaquin Valley Town Hall<br>
            P.O. Box 5149<br>
            Fresno, CA 93755-5149<br><br>
        <strong>Email</strong><br>
        <a href="mailto:valleytownhall@aol.com">valleytownhall@aol.com</a>
        <br><br>
        <div class="ui-bar">
            <a href="#buytix" data-icon="gear" data-theme="b">
             Buy Tickets</a>
        </div>
    </section>

    <footer data-role="footer">
        <h4>&copy; 2011</h4>
    </footer>
</div>
</body>
</html>
```

Figure 15-18   The HTML for the mobile web site (part 3 of 3)

Perspective

The use of mobile devices has increased dramatically over the past few years. Because of that, it has become increasingly important to design web sites that are easy to use from these devices. Although that usually means developing a separate web site, this can be a critical aspect of maintaining your presence on the Internet.

Fortunately, the task of building a mobile web site has become much easier with the advent of jQuery Mobile. No longer are mobile web pages limited to static pages that contain headings, paragraphs, links, and thumbnail images. With jQuery Mobile, web developers can now build feature-rich web sites that look and feel like native mobile applications.

Terms

media query	CDN (Content Delivery Network)
WURFL (Wireless Universal Resource File)	dialog box
	transition
viewport	theme
scale	collapsible content blocks
jQuery Mobile	accordion

Summary

- The best way to provide web pages for mobile devices is to build a separate web site for those devices. Then, you can redirect users from your full web site to your mobile web site.

- To redirect users to the mobile version of a web site, you can use JavaScript, server-side code, or *WURFL (Wireless Universal Resource File)*.

- The *viewport* on a mobile device determines the content that's displayed. To control how that works, you can code a viewport meta element in the head section of a page.

- *jQuery Mobile* is a JavaScript library that's designed for developing mobile web sites. jQuery Mobile uses the core jQuery library along with its own CSS file.

- To include the jQuery Mobile and jQuery libraries in a web page, you code script elements in the head section. Because jQuery Mobile uses jQuery, the script element for jQuery Mobile must be coded after the one for jQuery.

- jQuery Mobile lets you code the HTML for many mobile pages in a single HTML file. jQuery Mobile also supports the use of dialog boxes, transitions, buttons, navigation bars, collapsible content blocks, accordions, and more.

- By default, jQuery Mobile provides formatting that relies on a browser's native rendering engine. jQuery Mobile also provides *five themes* that you can use to adjust the default formatting without using CSS style sheets of your own.

Exercise 15-1   Test and modify the mobile web site for Town Hall

In this exercise, you'll first test the mobile version of the Town Hall web site that's presented in this chapter. Then, you'll make some modifications to it, like changing the Speakers page so it looks like the one that follows. This should demonstrate how easy it is to build mobile web sites when you use jQuery Mobile.

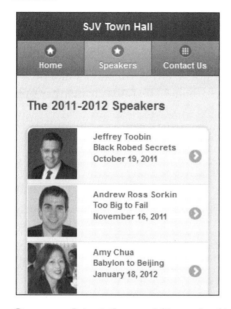

Open and test the mobile web site for Town Hall

1. Use your text editor to open this HTML page:

    `c:\html5_css3\exercises\town_hall_3\mobile\index.html`

2. Test this page and the navigation from one page to another within the site. The easiest way to do that is to run the page in Firefox and then reduce the size of the browser window so it's about the size of a mobile window. As you go from page to page, remember that all of the pages come from one HTML file.

3. Click on the image on the home page to go to the page for Scott Sampson, and then click the button at the bottom of that page to return to the home page. Next, click the Speakers button in the navigation bar and then the link for Scott Sampson to go to the page for Scott Sampson. This time, when you click on the button at the bottom of the page, you return to the Speakers page.

Modify the way the pages work and test these changes

4. Review the code for the button on Scott Sampson's page. Then, modify the code so it returns to the Speakers page no matter how the user got there.

5. In the HTML for the Speakers page, delete the second <a> element for each speaker. Then, test this change to see how the Speakers page has changed and how the navigation works.

6. Add the small images of the speakers to the Speakers page as shown in figure 15-16. Then, adjust the formatting for the text so the page looks something like the page above, but don't use CSS to do that. Instead, experiment with HTML elements like the h4, p, and strong elements. Without using CSS, this formatting can be time-consuming.

7. Add a page for Andrew Ross Sorkin that's like the ones for the other speakers. Use "Too Big to Fail" as the heading for the page and follow that with the large image for him, but don't bother adding any content beyond that. Then, test to make sure that this works and that the navigation to and from the page works.

Experiment on your own

8. Experiment with themes. Try using CSS to format the Speakers page. Add a page that uses a table. You'll soon see how quickly you can build a mobile web site with jQuery Mobile. Keep in mind, though, that this chapter has only presented about 25% of the features of jQuery Mobile.

16

Advanced HTML5 and CSS3 features

In this chapter, you'll learn how to use some of the exciting new features of HTML5 and CSS3. As you will see, you will be able to start using some of these features right away, but others aren't fully supported by all modern browsers. Nevertheless, you should at least know what these features can do so you'll be ready to implement them when they are fully supported. Beyond that, these features clearly indicate the direction that HTML5 is moving.

As you will see, all of these features except embedded fonts require the use of JavaScript. If you are familiar with JavaScript, you should be able to understand most of the code that's used in the examples. Otherwise, you can just focus on what the new features can do and make a note that you eventually need to learn JavaScript.

How to embed fonts in a web page

For many years, web designers have been frustrated by the limited number of fonts that have been available for a web site. In fact, web pages have been limited to the fonts that are available to each browser. That's why the font families throughout this book have been set to a series of fonts like Arial, Helvetica, and sans-serif. Then, each browser uses the first font in the series that's available to it.

But now, you can use a new CSS3 feature to embed fonts within your pages, That way, you know the fonts are available to the browser. You can also use third-party services like Google Web Fonts and Adobe Typekit to embed fonts within your pages. Although those services don't represent new HTML5 or CSS3 features, we've included them in this chapter so you know what your other options are for embedding or importing fonts.

How to use the CSS3 @font-face selector to embed fonts

Figure 16-1 shows how to use the CSS3 @font-face selector to embed fonts within your web pages. To start, you look in the folders that are listed in this figure where you'll see that you already have access to many fonts that most browsers don't have access to. Then, you find the font that you want and copy it into one of the folders for your web site. In this example, the Windows True Type Font named HARNGTON.TTF has been copied to the root folder of the web site.

Once you've copied the font to a folder, you code a CSS rule set for the @font-face selector that names and locates the font. In this example, the font-family property gives the name "Murach" to the font, and the src property points to the file, which is in the same folder as the web page.

After the font has been imported, you can code CSS rule sets that apply the new font to HTML elements. In this example, the second rule set applies the font to the h1 element with "booktitle" as its id. To do that, the font-family property is set to the name of the embedded font. Note, however, that a backup font is also specified for this property. This means that the default sans-serif font should be used by browsers that don't support the new @font-face selector. This also means that you can start using this feature right away because it will work on new browsers and won't cause any problems on old browsers.

A heading that uses a font imported with CSS3

Murach Books

The CSS for embedding a font

```
@font-face {
    font-family: Murach;
    src: url("HARNGTON.TTF"); }
```

The CSS for applying the font to an HTML element

```
#booktitle {
    font-family: Murach, sans-serif; }
```

The HTML for the element that the font is applied to

```
<h1 id="booktitle">Murach Books</h1>
```

Where to find the fonts on your computer

On a Windows system

```
C:\Windows\Fonts
```

On a Mac OS system

```
System\Library\Fonts
```

How to import a font

- Copy the file for the font family into a folder for your web site.
- In the CSS for the page, code a rule set for the @font-face selector. Use the font-family property to provide a name for the imported font family, and use the src property to locate the font file.

How to apply an imported font to an HTML element

- In the rule set for the HTML element, use the name that you gave the font as the value for the font-family property. Then, list one or more other font-families in case the browser doesn't support the CSS3 @font-face selector.

Description

- CSS3 provides a @font-face selector that can be used to import a font family.
- In this example, the file for a True Type Font (TTF) named HARNGTON has been stored in the same folder as the web page.

Figure 16-1   How to use the CSS @font-face selector to embed fonts

How to use Google Web Fonts

Figure 16-2 shows how you can use Google Web Fonts to import fonts into your web pages. Google Web Fonts is a free Google service that lets you select fonts from 263 different font families. Then, you can use those fonts in your web pages by including a link to a CSS file that Google provides.

To select a font, go to the web site for Google Web Fonts and browse through the font families. When you identify a font that you like, you can click on the Quick-use link to learn more about the font, including the load time for the font. You can also click on the Pop out link to get more information about the font, including what each character in the font looks like. If you want to customize the font by changing its thickness, slant, or width, you can also do that.

When you're ready to add a font to your collection, you click on the Add to Collection button. This adds the font to the blue collection pane at the bottom of the window. As you add more fonts to your collection, they will also appear within this pane. If you would like to preview what one of these fonts will look like in some randomly generated paragraphs, you can select the font and click on the Review button.

When you're satisfied that the fonts you've selected are the fonts that you want to use in your web pages, click on the Use button to display the Use page. Here, you have to select the way that you want to import the fonts into your web pages. One of these options is to use a link element provided by Google that imports the fonts. This is the option that's easiest to use, so it's the one that's used in this figure. The other two options are to use the @import selector or to use JavaScript code provided by Google that you include in the head section of your web page.

Once you copy the CSS link into the head section of a web page, you can use the font-family property to apply a font to an HTML element in that page. In the example in this figure, that property is set to "Sorts Mill Gowdy", which is the name of the font that has been imported. Here again, a backup font has been coded for those browsers that don't support this code.

The Google Web Fonts page (www.google.com/webfonts)

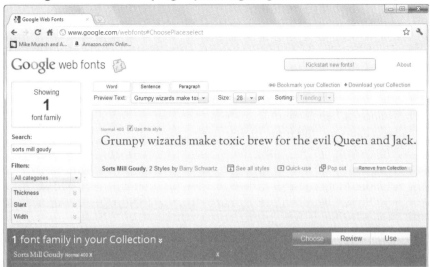

How to select Google Web Fonts

- Go to the Google Web Fonts page, browse through the fonts until you find one that you like, and click the Add to Collection button. If necessary, customize the font by using the options that are provided, like thickness, slant, and width.

- Click the Use button in the lower-right corner of the page to view the code that's required for using the font. This will be a link element that you need to copy into the head section of each web page that will use the font.

How to apply the imported font to an HTML element

- In the rule set for the HTML element, use the Google Web Font name as the value for the font-family property. Then, list one or more other font-families in case the browser doesn't support the Google font reference.

A heading that uses a Google Web Font

The CSS for importing a Google Web Font

```
<link href="http://fonts.googleapis.com/css?family=Sorts+Mill+Goudy"
      rel="stylesheet">
```

The CSS for applying the font to an HTML element

```
#booktitle { font-family: "Sorts Mill Goudy", serif; }
```

The HTML for the element that the font is applied to

```
<h1 id="booktitle">Murach Books</h1>
```

Description

- Google Web Fonts is a free Google service that lets you select and use any of the fonts in their current collection of 263 font families.

Figure 16-2   How to use Google Web Fonts

How to use Adobe Typekit fonts

Figure 16-3 shows how you can use Adobe Typekit to embed fonts into your web pages. Adobe Typekit is an Adobe service that lets you select fonts and add them to your kit. Then, you can use those fonts in a web page by including two JavaScript files in the head section of the page.

Unlike Google Web Fonts, which has no limitations, Adobe Typekit is restricted. For instance, a free account limits your service to a single domain. This means that you can't use the fonts in your web pages until they have been deployed to the web server that's hosting that domain. A free account also limits you to two fonts and limits the number of page views that use the font to 25,000 per month. To get more fonts and to lift these restrictions, you must buy one of the three packages that Adobe offers, which range from $24.99 to $99.99 per year.

To select and use Typekit fonts, you can use the procedure in this figure. When you find a font that you like, you can use the tabs to see how the font will look in various weights and styles, how the font will look for text that you enter, and how the font will look in every browser for these platforms: Mac OS X, Windows XP, Windows Vista, Windows 7, and even Ubuntu (Linux).

Once you select a font, you click on the Add to Kit button in the upper-right corner to add the font to your kit. This launches the Typekit Editor that's shown in this figure. In the Selectors pane, you can see one selector, which is a CSS class selector. This is a selector that you can use to apply the font later on, so you should record this. For more information about selectors and applying the imported fonts, you can click on the Using Fonts in CSS link in this pane. Then, when you're satisfied with the fonts in your kit, you click the Publish button.

After you publish your kit, you're ready to refer to those fonts in your web pages. To do that, click on the Embed Code link, which will display a dialog box that contains the two lines of JavaScript code that you need in your web pages. Then, copy these two lines of code to the head section of each web page that will use the fonts.

Last, to apply a Typekit font to an HTML element, you code a class attribute that uses the name that the Typekit Editor provided in the Selectors pane for the font. In this example, that name is "tk-blambot-pro", so that font is applied to the h1 element that's shown.

Other options for embedding fonts

Although the three options that you've just learned about are good ones, you should be aware that other font services are available. Of those, three of the most popular are Cufon, Font Jazz, and Font Deck. Two others are P+C DTR, which uses PHP scripts and CSS to produce fonts, and sIFR 3, which uses a combination of Flash, CSS, and JavaScript to embed fonts within your web pages. For more information, you can go to the web sites for these services.

The Typekit Editor web page (www.typekit.com/fonts)

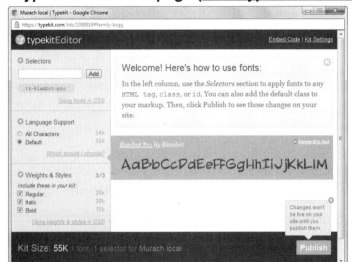

How to select Typekit fonts

- Go to the Typekit web page, and create an account that will include your domain name. That will be the only domain that the Typekit fonts that you choose will work in.

- Browse through the fonts or foundries until you find one that you like, and click the Add to Kit button, which will display the Typekit Editor. Then, record the selector that's in the upper-left corner of the editor because you'll use it to apply the font.

- Click the Publish button in the lower-right corner. Then, click on the Embed Code link in the top-right corner of the editor to display the JavaScript code for importing the font.

- Copy the JavaScript code and paste it into the head section of each page that uses the font.

How to apply the imported font to an HTML element

- Code the class attribute with its value set to the name that was displayed in the upper-left corner of the Typekit Editor.

The script elements for importing Typekit fonts

```
<script src="http://use.typekit.com/vxu5ibx.js"></script>
<script>try{Typekit.load();}catch(e){}</script>
```

The HTML for an element that a font is applied to

```
<h1 class="tk-blambot-pro">Murach Books</h1>
```

Description

- Adobe Typekit is an Adobe service that lets you select and use any of their fonts.

- Although the free Adobe service limits you to two fonts and one domain, you can lift these restrictions by buying one of the three Adobe Typekit packages.

Figure 16-3   How to use Adobe Typekit fonts

How to use the Geolocation feature

One of the most exciting new HTML5 features is its Geolocation feature. This feature lets you get the global position associated with a browser or mobile device. You do that by using the *Geolocation API* that's defined by HTML5.

How Geolocation works

Figure 16-4 shows how Geolocation works. Here, you can see the HTML for a button that starts a JavaScript function named initGeolocation when the button is clicked. The HTML does that by using the onClick attribute of the button. From that point on, it's all JavaScript.

The JavaScript for the initGeolocation function uses the objects of the API to call the getCurrentPosition method of the geolocation object. Then, that method calls the getLocation function and passes the position object to it.

Next, the getLocation function uses the properties of the position object to get information about the current position. These properties are summarized in the table in this figure. In this example, the getLocation function displays three of the position properties in a dialog box: latitude, longitude, and accuracy.

When the JavaScript initially calls the getCurrentPosition method, most browsers will display a dialog box that asks whether the user wants to allow the use of this feature. Then, the user can decide whether or not to allow it. If the user allows it, the JavaScript continues.

The position that is returned by the getCurrentPosition method is based on network signals such as IP addresses, cell phone IDs, cell tower triangulation, and the GPS coordinates for devices that have GPS capabilities. As a result, the position that's derived is an approximation, not an accurate set of coordinates. For instance, the accuracy property in the first dialog box in this figure shows that the position could be off by as much as 45,061 meters (25 miles).

For a device that has a GPS capability, though, the result should be much more accurate. For instance, the second dialog box in this figure was displayed by an iPhone. Its accuracy property shows that coordinates for the position are within 100 meters of the actual location.

At present, the Geolocation API is in draft form, and it isn't fully implemented by all browsers. As a result, the only properties that you can count in the browsers that do support Geolocation are the latitude, longitude, and accuracy properties. In contrast, few devices today include altimeters, so the altitude and altitudeAccuracy properties usually return null. Similarly, since the heading and speed properties imply the use of multiple readings and GPS data, these properties usually return null.

Properties of the position object that are defined by the Geolocation API

Property	Description
latitude	The geographic coordinate specified in degrees.
longitude	The geographic coordinate specified in degrees.
accuracy	The accuracy level in meters for the latitude and longitude coordinates.
altitude	The height of the position in meters.
altitideAccuracy	The accuracy level in meters for the altitude position.
heading	The direction of travel in degrees going clockwise relative to true North.
speed	The current ground speed in meters per second.

The HTML for the button that starts the initGeoLocation function

```
<input type="button" value="Get Location" onClick="initGeolocation()">
```

The JavaScript for the initGeolocation function

```
function initGeolocation() {
    navigator.geolocation.getCurrentPosition(getLocation);
}
function getLocation(position) {
    alert("Latitude: " + position.coords.latitude + "\n" +
        "Longitude: " + position.coords.longitude + "\n" +
        "Accuracy: " + position.coords.accuracy);
}
```

Dialog boxes that give the locations for a computer and an iPhone

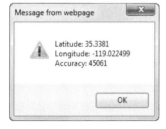

Description

- The Geolocation features lets you get the global position associated with a browser or mobile device. It does that by using the Geolocation API that's defined by HTML5.

- At present, this feature is supported by the current versions of Firefox, Chrome, Safari for iPhone, Internet Explorer, and Opera, but the API is still in draft form.

- When JavaScript calls the getCurrentPosition method, most browsers display a dialog box (not shown) that lets the user decide whether or not to allow the use of this feature.

- The getCurrentPosition method determines the latitude, longitude, and accuracy values based on network signals such as IP addresses, cell phone IDs, cell tower triangulation, and GPS coordinates.

- Since few devices today have altimeters, the altitude and altitudeAccuracy properties usually return null. Also, since the heading and speed properties imply the use of multiple readings and GPS data, these properties usually return null.

Figure 16-4   How Geolocation works

How to show the geolocation on a Google map

Figure 16-5 shows how to use the Geolocation API, Google's Map Services, and jQuery to display the user's position on a Google map. Here, the onLoad attribute in the body element is used to start the JavaScript function named initGeolocation. Then, just as in the previous figure, that function calls the getCurrentPosition method of the geolocation object, and that method calls the getLocation function, which accepts the position object.

This time, however, the getLocation function builds a URL that starts by referring to the Google Map Services API. This URL includes several parameters including the position coordinates twice. The first time, the coordinates are used to get the map for the current position. The second time, the coordinates are used to place a red marker at the current position.

After this URL value has been stored in the variable named "url", jQuery is used to set the src attribute for the img element with "map" as its id to the value in the url variable. This means that the map that is retrieved will be stored in that img element.

Here again, the map will reflect the accuracy or inaccuracy of the getCurrentPosition method. If you're using a device without GPS, your location on the map may be several miles from where you are. But if you're using a device with GPS, your location on the map should be close to where you are.

If you don't understand the JavaScript but would like to use this feature in your own application, nothing needs to be changed. You just code a script element in the head section and copy the code in this figure into it. You code the onLoad attribute for the body attribute. And you code an img element like the one in this figure.

Beyond that, though, you must include the jQuery library because the last statement in the getLocation function uses jQuery. To do that, you can use a statement like the one in figure 14-2 of chapter 14.

A web page with a Google Map that shows the user's location

The HTML that starts the JavaScript and receives the map

```html
<body onLoad="initGeolocation()">
    <p>Your current location is:</p>
    <img src="" id="map">
</body>
```

The JavaScript that gets the map and uses jQuery to place it

```javascript
function initGeolocation() {
    navigator.geolocation.getCurrentPosition(getLocation);
}
function getLocation(position) {
    var url =
        "http://maps.google.com/maps/api/staticmap?sensor=false&center=" +
            position.coords.latitude + "," + position.coords.longitude +
            "&zoom=14&size=300x400&markers=color:red|" +
            position.coords.latitude + "," +
            position.coords.longitude;
    $("#map").attr("src", url);
}
```

Description

- The onLoad attribute for the body element in the HTML starts the JavaScript function named initGeolocation() when the web page is loaded into the browser. That function calls the getLocation() function and passes the position object to it.

- The getLocation function constructs a URL that links to Google Maps and passes several values to it including the latitude and longitude coordinates for the user.

- After the URL is constructed, jQuery is used to put the URL into the value of the src attribute for the img element in the HTML. This gets the map and displays it in that element. Because jQuery is used, the jQuery library must be included in the head section.

Figure 16-5   How to show the geolocation on a Google map

How to handle Geolocation errors

When you use the Geolocation feature, several types of errors can occur. If the user won't allow the page to get the browser's location, that's one type of error. If the Geolocation service in the browser can't get the user's position or if the browser doesn't support the service, that's another type of error. If the service times out before it gets the user's position, that's a third type. Beyond that, other types of errors can occur like too much network traffic interfering with the service.

When an error occurs, you usually want to display an appropriate message or handle it in some other user-friendly way. To do that, you can use a JavaScript function like the one in figure 16-6.

To provide for error handling, the getCurrentPosition method requires two parameters. The first parameter is the function that is called if there aren't any errors. In this figure, this is the same getLocation function that was used in the previous figure. In contrast, the second parameter is the function that is called if there are errors. In this example, a function named errorHandling is called if there are errors, and an error object is passed to that function.

In the errorHandling function, a switch statement is used to handle three of the error codes that might be stored in the code property of the error object. In the API, these are named PERMISSION_DENIED, POSITION_ UNAVAILABLE, and TIMEOUT. For each of these codes, an appropriate message is displayed. But if the error code isn't one of these, an "Unknown error" message is displayed. Of course, if you know JavaScript, you can enhance this JavaScript code to handle the errors in more sophisticated ways.

JavaScript that handles Geolocation errors

```
function initGeolocation() {
    navigator.geolocation.getCurrentPosition(getLocation, errorHandling);
}
function errorHandling(error) {
    switch(error.code) {
        case error.PERMISSION_DENIED: alert("Not sharing your location.");
        break;
        case error.POSITION_UNAVAILABLE: alert("Cannot detect position.");
        break;
        case error.TIMEOUT: alert("Position retrieval timed out.");
        break;
        default: alert("Unknown error.");
        break;
    }
}
function getLocation(position) {
    var url =
        "http://maps.google.com/maps/api/staticmap?sensor=false&center=" +
            position.coords.latitude + "," + position.coords.longitude +
            "&zoom=14&size=300x400&markers=color:red|" +
            position.coords.latitude + "," +
            position.coords.longitude;
    $("#map").attr("src", url)
}
```

The message box that's displayed when permission is denied

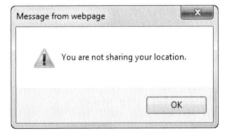

Description

- When you use the geolocation feature, it won't work if (1) the user won't share his location, (2) the Geolocation service in the browser is unable to detect the user's position, or (3) the retrieval of the position times out.

- To handle geolocation errors, you can code a second parameter for the getCurrentPosition method that specifies an error-handling function. Then, that function is executed if an error occurs, and an error object is passed to that function.

- In the error-handling function, PERMISSION_DENIED, POSITION_ UNAVAILABLE, and TIMEOUT are possible values for the code property of the error object.

Figure 16-6   How to handle Geolocation errors

How to use the web storage feature

In the past, you had to use cookies to store data on the user's system. But that meant that the data had to be processed by server-side code. That also meant that the data was passed to the browser with every HTTP request. Beyond that, the storage in a cookie is limited to about 4,000 bytes.

But now, HTML5 offers web storage that can be processed by JavaScript on the browser. Then, the data isn't passed to the server with every HTTP request. In addition, web storage can be used to store approximately 5MB of data.

How to use local storage

Figure 16-7 shows how to use the localStorage object that's defined by HTML5. This object provides for *local storage*, which is storage that persists between browser sessions. Then, you can use the setItem, getItem, and removeItem methods of the localStorage object to add, retrieve, or delete items that have been stored in this object.

The setItem method requires two parameters that provide the name of an item and the value for the item. For instance, you can use code like this to add items named "email" and "phone" that store the email address and phone number for a user:

```
localStorage.setItem("email", "gmm@yahoo.com");
localStorage.setItem("phone", "555-555-1212");
```

Then, you can use the getItem method with the item name as the parameter to retrieve the data for the phone item with a statement like this:

```
var phone = localStorage.getItem("phone");
```

To simplify, you can use the shortcut syntax in this figure. For instance, you can use this code to save the email and phone items:

```
localStorage.email = "gmm@yahoo.com";
localStorage.phone = "555-555-1212";
```

And this code to retrieve the items:

```
var phone = localStorage.phone;
```

The shortcut syntax is used in the example in this figure. Here, an if statement tests to see whether the "hits" item in local storage exists. If it does, it adds 1 to the number in that name/value pair. If it doesn't, it saves a new item named "hits" and saves the value of 1 in it. After that, the write method of the document object is used to write the value of the "hits" item.

How to use session storage

This figure also shows how to use the sessionStorage object to provide *session storage*. This works the same way that local storage works, but the storage is removed when the session ends.

The syntax for working with local or session storage

```
localStorage.setItem("itemname", "value")   // saves the data in the item
localStorage.getItem("itemname")            // gets the data in the item
localStorage.removeItem("itemname")         // removes the item
localStorage.clear()                        // removes all items

sessionStorage.setItem("itemname" "value")  // saves the data in the item
sessionStorage.getItem("itemname")          // gets the data in the item
sessionStorage.removeItem("itemname")       // removes the item
sessionStorage.clear()                      // removes all items
```

The shortcut syntax for getting or saving an item

```
localStorage.itemname                       // saves or gets the data in the item
sessionStorage.itemname                     // saves or gets the data in the item
```

JavaScript that uses local storage for a hit counter

```
<p>You have visited this page <output>
    <script>
        if (localStorage.hits) {
            localStorage.hits = Number(localStorage.hits) + 1;
        } else {
            localStorage.hits = 1;
        }
        document.write(localStorage.hits);
    </script>
</output> time(s).</p>
```

The text that indicates the current value of the hits field in local storage

You have visited this page 5 time(s).

Description

- *Web storage* is a new HTML5 feature that lets the web page use JavaScript to store data in name/value pairs. This feature is currently supported by every modern browser.

- One type of web storage is *local storage*, which is retained indefinitely. The other type of web storage is *session storage*. It works just like local storage, except that session storage is lost when the user closes the browser for the web site.

- Unlike cookies, web storage is meant to be accessed by client-side code, not server-side code. If the server-side code needs to access the data, use cookies, not web storage. Also, web storage isn't passed to the server along with each HTTP request.

- Although the storage limit for cookies is 4K, the HTML5 specification recommends a limit of 5MB for web storage. This limit is supported by every browser except Internet Explorer, which sets its limit at 10MB.

- To refer to web storage from JavaScript, you use the localStorage or sessionStorage object.

- At this writing, Chrome and Firefox provide browser extensions that let users access the web storage on their systems, but other browsers don't.

Figure 16-7   How to use web storage

How to use the Canvas feature

Canvas is a new HTML5 feature that lets you use JavaScript to create two-dimensional drawings. The *Canvas API* is supported by most modern browsers, and it provides a rich interface for drawings and animations. The benefit of using Canvas is that you don't have to depend on third-party, plug-in applications like Flash.

To give you some idea of what you can do with Canvas, the next four figures present some examples. If you understand JavaScript, you should be able to follow the code in these examples. If not, you can just review the examples to better understand what Canvas can do.

How Canvas works

To give you an idea of how Canvas works, figure 16-8 shows how to use Canvas to draw a black square. To start, you need to code a canvas element in the HTML for the page that includes id, width, and height attributes. You also need to code an onLoad attribute that loads the JavaScript function for drawing. In this example, this attribute is coded for the body element and the function that's called is "drawSquare".

In the JavaScript function, you start by using the getElementById method to create an object for the canvas element. Then, you use the getContext method of that object to create a *context object* for the canvas element. You can think of this context object as the container for all of the drawing features that are built into the Canvas API. Because the Canvas API currently supports only two-dimensional drawings, however, you need to use "2d" as the parameter for the getContext method.

Once you have a context object for the canvas element, you can use any of the methods in the Canvas API in your JavaScript code. In this example, the fillRect method is used to start a drawing 25 pixels from the left side of the canvas element and 0 pixels from the top. This method also specifies a rectangle that's 100 pixels by 100 pixels (which is a square). By default, this square is filled with the color black.

When you first start using Canvas, you may want to use CSS to put a border around the canvas element. That way, you get a better idea of how the coordinates work.

A black rectangle that's drawn with JavaScript's canvas API

The HTML for the canvas element

```
<body onLoad="drawSquare()">
    <h1>Black Square</h1>
    <canvas id="mySquare" width="200" height="150"></canvas>
</body>
```

The JavaScript code for drawing the square

```
function drawSquare() {
    var square = document.getElementById("mySquare");
    var contextSquare = square.getContext("2d");
    contextSquare.fillRect(25, 0, 100, 100);
}
```

How to get a context object for a canvas element

- Use the document.getElementById method with the id of the canvas element as its parameter.
- Use the getContext method of the canvas object to create a *context object* for the drawing. Its parameter should be "2d" to specify a two-dimensional drawing.

How to draw a rectangle

- Use the fillRect method to draw and fill the rectangle. Its parameters are the x coordinate for the start of the drawing, the y coordinate for the start of the drawing, the width of the rectangle, and the height of the rectangle.

Description

- Canvas is a new HTML5 API that lets you use JavaScript to draw, fill, and animate elements within a browser. This API is supported by most modern browsers.
- To support the Canvas API, HTML5 provides a canvas element that should be used to receive the output from the JavaScript. When you use this element, you should set its id, width, and height attributes.
- The benefit of using Canvas is that you don't have to depend on third-party, plug-in applications like Flash.

Figure 16-8   How Canvas works

How to draw shapes

Figure 16-9 shows how you can draw shapes like rectangles, circles, and arcs. Here again, just one canvas element is used, but this time it contains three drawings. Then, the JavaScript function that draws the shapes starts by getting the context object for the canvas element.

Once that's done, the JavaScript function uses the fillStyle property of the context object to set the fill color to red. That's followed by the use of the fillRect method, which creates the red rectangle. This time, the rectangle starts in the upper-left corner of the canvas, and it is 150 pixels wide and 100 pixels tall.

Next, the JavaScript function draws a circle by using the beginPath, arc, and closePath methods. Here, the first two parameters for the arc method specify that the center of the circle should be 200 pixels from the left side of the canvas element and 50 pixels from its top, and the third parameter says that the radius of the circle should be 50 pixels.

Then, the fourth and fifth parameters of the arc method specify the starting point and ending point for the arc, which in this case is from 0 degrees (the rightmost portion of a circle) to Math.PI*2 (all the way around the circle and back to 0 degrees). The last parameter, which doesn't matter for a full circle is set to true, which means that the drawing is counter clockwise. Finally, the fillStyle property is used to set the color of the circle, and the fill method is used to draw the circle and fill it with the green color.

The process for drawing a stroked arc is similar to the process of drawing a filled circle. Here again, the beginPath, arc, and endPath methods are used. This time, though, the fourth parameter is still the rightmost portion of the circle, the fifth parameter is set to Math.PI*1 (the leftmost portion), and the Boolean value is set to false, which means that the arc is drawn clockwise. As a result, the arc will be drawn for the bottom half of a circle. If the Boolean value were set to true, the drawing would be for the top half of the circle.

After the arc method is specified, the lineWidth property is used to set the width of the stroke. Then, the stroke method is used to draw the arc.

Of course, this figure is just designed to give you a general idea of how shapes can be drawn with the Canvas API. Keep in mind, though, that the API provides many other properties and methods for drawing shapes.

A red rectangle, green circle, and stroked arc drawn with the canvas API

The HTML for the canvas element

```
<body onLoad="drawShapes()">
    <canvas id="myShapes" width="600" height="150"></canvas>
</body>
```

The JavaScript code for drawing the shapes

```
function drawShapes() {
    //GET CONTEXT OBJECT FOR CANVAS ELEMENT
    var shapes = document.getElementById("myShapes");
    var contextShapes = shapes.getContext("2d");
    //DRAW RED RECTANGLE
    contextShapes.fillStyle = "red";
    contextShapes.fillRect(0, 0, 150, 100);
    //DRAW GREEN CIRCLE
    contextShapes.beginPath();
    contextShapes.arc(200, 50, 50, 0, Math.PI*2, true);
    contextShapes.closePath();
    contextShapes.fillStyle = "green";
    contextShapes.fill();
    //DRAW STROKED PORTION OF A CIRCLE
    contextShapes.beginPath();
    contextShapes.arc(300, 50, 50, 0, Math.PI*1, false);
    contextShapes.closePath();
    contextShapes.lineWidth = 3;
    contextShapes.stroke();
}
```

How to set the color for an object

- Use the fillStyle property of the context object.

How to draw an arc

- Use the beginPath method of the context object to indicate the start of a path.
- Use the arc method to specify the path of the arc. Its parameters are: the x coordinate for the center of the arc, the y coordinate for the center, the radius, the starting point for the arc, the ending point for the arc, and a Boolean value for which true means that the arc should go counter clockwise.
- Use the closePath method to indicate that the path should end.
- Use the fill method to draw the arc and fill it. Use the stroke method to draw the arc but not fill it. Use the lineWidth method to specify the width of the stroke in pixels.

Description

- To specify a point on an arc, you use a multiple of PI, where 0 PI is the rightmost point of a circle, .5 PI is the bottom, 1 PI is the leftmost point, and 1.5 PI is the top.

Figure 16-9   How to draw shapes

How to draw paths and text

Figure 16-10 shows how you can draw paths and text with the Canvas API. Here again, you use the properties or methods that are available in the API. In the example in this figure, you can see that the moveTo, lineTo, and stroke methods of the context object are used to draw paths. And the font and fillText methods are used to draw text.

Please note, however, that I'm not suggesting that you use these methods to create the footers for your pages. I'm just showing how easy it is to add lines and text to your drawings. Remember too that you can overlap lines, shapes, and text by adjusting the x and y coordinates for their starting points. You can also adjust the coordinates for a path so it isn't horizontal.

A footer with two paths and text that's drawn by the canvas API

Copyright 2011 - All Rights Reserved.

The HTML for the canvas elements

```
<body onLoad="drawFooter()">
    <canvas id="myFooter" width="500" height="40"></canvas><br>
</body>
```

The JavaScript for drawing the text and path

```
function drawFooter() {
    var footer = document.getElementById("myFooter");
    var contextFooter = footer.getContext("2d");

    contextFooter.moveTo(0, 0);
    contextFooter.lineTo(500, 0);
    contextFooter.stroke();

    contextFooter.moveTo(0, 40);
    contextFooter.lineTo(500, 40);
    contextFooter.stroke();

    contextFooter.font = "bold 14px sans-serif";
    contextFooter.fillText("Copyright 2011 - All Rights Reserved.", 0, 25);
}
```

How to draw a straight line

- Use the moveTo method of the context object to tell the browser where the line should start within the canvas element. Its two parameters are the x and y coordinates in pixels.
- Use the lineTo method to specify the width of the line and the y coordinate for where the line should end within the canvas element.
- Use the stroke method to draw the line.

How to add text

- Use the font property of the context object to specify the font weight, size, and font family.
- Use the fillText method to draw the text. Its parameters are: the text followed by the x and y coordinates for where the text should start.

Description

- If you vary the y coordinates for the moveTo and lineTo methods, you can draw a line that isn't horizontal.

Figure 16-10   How to draw paths and text

How to draw transparent shapes and use gradients

Figure 16-11 shows how you can draw shapes that are transparent or fill shapes with gradients. This time, the example uses two canvas elements, and the CSS for them displays them inline so they are side by side.

In the first canvas element, the CSS sets the background image to the Murach logo, which is 100-pixels square. As a result, this logo is repeated twice so it fills the 100x200 canvas element. Then, the JavaScript for this element overlays a portion of the first logo with a transparent blue square. To do that, it sets the globalAlpha property to .5, which means 50% transparency. Otherwise, this code is like the code that you've already seen.

In the second canvas element, the JavaScript draws a rectangle that contains a *gradient*. To do that, it first uses the createLinearGradient method to create a gradient object. Then, it uses the addColorStop method three times to add three colors to the gradient object. As a result, this gradient will start with red, end with blue, and have white in the middle (.5). After that, this code sets the fill style to the gradient object. Last, it executes the fillRect method to create the rectangle and fill it with the gradient.

The trick to using gradients is setting the x and y coordinates for the starting and ending points of the gradient area. In this example, the starting point is set to 50, 0, and the ending point is set to 150, 100. Since 0, 0 is the upper-left corner of the 200x100 rectangle that is later filled with the gradient, this means that the starting point is 50 pixels from the left at the top of the rectangle, and the ending point is 150 pixels from the left at the bottom of the rectangle. As a result, the gradient line is drawn so it bisects the rectangle that those two points represent, from corner to corner.

This is hard to visualize at first, but if you experiment with the coordinate settings, you'll soon see how this works. If, for example, you try these gradient settings (0, 0, 200, 0), you'll get a vertical gradient line in the middle of the rectangle. And if you try these settings (0, 0, 0, 100), you'll get a horizontal gradient line in the middle of the rectangle.

A transparent square over an image and a rectangle with a gradient fill

The HTML for the canvas elements

```
<body onLoad="drawShapes()">
    <canvas id="myCanvas_01" width="200" height="100"></canvas>
    <canvas id="myCanvas_02" width="200" height="100"></canvas>
</body>
```

The CSS for the canvas elements

```
canvas { display: inline; }
#myCanvas_01 {background-image:url("images/murach_100_square.jpg"); }
```

The JavaScript for the transparent shape and the gradient fill

```
function drawShapes() {
    // DRAW TRANSPARENT SQUARE
    var canvas_01 = document.getElementById("myCanvas_01");
    var context_01 = canvas_01.getContext("2d");
    context_01.fillStyle = "blue";
    context_01.globalAlpha = .5;
    context_01.fillRect(15, 15, 70, 70);
    // DRAW RECTANGLE WITH GRADIENT FILL
    var canvas_02 = document.getElementById("myCanvas_02");
    var context_02 = canvas_02.getContext("2d");
    var gradient = context_02.createLinearGradient(50, 0, 150, 100);
    gradient.addColorStop(0, "red");
    gradient.addColorStop(.5, "white");
    gradient.addColorStop(1, "blue");
    context_02.fillStyle = gradient;
    context_02.fillRect(0, 0, 200, 100);
}
```

How to draw a shape that's transparent

- Set the globalAlpha property for the context object to a value from 0 through 1, with 0 being completely transparent and 1 being opaque.

How to draw a shape with a gradient fill

- Create a gradient variable by calling the createLinearGradient method with four parameters that set the coordinates for the starting and ending points of the gradient area.

- Call the addColorStop method one time for each color in the gradient. Its two parameters are: a decimal value from 0 to 1 that says where to begin or end the color.

- Set the fillStyle property to the gradient object instead of a color.

Description

- In this example, a transparent blue square overlays a portion of the first logo that's used as the background image for the first canvas element, and a *gradient* is used for the second canvas element.

Figure 16-11   How to draw transparent shapes and use gradients

How to use the Drag and Drop feature

The new HTML5 *Drag and Drop API* lets you drag an HTML element like an image and drop it into an HTML container like a div element. For instance, you can use this feature to let the user drag items into a shopping cart. This feature is currently supported by all modern browsers, except Opera, and it is illustrated in the next three figures.

Here again, if you understand JavaScript, you should be able to follow the code. Otherwise, you can just review this example as another of the new capabilities that are available with HTML5.

How to use HTML to create draggable content

Figure 16-12 shows a web page that uses the drag-and-drop feature. Here, the user can drag any one of the four images at the top of the page and drop it into the shopping cart. Then, the value of the id attribute for the dragged image is displayed in the cart. The user can repeat this for all four books.

To make this work, the HTML must set the draggable attribute for each image to true. Also, the id attribute must be set for each image because that's the value that drops into the cart.

Incidentally, HTML5 web storage could be used in an application like this. To save the contents of the cart just for the session when the user moves to another page, session storage could be used. To save the contents so it is available the next time the user visits the site, local storage could be used.

A web page with objects that can be dragged into a cart

The HTML for the draggable elements and shopping cart

```
<img src="images/book1.jpg" draggable="true" id="SQL Server 2008">
<img src="images/book2.jpg" draggable="true" id="PHP and MySQL">
<img src="images/book3.jpg" draggable="true" id="Visual Basic 2010">
<img src="images/book4.jpg" draggable="true" id="ASP.NET 4 with VB 2010">
<div id="cart"><strong>Shopping Cart (Drag books here)</strong></div>
<input type="button" value="Checkout">
```

The CSS for formatting the images and shopping cart

```
img {
    float: left;
    margin: 10px; }
#cart {
    min-height: 100px;
    width: 275px;
    border: 3px dashed #ccc;
    margin: 10px;
    padding: 10px;
    clear: left; }
```

Description

- The drag-and-drop feature of HTML5 lets you drag one HTML element into a containing HTML element. At this writing, this feature is supported by all modern browsers except Opera.

- To make an HTML element draggable, you set the draggable attribute to true.

- In this example, when the user drags a book image into the div element for the shopping cart, the id for the book image will be displayed.

- In this example, the div element for the shopping cort is formatted with a minimum height. This lets the div element expand if needed.

- A drag-and-drop application like this would often be used with HTML5 web storage to save the contents of the shopping cart.

Figure 16-12   How to use HTML to create draggable content

How to use HTML to work with drag-and-drop events

When you use drag-and-drop, you use JavaScript to handle the events that are related to dragging and dropping. These events are summarized in figure 16-13. For instance, the dragstart event occurs when a drag is started, the dragenter event occurs when the mouse is first moved over a draggable element, the dragover event occurs when a drag moves over an object, and the drop event occurs when the user drops the object.

For the drag-and-drop example in the previous figure, the ondragstart event for all four images is handled by JavaScript code. To make that happen, the ondragstart attribute is coded for all four images. This attribute gives the name for the function that will handle the event (drag) and passes two parameters to it. The first one (this) represents the object for the book image that was dragged. The second one (event) is the event object. You'll see how these objects are used in the next figure.

To implement this drag-and-drop action, the JavaScript code must also handle the events that occur when an image is dropped into the cart. To make that happen, three attributes are coded for the div element that represents the cart. The ondrop attribute is used to specify that the JavaScript drop function should be executed when the drop event occurs. Here again, this function will receive the this and event objects.

Then, to handle the dragenter and dragover events, the ondragenter and ondragover attributes are coded for the div element. However, these attributes don't call a JavaScript event handler. They just specify "return false". This tells the browser to fire those events, but not do anything with them once they're fired.

Drag and drop events

Service	Description
dragstart	Fired for an element when a drag is started.
drag	Fired for an element after dragstart has started.
dragenter	Fired when the mouse is first moved over a draggable element.
dragleave	Fired when the mouse leaves an element while a drag is occurring.
dragover	Fired when the mouse is moved over an element when a drag is occurring.
drop	Fired for an element when a dragged object is dropped.
dragend	Fired when a dragged object has been dropped and the dragging operation is over.

HTML that handles four different types of drag-and-drop events

```
<img src="images/book1.jpg" draggable="true"
    ondragstart="drag(this, event)" id="SQL Server 2008 for developers">
<img src="images/book2.jpg" draggable="true"
    ondragstart="drag(this, event)" id="PHP and MySQL">
<img src="images/book3.jpg" draggable="true"
    ondragstart="drag(this, event)" id="Visual Basic 2010">
<img src="images/book4.jpg" draggable="true"
    ondragstart="drag(this, event)" id="ASP.NET 4 with VB 2010">
<div id="cart"
    ondrop="drop(this, event)"
    ondragenter="return false"
    ondragover="return false">
    <strong>Shopping Cart (Drag books here)</strong>
</div>
<input type="button" value="Checkout">
```

Description

- To use the drag-and-drop feature, you need to use JavaScript to handle some of the events that are in the table above. For instance, this example uses the dragstart, drop, dragenter, and dragover events.

- To specify the event handler for an HTML element that is draggable, you code an attribute for the event that will be handled, like ondragstart for the dragstart event. The value of this attribute should be the name of the JavaScript event handler. Then, within the parentheses after this name, you code "this, event". This will pass the object that is dragged (this) and the event object (event) to the event handler.

- To specify the event handler for the element that will receive a draggable object when it is dropped, you code an ondrop attribute. Here again, you code the parameters as "this, event" so the object for the receiving element and the event object will be passed to the event handler.

- To handle the dragenter and dragover events for the element that will receive draggable objects, you code ondragenter and ondragover events. In this example, the value of these attributes is set to false, which means "we understand that the events were fired, but we don't want to handle them right now."

Figure 16-13   How to use HTML to work with drag-and-drop events

How to use JavaScript for the event handlers

Figure 16-14 shows the JavaScript code for the drag and drop functions that are called by the attributes in the previous figure. Remember that both of these attributes pass one parameter that represents the object that the event occurred on and a second parameter that represents the event object. When these objects are received by the drag and drop functions, they are referred to as target and e.

In the drag function, the only statement uses the setData method of the dataTransfer property of the e object to get the data and save it in this property. Here, the first parameter specifies that this data should be treated as text, and the second parameter says that the data should come from the id attribute of the object that the event occurred on. Since that object is the image that is being dragged, the data is the id for the image.

In the drop function, the innerHTML property of the target object (the div element) is used to put HTML in that element. This time, the getData method of the dataTransfer property of the e object is used to get the text that the drag function retrieved, and that text is placed within <p> tags. As a result, the id is shown in the shopping cart when this function ends.

In the drop function, the code starts by testing to see whether the preventDefault property of the event object (e) exists. This property indicates whether the browser may take a default action for the event. In this case, if it does exist, the code issues the preventDefault method to cancel that default action. If this code isn't included in the drop method, it won't work correctly for some browsers.

A web page with an object that's about to be dropped

The JavaScript for the drag and drop functions

```
function drag(target, e) {
    e.dataTransfer.setData("Text", target.id);
}
function drop(target, e) {
    if (e.preventDefault) {
        e.preventDefault();
    }
    target.innerHTML += "<p>" + e.dataTransfer.getData("Text") + "</p>";
}
```

Description

- When the event handler for the drag or drop event is called, the events above are executed. These events receive an object for the element that caused the event and an event object.

- In the drag function, target refers to the image that's being dragged. In the drop function, target refers to the div element for the shopping cart.

- The dataTransfer property of the event parameter (e) that is passed to a JavaScript function has two methods: setData() and getData().

- The setData method accepts two parameters: the format for data and the data that's going to be set. In this example, the setData method sets the format to "Text" and the data to the id of the object that has been passed to it.

- The getData method gets the data that has been set by the setData method. Its parameter specifies the format of that data.

- The preventDefault property of the event object (e) indicates whether a default action for the event may be taken. The preventDefault method cancels that action.

- In this example, the drag function sets the data, which is the id of the img element that's being dragged. Then, the drop function gets that data and puts it in a paragraph within the div element for the shopping cart. This function uses the innerHTML property of the div element to add HTML within that element.

Figure 16-14   How to use JavaScript for the event handlers

Perspective

This chapter has introduced you to several of the new features that W3C is actively promoting. If some of these features aren't quite ready for prime time right now, it won't be long before they will be. Besides that, they are likely to be improved and enhanced. As a result, these features are likely to play ever larger roles in the web sites of the future.

Terms

@font-face selector	session storage
Geolocation API	Canvas API
web storage	context object
local storage	Drag and Drop API

Summary

- CSS3 provides a new @font-face selector that you can use to embed fonts from your libraries into a web page.

- You can also embed fonts in your web pages by using Google Web Fonts, Adobe Typekit fonts, and other services like Cufon, Font Jazz, Font Deck, P+C DTR , and sIFR 3.

- The HTML5 *Geolocation API* lets you use JavaScript to get the latitude and longitude for a browser. You can use this feature with the Google Maps Service to show the location of the user on a Google map.

- The HTML5 API for *web storage* provides for both *local storage* and *session storage*. To work with that storage, you use JavaScript to store and retrieve the data from name/value pairs in the localStorage and sessionStorage objects.

- The HTML5 *Canvas API* lets you draw shapes, paths, text, transparent shapes, and shapes with *gradient* fills. To do that, you code a canvas element in the HTML and use JavaScript to create a context object for that element. Then, you can use the methods of the context object to draw the shapes, paths, and text.

- The HTML5 *Drag and Drop API* lets you drag data from HTML elements and drop it into an HTML container element. To do that, you code the HTML draggable attribute for elements that can be dragged, and you use HTML to work with drag-and-drop events like the dragstart, drag, dragend, and drop events. Then, you use JavaScript to handle the events.

Exercise 16-1   Use web fonts, Geolocation, and web storage

In this exercise, you'll make three enhancements to a web page so it looks like this:

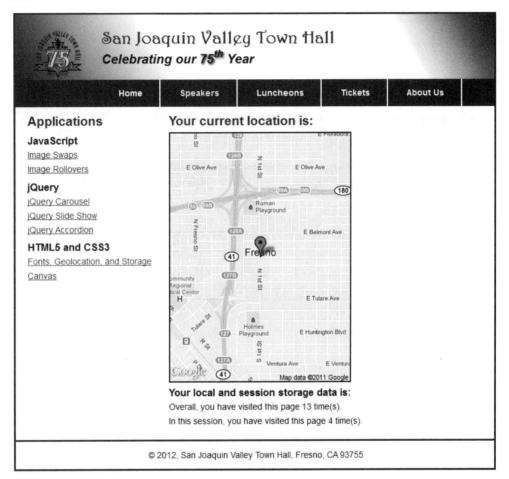

Open and review the HTML and CSS files for this page

1. Use your text editor to open the HTML and CSS files for this page:

   ```
   c:\html5_css3\exercises\town_hall_3\speakers\geolocation.html
   c:\html5_css3\exercises\town_hall_3\styles\speakers_pages.css
   ```

2. Test this page in Firefox and see that it displays the map.

Make three enhancements to this page and test after each one

3. Using figure 16-1 as a guide, choose a web font on your system and copy it into the styles folder. Then, use CSS3 to apply it to the h1 element in the header. You don't need to use an id selector for this.

4. Using figure 16-7 as a guide, use web storage to add the two messages that you see below the map. To start that, you can copy the code from the example for this figure into the body of the HTML file.

5. Using figure 16-6 as a guide, add error handling to the JavaScript code that gets the map. To start that, you can copy the code from the example for this figure into the script element in the head section of the HTML file.

Exercise 16-2   Use Canvas

In this exercise, you'll use Canvas to enhance a page so it looks like this:

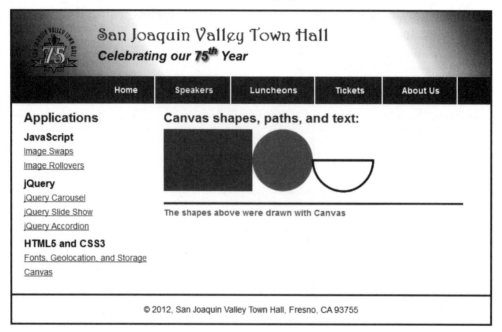

1. Use your text editor to open the HTML and CSS files for this page:

    ```
    c:\html5_css3\exercises\town_hall_3\speakers\canvas.html
    c:\html5_css3\exercises\town_hall_3\styles\speakers_pages.css
    ```

2. Test this page in Firefox to see that the shapes are already there.

3. Using figure 16-10 as a guide, add the path and text below the shapes to this page.

Section 4

How to design
and deploy a web site

In section 1, you learned how to use the professional subset of HTML and CSS for building web pages. Now, in the two chapters of this section, you can learn how to design and deploy a web site. You can read these chapters any time after you complete the chapters in section 1, and you can read these chapters in whichever sequence you prefer.

In chapter 17, you'll learn how to design the pages for a web site and how to design the navigation between those pages. You'll also learn the guidelines that will help you create an effective web site. Then, in chapter 18, you'll learn how to deploy your web site from your local computer or server to a web server that has Internet access. You'll also learn how to get your web site into the major search engines and directories.

17

How to design a web site

If you've read section 1, you know how to use HTML and CSS to develop web pages. Now, in this chapter, you'll learn the guidelines, methods, and procedures that you need for designing a web site. When you complete this chapter, you should be able to design and develop an effective web site.

Users and usability

Before you design a web site, you need to think about who your users are going to be and what they are going to expect. After all, it is your users who are going to determine the success of your web site.

What web users want is usability

What do users want when they reach a web site? They want to find what they're looking for as quickly and easily as possible. And when they find it, they want to extract the information or do the task as quickly and easily as possible.

How do users use a web page? They don't read it in an orderly way, and they don't like to scroll. Instead, they scan the page to see if they can find what they're looking for or a link to what they're looking for. Often, they click quickly on a link to see if it gives them what they want, and if it doesn't, they click on the Back button to return to where they were. In fact, users click on the Back button more than 30% of the time when they reach a new page.

If the users can't find what they're looking for or get too frustrated, they leave the site. It's that simple. For some web sites, more than 50% of first-time visitors to the home page leave without ever going to another page.

In web development terms, what the users want is *usability*. This term refers to how easy it is to use a web site, and usability is one of the key factors that determines the effectiveness of a web site. If a site is easy to use, it has a chance to be effective. If it isn't easy to use, it probably won't be effective.

Figure 17-1 presents one page of a web site that has a high degree of usability, and it presents three guidelines for improving usability. First, you should try to present all of the essential information "above the fold." This term refers to what's shown on the screen when a new page is displayed, which is analogous to the top half of a newspaper. This reduces the need for scrolling, and gives the page a better chance for success.

Second, you should try to group related items into separate components, and limit the number of components on each page. That will make the page look more manageable and will help people find what they're looking for.

Third, you should adhere to the current conventions for web site usability. For instance, clickable links should look like they're clickable and items that aren't clickable shouldn't fool users by looking like they are clickable.

If you look at the web site in this figure, you can see that it has implemented these guidelines. All of the critical information is presented above the fold. The page is divided into a header and six other well-defined components, including a set of tabs near the bottom of the page. It's also easy to tell where to click.

Of course, it's relatively easy to build a web site like this because it has a small number of products. In contrast, building usability into a large web site with dozens of product categories and hundreds of products is a serious challenge.

A web site that is easy to use

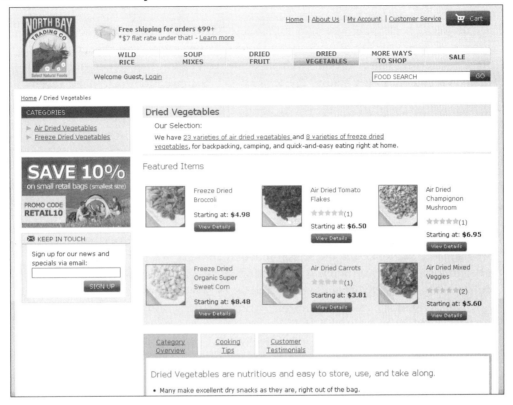

What web site users want

- To find what they're looking for as quickly and easily as possible
- To get the information or do the task that they want to do as quickly and easily as possible

How web site users use a web page

- They scan the page to find what they're looking for or a link to what they're looking for, and they don't like to scroll. If they get frustrated, they leave.
- They often click on links and buttons with the hope of finding what they're looking for, and they frequently click on the Back button when they don't find it.

Three guidelines for improving usability

- Present all of the critical information "above the fold" so the user doesn't have to scroll.
- Group related items into separate components, and limit the number of components on each page.
- Adhere to the current conventions for web site usability (see the next figure).

Description

- *Usability* refers to how easy it is to use a web site, and usability is a critical requirement for an effective web site.

Figure 17-1   What web users want is usability

The current conventions for usability

If you've been using web sites for a while, you know that you expect certain aspects of each web site to work the same way. For example, you expect underlined text to be a link to another web page, and you expect that something will happen if you click on a button. These are web site conventions that make a web site easier to use because they work the same on almost all sites.

Figure 17-2 summarizes some of the other conventions that lead to improved usability. By following these conventions, you give the users what they expect, and that makes your web site easier to use.

To start, a header usually consists of a logo, tag line, utilities, navigation bar, and search function. As a result, the users look for these items in the header. In the example in this figure, this tag line is below the logo: "Powered by Service." The utilities are in the top border, including "Logout", "My Account", "My Favorites", and "Help". The navigation bar contains links that divide the web site into sections. And the search function consists of a text box that's large enough for long entries followed by a Search button. All of these are web site conventions, and that's where experienced users look for these components.

The navigation conventions are also critical to the usability of a web site. In brief, clickable items should look like they're clickable, and items that aren't clickable shouldn't look like they're clickable. In other words, don't trick the users.

In addition, the last navigation convention says that clicking on the logo in the header should take you back to the home page. This is a more recent convention that isn't implemented on all sites, but is still worth doing. In the example in this figure, the navigation bar doesn't have a Home link so the only way to get back to that page is to click the logo.

If you implement all of these conventions on your site, you will be on your way to web usability. But that's just a start. In the rest of this chapter, you'll learn many other ways to improve the usability of a site.

A web page that illustrates some of the current web site conventions

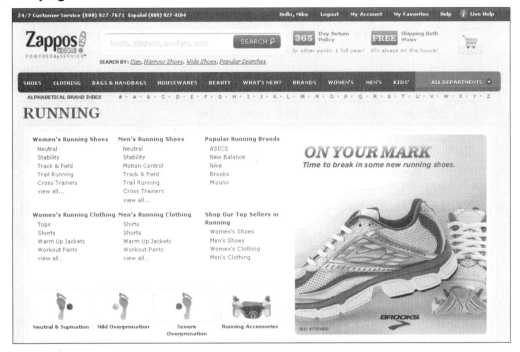

Header conventions

- The header consists of a logo, tag line, utilities, and a navigation bar.
- The tag line identifies what's unique about the web site.
- The navigation bar provides links that divide the site into sections.
- The utilities consist of links to useful but not primary information.
- If your site requires a search function, it should be in the header, and it should consist of a large text box for the text followed by a button that's labeled either "Go" or "Search."

Navigation conventions

- Underlined text is always a link.
- Images that are close to short text phrases are clickable.
- A small symbol in front of a text phrase is clickable.
- Clickable buttons should look like they're 3D.
- Short text phrases in columns are clickable.
- If you click on a cart symbol, you go to your shopping cart.
- If you click on the logo in the header, you go to the home page.

Description

- If your web site implements the current web site conventions, your users will be able to use the same techniques on your site that they use on other sites.

Figure 17-2   The current conventions for usability

Design guidelines

Did you ever think about what makes a good web site? Well, a lot of experts have. What follows, then, is a distillation of some of the best thinking on the subject.

Use the home page to sell the site

Figure 17-3 presents 10 guidelines for the design of a home page. Most important is the first one, which says to emphasize what's different about your site and why it's valuable from the user's point of view. In other words, sell the site to your visitors.

If you're a well-known company with a successful site, this isn't as important. That's why the home pages for the web sites of most large companies don't make any special efforts to sell their sites. But if you're developing the web site for a small company that still needs to develop a customer base, by all means use the home page to sell the site. That may determine whether or not your site is successful.

The other nine guidelines should be self-explanatory. For instance, you don't need to welcome users to your site because that space should be used to sell the site. You don't want to include an active link to the home page on the home page because it would just reload the page. You do want to limit the use of drop-down menus (which aren't presented in this book) because the users can't tell that the menus are there until they drop down. You do want to limit the length of the page title to 8 words and 64 characters because it's displayed in the results for search engines. And you do want to use a different design for the home page to set it off from the other pages of the site.

If you look at the home page in this figure, you can see that it tries to sell the site. Its tag line says: "love what you buy." Then, the copy in the top block adds: "We Simplify The Complex" and shows their three-step procedure for doing that. That encourages me to at least try one of their recommendations for a product category.

If you're competing with a known brand like *Consumers Digest*, and most of us are, you obviously need to let people know what you do better, and you need to do that on the home page. Nevertheless, not doing that is a critical failing of most web sites.

A home page that tries to sell the site

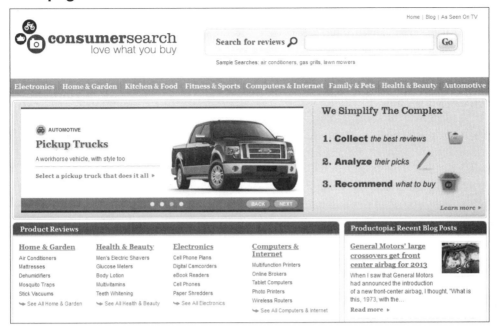

10 guidelines for developing an effective home page

1. Emphasize what your site offers that's valuable and how your site differs from competing sites.
2. Emphasize the highest priority tasks of your site so users have a clear idea of what they can do.
3. Don't welcome users to your site because that's a waste of space.
4. Group items in the navigation areas so similar items are next to each other, and don't provide multiple navigation areas for the same types of links.
5. Only use icons for navigation if the users will readily recognize them.
6. Use drop-down menus sparingly, especially if the items aren't self-explanatory.
7. Design the home page so it is different from the other pages of the site.
8. Don't include an active link to the home page on the home page.
9. Code the title for the home page as the organization name, followed by a short description, and limit the title to 8 or fewer words and 64 or fewer characters.
10. If your site provides shopping, include a link to the shopping cart on your home page.

Description

- *Homepage Usability* by Jakob Nielsen and Marie Tahir presents 113 guidelines for home pages, plus an analysis of the home pages for 50 web sites. Though dated, it is still worth reading.

Figure 17-3   Use the home page to sell the site

Let the users know where they are

As users navigate through a site, they like to know where they are. That's why letting the users know where they are is one of the current conventions for web site use. Remember too that many users will reach your site via search engines so they won't arrive at the home page. They have a special need to find out where they are.

As figure 17-4 shows, there are three primary ways to let the users know where they are. First, you should highlight the links that led the user to the current page. Second, the heading for the page should be the same as the link that led to it.

This is illustrated by the first web page in this figure. Here, the Fly Fishing link is highlighted in the navigation bar, which means that the user started there. Then, the Fly Rods and Freshwater Helios Rods are highlighted in the links of the left sidebar (they're red), which means the user first clicked the Fly Rods link followed by the Freshwater Helios Rods link. Last, the heading for the page is "Freshwater Helios Rods", which is the same as the link that led to the page.

The third way to let the users know where they are is to provide *breadcrumbs* that show the path to the page. This is illustrated by the second page in this figure. When you use breadcrumbs, the current convention is to do it just as this web site did it, with a greater than sign (>) to mark each step in the path.

A product page with the active links highlighted

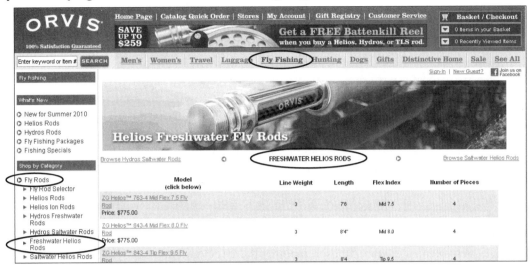

A product page that provides breadcrumbs

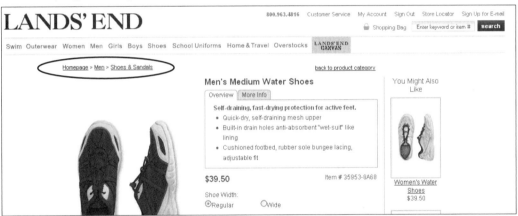

How to let the users know where they are

- Highlight the active links.
- The heading for the page should be the same as the link that led to the page.
- Provide breadcrumbs in this format: Homepage > Men > Shoes & Sandals.

Description

- As your site gets more complex, the users are likely to lose track of where they are in the site. But even simple sites should let the users know where they are.

Figure 17-4   Let the users know where they are

Make the best use of web page space

As you design a web page, remember that the part of the page that's above the fold is the most valuable space. As a result, you want to put the most important components of the page in that space. That's why many of the most successful web sites have relatively small headers. That way, they have more space for the components that make each page effective. In fact, the home pages of many of the best web sites have all of the components above the fold.

To emphasize this point, figure 17-5 presents an extreme example of a web page that doesn't get the most out of the space above the fold. In fact, none of the text of the page can be seen above the fold. You have to scroll down for all of the information. Granted that the photos are beautiful (if you're a fly fisher), but does the fish have to show on every page that relates to Bob Cusack's Alaska Lodge? This is a case where the graphics got out of control and diminished the usability of the page.

As you design your pages, remember the three guidelines in this figure. Keep your header relatively small. Prioritize the components that are going to go on the page. And then give the best space to the most important components.

Wasted space on a primary page

Guidelines for the effective use of space

- Keep the header relatively small.
- Prioritize the components for each page.
- Give the most important components the primary locations.

Description

- The most valuable space on each web page is the space above the fold. To get the most from it, you need to prioritize the components on each page and give the best locations to the highest-priority components.

Figure 17-5   Make the best use of web page space

Write for the web

Remember how web users use a web site. Instead of reading, they skim and scan. They want to get the information that they're looking for as quickly as possible, and they don't want to have to dig through several paragraphs of text for it. That's why writing for a web site is so different from writing for the printed page.

In figure 17-6, you can see a block of copy that isn't written for the web, followed by one that is. To present the same information in a way that is more accessible, the second example uses fewer words (135 to 177), which is the quickest way to improve your web writing. It also uses a numbered list to make it easy to find the flight information without having to dig through the text.

If you look through the other web writing guidelines, you'll see that they recommend what we implement in the figures of our books: an inverted pyramid style so the most important items are presented first; headings and subheadings to identify portions of the text; bulleted and numbered lists; tables for tabular information; and no headings with all caps. We do that so you don't have to read all of the text to review the information that you're looking for, and that's also the way web writing should work.

The last guideline is to make the text for all links as explicit as possible. For instance, "Find a job with us" is better than "Jobs", and "Apply for unemployment compensation" is better than "Unemployment". Remember that 30 to 40 percent of a user's clicks are likely to be on the Back button because a link didn't take him where he wanted. The more explicit your links are, the less that will happen.

Incidentally, the first example in this figure also illustrates poor typography. Above all, the text lines are 90 characters long, which makes the text difficult to read. In addition, three different font sizes are used in the first four lines, but the font sizes don't reflect the relative importance of the text. More about that in figure 17-8.

Writing that isn't for the web (177 words and 1041 characters)

> **The progressive air services you'll use to reach Cusack's Alaska Lodge are a wonderful reflection of your journey into the wilderness.** First, you will fly a major jet service from near your home to Anchorage, Alaska; arriving here, most itineraries will mandate an overnight stay. The next morning you will board a small plane piloted by one of the fine bush pilots of Iliamna Air Taxi (often one of their Pilatus aircraft, a high-flying, very comfortable aircraft), for the transfer between Anchorage and the little village of Iliamna. Upon arriving, Iliamna Air Taxi's Iliamna crew will switch your gear from the mid-sized plane to a smaller, float-equipped Cessna or Beaver, and after a short wait, you will be on the final leg of your adventure, touching down on the lake's surface in front of Bob's lodge a short thirty minutes later. For the remainder of your week, Bob will be your pilot, flying you into amazingly beautiful country in his two small airplanes, giving you a peek into the enormity and grandeur of his corner of Alaska.

The same copy, but written for the web (135 words and 717 characters)

> **The three-part flight to Bob Cusack's Alaska Lodge is a fascinating journey into the Alaskan wilderness**
>
> 1. You take a major jet service from your home to Anchorage, Alaska.
> 2. From Anchorage, you take the Iliamna Air Taxi to the little village of Iliamna. This flight will be piloted by one of the Air Taxi's fine bush pilots in a comfortable plane like the Pilatus.
> 3. In Iliamna, the Air Taxi's crew will switch your bags to a smaller, float plane like a Cessna or a Beaver. Then, after a short wait and a 30 minute flight, you will touch down on beautiful Lake Iliamna in front of Bob's lodge.
>
> For the remainder of your week, Bob will be your pilot as he takes you into the beauty and grandeur of his corner of Alaska.

Web writing guidelines

- Use fewer words.
- Write in inverted pyramid style with the most important information first.
- Use headings and subheadings to identify portions of the text.
- Use bulleted lists and numbered lists to make information more accessible.
- Use tables for tabular information.
- Don't use all caps (all capital letters) for headings. Usually, it's best to capitalize only the first letter in a heading, plus any required capitalization.
- Make the text for all links as explicit as possible.

Description

- Web users skim and scan; they don't read like book readers do. So when you write for the web, you need to change the way you think about writing.

Figure 17-6   Write for the web

Chunk long pages into shorter pages

Remember that web site users don't like to scroll. So a general guideline for web page design is to limit the amount of scrolling to one-and-one-half or two times the height of the browser window. But what if you need to present more information than that?

The best solution is to use *chunking* to divide the content into logical pieces or topics that can be presented on separate web pages. This is illustrated by the example in figure 17-7. Here, the copy for each book on the site has been broken down into six topics that are represented by the "About the book" links. If, for example, the user clicks on "What this book does", the first web page in this figure is displayed. Or, if the user clicks on "Meet the author", the second web page is displayed.

This approach lets the users select the topics that they're interested in so they have more control over their web site experience. This makes it easier for the users to find what they're looking for. And this reduces the need for scrolling. How much better this is than forcing the users to scroll through a long page of text trying to find what they're looking for.

Two pages with chunks of information about a book

What this book does

About the book

What this book does
Who this book is for
What software you need
Table of contents
Meet the author
Related books

Free downloads

Chapters 2 and 3
The book applications

Courseware

For trainers
For instructors

FAQs and correx

FAQs
Corrections

Our 100% Guarantee

When you buy books from

Murach's JavaScript and DOM Scripting

by Ray Harris
20 chapters, 764 pages, 337 illustrations
ISBN: 978-1-809774-55-4

List price: **$54.50**
Your price: **$38.15 (you save 30%)**
Ebook price: **$33.15**
Book and Ebook: **$48.15 (best buy)**

What this book does

To present the JavaScript skills in a manageable progression, this book is divided into four sections.

Section 1 gets you off to a fast start

It presents a complete subset of JavaScript that includes basic event handling and elementary DOM scripting. It also shows you how to use the Firebug extension of Firefox to test and debug your applications. When you finish this section, you're ready for rapid progress.

Section 2 presents the rest of the JavaScript essentials

This includes how to use arrays, functions, regular expression, libraries, and your own object types. The last application in this section puts all of the skills

Meet the author

About the book

What this book does
Who this book is for
What software you need
Table of contents
Meet the author
Related books

Free downloads

Chapters 2 and 3
The book applications

Courseware

For trainers
For instructors

FAQs and correx

FAQs
Corrections

Our 100% Guarantee

Murach's JavaScript and DOM Scripting

by Ray Harris
20 chapters, 764 pages, 337 illustrations
ISBN: 978-1-809774-55-4

List price: **$54.50**
Your price: **$38.15 (you save 30%)**
Ebook price: **$33.15**
Book and Ebook: **$48.15 (best buy)**

Meet author Ray Harris

Ray Harris is an expert JavaScript programmer. That will be obvious to you as soon as review the 20 complete applications that he presents in this book.
But Ray is much more than a JavaScript programmer. He has a Master's degree in Computer Science and Artificial Intelligence. He worked on advanced research projects at the Air Force Research Lab while he was in the USAF. He taught information security and web development at the College of Technology in Raleigh, North Carolina. In fact, Ray has been programming and teaching since he was 12 years old.
So when Ray said he wanted to write for us, it didn't take us long to hire

Description

- *Chunking* refers to the grouping of content into chunks that can be presented on separate web pages. This lets the users select the chunks of information that they're interested in.

- Chunking is one way to improve the web writing, make the information more accessible, and reduce the need for scrolling.

- You can also implement chunking with tabs (see chapter 13) and accordions (see chapter 14).

Figure 17-7   Chunk long pages into shorter pages

Know the basic principles of graphics design

Most web designers aren't graphics designers, but they should at least know the four basic principles of graphics design that are presented in figure 17-8. These principles are in common use on all of the best web sites, so it's easy to find examples of their use.

For instance, *alignment* means that aligning related items gives a sense of order to a web page, and all of the examples to this point in this chapter make extensive use of alignment. Similarly, *proximity* means that related items should be close to each other, and all of those examples illustrate this principle too. When proximity is applied to headings, it means that a heading should be closer to the text that follows it than the text that precedes it.

The principle of *repetition* means that you repeat some elements from page to page to give the pages continuity. This is natural for web pages, starting with the header, which is usually the same on all pages. This goes along with *contrast*, which is what draws your eye to a component. For instance, a component with a large heading or a yellow background will draw attention because it stands out from the other components of the page.

The home page in this figure illustrates what happens if you don't obey these principles. Because the principle of proximity isn't obeyed, the headings float above blocks of copy so it looks like the page consists of many small components. Because the contrast of the symbols in the middle of the page (what are they?) draws your eye to them, the user is drawn away from the text that matters. Besides that, the alignment isn't clean so the page looks disorganized.

If you aren't a graphics designer, you don't need to be intimidated by the use of these principles because there are thousands of good examples on the Internet. By copying them, you should be able to develop an attractive and inviting web site that delivers a high degree of usability.

But whether or not you're a graphics designer, you should at least get the typography right. That way, your readers are more likely to read what you've written. In section 1, you were introduced to some of the guidelines for effective typography, but this figure presents them again.

One common problem is text lines that are longer than 65 characters. This is illustrated by the first example in figure 17-6, which has 90 characters per line, and that makes the text unappealing and difficult to read. To fix that problem, you can increase the font size and shorten the line width. This is illustrated by the second example in figure 17-6.

Some less common problems are using a background image, using a background color that is too dark, centering text, and justifying text. Also, if you indent the first line of each paragraph, you don't need space between the paragraphs, but you do need space if you don't indent the first lines. Last, you should avoid the use of reverse type (white type on a dark background), especially for text, because it's difficult to read.

A home page that doesn't obey the graphics design principles

Four principles of graphics design

- *Alignment* means that related items on the page should line up with each other.
- *Proximity* means that related items should be close together.
- *Repetition* means that you should repeat some elements from page to page to give the pages continuity.
- *Contrast* is what draws your eye to the components on a web page. If everything is the same, nothing stands out.

Typographical guidelines

- Limit the line length of paragraphs to 65 characters.
- Use a sans serif font in a size that's large enough for easy reading.
- Show the relationship between a heading and the text that follows by keeping them close.
- Use dark text on a light background, and don't use an image for the background.
- Don't center text and don't justify text.
- If you indent the first lines of paragraphs, you don't need space between the paragraphs.
- Don't use reverse type (white type on a colored background) for text.

Description

- If you aren't a graphics designer, you can at least implement the basic principles of graphics design and get the typography right.

Figure 17-8   Know the basic principles of graphics design

Design methods and procedures

At this point, you should have a good idea of how the pages of a web site should look and work. That means you're ready to learn how to use the methods and procedures that will help you design a web site. But first, you should know how development teams are used.

The use of development teams

A large company's web site is usually designed and implemented by team members like those that are summarized in figure 17-9. To design the site, a typical team will consist of one or more web designers, one or more writers, a marketing specialist or two, and one or more graphics designers. Then, to implement the web site after it has been designed, a typical team will consist of HTML and CSS specialists, client-side programmers, server-side programmers, a database administrator, and a network administrator.

In short, you don't design a web site or even a portion of a web site by yourself when you work in a large shop. In contrast, a small web site may be designed and developed by a single person. In either case, though, you never work alone, unless you're designing your own web site. Instead, you review each phase of the design with the people you're developing it for: your boss, your client, the marketing team, or the other members of the design team.

This figure also summarizes the difference between a *web designer* and a *graphics designer*. This is an important distinction because they're usually two different jobs. In short, web designers participate in all phases of web design with the focus on usability. In contrast, graphics designers focus on the aspects of a web site that make it look more inviting and manageable so more people will use it.

In practice, then, good graphics design is an essential but relatively small part of the web design process. In fact, the trend is toward simplicity. So if you're designing a small site, don't be afraid to keep it simple.

A large web site that is managed by a team

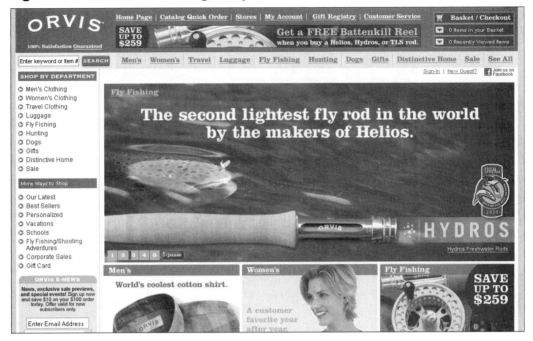

Typical members of a development team

For design	For implementation
Web designers	HTML and CSS specialists
Writers	Client-side programmers
Marketing specialists	Server-side programmers
Graphics designers	Database administrator
	Network administrator

Web designers vs. graphics designers

- *Web designers* participate in all phases of web design.
- *Graphics designers* focus on the graphics that make web pages work better and look more inviting.

Description

- In a large company, a web site is usually designed and implemented by a team. In a small company, a single person is likely to do everything.
- Unless you're designing your own web site, you will be working with others who will review and evaluate your work, such as your boss, marketing specialists, your customer, or potential users.
- *Web designer* is a term that's often confused with *graphics designer*, but graphics design is a relatively small part of web design.

Figure 17-9   The use of development teams

Top-down design, stepwise refinement, and prototyping

For all but the simplest web sites, designing a web site is a challenging process. To complicate that, your design usually has to please several reviewers so you can't just design the pages and be done with them. You usually have to design, review, adjust the design, and repeat that loop until the site is done.

With that as background, figure 17-10 presents three methods that can help the design process go more smoothly. These are proven methods that have been used on all types of projects for many years. And they work for web site projects too.

The first method is *top-down design*. This just means that you should design the most critical elements of a system first. Then, you can work your way down through the less critical elements until the entire system is designed.

For a web site, the most critical elements are the home page and the primary content pages. For instance, the primary content pages for a commercial site are the product pages. The primary content pages for a community service site are usually the pages that describe the services that the site provides. After those pages have been designed, which includes the navigation between them, you can go on to the other sections or pages of the web site.

The second method is *stepwise refinement*. This just means that you can't design a web page in a single step. Instead, you need to work the page through successive levels of refinement on the way to the final page design. For instance, the designer often starts by developing several sketches for the design of a page. Then, when the reviewers agree on one of those approaches, the designer develops a simple version of the page using HTML and CSS that shows more detail. This refinement process continues until the final version of the page is agreed upon.

Stepwise refinement is illustrated by the two examples in this figure. The first example shows a rough sketch of what the home page for a community service site might look like. This can be a hand-drawn sketch or a computer-drawn sketch. The second example is a web page that is a later step in the design of the page. Although it is only partially implemented, it will give the reviewers a better idea of what the designer has in mind.

The third method is *prototyping*. This just means that you need to develop a working model (*prototype*) of the critical web pages as early in the design process as possible. Then, the reviewers can actually use the pages to see how they work. That usually will raise all sorts of concerns that can be resolved early in the design process when the cost of fixing the problems is relatively inexpensive. If you don't prototype the web site, critical issues are likely to be raised late in the process when they cost more to fix.

The second example in this figure illustrates what an early prototype might be. At this stage, only one of the speaker pages needs to be developed to show the navigation to a speaker page and back. But if you get that right, you've got the top-level of your design project under control.

The sketch of a home page

Header	
Navigation bar	

Selling copy	News items
Lecture 1 with thumbnail photo and brief intro	
Lecture 2 with thumbnail photo and brief intro	
Lecture 3 with thumbnail photo and brief intro	
Lecture 4 with thumbnail photo and brief intro	
Lecture 5 with thumbnail photo and brief intro	
Lecture 6 with thumbnail photo and brief intro	

P.O. Box 5149, Fresno, CA 93755-5149 · (559) 444-2180

A prototype for the home page

Description

- *Top-down design* means that you start with the most difficult aspects of a system and proceed downwards through the less critical aspects. For a web site, this usually means that you start by designing the home page and the primary content pages.

- *Stepwise refinement* refers to the process of making step-by-step improvements to the design with review and evaluation after each step. This often means that you start the design for the pages of a web site with rough sketches before you implement them with HTML and CSS.

- A *prototype* is a working model of a web page or a portion of a web site. This gives reviewers an accurate view of how the web pages will work. The benefit of *prototyping* is that you detect problems early in the development cycle when they cost less to fix.

Figure 17-10   Top-down design, stepwise refinement, and prototyping

The lifecycle of a web site

The diagram at the top of figure 17-11 represents the *lifecycle* of every web site or business system. First, you design the web site. Then, you implement it. Last, you maintain it, usually for many years. In fact, the cost of maintaining a web site is likely to be far more than developing it in the first place. That's why it's so important to develop the web site in a way that makes it easier to maintain.

To make a web site easier to maintain, you need to implement it with HTML for the content and CSS for the formatting. That's most important, and that's what you've learned to do throughout this book. Beyond that, you should only use tables for tabular information, not for page layout. And you shouldn't use HTML frames, which aren't presented in this book.

Perhaps most important, though, is to take the time to get the design right in the first place. Then, you should be able to enhance and improve the web site with minimal change to what's already in place.

Next, this figure presents a simple procedure for designing a web site. This procedure will be illustrated in a moment, but here's the general idea. Like you would with any design project, step 1 has you define who is going to use the web site and what the goals of the web site are. As you do the steps that follow, these definitions should help you keep your focus.

In steps 2 through 5, you design the pages of the web site and the navigation between those pages. Here's where top-down design, stepwise refinement, and prototyping are essential. In short, you start with the most critical pages, move on to the less critical sections and pages, and you keep improving the design until everyone is satisfied and the prototype becomes the final design. Then, you can plan the folders for all of the files of the web site and go on to the implementation procedure.

In the implementation procedure in this figure, you start by developing the HTML and CSS templates for the pages of the web site. These should be at least partially complete as part of the design process, but some refinement is usually needed. These templates of course will make it easier to develop the web pages. Once they're done, you do the time-consuming work of developing the contents for all of the pages, and then implementing those contents with HTML. When all of the pages are ready, you test the entire site and deploy the web site to an Internet server as shown in the next chapter.

The last procedure in this figure is for maintaining a web site. In brief, you plan what the changes should be and then design, implement, and test them. If the changes are minimal, that may be all that's needed. But if the changes or enhancements are extensive, this might turn out to be another design project instead of a maintenance project. That's why it's so important to get the design right in the first place.

The lifecycle of a web site

How to make a web site easier to maintain

- Use HTML for the content and CSS for the page layout and formatting.
- Don't use tables for page layout. Only use tables for tabular information.
- Don't use frames (not presented in this book).
- Get the design right in the first place with full knowledge that each page is likely to be changed in the lifecycle of the web site.

A simple procedure for designing a web site

1. Define the audience and set the goals for the web site.
2. Design the home page.
3. Design the primary content pages.
4. Design the other pages.
5. Plan the navigation.
6. Plan the folders for the files of the site.

Top-down design, stepwise refinement, and prototyping

A simple procedure for implementing a web site

1. Develop the HTML and CSS templates for the pages.
2. Develop the web pages.
3. Test the entire site.
4. Deploy the site to a web server (see chapter 18).

A simple procedure for maintaining a web site

1. Plan the changes.
2. Design the changes.
3. Implement the changes.
4. Test the changes.

Description

- The *lifecycle* of all systems is (1) design, (2) implement, and (3) maintain. Often, more time is spent maintaining a web site than developing it in the first place.

Figure 17-11   The lifecycle of a web site

The design procedure applied to a small web site

To give you a better idea of how the design procedure in the previous figure works, this topic steps you through the design of a small web site.

Define the audience and set the goals

Figure 17-12 presents the description of a community service organization called Town Hall. Each year, this organization brings six speakers into the local community for lectures. This organization has been doing this for almost 75 years, and the lectures have enlightened and enriched the lives of the organization's members as well as students and non-members who attend the lectures. To balance its budget, this organization also relies on the donations from a core group of donors.

Before you can define the audience and goals of a web site, you need to get that type of information. Then, you can draft the definitions of the audience and goals as shown in this figure.

Usually, the *target audience* for a web site will consist of more than one type of visitor. In this case, that audience is defined as members, non-members, and donors. And usually there will be more than one goal for the web site. Because these definitions will guide the design of the web site, it's important to get them right and to get all of the design participants to agree on them.

About Town Hall

- Town Hall is a community service that runs six lectures each year that are available to all of the members of the community.
- The speakers for these lectures come from all over the country and are known experts in their fields.
- After each lecture, a luncheon is held in the same building and the speaker for the day answers questions from the audience.
- Eight days before each lecture, there's a meeting at the local library to discuss the subject of the lecture.
- Students are admitted to these lectures free.
- Town Hall will soon be celebrating its 75th anniversary.

The target audience

- Members of Town Hall
- Prospective members of Town Hall
- Donors and possible donors to Town Hall

The goals of the web site

- Provide all of the information that members need for attending the lectures.
- Provide all of the information that non-members need for attending one or more lectures.
- Convince non-members to become members.
- List current donors and encourage people to become donors.

Description

- Like all projects, you start by defining what you're trying to do and who you're going to do it for.
- Before you can define the audience and set the goals for the site, you need to learn about the company or organization that the site represents.
- The people who you want to use your web site can be referred to as the *target audience*.

Figure 17-12   Define the audience and set the goals

Design the home page

By now, you should know how to go about the design of a home page. Start with sketches for different approaches to the page. Then, prototype an early version of the page. And get reviews after each step in the refinement process.

When you design the home page for a web site, you also have to make some decisions about the navigation for the web site. This is illustrated by the prototype for the home page in figure 17-13. Here, the navigation bar indicates what the sections or pages of the web site will be. And the main column in the body of the page will provide the navigation to each of the six speakers. This too should be part of the stepwise reviews.

Design the primary content pages

Next, you design one of the primary content pages. This is illustrated by the prototype for a speaker page in figure 17-13, and it should be linked with the home page. This will give the reviewers a better idea of how the web site is going to work, including how the navigation will work. In this case, the user needs to click on the Back button or the Home link in the navigation bar to return to the home page.

Remember that one of the guidelines in figure 17-3 is to design the home page so it is different from the other pages, and the two pages shown here follow that guideline. In this case, even the header for the speaker's page is different from the home page header. Although most web sites use the same header for each page of the site, that isn't always necessary.

A prototype for the home page

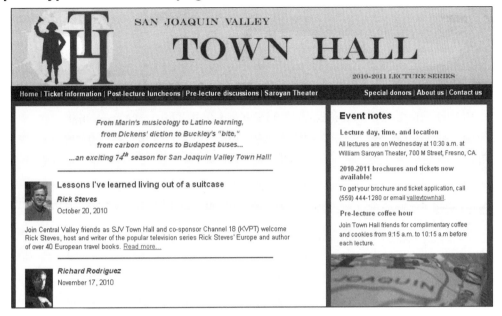

A prototype for a primary content page

Description

- To get the design started, sketch or prototype the home page. After you agree on the design of the home page, sketch or prototype one of the primary content pages.

- Use stepwise refinement to get these pages working the way you want them to.

Figure 17-13   Design the home page and the primary content pages

Design the other pages

After you've got the basic design for the home and primary content pages done, you can design the other pages. For a large site, you may need to design one section of the rest of the site at a time. But for a small site like Town Hall's, the other pages are mostly independent pages that can be designed one at a time.

This is illustrated by the example in figure 17-14. This is the page that provides the information for getting tickets. In this case, the designer decided that this page should also show the dates for the lectures so the users won't have to switch back and forth between the home page and the tickets page.

Then, she decided that she should also provide links to the speaker pages. As a result, the user can go to a speaker page from either the home page or the ticket page, and that clearly improves the usability of the site. So here again, the design of a page leads to navigation decisions.

The ticket information page

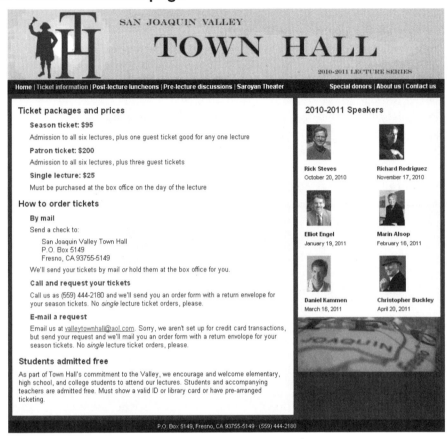

The other pages that are needed

- Post-lecture luncheon
- Pre-lecture discussions
- Saroyan Theater
- Special donors
- About us
- Contact us

Description

- After you've agreed on the design of the home page and the primary pages, sketch or prototype the other types of pages that are needed, working from the most important pages to the least important.
- Often, the pages for each section of a site are a separate design problem, and these pages don't have to be like the home page or the primary content pages.

Figure 17-14   Design the other pages

Plan the navigation

Whenever you have general agreement on how the navigation of the site should work, you can document the navigation by developing a *site plan*. This is illustrated by the first diagram in figure 17-15. This shows that the home page links to six speaker pages, and the about-us page links to two pages. Otherwise, the home page links go to single pages.

One of the benefits of developing a site plan is that it shows how many levels deep the navigation goes. In general, the deeper the navigation goes, the harder it is for the users to keep track of where they are in the site, and the harder it is to create and maintain the site. That's why most site plans don't go more than four or five levels deep.

When you develop a site plan, you can use whatever symbols you want for the web pages. Also, you usually have to show the site plan for a large web site over several pages. For instance, you can use one page to show the top two levels and maybe the third level for one of the sections of the site, and you can use other pages for the other sections of the site.

For a small web site, you may decide that you don't need a site plan. However, it can be useful when you're explaining the navigation to the people who are reviewing your design.

Plan the folders for the site

When all of the types of pages and the navigation are designed, you're almost ready to implement all of the pages. For instance, you will need to implement the pages for the other five speakers in the Town Hall web site. Before you do that, though, you should plan the folders that you're going to use for the files of your site.

For instance, the second diagram in figure 17-15 shows the plan for the folders of the Town Hall web site. Like all web sites, the top folder is the *root folder*. Beneath that, there is one folder for the style sheets of the web site and one for its images. Then, there is one folder for the speaker pages and one for the about us pages. The last folder is for all of the independent, single pages of the site, not including the index page that is in the root folder.

The benefit of planning the folders is that you will be able to find the files that you're working with more easily, and you will know where to put any new files that you create. For that reason, it makes sense to develop a preliminary plan for the folders early in the design process and enhance it as needed during the life of the project.

Here again, you may decide that you don't need a diagram for the folders that you're going to use. But you should at least create the folders that you're going to use on your computer or network early in the design process. That's especially true if you're working with other people on the design of the project.

The site plan for the web site

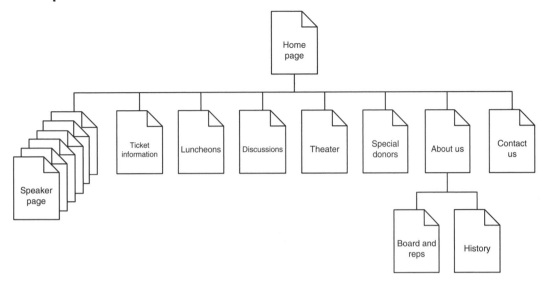

The folders for the web site

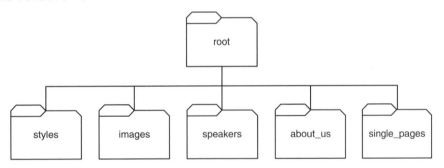

Description

- To document the navigation for a web site, you can develop a *site plan* that shows all of the pages that the web site requires. The site plan should also show the number of levels in the navigation structure.
- To a large extent, the number of levels in a site plan indicates how complicated the navigation is going to be.
- After you agree on the navigation that's represented by the site plan, you can diagram the folders that will be used for the files of the web site. This diagram should show the folders for the style sheets and image files, as well as any other types of files.

Figure 17-15   Plan the navigation and the folders for the site

Perspective

If you apply all of the guidelines, methods, and procedures that you've just learned, you will go a long way towards designing and developing an effective web site. But there's a lot more to learn. If, for example, you're going to do the writing for the site, you should learn more about effective web writing. Or, if you're going to do the graphics design for the web site, you should learn more about graphics design.

In short, designing a web site is a challenging process that requires a wide range of skills. And the more you learn about web design and development, the better your web sites will be.

Terms

usability	graphics designer
breadcrumbs	top-down design
chunking	stepwise refinement
alignment	prototyping
proximity	system lifecycle
repetition	target audience
contrast	site plan
web designer	root folder

Summary

- When you design a web site, *usability* is the primary issue. That refers to how easy a web site is to use, and to a large extent that determines the success of the web site. To achieve usability, a web site needs to implement the current conventions for web site use.

- The home page of a web site should be used to sell the site by emphasizing what's different about the site and why users should want to use it.

- To let the users know where they are as they navigate through a site, you can highlight the active links on the page, match the heading on the page to the link that led to it, and use *breadcrumbs*.

- Writing for the web isn't like writing for print. Instead, web writing should be written in inverted pyramid style, use headings and subheadings, and use bulleted and numbered lists.

- *Chunking* refers to the grouping of information into topics (chunks) that can be presented on separate web pages. This is a good way to convert one long page into two or more shorter pages.

- If you aren't a graphics designer, you should at least know the principles of *alignment*, *proximity*, *repetition*, and *contrast*. You should also know how to make the typography easy to read.

- With few exceptions, you will work with other people on the design of a site. In a large company, the design team may include web designers, writers, marketing specialists, and graphics designers.

- A *web designer* is involved with all aspects of web design. A *graphics designer* focuses on the graphics that make a web site look inviting and manageable.

- Three methods that should be used in the design of any non-trivial web site are: *top-down design*, *stepwise refinement*, and *prototyping*.

- The *lifecycle* of all systems consists of design, implementation, and maintenance. Because more time is likely to be spent on the maintenance than on developing the web site, you should design and implement a web site so it's relatively easy to enhance and maintain.

- When you design a web site, you start by defining its *target audience* and goals. Then, those definitions guide you as you design the home page, primary content pages, other pages, and navigation for the site.

- To design the navigation for a web site, you can develop a *site plan*. Then, that site plan can be used to plan the folders for the files of the site.

18

How to deploy a web site on a web server

Once you've developed and tested a web site on your local computer, you're just a few steps away from making that web site available to anyone in the world who is connected to the Internet. To do that, you just need to transfer the files for your web site to a web server that's connected to the Internet.

How to get a web host and domain name

Before you can *deploy* (or *publish*) a web site to the Internet, you need to have access to a web server that's connected to the Internet. If you already have access to an Internet web server, you can use that server. Otherwise, you can search the Internet for a web host as described in this topic. If you want to register a domain name for your site, a web host can usually do that for you too.

How to find a web host

Figure 18-1 shows how to find a *web host*, or *web hosting service*. To do that, you can search the web for "web host" or "web hosting service". Then, you can follow the links until you find a web host that has all the features you need. For small web sites like the ones presented in this book, you only need a small amount of disk space. For larger web sites, you may need more disk space, access to a database server, and a server-side programming language such as PHP, JSP, or ASP.NET.

In addition, most web hosts provide one or more *FTP (File Transfer Protocol)* accounts. This provides a way for you to transfer the files for your web site to and from your web host.

Most web hosts charge a monthly fee. For a small web site, the price may be as little as $5 per month. Also, some web hosts provide some services for free. If you search the Internet, you'll find a wide range of services and prices.

If you already pay an *Internet Service Provider* (*ISP*) to connect to the Internet, you can check to see if it provides free web hosting as part of its monthly fees. If so, you can check to see if it provides the web hosting features that you need for your web site.

When you get a web host, you will receive an *IP address* in this format: 64.46.106.120. You can use this address to access your web site. Later, when you get your domain name, you can access your site with either the IP address or the domain name. Internally, the Internet uses IP addresses to address web sites, but people use domain names because they're easier to remember.

A web host

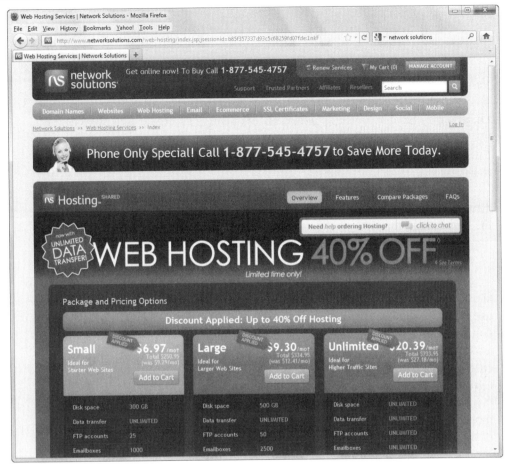

Description

- A *web host*, or *web hosting service*, provides space on a server computer that's connected to the Internet, usually for a monthly fee. You can use a web host to make your web site accessible via the Internet.

- *File Transfer Protocol* (*FTP*) allows you to transfer the files for your web site to and from your web host.

- To find a web host, search the web for "web host" or "web hosting service". Then, follow the links until you find a web host that has all the features you need.

- An *Internet Service Provider* (*ISP*) often includes free web hosting as part of its monthly fees. As a result, if you have an ISP, you can check to see if it provides the web hosting features that you need for your web site.

Figure 18-1   How to find a web host

How to get a domain name

If you're using a web host, you can often use its *domain name* to access your web site. For example, if your web hosting company has a domain name of

```
olive.forest.net
```

you may be able to access your web site using a *subdomain* like this:

```
www.valleytownhall.olive.forest.net
```

Or, you may be able to access your web site using a subfolder like this:

```
www.olive.forest.net/valleytownhall
```

Either way, the domain name of the web host is included in the URL that's used to access your web site.

For most professional web sites, you'll want to get your own domain name. That way, you can access your web site without including the domain name of the web host in the URL. For example, you can access a web site with the domain name valleytownhall.com like this:

```
www.valleytownhall.com
```

To get a domain name, you can use a web site like Network Solutions, as shown in figure 18-2. But first, you need to decide what extension you want to use for the web site. The .com extension was originally intended to be used for commercial web sites, .net was intended to be used for networking web sites, and .org was intended to be used for other organizations. However, many other extensions are now available, such as those for military (.mil), government (.gov), and business (.biz) web sites.

When you use a site like the one shown here, you typically enter one or more domain names. Then, the *domain name registry* is searched to see which of the names is available, and you can choose to purchase any available name for a specific amount of time. If you are using a web host, it may also provide a service like this.

A search for a domain name

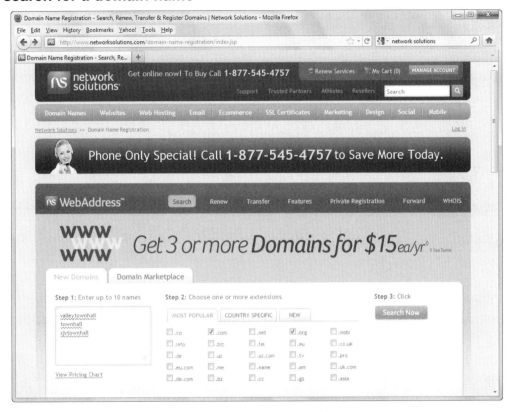

Description

- A *domain name* is a user-friendly name that's used to locate a resource that's connected to the Internet. For example, google.com is a domain name.

- A domain name can have one or more *subdomains*. For example, mail.google.com is a subdomain.

- The .com, .net, and .org extensions are popular endings for domain names. These extensions were originally intended to be used for commercial web sites (.com), networking infrastructure web sites (.net), and other types of organizations (.org).

- The *domain name registry* is a database of all registered domain names.

- If you are using a web hosting service, you can often use that service to register the domain name for you. To start, you can use your web hosting service to find a domain name that hasn't been registered yet. Then, you can have your web hosting service register that domain name for you.

Figure 18-2   How to get a domain name

How to transfer files to and from the web

Once you have a web host and domain name, you can publish your web site to the Internet by transferring the files for your web site from your local computer to the correct folder on the web host's server. To do that, you can use an FTP client like FileZilla, an IDE like Dreamweaver that includes an FTP client, or a tool for uploading files that's provided by your web host.

To give you an idea of how FTP clients work, the next three figures show you how FileZilla Client works. This is a free program that's easy to use. If you're using Aptana Studio 3, though, you may want to use the FTP program that it provides.

How to install FileZilla Client

Figure 18-3 shows how to install FileZilla Client. To do that, go to the FileZilla website and follow the instructions shown there. Since FileZilla runs on the Windows, Mac, and Linux operating systems, the directions for installing it vary depending on your operating system.

An FTP program

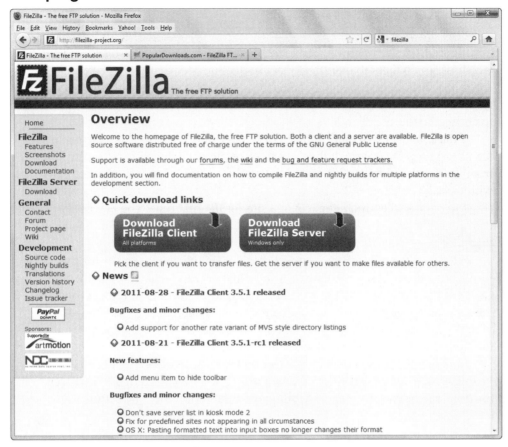

How to install FileZilla Client

1. Go to the FileZilla website (www.filezilla-project.org).
2. Click on the Download FileZilla Client link.
3. Follow the instructions to install the FileZilla Client application on your system.

Description

- FileZilla is a free FTP client application that runs on the Windows, Mac, and Linux operating systems.
- FileZilla supports basic FTP as well as FTP over SSL/TLS (FTPS) and SSH File Transfer Protocol (SFTP), which can be used for secure file transfers.

Figure 18-3   How to install the FileZilla FTP client

How to connect to a web site on a remote web server

Figure 18-4 shows how to use FileZilla to connect to your web site on your web host. To do that the first time, you use the Site Manager dialog box to create the new site and give it a name. Then, you specify the host name, server type, user name, and password for the site. Finally, you click the Connect button to connect to the site.

If the connection is successful, FileZilla displays a window like the one in the next figure. Otherwise, it displays an error message that you can use to troubleshoot the problem. If necessary, you can contact your web host for help with these FTP settings.

After you successfully connect to a site for the first time, you can easily connect to it again. To do that, you just select the site name in the Site Manager dialog box and then click the Connect button.

When you use FileZilla Client, you usually set the default folder for the local and remote sites. For example, you set the default local folder to the root folder of the web site on your computer, and you set the default remote folder to the root folder for your web site on the web host. That makes it easy to work with the web site each time you connect to it. To set the default folder, you use the Advanced tab of the Site Manager dialog box.

Note that the name of the root folder on the remote site varies depending on how your web server is configured. As a result, you may need to ask your web host for help or do some experimenting to set the root folder correctly.

FileZilla's Site Manager dialog box

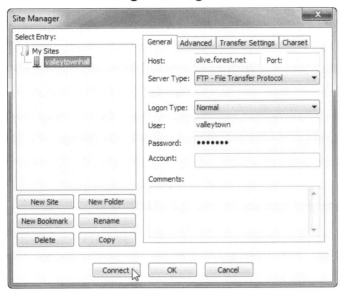

How to connect to a web site for the first time

1. Start FileZilla, and then use the File→Site Manager command to display the Site Manager dialog box.

2. Click the New Site button and enter a name for the site.

3. Enter the details needed to connect to the site, including the host name, user name, and password.

4. Click the Connect button to save the connection settings and connect to the site.

How to connect to a web site after it has been set up

- Open the Site Manager, click on the site name, and click the Connect button.

How to edit the settings for a web site

- Open the Site Manager, click on the site name, edit its settings, and click the OK button.

Description

- For the Server Type option, you typically use FTP. For sensitive data, though, you can use FTP over SSL/TLS (FTPS) or SSH File Transfer Protocol (SFTP).

- For the Logon Type option, you typically use Normal. See FileZilla help for a description of the other options.

- To set the default folders for the local and remote sites, use the Advanced tab.

Figure 18-4   How to connect to a web site on a remote web server

How to upload and download files

Figure 18-5 shows the FileZilla window after a connection has been made to a remote web site. Here, the right pane of the main window shows the folder tree for the remote site, along with the subfolders and files in the root folder. To display the contents of a subfolder, you can double-click on it, and to move up a level to the parent folder, you can double-click on the first folder (the one that's identified by two dots). You can use the same techniques to work with the files and folders on the local site, which are listed in the left pane of the main window.

To transfer one or more files or folders from your local site to the remote site, you can use the technique described in this figure. This is known as *uploading* files. You can use a similar technique to transfer files from the remote site to your local site, which is known as *downloading* files. Note that before you upload files, you must navigate to the folder on the remote site where you want to store the files. Similarly, before you download files, you must navigate to the folder on the local site where you want to store the files.

FileZilla when it is connected to a web host

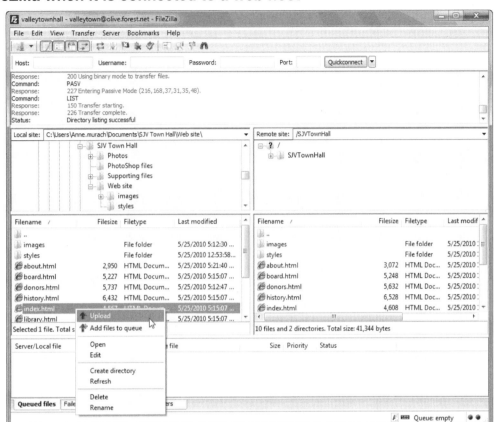

Description

- The top left pane of the main FileZilla window shows the folder structure of the local system, and the top right pane shows the folder structure of the remote system.

- If you select a folder in either folder tree, the subfolders and files in that folder are displayed in the lower pane. Then, you can use that pane to navigate through the folders.

- The folders that are identified by two dots at the top of both lower panes represent the parent folders.

- To *upload* a file or folder from the local site to the remote site, display the folder on the remote site where you want the file or folder uploaded. Then, right-click on the file or folder in the local site and select the Upload command from the resulting menu.

- To *download* a file or folder from the remote site to the local site, display the folder on the local site where you want the file or folder downloaded. Then, right-click on the file or folder in the remote site and select the Download command.

- You can also upload or download multiple files and folders by selecting them and then using the Upload or Download command.

Figure 18-5   How to upload and download files

Three more skills for deploying a web site

After you deploy your site to a remote web server, you need to test it. You also need to get your site indexed by the popular search engines so they will deliver people to your site.

How to test a web site that has been uploaded to the web server

Figure 18-6 shows how to test a new web page that has just been uploaded to an existing site. In that case, you need to check all the links that go to it and from it. You also need to check that all its content is there and working correctly, including images, JavaScript features, and jQuery features.

For instance, a web page often links to one or more HTML files, CSS files, and image files. Then, if you forget to upload a supporting file, one of the links won't work correctly. In that case, you can solve the problem by uploading the supporting file.

To test an entire web site that has just been uploaded to a web server, you need to methodically review each of the pages on the site, including all of the links to and from each page. The larger the site, the more difficult this is, and the more methodical you need to be. To complicate the task, you need to do this for all of the browsers that your users are likely to use.

A web site on the Internet

How to test a web page that you've just added to your site

- Start your web browser, go to your home page, and navigate to the new page using every route that your site has for getting there.
- Review the contents for the page, and make sure it's all there and it all works, including the images, JavaScript features, and jQuery features.
- Test all the links on the page to make sure they work correctly.
- Retest the page in all of the other browsers to make sure it works correctly in those browsers too.

How to test a new web site

- Methodically review all of the pages and test all of the links, one page at a time.
- Do this for each of the browsers that your users might be using.

Figure 18-6   How to test a web site that has been uploaded to the web server

How to get your web site into search engines and directories

After you deploy and test your web site, you will want to get your pages into the major search engines and directories so they can deliver visitors to your site. To do that, you go to the URLs in the table in figure 18-7, or you can search for "submit site to ..." These URLs take you to submission pages like the Yahoo! page shown in this figure.

At the submission page, you only need to submit the URL of your home page. Then, if your site is linked properly, the search engine's *robot* will "crawl" through the rest of your pages by following the links in your site. As it crawls, the robot will score your pages. Those scores will later determine how high your pages come up in the searches, and of course you want them to come up as high as possible.

The trouble is that the search engines use different algorithms for determining the scores of your pages. For instance, some search engines improve the score of a page if it has links to other sites. Some improve the score if the pages of other web sites link to the page. To complicate the process, the search engines change their algorithms from time to time without any notice.

To find out more about the scoring algorithms that are used, you can go to the sites for the search engines or directories that you're submitting your site to. Most of these sites also give advice for optimizing your site for their engines. You can also search the web for information on search engine optimization.

Once you've submitted your web site for indexing, you don't have to do it again, even if you've made significant enhancements to the site. That's because the robot for a search engine periodically crawls through all of the sites and indexes the pages again, sometimes with a new algorithm for scoring.

Last, you should be aware that most web hosts offer statistics packages that tell you where your visitors are coming from. You can also buy third-party packages that do that, or you can sign up for a free Google Analytics account (www.google.com/analytics). This data can help you figure out what's working...and what isn't working...so you can make changes that will improve your site.

Two additional free tools that you may find useful as you test and deploy a web site are Google Webmaster Tools (www.google.com/webmasters) and Web Site Grader by HubSpot (http://websitegrader.com). You can use Google Webmaster Tools to perform a variety of functions, including checking links site wide, showing search rankings per page, uploading a sitemap.xml file to provide for better crawling and rankings, and making recommendations for improvement to the site. You can use Web Site Grader to determine how much traffic your site is getting and whether it has any search engine optimization problems.

But what if you don't want a search engine to index some of your pages? And what happens if you delete a page that is still in the index for a search engine? You can find out how to handle those conditions in the next figure.

The URLs for the major search engines and directory

Site name	Site type	Web URL
Google	Search engine	http://www.google.com/addurl/
MSN/Bing	Search engine	http://www.bing.com/webmaster/SubmitSitePage.aspx
Yahoo	Search engine	http://search.yahoo.com/info/submit.html
DMOZ	Directory	http://www.dmoz.org/add.html

The Yahoo! page for submitting your site

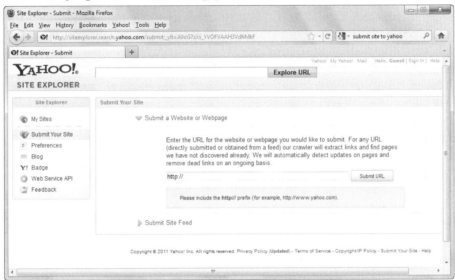

Description

- After you have deployed and tested your site, you will want to get your pages into search engines and directories that can deliver visitors to your site. To submit your site to the three major search engines and the major directory, go to the web sites in the table above.

- When you submit your site to a search engine or directory, you only need to provide the URL for your home page. Then, the *robot* (or *spider*) for that engine or directory "crawls" through the pages of your site and indexes them.

- After your site has been indexed the first time, the robot will periodically crawl through your site again to update the index based on the changes that you've made to your site.

- Each search engine or directory has its own algorithms for scoring pages, and those scores determine how high a page will be placed in the search results for specific keywords.

- At the site for each search engine or directory, you can get information that you can use to help your pages do better in the search results.

- Most web hosts offer statistics packages that track which sites and search engines are sending you visitors.

Figure 18-7   How to get your web site into search engines and directories

How to control which pages are indexed and visited

For many web sites, there are pages and maybe even folders of pages that you don't want indexed. For instance, you usually don't want your shopping cart pages indexed. To stop pages from being indexed, you can use one of the two methods shown in figure 18-8.

First, you can set up a robots.txt file in the root folder of your web site that specifies which folders or files to exclude from indexing. This is illustrated by the first set of examples in this figure. Here, the * for user-agent means that it applies to all search engines and directories. As these examples show, you can use a robots.txt file to eliminate one or more folders or files from indexing.

Second, you can code a robots meta tag with the content set to "noindex" and "nofollow". This means that the robot shouldn't index the page, and it also shouldn't follow any of the links on the page as it crawls through the pages of the site.

Now, back to the question of what happens if you delete a page on your web site that has already been indexed. Unfortunately, it will still come up in the search results until your site is re-indexed. In the meantime, if somebody clicks on its link, the page won't be found and a 404 error page will be displayed. Since this indicates to the user that your site isn't being properly maintained, you certainly don't want that to happen.

One way to get around this problem is to delete the content from the page, but not the page itself. Then, you can add a refresh meta tag like the one in this figure that will redirect the user to another page. In this tag, the content attribute should be set to zero (0) so the redirection is done right away (no delay). Then, the url attribute should be set to the page that you want the old page to be redirected to.

Unfortunately, the refresh meta tag isn't supported by all browsers, so you need to provide alternatives for it. Since your web server determines how each HTTP request is handled, this is usually handled by server-side code that redirects the request to a current page.

Three robots.txt files

A file that tells all search engines not to index the pages in the cart folder

```
User-agent: *
Disallow: /cart/
```

A file that tells all search engines not to index the pages in two folders

```
User-agent: *
Disallow: /cart/
Disallow: /private/
```

A file that tells all search engines not to index one folder and one file

```
User-agent: *
Disallow: /cart/
Disallow: /backlist/private.html
```

A meta tag that tells a robot not to index a page or follow its links

```
<meta http-equiv="robots" content="noindex, nofollow">
```

A meta tag that redirects the user from a deleted page to a current page

```
<meta http-equiv="refresh" content="0" url="../asp4_vb.html">
```

How to control which pages are indexed

- If you don't want the robot to index the pages in a folder of the site, you can add a text file named robots.txt to the root folder of your web site. You can also use this file to specify single pages that you don't want the robot to index.

- Another way to stop a robot from indexing a page is to add a robots meta tag to the page. In the content attribute, "noindex" tells the robot not to index the page and "nofollow" tells the robot not to follow the links on the page.

How to control which pages are visited from the search results

- When you delete a page from your web site, it will remain in the index for a search engine until the robot for that engine crawls through your site again, and maybe even longer.

- To prevent users from going to a page that you've deleted before your site is re-indexed, you can delete the content of the page but not the page itself. Then, you can add a refresh meta tag to the page.

- In the refresh meta tag, the content attribute should be 0 so the redirection is done immediately (0 delay), and the url attribute should specify the page that the user should be redirected to.

- Not all browsers support the refresh meta tag, though, so you should provide a server-side alternative to this whenever possible.

Figure 18-8   How to control which pages are indexed and visited

Perspective

If you understand the first three sections of this book, you can write and test the HTML and CSS code for a web site on a local computer. If you understand this chapter, you can make your web site available to anyone in the world who can connect to the Internet. Now, it's up to you to dream up a web site that's worth sharing with the world!

Terms

deploy	domain name
publish	subdomain
web host	domain name registry
web hosting service	upload a file
FTP (File Transfer Protocol)	download a file
ISP (Internet Service Provider)	robot
IP address	spider

Summary

- To *deploy* (or *publish*) a web site, you can use a *web host*, or *web hosting service*, that will make your web site accessible from the Internet.

- You can use *File Transfer Protocol* (*FTP*) to transfer the files for your web site to and from your web host.

- An *IP address* uniquely identifies a web site, and so does a *domain name*.

- To find a *domain name* for your web site, you search the *domain name registry*, which is a database of all registered domain names.

- Once you have a domain name, you can have one or more *subdomains* that address portions of the domain.

- You can use an FTP program to *upload* files from your computer to your Internet web server and to *download* files from your web server to your computer. FileZilla is a free FTP program that runs on the Windows, Mac, and Linux operating systems.

- To test a web page that has been uploaded to the Internet, start your web browser, navigate to the URL for the web page, and click on all links to make sure they work correctly.

- To get your web site into a search engine, go to the URL for its submission page. Then, its *robot* (or *spider*) will crawl through your pages and score them for later searches that are based on keywords.

- To stop pages from being indexed by a search engine, you can use a robots.txt file or robots meta tags. To redirect the request for an inactive page on your web site to another page, you can use a refresh meta tag.

Appendix A

How to set up your computer for this book

This appendix shows how to install the software that we recommend for editing and testing the web pages and applications for this book. That includes Aptana Studio 3 as the text editor for both Windows and Mac OS users, plus the Firefox browser for both Windows and Mac OS users. This appendix also shows you how to download and install the source code for this book.

As you read these descriptions, please remember that most web sites are continually upgraded. As a result, some of the procedures in this appendix may have changed since this book was published. Nevertheless, these procedures should still be good guides to installing the software.

How to install Aptana Studio 3

If you're already comfortable with a text editor that works for editing HTML and CSS, you can continue using it. But otherwise, we recommend that you use Aptana Studio 3. It is a free editor that offers many features, it runs on both Windows and Mac OS systems, and chapter 2 presents a quick tutorial on it that will get you started right.

On a Windows system

Figure A-1 shows how to download and install Aptana Studio 3 on a Windows system.

On a Mac OS system

Figure A-1 also shows how to download and install Aptana Studio 3 on a Mac OS system.

The web site address for downloading Aptana Studio 3

`http://www.aptana.com/products/studio3/download`

How to install Aptana Studio 3 on a Windows system

1. Go to the web site address above.
2. Click on the Download Aptana Studio 3 button near the bottom of the page, click on the Save File button in the resulting dialog box, and identify the location where you want the file saved in the Save As dialog box that's displayed.
3. When the Download finishes, use Windows Explorer to find the exe file, and double-click on it to start it.
4. As you step through the wizard that follows, you can accept all of the default settings that are offered.
5. After Aptana Studio 3 is installed, start it. Then, if you don't have a Git application installed on your system, Aptana will ask you if you want it to install a Portable Git application. Accept that option because Aptana won't run without it.

How to install Aptana Studio 3 on a Mac OS X system

1. Go to the web site address above.
2. Click on the Customize Your Download button, and select Mac OS X.
3. Click on the Download Aptana Studio 3 button, and click on the Save File button in the resulting dialog box.
4. When the Download finishes, double-click on the dmg file in the Downloads folder to display the Aptana Studio 3 window.
5. Use Finder to display the Applications folder. Then, drag the Aptana Studio 3 folder from the Aptana Studio 3 window to the Applications folder.
6. Start Aptana Studio 3. Then, if you don't have a Git application installed on your system, Aptana will ask you if you want it to install a Portable Git application. Accept that option because Aptana won't run without it.

Description

- Aptana runs on Windows, Mac, and Linux systems.
- Git is a source code management tool that Aptana requires. If necessary, Aptana will install it for you when you start Aptana for the first time.
- Chapter 2 of this book presents a tutorial that will get you off to a fast start with Aptana.

Figure A-1 How to install Aptana Studio 3 as your text editor

How to install Firefox

When you develop web pages and applications, you need to test them on all of the browsers that the users of the application are likely to use. For a commercial application, that usually includes Internet Explorer, Firefox, Safari, Opera, and Chrome. Then, if an application doesn't work on one of those browsers, you need to fix it.

As you do most of the exercises for this book, though, you can test your web pages on just two browsers. Windows users should use Internet Explorer plus Firefox. Mac OS users should use Safari and Firefox.

However, some of the advanced HTML5 features aren't fully supported or aren't supported at all by Firefox or Internet Explorer. Then, it's nice to be able to test those applications or run your exercise solutions on Chrome, Opera, or Safari. For instance, Firefox and Internet Explorer don't fully support the range or slider controls that are presented in chapter 10, but Chrome, Opera, and Safari do.

In figure A-2, you can see the procedure for downloading and installing Firefox. As you respond to the dialog boxes for the installer, we recommend that you make Firefox your default browser. Then, if you want to install Chrome, Opera, and Safari, you can use similar procedures.

The web site address for downloading Firefox

```
http://www.mozilla.com
```

How to install Firefox

1. Go to the web site address above.
2. Click on the Download Firefox - Free button.
3. Save the exe file to your C drive.
4. Run the exe file and respond to the resulting dialog boxes.

Other popular browsers

- Chrome
- Safari
- Opera

Description

- Microsoft's Internet Explorer and Mozilla's Firefox are the most popular browsers today. That's why we suggest that you test all of the exercises that you do for this book on both of those browsers.

- Because some of the HTML5 features aren't fully supported or aren't supported at all by Internet Explorer and Firefox, it's also good to install Chrome, Safari, and Opera on your system. Then, you can see the various levels of support that those browsers offer.

- If you have a Windows system, Internet Explorer will already be on it, but you will have to install Firefox.

- If you have a Mac system, Safari will already be on it, and you won't be able to install Internet Explorer because it doesn't run on Macs.

- To install Chrome, Safari, and Opera, you can use procedures that are similar to the one for Firefox.

Figure A-2   How to install Firefox

How to install and use the source code for this book

The next two figures show how to install and use the source code for this book. One figure is for Windows users, the other for Mac OS users.

For Windows users

Figure A-3 shows how to install the source code for this book on a Windows system. This includes the source code for the applications in this book, all of the significant examples, and the starting files for the exercises.

When you finish this procedure, the book applications, examples, and exercises will be in the three folders that are listed in this figure, but the exercises will also be in the second folder that's shown. Then, when you do the exercises, you use the subfolders and files in this folder:

```
c:\html5_css3\exercises
```

but you have backup copies of these subfolders and files in this folder:

```
c:\murach\html5_css3\exercises
```

That way, you can restore the files for an exercise by copying the files from the second folder to the first.

As you do the exercises, you may want to copy code from a book application or example into a file that you're working with. That's easy to do because the folders or files for the examples are preceded by the figure numbers that present them. For instance, this file

```
c:\html5_css3\book_examples\ch09\05_table_css3.html
```

is the HTML file that contains the code for the table example in figure 9-5 in chapter 9. And this folder

```
c:\murach\html5_css3\book_examples\ch14\06_accordion
```

is the folder that contains the files for the accordion example that's in figure 14-6 in chapter 14.

If you want to experiment with the code in the book applications or examples, you may want to copy the folders first so the original files won't be changed. For instance, you can copy the book_apps and book_examples folders from this folder

```
c:\murach\html5_css3\
```

to this folder

```
c:\html5_css3\
```

Then, you will have backup copies.

The Murach web site

`www.murach.com`

The default installation folder for the source code on a Windows system

`c:\murach\html5_css3`

The Windows folders for the applications, examples, and exercises

`c:\murach\html5_css3\book_apps`
`c:\murach\html5_css3\book_examples`
`c:\murach\html5_css3\exercises`

The Windows folders for doing the exercises

`c:\html5_css3\exercises\ch01`
`c:\html5_css3\exercises\ch02`
`c:\html5_css3\exercises\town_hall_1`
`c:\html5_css3\exercises\town_hall_2`
`c:\html5_css3\exercises\town_hall_3`

How to download and install the source code on a Windows system

1. Go to www.murach.com, and go to the page for *Murach's HTML5 and CSS3.*

2. Click the link for "FREE download of the book applications." Then, click the "All book files" link for the self-extracting zip file. This will download a setup file named htm5_allfiles.exe onto your hard drive.

3. Use Windows Explorer to find the exe file on your hard drive. Then, double-click this file. This installs the source code for the book applications, examples, and exercises into the folders shown above. After it does this install, the exe file copies the exercises folder to c:\html5_css3 so you have two copies of the exercises.

How to restore an exercise file

- Copy it from its subfolder in

  `c:\murach\html5_css3\exercises`

  to the corresponding subfolder in

  `c:\html5_css3\exercises`

Description

- The exe file that you download stores the exercises in two different folders. That way, you can do the exercises using the files that are stored in one folder, but you have a backup copy in case you want to restore the starting files for an exercise.

- As you do the exercises, you may want to copy code from a book application or an example into the file you're working on. That's easy to do because all of the applications and all of the significant examples are available in the book_apps and book_examples folders.

- In the book_examples folder, the prefixes on the files and folders refer to the number of the figure that presents the example.

Figure A-3   How to install the source code for this book on a Windows system

For Mac OS users

Figure A-4 shows how to install the source code for this book on a Mac OS system. This includes the source code for the applications in this book, and the source code for the exercises.

When you finish this procedure, the book applications, examples, and exercises will be in the three folders that are listed in this figure, but the exercises will also be in the second folder that's shown. Then, when you do the exercises, you use the subfolders and files in this folder:

    documents\html5_css3\exercises

but you have backup copies of these subfolders and files in this folder:

    documents\murach\html5_css3\exercises

That way, you can restore the files for an exercise by copying the files from the second folder to the first.

As you do the exercises, you may want to copy code from a book application or example into a file that you're working with. That's easy to do because the folders or files for the examples are preceded by the figure numbers that present them. For instance, this file

    documents\html5_css3\book_examples\ch09\05_table_css3.html

is the HTML file that contains the code for the table example in figure 9-5 in chapter 9. And this folder

    documents\murach\html5_css3\book_examples\ch14\06_accordion

is the folder that contains the files for the accordion example that's in figure 14-6 in chapter 14.

If you want to experiment with the code in the book applications or examples, you may want to copy the folders first so the original files won't be changed. For instance, you can copy the book_apps and book_examples folders from this folder

    documents\murach\html5_css3\

to this folder

    documents\html5_css3\

Then, you will have backup copies.

The Murach web site

```
www.murach.com
```

The Mac OS folders for the book applications and exercises

```
documents\murach\html5_css3\book_apps
documents\murach\html5_css3\book_examples
documents\murach\html5_css3\exercises
```

The Mac OS folders for doing the exercises

```
documents\html5_css3\exercises\ch01
documents\html5_css3\exercises\ch02
documents\html5_css3\exercises\town_hall_1
documents\html5_css3\exercises\town_hall_2
documents\html5_css3\exercises\town_hall_3
```

How to download and install the source code on a Mac OS system

1. Go to www.murach.com, and go to the page for *Murach's HTML5 and CSS3*.
2. Click the link for "FREE download of the book applications." Then, click the "All book files" link for the regular zip file. This will download a setup file named htm5_allfiles.zip onto your hard drive.
3. Move this file into the Documents folder of your home folder.
4. Use Finder to go to your Documents folder.
5. Double-click the htm5_allfiles.zip file to extract the folders for the book applications, examples, and exercises. This will create a folder named html5_css3 in your documents folder that will contain the book_apps, book_examples, and exercises folders.
6. To create two copies of the exercises folder, copy this folder

   ```
   documents\murach\html5_css3\exercises
   ```

   to

   ```
   documents\html5_css3
   ```

How to restore an exercise file

- Copy it from its subfolder in

  ```
  documents\murach\html5_css3\exercises
  ```

  to the corresponding subfolder in

  ```
  documents\html5_css3\exercises
  ```

Description

- This procedure stores the exercises in two different folders. That way, you do the exercises using the files that are in one folder, but you also have a backup copy.
- If you want to copy code from a book application or an example into an exercise file that you're working on, you can find all of the applications and significant examples in the book_apps and book_examples folders.
- In the book_examples folder, the prefix on a file or folder refers to the number of the figure that presents the example.

Figure A-4 How to install the source code for this book on a Mac OS system

Index

!important rules, 138, 139
* selector, 135
@font-face selector, 526-527
@media rule, 402, 403

A

a element, 104, 105, 248-263
   colors, 250-251
   email, 250-251
   media file, 256-257
AAC (Advanced Audio Code), 376, 377
AAC codec, 380, 381
abbr element, 90, 91
Above the fold, 426, 427, 568, 569
Absolute measurement, 124, 125
Absolute positioning, 220-225
Absolute units of measurement, 124, 125
Absolute URL, 102, 103
accept attribute, 336, 337
Accessibility, 32, 33
   access keys, 342, 343
   images, 271, 278
   labels, 332, 333
   links, 249, 251
   pseudo-class selectors, 250, 251
   radio buttons, 332, 333
   tab order, 342, 343
   tables, 308, 309
accesskey attribute, 342-343
   a element, 248-249
Accordion, 464-465, 474-479
   jQuery Mobile, 512-513
action attribute, 318, 319
active pseudo-class, 136, 137
active pseudo-class selector, 250-251
Address bar, 27
address element, 88, 89
Adjacent sibling selector, 132, 133
Adobe Creative Suite, 22
Adobe DreamWeaver, 22, 23
Adobe Flash, 22
Adobe Flash Player, 376, 377
Adobe Illustrator, 22
Adobe Media Encoder, 384, 385
Adobe Photoshop, 22, 284-285
Adobe Reader, 257
Adobe Typekit fonts, 530-531

Advanced Audio Coding (AAC), 376, 377
Alignment, 574-575
   controls, 338-339
   image, 272-273
   text, 144, 145
alt attribute, 270, 271, 282, 283
   button, 320, 321
   img element, 108, 109
Anchor, 254
Animated image, 268, 269, 284
Apache web server, 10, 11
Application server, 8, 9
Aptana Studio, 3, 20, 21, 54-67
   auto-completion, 60, 61
   create project, 54, 55
   error marker, 61, 64
   installing, 612, 614
   open file, 56, 57
   project, 54, 55
   run, 66, 67, 68, 69
   save, 66, 67
   syntax highlighting, 60, 61, 64
   template, 58, 59, 62, 63
   tidy validator, 70, 71, 74, 75
area element, 282-283
article element, 98, 99, 214, 215
ASF, 377
aside element, 98, 99, 200, 201
ASP.NET, 10, 11
Attribute, 14, 46, 47
   accept, 336, 337
   accesskey, 248-249, 342-343
   action, 318, 319
   alt, 108, 109, 282, 283, 320, 321
   autocomplete, 344, 345
   autofocus, 322, 323, 342, 343, 444, 445
   autoplay, 391
   caption, 308, 309
   checked, 324, 325
   class, 46, 47, 52, 53, 94, 95, 130, 131, 502-503, 506-507, 508-509
   cols, 330, 331
   colspan, 306, 307
   controls, 391
   coords, 282, 283
   core, 94, 95
   data, 386, 387
   data-icon, 500-503
   data-inline, 500-501
   data-inset, 514-515
   data-rel, 498-501
   data-role, 494-495, 500-503, 510-511, 512-513, 514-515

email control, 350, 351
Email message, 248-249
embed element, 388, 389
Embedded fonts, 526-531
Embedded JavaScript, 418, 419, 424, 425, 428, 429
Embedded style sheet, 120, 121
Embedding media types, 386-389
Empty tag, 44, 45
Emulators (mobile devices), 488-489
Encoding (media), 384, 385
enctype attribute, 336, 337
Error Console (Firefox), 438, 439
Event, 422, 423
    drag-and-drop, 550-551
Event handling, 422, 423
    drag-and-drop, 552-553
Expression Web, 22, 23
Extensions, 596, 597
External JavaScript file, 424, 425
External style sheet, 16, 17, 120, 121

F

Fantasy font, 141
Favicon, 82, 83
FavIcon from Pics, 289
Fetch, 25
FFmpeg, 384, 385
fieldset element, 334-335
figcaption element, 100, 101, 276-277, 304, 305
figure element, 100, 101, 276-277, 304, 305
File Transfer Protocol (FTP), 24, 25, 594, 595
File upload control, 336-337
Filename, 26, 27
FileZilla, 25
FileZilla Client, 598-603
Firefogg, 384, 385
Firefox, 10, 11
    Error Console, 438, 439
    installing, 614-615
    JavaScript error, 438, 439
first-child pseudo-class, 136, 137
first-letter pseudo-element, 136, 137
first-line pseudo-element, 137
Fixed column, 202, 203
Fixed layout, 164, 165
Fixed positioning, 220-223
Fixed-width page layout, 200, 201, 204, 205
FLAC (Free Lossless Audio Codec), 381
Flash, 22, 257, 392, 393, 489
Flash Video, 377
float property, 150, 151, 198, 199, 274-275

Floating, 198-201, 204, 205
    images, 150, 151, 218, 219, 274-275
    labels, 338-339
focus pseudo-class, 250-251, 340-341
Folder structure, 588, 589
Font family, 140, 141
font property, 142, 143
Font size, 140, 141
font-family property, 140, 141
font-size property, 140, 141
font-style property, 142, 143
font-variant property, 142, 143
font-weight property, 142, 143
Footer element, 98, 99
for attribute
    label, 332, 333
    output controls, 360, 361
Form, 318-363
    for search function, 356-357
form element, 318, 319
    file upload control, 336, 337
Formatting
    controls, 340-341
    web page for printing, 402-405
Frame, 268, 284
FTP (File Transfer Protocol), 24, 25, 594, 595
FTP plug-in, 24, 25
FTP program, 22, 24, 25
FTP Voyager, 25
FTPS, 600, 601

G

General sibling selector, 132, 133
Geolocation feature, 532-537
get method, 318, 319
GIF (Graphic Interchange Format), 108, 109, 268, 269
GIMP, 284-285
Glossary, 240
Goals, 582-583
Google, 10, 11, 475
Google Analytics, 606
Google Site Search, 324, 325
Google Web Fonts, 528-529
Google Webmaster Tools, 606
Gradient
    Canvas, 546-547
    linear, 186, 187
Graphic Interchange Format (GIF), 108, 109, 268, 269
Graphics designer, 576-577
Grouping controls, 334-335

H

H.364 codec, 378, 379
h1...h6 elements, 86, 87
Handbrake, 384, 385
Handheld media, 484-485
head element, 14, 15, 42, 43, 112
Head section, 82, 83
Header cell, 294, 295
Header conventions, 562-563
Header element, 98, 99
Headers, 568, 569
headers attribute, 308, 309
height attribute, 270, 271
   audio and video elements, 391
   button, 320, 321
   element, 108, 109
   embed element, 389
   object element, 386, 387
Height formula (box model), 164, 165
height property, 168, 169, 270, 271
Hex, 126, 127
Hexadecimal, 126, 127
hgroup element, 100, 101
Hidden field, 322, 323
   for search functions, 356, 357
high attribute, 362, 363
Hot linking, 286
hotspot, 282, 283
hover pseudo-class, 136, 137, 250-251
   with image rollovers, 280-281
href attribute, 104, 105
   a element, 248-249
   image map, 282, 283
   media file, 256-257
   placeholder, 254-255
HSA values, 128, 129
HSLA values, 128, 129
HTML (Hypertext Markup Language), 7, 14, 15
   attributes, 46, 47
   coding errors, 61, 68
   comment, 48, 49
   document, 14, 15, 42, 43
   elements (see Element)
   html element, 42, 43, 112
   source code, 28, 29
   specialist, 576, 577
   standards, 18, 19
   structure, 42, 43
   syntax, 42-49
   tag, 44, 45
   validation, 70-73

HTML (continued)
   vs. XHTML, 18, 19
   whitespace, 48, 49
HTML5 attribute
   autocomplete, 344, 345
   autofocus, 322, 323, 342, 343
   data validation, 344, 345
   draggable, 548, 549
   high, 362, 363
   list, 348, 349
   low, 362, 363
   max, 352, 353, 362, 363
   min, 352, 353, 362, 363
   novalidate, 344, 345
   optimum, 362, 363
   pattern, 346, 347
   placeholder, 322, 323
   required, 344, 345
   step, 352, 353
   title, 346, 347
   value, 362, 363
HTML5 controls, 350-363
HTML5 element, 362, 363
   article, 98, 99
   aside, 98, 99
   audio, 390, 391
   canvas, 540-547
   datalist, 348, 349
   embed, 388 389
   figcaption, 100, 101, 276-277, 304, 305
   figure, 100, 101, 276-277, 304, 305
   footer, 98, 99
   header, 98, 99
   hgroup, 100, 101
   nav, 98, 99
   on*event*, 550, 551
   output, 360, 361
   progress, 362, 363
   section, 98, 99
   source, 390, 391
   time, 100, 101
   video, 390, 391
HTML5 features
   Canvas, 540-547
   Drag and Drop, 548-553
   Geolocation, 532-537
   web storage, 538-539
HTML5 ratings, 31
HTML5 semantic elements, 98-101, 112
HTML5 validation, 84, 85
HTTP (Hypertext transport protocol), 6, 7
HTTP request, 6, 7, 8, 9
HTTP response, 6, 7, 8, 9

T

Tab order, 342-343
Tabbed data, 434-437
tabindex attribute, 248-249, 342-343
Table, 294-313
Table body, 294, 295
table element, 296, 297
Table footer, 294, 295, 300-301
Table header, 294, 295, 300-301
Tabs, 434-437
Tabular data, 295
Tag (see also Element), 14, 44, 45
    content, 44, 45
    name, 44, 45
    nested, 44, 45
Tag line, 562, 563
target attribute, 318, 319
    a element, 252-253
Target audience, 582-583
tbody element, 300, 301
td element, 296, 297
Team, 576-577
Tel control, 350, 351
Testing, 68, 69
    JavaScript application, 438, 439
    mobile web pages, 488-489
    web site, 604-605
Text area, 330-331
Text box, 322, 323
Text editor, 20, 21
Text field, 322-323
Text node, 420
text-align property, 144, 145, 298, 299
text-decoration property, 146, 147, 250-251, 258-259, 260-261
text-indent property, 144, 145
text-shadow property, 148, 149
text-transform property, 146, 147
textarea element, 330-331
TextWrangler, 21
tfoot element, 300, 301
th element, 296, 297
thead element, 300, 301
Theme
    jQuery, 452-453
    jQuery Mobile, 506-507
Theora codec, 378, 379
Three-column page layout, 204, 205
Thumbnails, 278-279
Time control, 354, 355
time element, 100, 101
Title (web page), 564, 565

title attribute, 94, 95, 248-249, 346, 347
title element, 82, 83
Tooltip, 94
top property, 220, 221
Top-down design, 578-581
tr element, 296, 297
Transition (jQuery Mobile), 498-499
Transparency (image), 284-285
True Type fonts, 527
Two-column page layout, 200-203
Type, 52, 53, 130-131
type attribute, 318, 319
    button, 320, 321
    check box, 324, 325
    embed element, 389
    file upload control, 336, 337
    media player, 256-257
    object element, 386, 387
    radio button, 324, 325
    source element, 390, 391
    text field, 306, 307, 322, 323
Typography, 570, 571, 574, 575

U

UI library (jQuery), 452-455
ul element, 106, 107, 234-235
Uniform Resource Locator (URL), 26, 27, 102, 103
Units of measurement, 124, 125
Universal selector, 130, 131, 134, 135, 178
Unordered list, 106, 107, 234-235
Uploading files, 602-603
URL (Uniform Resource Locator), 26, 27, 102, 103
url control, 350, 351
Usability, 560-563
usemap attribute, 282, 283
User accessibility, 32, 33
User characteristics, 560, 561
User style sheet, 138, 139
UTC, 354, 355
Utilities, 562, 563

V

valid pseudo-class, 344, 345
Validating data, 344-349
Validation
    CSS, 74, 75
    data, 12, 13, 344-349, 442, 443
    HTML, 70-73
value attribute, 362, 363
    button, 320, 321

XYZ

For more on Murach products, visit us at
www.murach.com

Books for web developers

Murach's HTML5 and CSS3	$54.50
Murach's JavaScript and DOM Scripting	54.50
Murach's PHP and MySQL	54.50
Murach's MySQL for Developers	54.50

Books for Java developers

Murach's Java Programming	$57.50
Murach's Java Servlets and JSP, Second Edition	52.50
Murach's Oracle SQL and PL/SQL	52.50

Books for .NET developers

Murach's C# 2010	$54.50
Murach's ASP.NET 4 Web Programming with C# 2010	54.50
Murach's ADO.NET 4 Database Programming with C# 2010	54.50
Murach's Visual Basic 2010	$54.50
Murach's ASP.NET 4 Web Programming with VB 2010	54.50
Murach's SQL Server 2008 for Developers	$52.50

Prices and availability are subject to change. Please visit our website or call for current information.

Our unlimited guarantee...when you order directly from us

You must be satisfied with our books. If they aren't better than any other
programming books you've ever used...both for training and reference...you can
send them back within 90 days for a full refund. No questions asked!

Your opinions count

If you have any comments on this book, I'm
eager to get them. Thanks for your feedback!

To comment by

E-mail:	murachbooks@murach.com
Web:	www.murach.com
Postal mail:	Mike Murach & Associates, Inc.
	4340 North Knoll Ave.
	Fresno, California 93722-7825

To order now,

 Web: www.murach.com

 Call toll-free:
1-800-221-5528
(Weekdays, 8 am to 4 pm Pacific Time)

 Fax: 1-559-440-0963

 Mike Murach & Associates, Inc.
Professional programming books

What software you need for this book

- To enter and edit HTML and CSS, you can use any text editor, but we recommend Aptana Studio 3 for both Windows and Mac OS users. It is a free editor with many excellent features.

- To help you get started with Aptana Studio 3, chapter 2 provides a short tutorial.

- To test the web pages that you develop on a Windows system, we recommend that you use Internet Explorer and Firefox. On a Mac OS system, we recommend that you use Safari and Firefox. All three browsers are free.

- To help you install these products, appendix A provides the web site addresses and procedures that you'll need.

The downloadable applications and files for this book

- All of the applications that are presented in this book.

- All of the significant examples that are presented in this book.

- The starting files for the exercises in this book.

How to download the applications and files

- Go to www.murach.com, and go to the page for *Murach's HTML5 and CSS3*.

- Click the link for "FREE download of the book applications."

- If you're using a Windows system, click the "All book files" link for the self-extracting zip file. That will download an exe file named htm5_allfiles.exe. Then, find this file in Windows Explorer and double-click on it. That will install the files for this book in this directory: c:\murach\html5_css3.

- If you're using a Mac, click the "All book files" link for the regular zip file. That will download a zip file named htm5_allfiles.zip onto your hard drive. Then, move this file into the Documents folder of your home directory, use Finder to go to your Documents folder, and double-click on the zip file. That will create a folder named html5_css3 that contains all the files for this book.

- For more information, please see appendix A.

www.murach.com